RIOTING *in*
AMERICA

Paul A. Gilje

RIOTING *in* AMERICA

INDIANA UNIVERSITY PRESS

Bloomington and Indianapolis

This book is a publication of

Indiana University Press
601 North Morton Street
Bloomington, Indiana 47404-3797 USA

www.indiana.edu/~iupress

Telephone orders 800-842-6796
Fax orders 812-855-7931
Orders by e-mail iuporder@indiana.edu

First reprinted in paperback in 1999.

© 1996 by Paul A. Gilje

The paper used in this publication meets the minimum requirements of American National Standard for Information Sciences—Permanence of Paper for Printed Library Materials, ANSI Z39.48-1984.

Manufactured in the United States of America

Library of Congress Cataloging-in-Publication Data

Gilje, Paul A., date
  Rioting in America / Paul A. Gilje.
    p. cm. — (Interdisciplinary studies in history)
  Includes index.
  ISBN 0-253-32988-4 (cloth : alk. paper)
  ISBN 0-253-21262-6 (paper : alk. paper)
  1. Riots—United States—History. I. Title. II. Series.
HV6477.G55 1996
303.'23'0973—dc20   95-35446

2 3 4 5 04 03 02 01 00 99

FOR ERIK AND KARIN

Contents

Preface

Although I did not know it at the time, I began this book twenty years ago in my first year of graduate school. I was in a seminar in early American history with Gordon Wood and decided to write a paper on rioting in the early national period. I selected my topic almost capriciously. I had been reading about European popular disorder in other classes, Wood indicated that there was little published on the subject, and I thought that it might be appropriate for a working-class kid from Brooklyn to study collective violence. I had no particular political axe to grind and, even though it was the mid 1970s, I felt no compunction to rehash the radicalism of the 1960s.

What started out as almost a lark soon became more serious. Wood admonished his students to conceptualize their topics in broad terms and fit the detail of their research into a larger interpretive framework. As a novice to professional history I struggled along with the rest of the class and produced an essay on the Baltimore riots of 1812 and several years later completed a dissertation on rioting in New York City after the American Revolution. Eventually those works, after much revision, found their way toward publication in articles, essays, and a book. All the while, however, I kept in the back of my mind the need to look at the big picture urged upon fresh graduate students in 1975. I sought not only the changes that occurred in my immediate period, but the grand shifts and movements that preceded and followed it.

When Harvey Graff suggested in 1988 that I write a synthetic examination of rioting in American history I seized the opportunity to put my inchoate ideas into more definite form. I naively thought I could complete the book in two to three years. Time has proved that assumption wrong and shown the wisdom of the sage warning from a wary advisor that writing history out of one's own period is difficult. This book, then, is my effort at pulling together an interpretation of rioting that has been germinating for most of my life as a professional historian.

The task has been daunting. My first problem was determining how much rioting took place. Although for some periods lists of popular disorder exist, there is no comprehensive guide. Instead I had to compile my own file of rioting drawn from many different sources. Although this file now contains over four thousand entries, I know that it is still not complete. Every time I pick up a book or article close to the subject I find yet another example to add. At some point in my research I had to draw the line and decide that I have looked at the most significant examples as well as many less significant examples, and may therefore come to my conclusions. I expect experts—especially those who have concentrated on areas beyond the revolutionary and early national periods—may disagree with me. I only hope that they can be a little forgiving and keep my larger goal of synthesis in mind when making their criticisms.

I also had the problem of wanting to tell the reader too much. Each riot represents a special human drama that had great impact on the participants' lives. I have striven to keep that drama in focus in the hope of bringing some of these people to the historical light that they have deserved. When I read of the lives lost or shattered by fervent moments of popular violence I took the stories personally. The fear of showing my sympathies too openly, space limitations, and the desire not to try the patience of my readers too much has forced me to shorten many of the descriptions of these episodes.

In the course of writing a book like this I have incurred many debts. The notes to the text acknowledge some but not all of the intellectual debts I owe to the many scholars who have gone before me. Without the interest in social history that began in the 1960s, and without a renaissance in riot studies that went with it, this book would not have been possible.

I have already acknowledged the aid and inspiration offered by Gordon Wood. Others from my years at Brown University contributed to my thinking about rioting. These include R. Burr Litchfield, Jack Thomas, and David Underdown. Since 1980 I have been a member of the history department at the University of Oklahoma, where I have received special encouragement from H. Wayne Morgan, David Levy, Robert Nye, Robert Griswold, Gary Cohen, and Donald Pisani. Barbara Million and Lucy Butler, the office staff at the department, have also aided me on many occasions. The University of Oklahoma and its research council have provided much needed support including travel grants, a reduced teaching load for a semester, and a Southwestern Bell Fellowship. While working on this book in the spring of 1991 I had the pleasure of being a fellow at the Center for the History of Freedom, Washington University, St. Louis. I want to thank the other fellows—Jan Lewis, David Konig, Peter Onuf, and Alan Taylor—for their friendship, and the Center for the History of Freedom for its support. I must also single out my collaborator, Howard B. Rock, for his understanding and comradeship as I worked on this book while editing and writing other projects with him.

Libraries are the most important tools the historian has at his disposal. The libraries at the University of Oklahoma and Washington University, St. Louis, have been particularly helpful with their own resources and in obtaining other items from inter-library loan.

The most difficult acknowledgments are personal. As always, my wife, Ann, has been my partner and friend. During the writing of this book both my mother and father died. This loss has slowed me down. I would have liked for Arne and Wladja Gilje to have seen the final product. While I was growing up my father worked in a machine parts factory and belonged to a union that went on strike every few years. I have often thought of the concern and worry on my mother's face when my father went off to the picket line. She lived through the 1920s and 1930s and knew, but never expressed to me, the dangers inherent in a strike. My father had a different attitude. He almost looked forward to picketing, enjoying its fellowship and holiday spirit. His experience, since he had only arrived in this country in 1936, was largely of the 1940s, '50s, and '60s, when the strike and picket line had assumed ritual aspects. This book helps to explain some of the difference in my parents' attitudes in those difficult moments when my father joined in strikes.

My parents taught me to face the future—an odd trick for a historian. In their declining years they always stressed the importance of preparing the next generation for a better life. That was their one great goal concerning their own children, and is certainly my goal for my children. I want my children, when they are old enough, to read this book to see the troubled course of American history and to understand that the fragile gains of American democracy have come at a gruesome cost. To this end I dedicate the book to Erik and Karin.

RIOTING *in*
AMERICA

INTRODUCTION

Why Study Riots?

Because Riots Are There

Rioting is part of the American past. All too often riots are seen as brief moments of spontaneous collective violence that erupt unto the scene, but only temporarily interrupt the constant and peaceful pulse of American politics and society. The answer to the question "why study riots?" is deceptively simple: because riots are there.

Riots have been important mechanisms for change. In the story of America, popular disorder has expressed social discontent, altered economic arrangements, affected politics, and toppled regimes. Without an understanding of the impact of rioting, we cannot fully comprehend the history of the American people.

The United States of America was born amid a wave of rioting. Textbooks obscure this fact, not hidden from contemporaries, by emphasizing labels like the "Boston Massacre" or the "Boston Tea Party." Yet each of these incidents, and hundreds of others like them during the 1760s and 1770s, were riots. The "Boston Massacre" was a riot that took place in 1770 and was more concerned with competition over scarce jobs between off-duty soldiers and civilians than with the imperial crisis. The "Boston Tea Party" of December 1773—a ritual repeated in 1774 several times—was a concerted effort by the rioters to destroy property to register local opposition to imperial regulation. These riots, combined with the Stamp Act disturbances, liberty pole frolics, effigy processions, rail riding, tarring and feathering, and countless other episodes of popular outrage helped to transform a colonial rebellion into a revolution.[1]

Scholars now know that the boisterous crowds of the 1760s and 1770s built upon popular practices inherited from English traditions that were well rehearsed in the years before resistance began. Underneath a veneer of political stability in eighteenth-century colonial America lay a tradition of popular disorder that traced its roots back to the more turbulent seventeenth century. Colonial Americans thus rioted repeatedly in carnivalesque rituals on Pope Day and New Year's, as well as less regular instances against impressment, the exporting of flour, conflicting land claims, and a host of local causes.

Rioting continued after independence, flaring into open rebellion on the frontier in the movement against legal land seizures in western Massachusetts in 1786 and 1787 and the opposition to the excise duties in western

Pennsylvania in 1794. The Shays' and Whiskey Rebellions, however, were not isolated occurrences. Riotous confrontations reappeared as white settlers struggled to establish themselves in one area after another. Even "bleeding Kansas" in the 1850s, thought to presage the Civil War, might best be seen as another outburst of this rural rioting.

More established regions also sustained rioting after the break with England. Alexander Hamilton wanted the readers of the *Federalist Papers* to believe that the new constitution of 1787 did away with civil discord like Shays' Rebellion. The ratification of that document, however, brought with it some rioting between pro- and anti-constitution forces. In New York City Federalist rioters sacked the office of a leading anti-Federalist newspaper, while in Carlisle, Pennsylvania, and Albany, New York, Federalists and Anti-federalists battled with one another.

Americans persisted in rioting throughout the nation's history. In the years after the revolution, Americans rioted to regulate communal morality by attacking bawdy houses and objecting to grave robbing to provide medical schools with cadavers to dissect. Political contests between Federalists and Jeffersonians were often marred by riots, especially over the Jay Treaty in 1795 in Boston and Philadelphia. Political partisans rioted periodically throughout the nineteenth century.

Patterns of popular disorder were established during the era of the early republic that would endure for more than one hundred years as ethnic groups fought over Paddie processions, holidays, neighborhoods, and the work place. These riots were not limited to the Irish. In the 1840s Protestants battled Catholics over the use of the Bible in public schools and in the 1850s nativists strove to limit immigrant political participation in popular disorder that led to extremes of violence, including the use of cannon during elections. Ethnicity was important in the New York draft riots of 1863, the Orange riots of 1870 and 1871, and many other conflicts in the late nineteenth and early twentieth centuries.

In the early 1800s racial animosities intensified, leading to anti-black disturbances; this hostility escalated after that and white Americans began to vent their full racist fury in riots during the 1830s and 1840s. Whites sustained those same antagonisms until the mid twentieth century with the most brutal and vicious rioting imaginable. The litany of anti-black rioting in America is punctuated with blood and tragedy that leaves a trail from Jacksonian America to the New York Draft Riots of 1863, to Reconstruction when whites killed thousands of southern blacks, to the rural lynching of the post-1877 South, to the urban centers of East St. Louis in 1917, Chicago in 1919, and Tulsa in 1921.

As laborers struggled to gain or maintain an identity and sense of well-being in the face of unrelenting forces altering the work place and work relations, they, too, had recourse to rioting. Most workers preferred simply to strike—to walk off the job until economic pressure forced their employers to relent. Even in the opening years of the nineteenth century, just as workers refined their strike tactics, coercion was needed to enforce unity and to persuade owners of the legitimacy of the laborers' demands. That coercion frequently took the form of rioting—whether it was tarring and feathering a recalcitrant shoemaker in Baltimore, or brawling with strikebreakers on New York docks. Force was often garnered to meet force, and riots and violence represent the signposts of American labor history from the 1830s to the twentieth century. Before 1865 most violent strikes were limited to cracked heads and were local affairs. After 1865, the rioting became national in scope. In the great railroad strike of 1877 workers fought the military from Baltimore to San Francisco. The dimensions of these labor wars continued to capture national headlines with battles at Homestead in 1892, Pullman in 1894, Ludlow in 1914, and Blair Mountain, West Virginia in 1921. Add to these major cataclysms countless skirmishes in the cities, towns, and countryside, and we can see that much of the history of American labor is written in blood as riots.

Popular disorder, however, encompassed many other areas of strife, ranging from the price of food in Civil War Richmond to the rise of the Ku Klux Klan in the 1920s. Some of this rioting appeared traditional, like the food riots, though much of it was more brutal. Some Americans eagerly attacked political groups labeled as radical in the early twentieth century, and patriotism became a screen to mask political persecution during World War I. Wobblies fighting for the right to free speech became the victims of conservative mobs during the first two decades of the twentieth century. Crowds took similar action against opponents of America's entry into the First World War and even draped a German-American in the stars and stripes, marched him through town, and then killed him because of his accent.

Against this backdrop we need to view more recent rioting. Rioting has played an important part in our perceptions of the nation. The disorder accompanying the civil rights movement of the 1950s and 1960s helped to convince many Americans of the righteousness of social equality. The race riots of the 1960s brought urban renewal and further efforts at racial harmony. Campus unrest defined a generation and altered higher education, while the antiwar movement forced a shift in foreign policy that continues to influence every decision on international affairs.

Despite the apparent supineness of the late 1970s and the 1980s, riots have not left American society. The blackout disorders of New York in 1978 and 1982, the Boston bussing wars of 1974–1976, the Miami riots of 1980, 1982, 1984, and 1989, the racial "incidents" in 1987 in Jamaica Plains, New York, and the cataclysm that rocked Los Angeles in April 1992 all show that rioting is an American phenomenon that is still with us.

Problems of Definition

As the catalogue of rioting above—and the list is almost endless—indicates, the term "riot" encompasses many different types of activity. Depending on the context, a riot could be a parade with an effigy, or brutal manslaughter by a crowd, with a wide range of possibilities in between. Much depends on the perspective of the individual; one person's peaceful demonstration is another person's riot. Moreover, what rioters do in specific instances changes with time and location.

In order to make sure we understand what is meant by rioting for this study, a working definition needs to be spelled out. Dictionaries generally define *riot* as a "public violence, tumult, or disorder" or more specifically "a tumultuous disturbance of the public peace by three or more persons assembled together and acting with a common intent." This definition makes a good beginning, but lacks specificity. "A tumultuous disturbance of the public peace" can be interpreted variously. It does not imply any direction, nor does it give any indication that anything more has occurred than that three drunken individuals have reeled down the street, shouting obscenities. This may legally be a riot, but for this study refinement is needed to indicate the purpose of a crowd. Moreover, although dependent upon statutes concerning riots, the three person limit probably is too small. Therefore the definition followed here, and based in some legal precedent, is that a riot is any group of twelve or more people attempting to assert their will immediately through the use of force outside the normal bounds of law.[2]

Even this definition, however, contains important gray areas. Two of these trouble spots relate to an understanding of the terms used in the definition. The first concerns the "use of force." As will become clear in this book, the level of violence in riots varies from incident to incident. Force is thus not simply a matter of violence. It implies coercion that sometimes includes physical violence and sometimes does not. For this study *force* will mean coercion or compulsion based upon violence, or based on the threat of violence, or based, within indefinite boundaries, on the ritual and habits of mob action. This last meaning of "force" is admittedly vague and depends heavily upon local and historical circumstances.

The second problem with the definition of riot revolves around the meaning of the "normal bounds of law." There have been periods when the "normal bounds of law" were either not clear or nonexistent. During the American Revolution there were two legal systems competing for legitimacy, one British and one American. From the point of view of King George, Washington's Continental Army was a mob. This ambiguity over the "normal bounds of law" recurred in American history on the frontier and accounts for much of the violence, vigilantism, and rioting there. Recognizing the relativity of "normal bounds of law," in this book we will assume the standard conventions concerning the concept—normal bounds of law devolve from legitimate government as viewed from our current perspective.

The definition of "riot" above avoids the issue of spontaneity. Some popular disturbances were planned, others erupted without previous collusion. The Sons of Liberty organized the Boston Tea Party. Does that make it less of a riot? Did every participant join in the ritual only because of the schemes of opposition leaders? As far as this study is concerned, the Tea Party was a riot that included many participants who were there for any number of different reasons. If we can assert with relative confidence that this affair was planned, in most situations we do not know whether a disturbance was prearranged. Officials often charged that there was some sort of plot whatever the actual evidence. Many ghetto riots of the 1960s initially were blamed on black extremists pushing for revolution. In other riots there may have been some plan, but the action took unanticipated directions. The New York City Draft Riot of 1863 opened with an orchestrated protest, but quickly spread and became more violent. Because of the difficulty of determining spontaneity and this blend of planned, partially planned, and unplanned disorder, most action that fits our definition will be considered a riot.

Beyond the language in the definition of rioting and the issue of spontaneity, other problems occur concerning labeling specific types of behavior by certain identifiable groups as riots. Criminal activity by twelve or more persons might be described as rioting. A gang of street toughs romping through a neighborhood and terrorizing all who stood in their way was a riot, but what can we say about organized crime such as that perpetrated by the Mafia and urban drug gangs in the twentieth century or Chinese tongs in the nineteenth century? These groups enforced their will outside the normal bounds of law in groups of twelve or more. For the sake of this study, criminals routinely breaking the law as a group will be excluded from the category of riot. If a criminal gang joins extemporaneously in popular disorder, then they will be considered as participating in a riot.

Certain racial conflicts also create difficulties. Relations between native Americans and white Anglo-Americans often have been marred by collective violence. Frequently this struggle has led to war. But what about those instances when whites already assumed sovereignty over a specific Indian tribe and that tribe began to fight against the whites? Is that an Indian uprising? An Indian war? An Indian riot? Moreover, how do we categorize actions against Indians by the government or by white settlers that were violating their own laws? Certainly the Paxton Boys massacre of Conestoga Indians in 1763 was a form of rioting? Should we also include the massacre at Wounded Knee in 1890 when the Seventh Cavalry mowed down 200 to 250 Sioux because one Indian apparently fired a rifle? This study of rioting will exclude Indian-white conflicts when the issue of Indian sovereignty is at stake or when the two groups engaged in what is usually described as warfare, while it will consider incidents like the Paxton Boys massacre in which Indians had accepted white rule.

Similar problems arise concerning violent interactions between blacks and whites, especially before emancipation. Were slave rebellions, like the one led by Nat Turner in 1831, riots? While an argument can be made to include slave rebellions as a form of rioting, they will not be examined in this work. Slavery as an institution dictated white domination over African Americans both legally and socially. This control may not have been complete and could be challenged subtly on a day-to-day basis, but the extreme nature of American slavery prevented any overt group challenges short of rebellion. Given these circumstances the only way Nat Turner and other slaves could strike a collective blow at slavery was with a violence that erupted only periodically and changed little as long as the African Americans concerned were held in bondage.

Strictly following the definition outlined above might include all these incidents. There is no satisfactory way to resolve this dilemma. Drawing fine distinctions between "criminal activity," "uprisings," "rebellions," and "riots" would lead to a semantic jungle from which we might never emerge. Instead, compromise and artificial distinctions must be relied upon. This study will adhere to the definition of riot as any group of twelve or more people attempting to assert their will immediately through the use of force outside the normal bounds of law, but will arbitrarily exclude some activity by organized crime, by Indians, by soldiers at Wounded Knee, or by blacks revolting against slavery, while including other activity—by gangs of street toughs, by the Paxton Boys, and by African Americans in a free society.

Rioting and Social History

Rioting is a key field in social history.[3] Social history deals with how different groups of people interacted over time along economic, racial, ethnic, and gender lines. Since the 1960s scholars have emphasized the need to examine more carefully the "inarticulate." We must therefore focus our attention on the little guy—the man in the street—and determine what he thought and believed. Riots are moments when people in the street—*le menu peuple* ("the little people")—make themselves heard and reveal how they interact with others in society. Suddenly, in a luminescent moment, amid the shouting roar of the crowd, the "inarticulate" become articulate. Rioters demonstrate what they are thinking not only by uttering slogans and obscenities, but by the actions they take and by the objects they attack. Authorities, too, reveal in their reactions to the crowd their assumptions about how various groups ought to interact within society. Both rioters and authorities act and react differently in different circumstances and contexts. Changes in behavior during a riot are not random; patterns emerge over time. By studying changes in those patterns of rioting we can gain an understanding of how the ideas and beliefs of the little people shifted and how, too, the interaction between different groups within society became altered.

Basic to this approach to rioting is the assumption that mobs are rational. In other words, riotous crowds do not act merely on impulse and are not fickle. There is a reason behind the actions of rioters, no matter how violent those actions may be. This rationality has two major components. First, the mob's behavior is directly connected to grievances of those involved in the riot. A tumultuous crowd does not ordinarily engage in wanton destruction of persons and property. Instead they seize upon some object or objects that represent the forces that propelled them into the riot originally. A Salem crowd in September 1768, for instance, captured a customs informant, tarred and feathered him, and carted him through town with a halter on his neck. The informant embodied not only a willingness to ensure compliance with detested customs duties, but also a repudiation of communal solidarity in the face of intrusion by the external imperial forces. The more brutal violence of a century later also was not mindless. Lynching of blacks, a ritual practiced thousands of times, often included humiliation and physical desecration of the victim that had a variety of psychosexual connotations aimed at publicly asserting white racial dominance. In the consumer age of the late twentieth century, urban rioters usually confiscated or destroyed material goods they believed ordinarily denied to them.

The rationality of the mob can be seen not only in the grievances expressed, but also in the choices of the particular crowd. In any given situation, rioters have an infinite number of options. But the activity selected by rioters is not capricious nor random. Instead it is dictated by specific historic circumstances. Rioters in eighteenth-century colonial America seldom killed anyone. Revolutionary Americans turned to ritual punishments that had deep roots in Anglo-American culture to single out a violator of communal norms. By the mid nineteenth century Americans were much more willing to kill during a riot. Even in what might be perceived as mindless slaughter, rioters revealed some discrimination. Police officers in a New Orleans race riot in 1866 covered their badges, and fired revolvers at unionists and blacks holding a political meeting at Mechanics' Hall. They did not blow up the entire building. They did not murder everyone in it. Physical attacks in more recent riots, like the assault on white trucker Reginald Denny in Los Angeles in 1992, had an eerie resonance reflecting the image of the white police beating of Rodney King that triggered the disturbance. Even in the frenzy of the moment some rationality, connected to ideas about intergroup relationships within society, was evident.[4]

Having asserted the idea that the mob is rational, it is also important to note that there is always a certain element of the irrational in any given tumult. Rioting was not a daily routine. Each participant in a riot knew that he was involved in an exceptional episode of his life. Emotions and passions surfaced; people got carried away with what they were doing. Normally reserved individuals might find themselves cheering on the tarring and feathering, or worse, firing away at the helpless victim.[5]

Riots had important meanings to the individual and the community. They could also be a form of amusement. During the tumult, rules and society were turned upside down and put aside; a carnival-like atmosphere prevailed. Each member of the crowd came to the riot for his or her own complex of reasons and thus participated in the collectivity for his or her own purposes. Many Salemites in 1768 might truly have been angered at the new customs duties. Others might have been distressed over the sour economic conditions of Massachusetts in the 1760s. Some might have harbored a special personal grudge against the victim. Others might have been out on the street on a lark and decided to join in the frolic. A mix of motives might be delineated for the New Orleans police rioters in 1866—opposition to Reconstruction, personal hatred of blacks or of one black in particular, or some pet peeve that allowed itself to vent in a welter of angry bullets fired at the most available target. This mixture of motives, combined with the passions released in rioting, makes it more difficult, but not impossible, to understand rioting within its historical context.

During riots the normal rules of society are put aside and new rules, connected to previous patterns of popular disorder, suddenly and briefly come into force. Thus ghetto rioters might loot a store proclaiming in mid summer that it is "Christmas," and an early-nineteenth-century rioter might turn his coat inside out in a symbolic gesture indicating a suspension of the usual social restraints. The form of this breaking of the rules is important and pushes the boundaries of society to new limits, while remaining within certain bounds. In the process, like the criminal whose behavior tells us what is and is not acceptable, riots reveal the boundaries of social interaction, whether it be the tarring and feathering of a customs informant, or the shooting of blacks at a political meeting, or the beating of someone of a different race.[6] Ultimately, riots enable us to trace crucial areas of social change because what people do in riots changes over time and those changes are related to larger social and economic developments.[7] This change is not necessarily linear. The complex reasons and emotional base of rioting guarantees some variety. Differences exist between regions. Southern rioters might behave one way, northerners another, westerners still another. Within a single state or location there could be variation. People are not always consistent in what they do in a riot. One group of rioters is not necessarily aware (although sometimes they are) of what another group of rioters did in another time and another place. Exceptions to patterns haunt generalizations—yet generalizations can be ventured.

Riots and American History

The examination of rioting entails rethinking basic assumptions about American history. Standard periodizations, like those wedded to presidential administrations, do not help us. The focus here is on the *longue durée*—changes that occurred not measured in years or decades, but in centuries. The chronology that arises from this analysis reflects major shifts in American history. From this perspective, the central mechanisms for change combine several areas. Although the standard political benchmarks of 1776 and 1861 are important, by themselves they do not mark major transformations. Independence did not alter rioting dramatically. But revolutionary ideals of equality inaugurated a shift in perceptions of society that created change in the nineteenth century. Collective violence before, during, and after the Civil War represented a continuum, despite a shifting context that provided new and different reasons for rioting. In the twentieth century several movements—largely derived from the extension of the democratic ideal to more Americans—coalesced to provide another reason for change.

The interpretation that emerges from this study offers one angle from which to view American history, and the periodization outlined in this book for rioting does not necessarily hold for all areas of change. As social historians undertake synthesis of other topics, different organizational frameworks will emerge. The task for historians will then be to seek lines of both intersection and divergence between areas of study, not only to understand the particular problem they are concerned with, but also to gain greater insight into what are the significant transformations.

Four hundred years of rioting, including thousands of riots, have been examined to determine changes in patterns of American popular disorder. By stepping back and looking at this larger picture, distinct trends appear. There were four major phases of rioting related to key changes in American society.

I explore the first and second phases in chapter 1. In the seventeenth century there were two broad categories of rioting: disturbances that emphasized ritual and custom that featured a minimum of violence against persons; and extensive, sometimes violent, rebellions. Both forms emerged out of the turbulent conditions in England. Americans and the English strove to capture a world that they had lost—an ideal village community that may never have existed—through communal action that often took the guise of popular disorder. These disturbances highlighted a sense of identity among those in a community and avoided violence against persons. The upheaval that propelled many across the Atlantic, however, sometimes expressed itself with more vehemence in an unsettled society. As colonists struggled to establish themselves in a new world, and to replicate a social hierarchy that was even then being challenged in England, they were all too willing to turn to blows to settle disputes. The violent rebellions that swept across the colonies from the middle to the end of the century were indicative of this trend.

The second phase of rioting began sometime in the early eighteenth century during a period of growing social stability as the rules of the game—that is, the proper interaction between social groups—became more clear. A better defined social hierarchy established itself. The result was that the level of violence decreased. Ritualized crowd behavior became the norm, and people in riots avoided smashing heads and spilling blood. Riots became a means of maintaining community solidarity in the face of those few challenges posed by a market economy, by outsiders, and by violators of local morality. Even as Americans moved toward revolution, the subject of chapter 2, they sought to keep within the bounds of accepted patterns of popular disorder. Despite the great political upheaval that marked the later part of the eighteenth century, rioters clung to ritual forms of behavior practiced earlier in the century and ratified by the riotous experience of the American Revolution.

Chapters 3, 4, and 5 trace the many expressions of the third major phase of rioting that started during the opening decades of the nineteenth century. The American Revolution initiated a process that changed the rules that guided society and upset the social stability that had been based upon ideas of hierarchy. Chapter 3 focuses on the unleashed democracy that in part grew out of widespread participation in popular disorder, and that spelled the end of hierarchy and the traditional eighteenth-century world. Equality cut the ties that had bound people to their community and created a world of individuals competing with one another. To help in this new aggressive cutthroat egalitarian atmosphere, individuals formed associations based on ties of affinity. Riots reflected this upheaval, becoming increasingly violent and bloody as different social groups—divided by politics, ethnicity, class, and race—squared off against each other in brutal conflicts. Americans could kill each other because they did not identify with each other. This phase, commencing by the 1820s and lasting to about 1940, was the most gruesome and sanguine for civil strife in American history. Chapter 4 details the failure of American democracy in race relations from the Civil War to the early twentieth century. Chapter 5 covers post–Civil War violent labor strife, ethnic conflict, and political polarization that led to riots with large death tolls and brutal attacks on individuals.

By the middle of the twentieth century the fourth phase began and popular disorder became less violent. This shift, examined in chapter 6, does not signify a pendulum swinging back to patterns of rioting from an earlier age. New conditions established a new context for this less violent rioting. Eighteenth-century popular disorder had been born out of a world of hierarchy marked by deference, paternalism, and a sense of local community. Late-twentieth-century rioting arose from the greater extension of democracy, the destruction of local community, the rise of a national state, and the creation of a national media. In the mid twentieth century political leaders came to accept the full implications of democracy, and the rules that dictated social interaction became clear to most contenders. The national government wielded both the power and the will to step in and mediate disputes guaranteeing equal rights. It now became more difficult to hide from an enlarging bureaucracy and a roving media that put all before the national eye. Other factors came into play. The decline in the rate of immigration in the 1920s helped to homogenize

American society, while the acceptance of the strike as a bargaining tool in the 1930s and the rise of the civil rights movement after 1950 minimized two of the most violent areas of confrontation in the previous century.

Yet rioting did not disappear. The student protest movement, ghetto riots of the 1960s, and a range of incidents in the 1970s and 1980s all attest to continuing popular disorder. As distressing as these events were to many of those in authority at the time, these rioters concentrated more on symbolic gestures and the destruction of property than brutal assaults on persons. If by the 1990s Americans did not riot as frequently, nor engage in as many brutal acts of collective murder as they once had, the Los Angeles riot of 1992 loomed as a warning of greater strife. Patterns of popular disorder have changed before, and may change again.

DISORDER AND ORDER IN COLONIAL AMERICA | 1

English Background

Rioting in the colonial period can be divided into two distinct phases. During the seventeenth century rioting varied from brutal upheaval often aimed at toppling government to more limited collective violence aimed at protecting a community from outside intrusion or asserting community morality. In the eighteenth century the benign type of rioting became more frequent and focused on issues such as the exportation of grain, bawdy houses, violators of local mores, customs collectors, and impressment. In this second phase colonial Americans borrowed rituals and patterns of behavior from their English and European forebears, enhancing them with practices of their own.[1] By the 1760s—when colonists used these rituals in a new and ultimately more revolutionary cause—an elaborate repertoire of behavior existed that could be relied upon in any given tumultuous moment.

To understand best both the diversity and patterns of colonial American rioting we need first to survey English popular disorder before and during colonization.[2] Much of the violence and disruption of seventeenth-century colonial America reflected the violence and disruption in England. Likewise, the predominance of less personal physical violence in the eighteenth century in colonial America represented a delicate balance between various social groups that was first worked out in England. In other words, both England and its colonies shared a political and social instability before 1700, just as they came to share political and social stability for most of the eighteenth century.

The English society that spawned the North American colonies was in upheaval. Ideals were wedded to notions of hierarchy and patriarchy. The perfect English world revolved around the village community. There, the local gentry, tied to a great lord and through him to the king above, paternalistically guarded the good of all, and each family lived in harmony with itself and its neighbors. Reality crashed in upon this ideal as demographic growth, inflation, and a new agricultural economy created a more complex society. The increased population put greater pressure on land use and led to higher grain prices. It also convinced large landholders to engross as much land as possible, leading to the enclosure of commons land, the draining of swamps and fens, and the stripping down of forests. European-wide inflation, caused by the influx of New World gold and silver, accelerated these developments. Some villages became overcrowded, others were almost empty. People were cast upon the kingdom, drifting from one area to the next, making existing relationships more difficult to maintain.[3]

This social change had a profound impact on rioting. On the one hand the English used popular disorder to reassert their traditional values. On the other, the tangled forces for change pushed some rioting to extremes, unleashed pent-up antiauthoritarianism, and led to rebellion.

Both those on top (patricians) and those on the bottom (plebeians) of society vaguely recognized the threat to their world view from new economic forces. Acting to shore up the disintegrating customary society, they brought it into bolder relief. The public spectacle, so important to a semiliterate world that stressed the oral and dramatic aspects of society, was instrumental in reasserting traditional values. This development can be seen on ritual holidays like Pope Day and in rioting.

In most popular disorder during the Tudor and Stuart era rioters generally limited their violence against persons and destroyed property that symbolized their grievances. Based upon the community interests, these disturbances at times expressed personal rather than class concerns, and the participants "were guided by tradition and custom and were vainly attempting to restore a lost world which may never have existed."[4] Enclosures probably triggered the greatest number of riots during this era and often expressed the local resentment of the community against the engrossing of land. Rioters also protested acts of deforestation and opposed the export of grain. There were other reasons for rioting as well, including protest against taxation, attacks on foreigners, festive misrule taken too far, mutinies of soldiers and sailors, and issues of communal regulation.[5]

Serious popular disorder and dynasty-shaking rebellion, however, rocked English society during the sixteenth century under the Tudors and persisted into the seventeenth century. The best known Tudor rebellions include the Pilgrimage of Grace in 1536, the Western Rebellion of 1548–1549, Kett's Rebellion of 1549, Wyatt's Rebellion of 1553–1554, and the Northern Rising of 1569–1570. The Stuarts were not immune to the same difficulties. The English Civil Wars of the 1640s and the Glorious Revolution of 1688–1689 ought to be considered as successful rebellions that overthrew the monarch. Although some of these rebellions were led from the top down, some included a strong impetus from the bottom up.[6]

The distinction between frequently practiced ritualistic disturbances, like the antienclosure riots, and the rebellions was vague. Opposition to enclosures, for instance, produced rioting during the Lincolnshire Rebellion of 1536 as well as the disturbances of 1548 and 1549. Antienclosure rioting became so widespread at one point from 1628 to 1632 that these disorders are sometimes lumped together as a separate "rising" of the people. This hazy connection was important. Although antienclosure disturbances were ordinarily tame and centered around the destruction of bushes and fences erected to prevent common use of land, they could be associated with more violence that threatened the state. Rioters during the mid Tudor rebellions killed at least ten persons during the 1530s and 1540s. Officials thus reacted to many outbreaks of rioting seriously, recognizing the potential for greater unrest. When rebellion occurred, the government exacted a heavy toll not only against the rebels, but also against any rioting that took place in tandem with the rebellion.[7]

Thus, in this turbulent society physical violence was never very far from the surface. For a few forms of popular disorder such violence was endemic. Widespread poaching, which could either be an individual act or a group movement that was tantamount to rioting, often included violence against persons. In part this situation derived from the fact that poaching explicitly challenged the prerogatives of the gentry—only the highborn had the right to hunt—and in part it was because poaching necessitated being armed and therefore placed the perpetrators in a situation to use forceful and violent means.[8] Even when explicit violence in popular disorder was lacking, there developed a language and rhetoric that promised greater bloodshed.

Violent rebellion, ritualistic rioting, poaching, and uttering threats to the gentry all relied upon a tradition of antiauthoritarianism and resistance that belied the deferential and hierarchical nature of Tudor-Stuart society and reached back to the middle ages. The root of that tradition lay in the myth of the Norman yoke. In its most radical interpretations this myth held that Anglo-Saxon England before the invasion of William the Conqueror had minimized privilege and guaranteed the rights of all.[9]

English historians have begun to etch in some of the outlines of this tradition of rebellion and disorder among the common people. In 1596 there was a conspiracy to rebel against both the local and national regime begun by a carpenter and another laborer in the hope of knocking "down the gentlemen." The rising came to nothing as it failed to garner support before the local gentry uncovered it. Officials brought the plotters to London to stand trial for treason and then executed them not far from the intended rendezvous in Oxfordshire. What is truly fascinating about this story is that the individuals involved had been aware of the far more serious 1549 rebellion and used that legacy to encourage support. Moreover, the organizers had a good idea of what was necessary to sustain a rebellion and knew of contemporary disturbances by apprentices in London. Suggested here, in other words, is an undercurrent of resistance that reached deep into the hearts and souls of many commoners.[10]

The core of this heritage posed a political threat to the regime and the entire social order. That threat can be seen in the 1381 rebellion, the rebellions of 1548–1549, and most dramatically in the 1640s. In the latter case, London mobs underwent an important transformation in the years immediately before the civil war. Building on customary misrule that had long been a part of the popular culture, rioters centered their attention on specific objects, like Catholics and foreigners, in 1640 and 1641. With the calling of the Long Parliament these mobs, now composed of individuals from a broader spectrum of society, expanded their demands and helped to propel the entire English nation into revolution. Pressure from the clamoring mobs in the streets and surrounding parliament divided the Commons into a popular party and a party of order. The popular party, acting on behalf of the street demonstrators, pushed for reform until they precipitated armed conflict. These mobs did not operate from an ideological void. Both economic grievances and religious radicalism motivated them. Their ideas continued to crystalize in the heated atmosphere of revolution, finding expression not only in the political program of the levellers, but also in various social blueprints offered by a host of seers, prophets, and would-be messiahs who hoped to seize the moment to turn the world upside down. Nor did the ideological content of the crowd evaporate in the cavalier world of the Restoration. Political divisions based upon religious differences continued to reach down to the lowest levels of society, with nonconformists supporting the whigs, and Anglicans backing the tories.[11]

The desire to protect the community, ritual misrule, and antiauthoritarianism modified notions of popular resistance. Opposition to intrusions upon a community, whether in the form of enclosures, market conditions, or whatever, helped to bind the village together and could thus reinforce the bonds of hierarchy within the community. Ritual misrule on festive holidays often served a cathartic function, channeling disruptive urges into socially accepted paths. Yet some elements of antiauthoritarianism persisted even in the most benign of customary riots and the most innocuous of popular festivities. In the changing and turbulent social conditions of the sixteenth and seventeenth centuries those elements repeatedly appeared and intensified conflict. The domination of those elements was always short lived. During the 1640s and 1650s, rioting and misrule helped to topple the Stuart dynasty and contributed to the call for a new order. The confused world that emerged so disrupted the older notions of hierarchy and community that almost all England welcomed the restoration of the Stuarts. Despite the joy of a return to a "merry England," the tradition of resistance did not lie far under the surface as the popular support for Monmouth's Rebellion in 1685 and the success of the Glorious Revolution attest.[12]

Rioting continued its importance in England in the eighteenth century, even if it no longer periodically posed a serious threat to the crown. In London, mobs were politically important from the early to the closing decades of the century. Thus the Sacheverell riots, which targeted dissenter churches and whig institutions, expressed popular support for tory policies in 1710. Demonstrations against an excise bill in 1730 compelled Sir Robert Walpole to withdraw the matter, and three years later anti–Gin Act riots left a measure aimed at limiting alcoholic consumption inoperable. In 1753 riots convinced officials not to pass a law designed to make naturalization easier for Jews. Most significant, starting in the 1760s there was a series of disturbances, first celebrating John Wilkes and then turning to general issues of reform, that signaled an awakening of greater political consciousness among Londoners.[13]

In the rest of England rioting was much more traditional in its orientation. There were countless riots opposing the sending of grain and bread outside of a region simply because it might find a higher price somewhere else. Rituals of communal regulation, however, had several purposes. For instance, the charivari or rough music—ranging from banging on pots and pans to rail riding, effigy burning, and mock murder—practiced against newlyweds when there were great discrepancies of age, might also be utilized against sexual deviants, wife beaters, or someone who violated an agreement with fellow laborers. Riots occurred in the countryside over labor issues as well. "Collective bargaining by riot" appeared early in English history and continued throughout the eighteenth century.[14]

While English rioting in the eighteenth century was an extension of previous patterns, the level of overt challenge to political authority, and even the level of violence, declined. In part this development is a function of the so-called political stability of Georgian England. And in part it is a function of the acceptance of social hierarchy and a deferential world view.[15]

Repeated cases of rioting, however, indicated that conflicts recurred. Within the villages and across the countryside some men pursued new notions of market economics and others, often resorting to popular disorder, reasserted older values. The process of crowd action to defend the old order gave greater shape and meaning to values than had existed in the tumultuous world of the previous centuries. Moreover, this rioting testified to the resilience of a tradition of rebellion and disorder. Modified in the eighteenth century as it may have been, that tradition was evident in the contrasts between plebeian and patrician culture, especially in the counter-theater of the plebs. When a crowd parodied the gentry, celebrated a mock election, or riotously assumed the power of the courts and humiliated an offender of local custom, it asserted an antiauthoritarianism that had deep roots in the social soil of England. In some areas antiauthoritarianism was pervasive. The Kingswood colliers near Bristol sustained a reputation for lawlessness throughout the eighteenth century, and certain areas of the coastline were infamous for the aplomb with which the locals, in defiance of authority, pursued the plundering of wrecked ships.[16]

English rioting combined nonviolent and violent traditions. There was, however, a shift from seventeenth-century tumult, which included many examples of both types, to the eighteenth century when more limited activity was likely. In both centuries there remained a strain of antiauthoritarianism in rioting.

Popular Disorder in the Seventeenth Century

Rioting in seventeenth-century colonial America followed the patterns of popular disorder established in England during the same era. Several major rebellions took place, interspersed with smaller episodes of collective action. Both the larger and smaller events contained varying degrees of violence depending on the specific circumstances. Spawned by the same world of the "vexed and troubled" English, each group of colonists came to the New World with their own separate motives and organized distinct communities ranging from the peaceable kingdoms of Puritan New England to the raucous competitiveness of the nascent tobacco culture of the Chesapeake. Despite these contrasts, and despite a small population, almost all of colonial America experienced disorder in the seventeenth century.

Although some scholars may not consider the seventeenth-century rebellions rioting, closer examination suggests otherwise. Nathaniel Bacon may have raised his army to fight Indians, but he easily turned to arms to assert his will, and the will of his followers, outside the normal bounds of the law against Governor Berkeley. The overthrow of Governor Andros in Boston began with crowds in the street arming themselves and seizing government officials loyal to Andros. Ill-conceived threats uttered by the lieutenant governor led to the expulsion of Francis Nicholson during Leisler's Rebellion in New York City. Many of these disturbances started in reaction to disruptions on the other side of the Atlantic. Maryland's "time of troubles" in 1644–1647, and the Protestant and Catholic confrontation at the Severn in 1655, were mere extensions of the civil war raging in England. News of William of Orange's successful invasion and coup d'etat against James II convinced the Puritans to overthrow Andros in New England. The same is true for Leisler's uprising in New York, and the Protestant Association uprising against the Catholic proprietary in Maryland.

Internal social instability also contributed to this popular disorder. In England there was supposed to be a clear identity between the social, economic, and political elite. The upheaval of the seventeenth century suggests that even in the old country there was some difficulty in sustaining this ideal. The North American wilderness compounded these problems, creating an environment that was too capricious and too harsh to allow the ideal to become reality. In the first few years aristocratic leaders came to the new world, but they either died or returned to England. In Virginia a period of transition followed that left a void filled first by individuals ill suited to the task, and then, during the second half of the century, by scrambling younger sons of English gentry who hoped to establish themselves as a new aristocracy in America. Similar developments and competition among the elite helped to fuel the rebellions that shook North Carolina, Maryland, New York, and New England.[17]

To explain fully the origins of seventeenth-century popular disorder, we need to go beyond the elite and ask what the collective violence meant for those individuals who lived through and participated in the upheavals. How, after all, did Bacon, Leisler, John Coode (in Maryland in 1689), and Thomas Culpepper (in North Carolina in 1677) attract others to follow them and revolt? In Virginia, a combination of factors, including a rise in the number of men who lived through the years of servitude and had a limited access to land, contributed to the ranks of the discontent. Tension in New York cut more along ethnic lines as the Dutch resented the loss of status and political power to others, while in Maryland, New England, and New York entrenched anti-Catholicism came into play. The intensity of this discontent and resentment had important ramifications for the degree of violence expressed in each rebellion.[18]

Perhaps the most bitter social distress and deepest resentments were in the Chesapeake. Bacon's Rebellion in 1676 started as an Indian war. Nathaniel Bacon wanted to unleash the vengeance of frontier settlers on all Indians to open new lands for the growing number of freed ex-servants in Virginia. Governor Berkeley argued for a more measured Indian policy and therefore denied Bacon official sanction for his war of extermination. A series of political maneuvers ensued, including Bacon's marching on Jamestown. In his first occupation of the seat of government, Bacon had his followers surround the House of Burgesses to wrest from Berkeley the desired commission to fight Indians. Bacon managed this feat by threatening to fire upon all who were within. A second attack later drove Berkeley into retreat and ended in the burning of the capital. At least two men died in the battle for Jamestown. Although there was not more bloodshed, both sides exhibited a frightful willingness to use physical violence as well as steal one another's property.[19]

Maryland also experienced a series of violent episodes. The so-called time of troubles was a period of total anarchy in the 1640s during which there was no real government. Whoever had the strongest party at a given moment and at a given spot was able to do what they wanted; no one was safe. In the 1650s the province's Puritans seized the government. When the proprietor's governor tried to unseat the rebels at the Battle of the Severn, almost half of his one hundred–man force was either killed or wounded, while the Puritans suffered at least three dead.[20]

When the social tensions were more diffuse then the amount of violence was less. The impact of social stability affected the activity that accompanied the ouster of Governor Andros in the land of steady habits. In Boston popular opposition to the royal governor was so extensive that the presence of armed mobs in the street was almost enough to ensure the demise of his regime. Popular support for Leisler led to a fairly united and peaceful collective action in New York in 1689, although in 1691, when Major Richard Ingoldsby successfully deposed Leisler, that same popular support led to some hard fighting and deaths.[21]

Superior numbers could also help to limit violence. During Culpepper's rebellion in North Carolina in 1677 the men who deposed Thomas Miller were armed and ready for a fight, but Miller could generate little support. The rebels thus confined themselves to clamping Miller and a handful of his supporters in irons while a boisterous crowd toppled the pillory into the water.[22]

The successful Protestant overthrow of the proprietary government of Maryland in 1689 is a case that combined both factors. When John Coode and his supporters captured the capital at St. Mary's and the proprietor's plantation, the opposition dared not fire a shot. Not only had social conditions stabilized, but the size of his force intimidated his opposition into surrendering.

The same shared English and European heritage that provided the context for these rebellions, also lay behind moments of riot when the objective was not to overthrow government. Colonists rioted for several reasons during the seventeenth century, including opposition to government actions, boundary disputes, and ethnic hatred. Some of this disorder followed English patterns; some of it was more brutal.

One traditional form of rioting was the tobacco cutting in Virginia in 1682. Distressed over the inability and unwillingness of the colonial government to enact legislation to limit crop production, planters in several counties destroyed tobacco seedlings to reduce total production. There were two waves of this rioting. One started on a customary day of the celebration of spring (May Day) and the other commenced during cider-making season in August. Both were periods of frolic and expressions of group solidarity, and thus connected to celebrations of misrule. The tobacco cutting itself was also purposeful. The rioters, like their English cousins protesting enclosure by tearing up bushes, limited their destruction to tobacco seedlings.[23]

The nastiest riot in seventeenth-century colonial America was in Marblehead, Massachusetts, in 1677. A group of fishermen returned to Marblehead with two Indians that they hoped to ransom for goods captured by other Indians while they were fishing off the coast of Maine. They did not reckon with the passions that had been worked to a feverish pitch by the losses to Indians during King Philip's war. As soon as the fishermen arrived with their prisoners, the Marblehead women stoned and clubbed the Indians. Then, when the victims' bodies fell lifeless to the ground, the women mutilated the corpses and severed their heads.[24]

Most rioting in this era was not that bloody. Riotous opposition to colonial governments took place frequently and usually included intimidating demonstrations, some jostling, and a limited amount of force. After the Lancaster County court in Virginia sentenced a man to the stocks for uncivil behavior in 1665, a crowd of bystanders threatened the judges, forcing them to close the court. New York townsmen rioted several times in opposition to the arbitrary behavior of colonial officials. In 1666 the people of Brookhaven, Long Island, assailed a constable collecting taxes. Twenty years later, the suspension of the

newly granted assembly and retention of higher taxes led to disturbances in
Jamaica and Richmond. Jacob Leisler ran into opposition in Queens County
in 1690 that suspended courts there. Taxation also triggered disturbances in
Virginia in 1673 and 1674, and it was local resentment to import duties
that compelled Governor William Phips to lead a mob in an attack on the
customshouse in 1693.[25]

Border and land riots followed the same general pattern in the seventeenth
century. Marylanders perpetrated the most violent of these disturbances, not
surprisingly given that colony's own tumultuous history, when they sacked and
burned to the ground what is now Lewes, Delaware, in a dispute with the
Duke of York in 1673. Less destructive were the supporters of the New York
Dutch Reformed Church in 1688 when they forcefully evicted a tenant of
Westchester town in a land dispute. In 1699, New Jersey rioters, armed with
clubs and stones, freed Lewis Morris from a Woodbridge jail and mistreated a
sheriff in Middletown while opposing proprietor demands for quit-rents.[26]

Rioting connected to ethnic tensions was most prevalent in the colonies that
had once been under Dutch rule. Not only was ethnicity an important factor in
Leisler's Rebellion, but it caused tension throughout the closing decades of the
seventeenth century. In 1667 Dutch villagers and an English garrison faced
each other in a riot in Eospus (Kingston), New York, that barely avoided
greater personal violence. A Swede named "Long Finn" led an aborted uprising
in Christiana (in Delaware) in 1669.[27] For most colonies during this period,
with a relatively homogenous population, ethnic tensions were at a minimum.[28]

Taken together, popular disorder in seventeenth-century colonial America
paralleled the situation in England and left a mixed legacy for the ensuing
generations. The English on both sides of the Atlantic experienced rebellions
and rioting that often shaded into each other and that had varying degrees of
violence. These incidents of disorder revolved around several different issues—
some of which were of special importance to the elite, others of which explain
the participation of the little people. Certain key conceptual points need to be
emphasized as we move from the seventeenth to the eighteenth century. First,
the ideals centered on a belief in hierarchy and the need for a stable social
order stayed intact despite the challenge implicit in both rebellion and riot.
The English and the colonial Americans strove to make those values a reality,
even if they had to do so utilizing violent means. Second, the propensity to riot
demonstrated a fundamental belief, by those on top and those on the bottom
of society, that they had a right to rely on force and violence in certain circumstances. During the eighteenth century that legitimization became even further entrenched in Anglo-American culture.

Legitimizing the Mob

Rioting never became completely legitimate. Confidence in the right to riot
may have grown in the eighteenth century, yet all moments of popular disorder

were viewed as potentially dangerous. The experience of the seventeenth century, with all of its upheaval in both England and America, stood as a testament to the dangers of mob rule. Yet having made this qualification, what stands out in examining eighteenth-century popular disorder is not the doubts and threats it posed; instead, it is the general acceptance of the mob as a quasi-legitimate part of the standing social and political order. This sense of legitimacy had two crucial sources. One was based in ideology, the other was based on experience. One reflected the ideas and interests of the patricians, the other the lives and world of the plebeians.

Anglo-Americans never forgot the upheaval of the mid seventeenth century. The main ideological legacy of that political disruption was a belief in the need to limit the power of government. For colonial Americans the most important transmitters of this legacy were a group of English coffeehouse radicals known as the True Whigs or commonwealthmen. These men developed an elaborate critique of Georgian government and derided the alliance between politicians and business centering on the engrossing of power at the expense of the people's liberty. To protect liberty it was necessary to limit the power of government.[29] One means of doing so was through the people in the streets. Commonwealth writers recognized that mobs could create problems since "one may at any Time gain an interest in a Mob with a Barrel of Beer" or "by Means of a few odd Sounds, that mean nothing, or something very wicked." But some popular disorder was preferable to granting the monarch too much power, since "all tumults are in their nature, and must be, short in duration" and "must soon subside, or settle into some order," while "Tyranny may last for ages, and go on destroying till at last it has nothing left to destroy."[30] In other words, rioting could be tolerated because it offered an important check on the power of government.

Connected to these ideas on government was the commonwealth belief that there are two kinds of law: fundamental law based on nature and reason (note the Enlightenment influence) and the laws of the land as enacted by the government. Ideally there ought to be many similarities between the two. But people are not perfect, and there was always the fear that the power of individuals in government might lead them astray. Hence differences arose between the natural law and the civil law. When those differences became too great, something had to be done to realign them.

The ideal of corporatism—the view of society as a single organic entity—reenforced the legitimization of the mob. Corporatism held that everyone within a given society shared the same essential interest. In the seventeenth and eighteenth centuries this concept received a severe pounding by the repeated conflicts that tore communities apart. Yet the ideal retained a certain resiliency, underpinned many basic social assumptions, and continued to be one of the essential rationales behind the acceptance of hierarchy. If corporatism allowed the high born to argue that it was their paternalistic duty to protect those beneath them and defend the current social system, it also offered a rationale for rioting. In a community with a single identifiable interest it was perfectly acceptable to rise in unison to defend that interest through extralegal means, including the riot.

The ideal of corporatism was also crucial to another important source of the legitimization of the mob—plebeian experience with the crowd. In a culture in which oral communication and dramatic gesture were central to the expression of social values, group gatherings held special meaning. Patricians recognized this significance and took every opportunity to assert corporate ideals, faith in hierarchy, and their own hegemony. Through court day ritual the local elite mustered as much of the community as possible, and in a display of public theater merged their own social, political, and economic identity with the authority of the state. The calendar was full of other opportunities to effect the same goal. Anglo-Americans gathered in crowds to celebrate royal birthdays and anniversaries, the arrival or departure of colonial governors, military victories, elections, and a host of other occasions. In each, plebeian and patrician joined to sanction their theoretically shared interests, while maintaining the proper social distance demanded by notions of hierarchy.[31]

Although these moments of celebration often strengthened the hand of the elite, the plebs, too, benefited. They not only got a day off from work, and perhaps were treated to a meal and plenty of drink, but a subtle confirmation of their own political role occurred. A procession of court officials through a colonial town was meaningless without people in the streets cheering them on. Actors on a stage need their audience perhaps more than the audience needs its actors. Because of that need, the ritual public theater of the patricians reminded the common folk of their power as a crowd and as a community. Those who stood on the sidelines huzzahing for the governor, and those who stood gazing into the flickering flames of a celebratory bonfire, shared an important experience that solidified their faith not only in the hierarchy, but also in the corporatism of the crowd.

The significance of that experience becomes even more apparent when we shift our attention from the rituals of communal affirmation to other forms of crowd ritual. On many occasions of celebration, as drink flowed freely and as spirits soared, the cheering crowd might go in directions of its own. Having observed the theater of the elite, the common people might engage in counter-theater. These rituals of misrule might merely take the form of excessive frolicking and include the shattering of some windows, the overturning of barrels, or noise making late into the night. The rituals of misrule might well assume a more organized and intricate form that contained several layers of meaning. In colonial America the most famous of these rituals were the Pope Day celebrations.

Long before Guy Fawkes attempted to blow up King, Lords, and Commons in 1605, the English found cause to have a holiday in early November. The foiled Catholic plot only added a newer and more Protestant reason to do so. Celebrations of the anniversary of this event occurred in both England and America before the 1740s. Sometime during that decade the holiday took a plebeian cast in Boston, and for the next twenty years townsmen paraded the streets on November 5 with effigies, not of Guy Fawkes, but of the Pope, the pretender, and the devil. On this day the streets were turned over to apprentices, young journeymen, sailors, and others. In the weeks before the event, and in a ritual that marked a role reversal, the organizers raised a levy for their celebration. Misrule dominated on November 5 as North Enders and South Enders vied with each other for honors in a battle royal that ended in the burning of each group's effigies.

In its origins the Guy Fawkes holiday was marked by rituals of affirmation—bonfires, official processions, and distribution of public treats—to celebrate the saving of the Stuart monarchy. But in Boston in the 1740s, and in New York starting in 1748, the meaning of the ritual became extended. In both cases the processions began in the wake of the Stuart pretender's efforts to recapture the throne and in the context of local economic difficulties. At minimum this public misrule can thus be interpreted as "a ritual of detestation of the Stuarts, and a constant reminder of their pretensions to power and, by implication, of the heroes [like Oliver Cromwell] who fought them." Pushing the evidence a little further, the rituals might have also represented a submerged resentment of all arbitrary government and, in the most liberal reading of the evidence, of all hierarchy.[32]

Yet even if there was resentment to the standing social order implicit in the Pope Day celebration, the context of the expression of that resentment helped to limit and channel any serious challenge to the hierarchy. Misrule, like rituals of affirmation, reminded the crowd and community of its own strength. But it also served as an important safety valve. Moments of misrule could be tolerated because they were only moments. More importantly, performance of ritual serves a crucial function in society, allowing that society to deal with tensions and difficulties that might otherwise tear it apart. Symbols, like the effigies in the Pope Day processions, are thus useful because they can simultaneously express different messages. All of those messages have some utility, whether it be an affirmation of the current monarchy or a challenge to hierarchy. Status reversal mocked those of higher status and legitimized the normal social order. Pope Day organizers may have exacted a tax on Boston inhabitants, but they got the idea of doing so from the regular tax levies.[33] African-American parodies of white behavior sometimes exhibited during Pinkster celebrations in New York and during the "nigger elections" of New England ratified the daily status of blacks in those societies.[34]

The experience with rituals of affirmation and rituals of misrule reminded common folk of the power of the crowd. Aware of that strength, and based upon the corporate assumptions of a single interest shared by members of the community, crowds sometimes moved to regulate or to protect their community. Such activity, taken when the local elite did not or could not act for the community, further enhanced the sense of legitimacy behind the crowd. English and colonial bread rioters believed that the community had a duty to protect its poorest residents and enable them to purchase bread at a reasonable or "just price."[35]

Ultimately, that faith in the right to riot to protect the community interest shaded into a more dangerous tradition—the tradition of rebellion that arose repeatedly in the sixteenth and seventeenth centuries. In the eighteenth century expressions of that tradition were submerged and appeared in the Jacobite utterances of some rioters or in the passing references to Cromwell and the Interregnum. During the American Revolution references to both challenges to the English monarchy can be seen in the prominence of the number 45, representing the Pretender's invasion in 1745 and taken from the Wilkites, and in repeated use of Cromwellian imagery.

Eighteenth-Century Rioting

A combination of social and economic crosscurrents that marked the colonial American world in the eighteenth century had an important impact on rioting. Compared to the previous century, there was great political and social stability, at least before 1765. Most of the controversies that had set Anglo-Americans at each other's throats in rebellions and civil wars had subsided. A clearly identifiable Anglo-American hierarchy had emerged, and ideas about deference and paternalism served as a lubricant keeping the social and political mechanisms working. Yet, just as the values of hierarchy and corporatism seemed transcendent, more and more colonists began to participate in a market economy and to pursue their individual interest regardless of the interest of the community. This development did not create a simple dichotomy between modernist capitalists and traditional corporatists. Instead, both ideals tended to swirl about in the heads of most Anglo-Americans, leaving them confused, dizzy, and uncertain. Under these circumstances, riots often offered an opportunity to clear the head and reassert older values as a community took to the outdoors to find its corporate voice. Moreover, as some individuals, driven by market conditions or attached to an exterior and cosmopolitan world, violated community values, opportunities to riot and resist that intrusion increased. All members of society may have found themselves pulled in contrary directions, but given the prevalent ideas on the legitimacy of the mob, rioters most often demonstrated in the spirit of shared community values. Indeed, their actions brought those values into bolder relief.[36]

Yet as rioters huzzahed, pulled down a house, rescued a comrade, or threatened a government official, they could not entirely separate themselves from the mass of contradictions confusing their lives. In any given moment of popular disorder there were probably countless reasons propelling those individuals into that crowd on that particular night. Thus, no two riots were exactly the same in action, motivation, or result. Despite this diversity, and despite dramatic exceptions, based upon approximately 150 examples of popular disorder, it is possible to describe a typical colonial riot in the eighteenth century.[37]

What was the typical eighteenth-century colonial American riot like? In all probability the crowd would be about fifty to one hundred strong, armed with clubs, and rioting in a village or one of the colonial cities. The rioters came from a wide social and economic spectrum within the neighborhood, including the affluent and the impoverished, but were almost always male. Maybe members of the mob had disguises, either blackened faces, like some of their English counterparts, or Indian dress. The crowd limited itself to the destruction of property, such as tearing down a house or jail, and would last at most for a couple of hours. Waving cudgels, the rioters would threaten greater violence, huzzah, and make noise. The owners of the property in question, as well as local officials who might oppose the purpose of the riot, ordinarily acquiesced in the riot. Indeed, it was almost as if both sides, those rioting and those against the rioting, knew the prescribed rituals and understood their role in them. Usually the rioters believed that they acted in the spirit of their corporate community defending land titles, morals, prices, or local interests against government intrusion.

There were many exceptions to this brief composite portrait of a colonial riot between 1700 and 1765. Crowds sometimes were smaller than fifty and, especially in the cities, could run into the hundreds. A mob of three hundred reportedly broke open Newark (a village) jail in 1746, and approximately five hundred participated in the tearing down of two of Boston's regulated markets in 1737. Some mobs, like the one composed of gentlemen who aided Oliver DeLancey in harassing a Jewish couple in 1749, contained only members of the elite. Other riots, like Pope Day processions and most impressment disturbances, had a more plebeian cast. In a few cases there is explicit mention of the participation of women. For example at Scarlett's Wharf in Boston, women greeted returning soldiers, after an abortive invasion of Canada in 1707, with jeers, shouting "So-ho, souse ye cowards" and bombarded the men with chamber pots. On another occasion, a crowd of men and women, "with Axes, Clubs, sticks, hot water and hot soap," met deputy sheriff Solomon Boltwood on his way to Pelham, Massachusetts, in 1762 and prevented him from carrying on his official functions.[38]

Physical violence leading to fatalities occurred in some riots. Although the preferred weapon of rioters was the club, colonial Americans sometimes carried guns into riots. When they did so the potential for violence increased greatly. Besides the Paxton Boys in Pennsylvania (1763–1764), who killed twenty peaceful Indians, there were at least nineteen deaths in colonial riots between the opening of the century and 1765.

Officials and the forces of law and order were responsible for most fatalities in eighteenth-century English popular disturbances.[39] This was not exactly the case in colonial America. As many as ten men were killed in riots involving the military—a group that had access to and knowledge of weaponry. In 1705 a brawl among privateersmen in New York City led to the deaths of a navy lieutenant who tried to disperse the crowd, and one rioter. In Boston a press-gang killed one of its unwilling recruits in a disturbance in 1745. There were two separate incidents of impressment resistance in New York harbor in August 1760. Cadwallader Colden described how a press-gang boarded a privateer as it arrived in port. The sixty-three-man crew resisted, beat off the men of his majesty's navy, killing four, and then escaped ashore. A newspaper of the same month reported a boarding of a recently arrived salt ship from Lisbon. Again the British navy sent a boat to press some of the crew, and again the sailors resisted. One man died in this scrape. Finally, in 1764 a mob of soldiers attempted to rescue Colonel Robert Rogers from debtors gaol. Officials called out the militia. Several rioters were wounded and one redcoat was killed in the affray.[40]

Five people were killed in disturbances connected to land and border controversies. In each instance, the fatalities came after a string of other confrontations and in circumstances in which both sides believed that they operated under the cloak of legality. In 1734 a Pennsylvania sheriff and his so-called posse attempted to arrest Thomas Cressap, the defender of Maryland's claim in the contested Susequehanna region. Cressap and his followers fought off the sheriff, killing one of his party. Two years later Pennsylvania officials gained the upper hand when another posse forced Cressap to surrender, but not before the Pennsylvanians had killed a Marylander. Similar circumstances explain the three deaths in New York in the 1750s. Forces working for the New York landlords shot and killed one man in 1755 as they evicted New Englanders. In 1757 further proceedings led to a gun battle in which one man from each side died.[41]

The four remaining deaths were in disturbances less anomalous in the eighteenth century. Oystermen from Perth Amboy, New Jersey, killed two Long Islanders when they discovered a party of men from Jamaica, New York, raiding their fishing territory in 1748. There is also a report of two men being killed in election rioting in Baltimore County in 1752.[42]

Rather than always representing a community speaking in a single voice, sometimes the rioting revealed a divided community. Several disputes concerning the local church broke into rioting. In Jamaica, New York, dissenters in 1715 took over the church and parsonage, driving out the deceased Anglican minister's wife. Petitioners in 1736, who wanted to be relieved from supporting the minister in Charlestown, Massachusetts, twice attacked the parsonage. Politics was another area of rioting that revealed divisions in the community. In the "bloody election riot" in Philadelphia in 1741, festering animosity against the dominant Quaker-German alliance led to an assault of about seventy sailors during the voting for election inspector. The rioters on both sides used clubs in the brawl. Some cracked skulls resulted, but no fatalities.[43]

There were also cases of sheer rowdyism that revealed the disorder endemic in the eighteenth-century world. An unidentified group of Philadelphia mischief makers in 1729 broke into the mayor's garden and destroyed many of his plants. Sailors riotously carried off public pumps in Philadelphia in 1741, and "young rakes" in New York tore down private lamp posts in 1752. This form of misbehavior ranged from smashing windows or smearing signs with tar, to attacks on the watch and forces of law and order. Often such rowdyism took place during holidays like New Year's, or patriotic celebrations.[44]

Although there are exceptions to every facet of the composite portrait of eighteenth-century colonial American rioting, the overall picture still rings true. The vast majority of riots identified between 1700 and 1765 consisted of relatively limited action, either destroying property or intimidating and ritually humiliating an individual. Most riots, too, were raised to defend the community. These disturbances can be grouped roughly into three categories: riots concerning land, riots of communal regulation, and riots against imperial intrusion.

Not surprisingly in an agrarian society, about one third of all the disturbances identified concerned land. In fact, in some areas this kind of disturbance became so frequent that it would probably be impossible to discover every incident. These riots derived from the helter-skelter nature of English colonization in North America, with vaguely drawn colonial boundaries, overlapping land claims, and unclear jurisdictions. Compounding these difficulties of European origins was the further problem of Indian land titles. With different conceptions of property, native Americans signed or were coerced into agreements that added to the confusion of proper land ownership. Given the Anglo-American preoccupation with "legality," the previous English experience with land rioting over enclosures, and the demand for land in the eighteenth century, these disturbances could almost be expected.

The conflicting motives that beset colonial Americans in the eighteenth century can be seen in land riots. In most cases, communities acted together to protect themselves from land claims outside their immediate little world. Towns like Newark and Elizabeth, New Jersey, stood united against ancient quit-rent claims of would-be proprietors. Yet, at the same time, the value of the contested lands, and the desire to own unhindered a piece of property, derived from market forces. Despite this contradiction, the experience of joining together in a collective activity tended to reinforce notions of corporatism and protected the property that was to become the hallmark of individualism.

Land riots could take a number of different forms. One favorite tactic was to disrupt the legal process either by preventing a court from sitting, which happened in New Jersey as early as 1700, or by obstructing an official in the process of serving an official writ. If the law had already intruded upon the lives of the farmers, a jail rescue might be in order. Dispute over lands in eastern Connecticut led to jail rescues in Hartford in 1722 and 1723. During the 1740s and 1750s there were several jail breaks in New Jersey. Similar disorder arose in the Maryland/Pennsylvania border troubles in the 1730s and in Massachusetts. Rioters in New Jersey, New York, Maryland, and elsewhere often attacked property—destroying fences, pulling houses down, or simply evicting a tenant. These rioters did so to challenge directly the legitimacy of their opponents' land titles.[45]

Many other disturbances can be labeled actions of communal regulation. These riots revolved around three major areas: issues of customary rights concerning both the market and natural resources, the morality of people in the neighborhood, and expressions of loyalty and identification with the community. In contrast to England in the same century, the marketplace was relatively immune to rioting in the colonies. Only Boston suffered repeated bouts of bread riots, with disturbances in 1710, 1713, and 1729. These outbreaks followed the basic patterns of collective behavior of their English counterparts. Twice rioters prevented grain from being exported to higher priced markets by cutting a ship's rudder and similar limited behavior. In the third riot the mob broke into the storehouse and distributed its contents, thereby convincing officials to provide more relief to the poor. Traditional ideas about markets came into play in at least three other disturbances. Bostonians in March 1737 objected to the monopolistic regulated markets recently erected, so they pulled two of them down one evening. Controversy over coinage led to a bakers' strike in Philadelphia in 1741. In turn, Philadelphians mobbed some bakers. When merchants devalued pennies, which decreased wages and increased the price of bread, New Yorkers riotously demonstrated their opposition one chilly January morning in 1754.[46]

Anglo-American patterns of popular disorder concerning control and marketing of natural resources in the eighteenth century developed from both the English and American experiences of the previous century. When tobacco prices sagged in the early 1730s, planters again had recourse to the methods of limiting production utilized in the 1680s. In Prince Georges County, Maryland, in 1732 rioters chopped down green tobacco plants. Their compatriots in the nearby northern neck of Virginia destroyed tobacco warehouses in the same year. Several colonial American communities—just as in English towns concerned with commons land, forests, and nearby game—developed a proprietary interest in local resources. During the 1730s the poor settlers living near the banks of the Schuylkill River fought with colonial officials over fishing rights. The fishermen set up weirs and racks in the river and its tributaries, thus hindering commercial traffic. Laws to prevent these obstructions met concerted resistance. When officials sent constables to enforce the law, the fishermen drove off the peace officers. A similar sense of proprietary interest explains the fatal attack of Perth Amboy oystermen on the Long Island intruders in 1748. Likewise, foresters in New England forcefully opposed the White Pines Act, which reserved the best timber for the crown. In 1734 in Exeter, New Hampshire, about thirty colonists prevented ten deputies from placing the crown's mark, a broad arrow, upon illegally felled trees. One of the most prominent men in the community led these rioters, who, paralleling the blackened faces of men in riots in England, donned Indian costume as a disguise.[47]

Mobs also acted to assert moral values within the community. In 1705 Arthur Lawson was a little too open about his adulterous affair for the sensitivities of most Bostonians. Because of his connections with the politically influential, complaints to the sheriff fell upon deaf ears. One night during Lawson's visit to his lover, a crowd gathered outside, and in charivari-like fashion raised a great cacophony, shouting that they would pull the house down if Lawson did not return to his wife. Similar incidents occurred in Dedham in 1758, Northhampton in 1761, and Attleborough in 1764.[48]

A group of men in Elizabeth, New Jersey, in 1752 resorted to English crowd ritual to restrain some husbands from beating their wives. Calling themselves "regulars" and painting their faces and assuming women's clothing, these guardians of community morality flogged reputed wife beaters. This behavior was loaded with ritualistic symbolism. English rioters often darkened their faces and sometimes wore female dress as a disguise and as a signal that normal rules were suspended during the disorder. Moreover, both the government and rioters frequently relied on the lash in the eighteenth century as a means of punishment because it not only inflicted corporeal pain, but ritually humiliated the victim. The female disguise only strengthened the symbolic message of that humiliation for a wife beater. Apparently this practice had a certain appeal. Within two months "Regulators" in Philadelphia "flagilated" a man's "Posteriors with Birchen Rods, till the Blood trickled down to his Heels" for having horsewhipped his wife.[49]

Prostitutes, too, ran into the wrath of urban mobs in colonial America. During the 1730s there were two bawdy house riots in Boston. In 1734 rioters pulled down one house of ill repute, apparently "under the countenance of some well-meaning Magistrates." In 1737 Bostonians limited themselves to breaking the windows and doors of a bawdy house, driving the woman occupant out. Again, there were some reports that magistrates watched the show from the sidelines. A similar combination of riotous and official action also took place in New York City in 1753. The magistrates undertook one of their periodic sweeps of the street. Sending many of the prostitutes to the work house, they also freed several after "an Examination." A mob then captured some of the released women and "severely handled" them.[50]

Expressions of loyalty and identification with the community, while dealing with perceived violators of moral sensibilities, often marked a bridge between the community and the cosmopolitan world of the British empire. Thus revelers celebrating the 1745 colonial victory at Louisburg in both Philadelphia and New York City became incensed at the owners of houses who did not properly illuminate the windows. Failure to put candles in your windows, then, brought a hail of rocks and shattered glass. Philadelphians singled out the homes of Quaker pacifists in 1746 during the celebration of the defeat of the Pretender's invasion of Great Britain. The same tendencies also were evident in some Pope Day celebrations. These patriotic disturbances, which were often mild affairs, testify to the many currents pulling on all colonial Americans; although usually focused on local matters, at certain times, especially during the various wars against Catholic powers in Europe, the community could eagerly identify with the British nation.[51]

Popular disorder also broke out when local interests ran counter to the needs and desires of English officials. After the intensification of international rivalries in 1745, riots triggered by the intrusion of the British bureaucracy into the daily life of colonial Americans became more frequent. Approximately two thirds of the riots between 1700 and 1765 concerning customs collection, impressment, and civilian/military tension were after 1744. Although some impressment disturbances led to fatalities, the vast majority of these disturbances fit the pattern of limited collective action typical of colonial American rioting.

Motivation in the anti-customs enforcement riots reflected the contradictory impulses that confronted colonial Americans. Imperial regulations setting up customs duties and prohibiting certain types of trade pitted the interest of the local community against the interest of the British empire. But if opposition to customs can be construed as protecting the community interest, it also adhered to the benefit of specific individuals who were aggressively pursuing their own capitalist aims by smuggling. Regardless of motivation, colonial anti-customs crowds behaved as if they were only protecting their community from intrusive outside forces. When confronted with a zealous customs collector, or one who would not take a bribe, colonial Americans turned to their tradition of mob violence. Typical was the action of seventy disguised Philadelphians in 1724, who cut a vessel from its moorings, carried it down river, and then unloaded the smuggled goods, much to the chagrin of the collector. Forty Rhode Islanders in 1764 performed a similar feat in Narragansett Bay, blackening their faces in eighteenth-century riot style.[52]

Informers, too, found themselves victims of collective violence. When a few Boston sailors from aboard a seized vessel in December 1723 decided to testify for the Crown, no doubt for a fee, men in the gallery during the court proceedings shouted threats and intimidated the witnesses. After the trial a mob grabbed the informants, dragged them through the streets, and physically abused them. During the French and Indian War a New York informer attempted to publish an expose of the smuggling with the enemy. This tactic violated the mercantile interests of the community. Every printer refused him. A mob captured him, "hauled him through the streets in a cart"—a punishment used by both city government and mobs—and bystanders pelted him with "filth and offal." Finally, in an action that revealed the conjunction of interests between local officials and rioters, the magistrates threw the culprit in jail.[53]

Most impressment disturbances were raised in the spirit of eighteenth-century riot traditions and expressed both individual and community interests. Merchants wanted to maintain an expansive labor pool for their ships to keep wages low and costs down. Waterfront workers and sailors had more at stake; they wanted to stay out of the navy. Impressment for these men meant practical imprisonment, horrid conditions, and an earlier death. Somehow the conjunction of these concerns became subsumed into a sense of shared community.

The Knowles riot in Boston in 1747 was the most famous and most representative anti-impressment crowd action. Hundreds, perhaps thousands of sailors and Bostonians, angered by recent impressments, captured several naval officers and threatened to hold them hostage. Yet they did little bodily harm to them. When they brought their prisoners to the gate of Governor William Shirley's house, the mob showed enough deference to surrender the naval officers to Shirley. The governor was able to address the crowd on this and another occasion unscathed. Nor did the rioters commit any depredation on the governor's residence. They did take an under sheriff, physically abused him, and, in a nice bit of role reversal, locked him in the town stocks. But that action was the most violence perpetrated against any individual. The mob also marched to the town house, where they smashed windows, occupied the bottom floor—the building after all belonged to the community—and convinced local officials to negotiate with the navy for the suspension of the press and the release of those already taken. In a final act of insolence they threatened to burn a vessel then being built for the navy, but decided instead to use a navy barge. Oddly, the long boat consumed by fire on the Commons belonged to a riot ringleader, and thus was a safe and effective means of expressing anti-impressment sentiments. It was safe because the ownership prevented any legal liability, and effective because at the time of the conflagration most of the crowd believed they were witnessing the destruction of royal navy property.

This pattern of behavior can be seen in other impressment disturbances. In 1764 New Yorkers rioted against the impressment of some fishermen in an action that paralleled the Knowles riot. When the captain of the naval vessel came ashore, a mob surrounded him. But he was not injured. Instead, the crowd convinced him to publicly declare his opposition to the impressment and sign an affidavit to that effect. The rioters, however, also dragged his long boat to New York's Common, and there burned it to the delight of all assembled.[54]

In many ways impressment disturbances were a variant of a civilian/military tension that expressed local opposition to intrusion by forces outside the community. That tension found other outlets of expression as well. Animosity often built up between soldiers stationed in an area and the civilians. Each side might take advantage of any opportunity to strike a blow at the other. Mutual antagonisms, no doubt, lay behind the willingness of colonial Americans to defend deserters from recapture. In December 1757 a crowd at Brintwood, New Hampshire, rescued such a deserter from a recruiting party, then, with axes in hand, they chased the soldiers for several miles. Newporters in July 1764 brawled with sailors along the waterfront for similar reasons. Such incidents also occurred elsewhere. At other times it was the military that took the offensive against the civilian population. In 1764 drunken officers and enlisted men rampaged through Albany, beating civilians and magistrates, breaking windows and doors, and destroying property. These incidents were more frequent in the 1750s and 1760s as the number of soldiers and sailors increased in the colonies.[55]

Colonial American rioting reflected the English experience in the seventeenth and eighteenth centuries. Rioting in England and in America during the seventeenth century was a mixture of limited affairs in defense of a community and more dramatic events that challenged the government. The latter category expressed strong currents of antiauthoritarianism and sometimes included greater levels of violence. During the eighteenth century the first type became more predominate as the social and political order stabilized on both sides of the Atlantic.

For the eighteenth century we can draw distinctions between categories of disturbances such as riots over land rights, communal regulation, and imperial policy, but the boundary between these must remain vague. The 1734 white pine riot in Exeter, New Hampshire, might be considered an action against imperial controls, or an effort to control land, or a move by a community to regulate a local natural resource. One thing ties together almost every riot between 1700 and 1765: a belief in the corporate interest of the community. Most riots thus started as a defense of community interest. Often that interest was pure chimera, hiding in its shadows personal motives. Even when other concerns were evident, they were disguised and cast into an acceptable form. Despite the hidden psychology within each rioter, crowd actions taken under the umbrella of communal values brought those communal values into sharper relief.

The clearer definition of corporatism that emerged out of the shared experience of participating in a crowd rescuing a neighbor from the clutches of a greedy landlord, or humiliating an adulterer, or harassing a customs informer, enhanced the legitimization of the crowd. The noise, the excitement, and the break in the daily routine all contributed to the effect. Although ultimately the activity of a riot is rational, riots were emotional experiences. Any youth, with liquor flowing through his veins perhaps for the first time, mesmerized by the bonfire's orange and yellow flames etched against the darkness of night, shared in a group experience that would be difficult to forget.

That legitimization had an impact on social relations. If the magistrates responded positively to a disturbance, as in Boston's bread riots, notions of hierarchy and deference might be strengthened. If a member of the local elite led the crowd, as frequently happened, the effect might also be the same. Even with the involvement of patricians, the riot reminded the plebs of their own power and strengthened the antiauthoritarian and egalitarian impulses of the mob—impulses that harked back to the English heritage of rebellion and resistance.

Those older impulses took on greater shape and meaning with every crowd action as the special repertoire of the colonial American crowd developed. These forms of mob behavior were an amalgam of old and new. Thus, like English rioters in the eighteenth century, colonial Americans tended to limit their destruction of property to only a few items that somehow symbolically represented very specific grievances. So, too, Anglo-American rioters emphasized the ritual humiliation of their victims by carting them through town, whipping them, or otherwise holding them up to general opprobrium. As a part of this effort there began, at least in the Pope Day procession, the use of the effigy to focus the crowd on certain issues. Some mob practices were taken directly from previous English and European experience, others adapted, still others invented anew. Disguises used by colonial rioters show how this process operated. Like their English cousins, rioters might blacken their faces, and at least once, in New Jersey, they wore women's clothing. In other riots the disguises were more nondescript, showing some adaptation, but in Exeter, New Hampshire, along the Massachusetts and New York border, and in the woods of Maine, colonial rioters donned Indian costume decades before the good citizens of Boston immortalized that ritual habit in the Tea Party of 1773.

Colonial Americans had the opportunity to develop and inculcate ritual because they tended to riot in clusters. The Knowles riot in 1747 culminated a series of Boston impressment disturbances in the four or five previous years. New Jersey settlers rioted in the opening years of the eighteenth century and again in the 1740s. Disturbances broke out in clusters on the Maryland/Pennsylvania border in the 1730s, and on the New York/Massachusetts border in the mid 1750s. Less than a month after a mob attacked a bawdy house in 1737, another mob tore down two markets in Boston. Although these clusters might be explained by local circumstances in each situation, like evictions by proprietors in New Jersey, the uniformity of behavior cannot be. Colonial Americans saw the riot as a legitimate response, and having participated in one disturbance, they were likely to do so again.

All of these various currents—the clustering of riots, the use of prescribed ritual, the antiauthoritarianism and egalitarianism, the corporatism despite the presence of individualism—burst onto the scene in 1765. Following the crisis and rioting of that year came over a decade of popular disorder that catapulted Americans toward independence. That transformation in turn necessitated a reconceptualization of the social, political, and economic landscape that dramatically altered both the perceptions of popular disorder and ultimately the rioting itself.

RIOTING IN THE REVOLUTION | 2

The Epidemic of Rioting

In 1765 an epidemic of rioting broke upon the American scene. Between the beginning of that year and the end of 1769 there were at least one hundred fifty riots. During the 1770s the pace of rioting did not slacken. Mobs shattered the peace in community after community, and in the process Americans propelled themselves into a revolution.

Why did this rioting take place? The resistance movement against British imperial measures led to many of these disturbances. But it did not trigger all of them. Moreover, opposition to customs regulations and taxes like the Stamp Act did not necessarily have to take a riotous form. Constitutional and legal objections to actions by parliament cannot explain the angry mechanics and seamen in the streets, nor can it explain the hostility of farmers when they closed county courts. Motives for these disturbances twisted in a maze of currents that suggest that there was something wrong with American society.

In the second half of the eighteenth century the British North American colonies experienced several crises. First, there was rapid population growth from both reproduction and immigration. Several colonies doubled in population between 1750 and 1770 and all colonies shared in this extraordinary population explosion. With economic expansion paralleling the population growth, this largely agrarian society put pressure on the available land. The back country filled to the ridges of the Appalachians, and many wondered where their children would find enough room to establish their families. The demand for land contributed to the outbreak of the French and Indian War and led to disputes over ownership of property. It also created tension between the eastern and western sections of colonies over issues like administrative corruption, representation, Indian policy, and inequitable tax burdens.[1]

Compounding these demographic and land difficulties were several economic problems. As trade expanded with Great Britain, debt levels also increased. The colonies produced agricultural commodities and imported finished goods, making a negative balance of payments between the colonies and England. Despite a rise in overall wealth, its distribution became more lopsided in the 1750s and 1760s. Added to these hardships was a postwar

depression during the 1760s. Many of those people eager to join the mobs of
1765 and 1766 in the colonial ports were unemployed sailors and mechanics
who otherwise might have had other things to do.

Corporatism called for all in a community to share a common identity.
Against the rising tide of diversity that ideal appeared awash in a sea of differences. The growth of economic inequality brought several social cleavages into
bolder relief. Rich merchants, trying to maintain their exalted position, were
pitted against laborers and artisans in the cities, and against farmers in the
countryside. These economic conflicts did not cut simply along class lines.
Merchants competed among themselves, as did many farmers. Everyone
seemed to be struggling to guarantee that they would get a sufficient slice of
what they thought was the fixed economic pie.

Other differences divided society. Immigration in the eighteenth century
contributed to ethnic diversity, as Scotch, Scotch-Irish, and Germans entered
the colonies. These non-English groups brought strange accents, languages,
and cultures. New religious beliefs made it impossible to maintain the customary identity between the community and the church. Further shattering religious harmony were the revivals, known as the Great Awakening, that began
in the 1740s and continued into the 1770s. Many of the tensions over demographics, land, and economics were played out in the contest between those
inspired by religious revival—new lights—and those who opposed it.

Without any external problems colonial Americans would have experienced
disruption and disorder during the 1760s and 1770s. The tension evident
throughout the first half of the eighteenth century between traditional values
such as hierarchy and corporatism, and those that centered on individualism
and the rule of the market, would have combined with these social problems to
produce turmoil. As it was, many riots after 1764 had little to do with imperial
relationships. Riots concerning land and property had occurred earlier in the
century; after 1764 the volume and intensity of such disturbances increased as
men violently confronted each other in northern and western New England,
New York, New Jersey, Pennsylvania, and North and South Carolina. With
the intrusion of added impositions and taxes from England the situation
became explosive.[2]

Starting in the summer of 1765 Americans riotously demonstrated against
imperial regulation, laying bare the innermost frictions within their society.
Colonial American leaders strove to sustain a delicate balance between encouraging popular disorder and struggling to cover deeper divisions. Rioters
adhered to eighteenth-century traditions and looked backward to a corporate
and hierarchical world, while driving toward a divisive, egalitarian world
marked by individualism. This odd combination of impulses helps to explain
a central paradox of revolutionary rioting; the overthrow of the political
system through the restrained forms of behavior that had marked earlier
rioting.

Patterns of behavior in prerevolutionary collective action followed and built upon the patterns of behavior in earlier disturbances. One of the main features of many riots after 1765 was the parading of effigies of government officials or local persons who violated the sanctions of the resistance movement. Effigies allowed crowds to express themselves without damaging the individual in question. The idea and form of the effigies was borrowed from Pope Day celebrations in Boston and New York. Moreover, the treatment of the effigies, often displayed with an image of the devil, hanging from a gallows or liberty tree, carted through town, and then burned in a night bonfire, dramatically mimicked earlier crowd behavior and judicial punishments designed to unify a community.[3]

Imbedded within Anglo-American traditions of mob activity were also some contrary messages and meanings that boded ill for those who hoped to guide the crowd along set paths. If a popular demonstration could contribute to the unity of the community, it also marked a moment when someone violated that unity. When those divisions became severe, or where even the identity of the community became indistinct, violence could increase. Violent and divisive disturbances flared in frontier and land disputes during the 1760s and 1770s as well as during the Revolutionary War when passions were at their highest and divisions at their deepest.

Anglo-American rioters earlier had expressed some antiauthoritarian tendencies; after 1765 these strains appeared with greater frequency and took on more of the characteristics of egalitarianism. This antiauthoritarianism harked back to the turbulent political atmosphere of the mid seventeenth century and the older patterns of social disorder and rebellion in England. Although initially these impulses operated within a corporate framework, suggesting a new social order of a community of equals based on a moral economy, the challenge to notions of hierarchy contained an implicit threat to corporatism that became more explicit during the 1770s and 1780s. With the epidemic of rioting that started in the summer of 1765 and continued throughout the revolutionary era, the mob took on a life of its own. Slowly, as Gouverneur Morris, a whig leader, noted in 1774, the mob began "to think and reason," and that thinking reasoning moved the resistance movement in unanticipated directions.[4] Ultimately this push for change from below contributed to, if it did not direct, the new democratic order of the American Revolution.

The dramatic political and ideological changes that came out of this period had a profound effect on patterns of rioting and the role of popular disorder in society. Democratic forms of government removed one of the rationales behind the legitimacy of the mob. If the people are represented in government, so the argument now went, they had no reason to take extralegal means to express themselves. Instead they were to use the ballot box. Yet the decades of some of the most intensive rioting in American history provided a different lesson. There also emerged the idea that the people's democratic will might still be best reflected immediately through the crowd. The ramifications of this contradiction were part of the legacy of independence and the formation of a new political order.

The Stamp Act

No one predicted the violent reaction to the Stamp Act. Before 1765 colonial Americans brawled with British soldiers, mobbed press-gangs, and rioted against overzealous customs officials. Even though this activity became more frequent in the decades before 1765, colonial Americans acted no worse than rioting English on the other side of the Atlantic. After the summer of 1765, the situation changed. Between August 14, 1765, when the Boston mob first mobilized against stamp agent Andrew Oliver, and May 19, 1766, when Philadelphians riotously celebrated the repeal of the Stamp Act, there were at least sixty riots at over twenty-five different locations. During some of these months in port cities like Boston and New York, mobs were in the streets almost every night and government ground to a halt.[5]

The significance of these riots should not be underestimated. A pattern of crowd behavior and of resistance to British imperial power developed that Americans then repeated in reaction to the passage of the Townshend Duties of 1767 and the Tea Act of 1773. During the heated months of the Stamp Act controversy, colonial Americans took the important first steps of translating popular culture with implicit political meaning to forms that had explicit political meaning.

The rioting of the 1760s and 1770s also revealed crucial divisions within American society. On the one hand there were the people clamoring in the street—mechanics, sailors, and others—who found they wielded a new and exhilarating power. On the other hand were the organizers of the resistance movement—generally recruited from higher up in society—who needed the mobs but struggled to restrain them. Previously rioting had been practiced intermittently. Now, it seemed it was permissible to riot every day, and the threshold for rioting decreased. After the experience of the Stamp Act crisis, colonial Americans readily turned to extralegal violence for many reasons.

Older practices borrowed from popular culture surfaced in the first outbreak of anti–Stamp Act activities in Boston. Shoemaker Ebenezer McIntosh, who had orchestrated several effigy parades on Pope Day and had led the South Enders in a triumphant street battle against their rivals from the North End the previous November, served as mob captain of the anti–Stamp Act demonstrations that began with the exhibition of two effigies hanging from a tree. One was of stamp man Andrew Oliver; the other showed a boot—as a pun to mock the king's advisor the Earl of Bute—with a devil popping out of it. This display, combining a figure detested by the community with Satan, typified earlier Pope Day celebrations where the Pope, the

Stuart pretender, and the devil might be shown together. Bostonians marched with the effigies past the town hall where colonial officials could hear, if not see, the mob's command of the streets. Then, following earlier practices which mimicked formal judicial procedures, the crowd defaced and burned the effigies.[6]

In the next few months, both New York and Charleston descended into near anarchy after effigy processions. The practice spread to several Connecticut towns: Newport; Philadelphia; Newburyport; Wilmington, North Carolina; Savannah, Georgia; and many other locations. The message of these demonstrations was the same: anyone who supported the Stamp Act had best change their mind before the crowd turned upon the real person instead of vicariously abusing his effigy.[7]

Another crowd ritual borrowed its pageantry from both the elite and common folk and emphasized the relationship between the imperial measures and the popular idea of liberty—the funeral procession for liberty. Usually the organizers prepared a coffin with the word liberty emblazoned upon it. Then, similar to the funeral rites practiced at the death of a leading citizen, and with mock solemnity, a procession marched through town with the coffin, which was interred or destroyed. Such "services," sometimes with an effigy demonstration, took place in late October about the time the Stamp Act was to go into effect in New York City; Newport; Wilmington, North Carolina; Charleston; and elsewhere.[8]

Had these mobs been content with the effigy parades or with the ritual of burying liberty, leaders of the resistance movement would have breathed more easily. But the people in the street quickly revealed that they had certain grievances of their own—especially resentment of wealth—that made for a more volatile situation. On August 14, 1765, after an effigy parade Bostonians tore down wharf buildings belonging to Andrew Oliver, and then, as the last embers of the bonfire were about to be extinguished, broke into Oliver's house and demolished furniture, drank his wines, and in other ways assailed symbols of his wealth. The Boston mob at Oliver's house was restrained, however, compared to the group that gutted Lieutenant-Governor Thomas Hutchinson's house twelve days later.[9]

Events in Boston were not isolated. A Newport mob sacked several houses belonging to crown officials on August 28. In New York City, after a rugged evening of frolic on November 1, a mob gutted the house occupied by the British officer Major James. On September 2, 1765, a crowd in Annapolis hauled down the house of stamp officer Zachariah Hood, forcing him to flee the province. Crowds also focused upon other symbols of wealth. New Yorkers captured Lieutenant-Governor Cadwallader Colden's carriage and two of his sleighs, displayed his effigy in the carriage, and burned all three vehicles. In Albany a mob defaced the house of a suspected stamp distributor, destroyed some furniture, and drew his carriages through the streets in flames.[10]

At times mobs came precariously close to challenging their whig leaders. In Newport the opponents of the Stamp Act had encouraged a sailor, John Weber, to head the mob. They soon discovered that Weber enjoyed his power too much. The whig leaders plied him with gifts. When that did not appease him, they prepared for the worst. Fortunately for these merchants, lawyers, and other prominent Newporters, a royal official arrested Weber. Despite the threat of a rescue, Weber stayed in custody while whig leaders orchestrated more organized demonstrations to occupy the mob.[11]

The conservative and affluent leaders of the resistance movement understood the threat to the social order when lower-class sailors, mechanics, and others threatened symbols of wealth and hierarchy. Soon after the mob broke into Oliver's house, several whig leaders tried to persuade the rioters to leave. Boston leaders were nearly unanimous in condemning the "licentious" proceedings and looting of Hutchinson's house on August 26. When radical Boston minister Jonathan Mayhew discovered that one of his sermons on liberty was seen as inciting the anti-Hutchinson mob, he was aghast and asserted that he needed "to moderate and pacify than to risk exciting so sensitive a people."[12] Fear of more extensive mobbing convinced New York merchants to take to the streets on the nights after November 1 to quell further disturbances. Finding their influence more limited than they expected, men like Robert R. Livingston turned to ship captains who knew many sailors in the crowd personally and who therefore might effectively dissuade them from violence. In Philadelphia the opposition to rioting was more extensive, in large part due to the political connections of stamp master John Hughes. There, hundreds of artisans, calling themselves the white oaks, patrolled the streets and broke up several effigy processions, allowing the whig leaders time to meet with Hughes and convince him not to uphold the law before mob violence became too extensive.[13]

Eventually, ad hoc committees organized, called Sons of Liberty, that simultaneously struggled to limit the activity of the mob, while using crowds as their main tool of coercion. Although able to prevent another Hutchinson-like attack, the Sons of Liberty did not always have an easy time of it. In New York City, they excoriated violators of the nonimportation movement and utilized a shouting crowd as enforcement, but limited the actual violence against both property and persons. Newburyport Sons of Liberty also struggled to limit crowds. In February 1766, they hauled John Boardman before a local justice to swear he would never again use stamp paper. Although the committee then dismissed him as absolved, to three cheers from the assembled crowd, a mob paraded with his effigy again the next day with drums beating and flags flying.[14]

If the Sons of Liberty often managed to control and guide crowd action against the Stamp Act, their position remained precarious. They faced the possibility, of which whig leaders were acutely aware, that they would be consumed by the monster—mobs—that they had conjured to thwart imperial regulation. As they watched shoemaker Ebenezer McIntosh, sailor John Weber, and others lead the tumultuous crowd composed of men of lower social standing, not a few whig leaders began to wonder where it might end.

Beyond the Imperial Crisis

In the months and years after the Stamp Act controversy the contagion of rioting spread. There was a certain continuity in popular disorder that ran from the colonial to the revolutionary period, but the imperial crisis provided a new atmosphere for rioting. Land riots, conflicts between different sections of colonies, and questions of community regulation persisted. At times these issues overlapped and interacted with the imperial crisis, and at times they did not. Usually rioters followed nonviolent rituals practiced earlier, but in several instances the violence got out of hand, and men fought pitched battles leading to fatalities. The wave of rioting sweeping through the colonies seemed to convince the rioters that they could push to extremes, and it persuaded those against disorder of the necessity of firm measures.[15]

The tenant uprising in New York suggests how the context, even the intensity, of these riots differed as a result of the imperial crisis. The great Hudson River landlords, several of whom were leaders of the opposition to British taxation, faced their steepest challenge during the anti–Stamp Act hoopla. Starting in November of 1765 there was a revival of the tenant and squatter riots of the previous decade. Crowds, numbering as many as two hundred, forcefully evicted rent paying tenants of the landlords in Dutchess County. By the following spring the rebellion had spread. In late April 1766 aggrieved tenant farmers and squatters, although driven by issues distinct from the imperial crisis, called themselves Sons of Liberty and marched on New York City. About five hundred gathered at Kingsbridge, the main entry point to Manhattan Island. These men believed that they would be joined by the mechanics, laborers, and sailors that had been rioting against the Stamp Act. No such urban/rural alliance materialized. The governor refused to hear their petition. After he threatened to use force to disperse them, they returned to their farms. But the rioting continued. In June there were several confrontations between the landlords and their opponents, culminating in a violent affray at Nobletown in which at least four men were killed. A month later British troops arrived to drive off the squatters.[16]

The North Carolina Regulator movement ended in a similar flurry of violence and also occurred against the backdrop of the British imperial crisis. Several Stamp Act riots toook place in coastal North Carolina, ranging from effigy processions and crowd intimidation of officials, to an extended quasi-military operation in which several hundred men marched on Brunswick, temporarily captured the governor, and compelled Crown officials not to enforce the measure.

Like the tenant uprising in New York, the North Carolina Regulation had no direct link to the imperial crisis, yet there were connections in both ideology and the forms of crowd behavior. North Carolina Regulators had a whig fear of corruption, introduced on the colony level by merchants and lawyers, and wanted fair representation and a court system purged of place holders. Their rioting included court closing and intimidation of officials and mirrored the anti–Stamp Act riots in North Carolina and land riots of other colonies. In September 1770, hundreds of Regulators gathered at Hillsborough. Armed with sticks and switches they took over the county court. By stopping legal processes they halted suits against any of their number, and symbolically humiliated the judicial process. Driving the judge off the bench they captured and whipped several lawyers. Since this common form of corporal punishment was used by the court, it therefore was an appropriate punishment for the court's minions. Exhibiting resentment like that expressed by the Bostonians against Thomas Hutchinson, they abused placeman Edmund Fanning, broke into his house, burned his papers, ransacked the furniture, and demolished the building. Fanning had long been singled out for what Regulators believed were his ill-gotten gains. As with Hutchinson's house, the destruction of the building and the furniture was an assault on wealth, especially wealth earned through nefarious means. The burning of the papers held at least two important meanings. On a symbolic level the papers signified Fanning's official duties; on a more pragmatic plane they may have been legally relevant and threatening to many Regulators. Finally, taking ritual role reversal even further, they held a mock court.

Unfortunately for the Regulators their movement collapsed in 1771 when serious opposition from the tidewater region escalated the confrontation and led to greater violence. In May two thousand to three thousand men gathered hoping to get Governor William Tryon to redress their grievances. Tryon, however, arrived with 1,185 militia men from the eastern counties of North Carolina. Supported by artillery and a well-equipped army, he was in no mood to parley. Instead, Tryon sent the Regulators an ultimatum. When they failed to respond, he attacked. The subsequent Battle of Alamance on May 16 ended in approximately thirty deaths and two hundred casualties on both sides. Tryon also had seven men executed.[17]

The Regulator movement of South Carolina differed from its North Carolina counterpart and reflected less the traditions of popular disorder and the rioting of the ongoing imperial crisis. Yet the lawlessness that the Regulators reacted against was in part a product of the near anarchy and political paralysis brought on by the colonial resistance movement.

Starting in the fall of 1767, and running to 1769, a nascent planter class in South Carolina strove to establish the rule of law and order on the frontier through crowd action. The issue here was not the closing of courts, but the administration of ad hoc justice against bandits, slave stealers, gamblers, and other undesirables. Following legal precedent for the regional treatment of slaves and other rioters, the Regulators relied on the lash as punishment.[18]

During the 1770s two other major conflicts, based in overlapping boundary claims and the search by New England settlers for more land, erupted on the frontier. Each also merged with the movement for independence.

Extreme violence, shading into actual warfare, marred the controversy over Pennsylvania lands in the northern Susquehanna River valley. The Yankee-Pennamite contest began in 1769 when settlers from Connecticut, staking their claims on a land company charted by Connecticut, made their way to the area of northeastern Pennsylvania called Wyoming. Upon their arrival they discovered a trading outpost of newly appointed Pennsylvania proprietors. The Connecticut men drove off the Pennamites. Sieges and countersieges followed. This was a shooting war, and in the next few years several men were killed. Meanwhile more New Englanders poured in, especially after 1772 when some peace was established in the region and the settlers organized towns that were an extension of Litchfield County (Connecticut claimed the territory based on its sea-to-sea charter). The controversy was caught in the maelstrom of revolution when an army of seven hundred Pennamites, under tory leadership, shattered that peace in 1775. Beating back this invasion force, the Connecticut men soon found themselves enmeshed in a brutal frontier war with Indians, tories, and the British. After Independence, despite United States ratification of Pennsylvania's claim, some outbreaks of violence continued.[19]

The Green Mountain boys, meeting less resistance, generally limited themselves to the standard techniques used in most other land riots of the day—eviction of settlers whose land was patented by their opponents, destruction of houses and property, frequent threats, and some physical abuse. Both New York and New Hampshire claimed what is now the state of Vermont. A royal decision granting the territory to New York did not change the minds of many in the region. In July 1771 Sheriff Henry Ten Eyck of Albany arrived to evict James Breakenridge. The sheriff's posse, however, evaporated in the face of well over one hundred men defending Breakenridge. With little support, Ten Eyck's writ, and the long arm of New York law, became meaningless. For the next couple of years, the Green Mountain boys interrupted New York surveyors, drove off settlers who registered their land in New York, pulled down and burned homes, and defied New York officials. They also intimidated New York justices and joined in some court closings. By 1775 any semblance of New York's authority had disappeared. In the same year, Ethan Allen led the Green Mountain boys in the capture of Fort Ticonderoga and Crown Point. Within two years after that Vermonters wrote a constitution and proclaimed themselves a state.

The rebellion in Vermont provides a good example of the influence of pervasive revolutionary disorder on other conflicts. Men like Ethan Allen, who was something of a propagandist, purposefully referred to the term "mob" to describe the intimidation and collective action perpetrated by the Green Mountain boys during the 1770s and used the opportunity presented by the revolution to redefine the political map. Others acted in a similar vein. Court closings in eastern Vermont in 1775, for example, were not directly related to the contest with New York. Instead, farmers who found themselves in economic difficulty rioted to suspend the legal process that threatened their property. The hundreds of irate Massachusetts farmers who occupied and closed county courthouses in 1774 may have been resisting the Coercive Acts, but they also protected themselves from debt seizures. The overlapping of local and imperial concerns also appeared in frontier Maine as early as 1766 when a mob raided the property of rich merchant and creditor Richard King during the anti–Stamp Act rioting of that spring.[20]

Combinations of motives can be seen in some riots of communal regulation away from the frontier. During the Stamp Act disturbances in New York City, for instance, rioters demolished several houses of prostitution. Although the exact cause for this activity was unclear, the houses in question not only stood as a moral affront to the community, but also were probably frequented by the detested British military.[21]

Two sets of riots against smallpox inoculation reveal further the impact of the spread of rioting during this period. They also exposed certain strains of egalitarianism. In the eighteenth century those who supported inoculation often saw themselves as part of the enlightened world of the elite and opposed to superstition and popular traditions. Inoculation instigated by either whig or tory patricians may have signaled a challenge to plebeian beliefs that might best be countered with crowd action.

The Norfolk riots in 1768 and 1769 show how the reasons for communal regulation mixed with imperial concerns. The majority in Norfolk feared inoculation because it threatened those not inoculated. In June 1768 crowds twice besieged the plantation housing inoculated families, breaking windows and doors and finally compelling the residents to go to the pest house where all those with infectious diseases were kept. Almost a year later, more rioting broke out when Cornelious Calvert inoculated three slaves and an apprentice. Again, the crowd shattered windows and behaved uproariously. It also assailed a ropemaker who gave evidence at a trial for the last riots. Beneath the surface of this rioting, however, were stark whig/tory divisions and antiauthoritarian proclivities. Those advocating inoculation also tended to be affluent individuals in Norfolk who supported the King. The anti-inoculation mobs contained many plebeian whigs.[22]

The inoculation riots in Marblehead in January and February 1774 undercut the position of the leading whig politicians and revealed the influence of the resistance movement on the forms of disturbance. Even more so than in Norfolk, the riots threatened authority. The proprietors of the smallpox hospital in this New England mercantile community were John and Jonathan

Glover, Elbridge Gerry, and Azor Orne. These men were wealthy leaders of the whig cause. The challenge to their inoculation efforts also challenged their wealth and position. Although the crowd never went further than breaking the windows of the proprietors' homes, it used threats and coercion, like that applied against stamp agents and loyalists, to wrangle agreement from the proprietors to close the hospital. More resonant of revolutionary rioting was the tarring and feathering of some men who had stolen clothes from the hospital. The riots in Marblehead lasted for several days and also included practices used by crowds before 1765. Rioters blackened their faces several times, burned a small boat used to bring supplies to the island, rescued imprisoned comrades, and eventually wrecked the hospital itself. The proprietors of the hospital not only lost their investment, but also surrendered their political influence and wondered where all the talk about liberty and the heavy-handed use of mobs was leading.[23]

They had good cause for concern. Rioting seemed to be breaking out everywhere for many different reasons. In New York City a lawyer's comment in support of the Stamp Act in March 1766 triggered not only an effigy display, but also an odd demonstration against the legal profession in which a crowd of boys mockingly dragged around the city a goat, which was a popular symbol for lawyers in the eighteenth century.[24] On May 5, 1766, after news of the repeal of the Stamp Act arrived in New York City, a mob broke up the reestablished local theater. This action defied the immorality of the stage and expressed resentment to ostentatious displays of wealth during a time when many in the community were suffering economically. During the subsequent years crowds throughout the colonies rioted over many issues, including the collection of debts that were considered unfair, prostitutes plying their wares, adulterers, and radical religious sects. Even the students of Harvard seized the moment to protest rancid butter and college rules.[25]

From Resistance to Revolution

The imperial crisis lay at the core of most rioting in the 1760s and 1770s. The repeal of the Stamp Act did not mark the end of this type of collective violence, nor did it mark the triumph of groups like the Sons of Liberty in their efforts to rein in the mob; instead, in the months and years that followed, the people in the street continued their clamor and refined the techniques of popular disorder. In the late 1760s soldiers and civilians confronted each other several times, leading to the rising significance of the liberty pole in New York City and the violent outburst of the Boston Massacre on March 5, 1770. During the same period, opposition to customs enforcement increased, and although mobs continued to use effigy parades and other tactics developed during the Stamp Act controversy, a public ceremony—tar and feathers—emerged that seemed well suited for customs informants. The Tea Act brought on new rioting, beginning with the Boston Tea Party of December 16, 1773. Other tea parties, renewed crowd activity to enforce trade sanctions, and harassment of tories gradually shaded into a form of warfare from 1774 to 1775. Even after independence, however, rioting did not subside. Mobs molested tories, affected elections, and participated in bread and draft riots.

The New York City civilian and military confrontations began within months of the repeal of the Stamp Act. New Yorkers had erected two flagpoles on the common to celebrate the King's birthday in June. The public ceremony, however, was more a celebration of the repeal of the Stamp Act and a typical fertility rite of spring (the poles looked like maypoles), than a commemoration of the Hanoverian dynasty. Moreover, the New York assembly's refusal to comply with the British Quartering Act in the summer of 1766, just as additional British troops arrived to garrison the city, intensified the animosity between locals and the army. That the flagstaffs sat on the parade ground used by the British troops, and in front of some barracks, only added to the affront.

One night in August 1766, several soldiers cut one of the poles down (it is not clear what happened to the other one). The next day New Yorkers held a meeting in protest. A party of soldiers with drawn bayonets attacked those attending and prevented the raising of another pole. Suddenly a flagpole became a "Tree of Liberty"—Bostonians had identified such a tree in their town during the Stamp Act crisis.[26] In the coming months that tree of liberty metamorphosed into a liberty pole as New Yorkers repeatedly reerected it after each military assault. New Yorkers organized their 1767 celebration of the repeal of the Stamp Act around the pole. Each public ritual and every civilian-military clash added to the pole's symbolic weight.

The animosity between civilians and military ran deeper than questions of imperial policy. Off-duty soldiers competed for the attention of young women, often behaved in a rowdy and imperious manner, and took scarce jobs away from laborers. During the fall of 1766 soldiers became particularly offensive in their behavior, sacking houses of prostitution when they believed they were treated unfairly, and assaulting several civilians in the streets. This tension culminated in a riot in January 1770, also known as the Battle of Golden Hill, when two civilians distributing handbills deriding the military seized a soldier, and his comrades tried to rescue him. Several injuries but no fatalities resulted.[27]

New York was not the only community to experience this type of disorder. In July 1767 in Elizabeth, New Jersey, British officers, who refused to pay their debts to local proprietors, marched through town with fife and drum, broke windows, rescued comrades held in jail, and fought with townsmen.[28] More serious, and following a close parallel to the affairs in New York, was the situation in Boston.

In the months before the Boston Massacre of March 5, 1770, there were many brawls between laborers and soldiers, with crowds harassing British soldiers on and off duty. The riot on King Street the night of March 5 started as another one of these incidents. For several hours preceding the shooting, soldiers and Bostonians fought throughout the city. Attention, however, focused around King Street and the sentry at the customs house. A small reenforcement of seven men came up to support the sentry. As they were pressed hard by the crowd that hurled ice and snow balls, and amid clamor and tumult, a gun went off. No one knows for sure how the shooting started; some say in a scuffle, others say they heard the command "fire." Regardless of how it began, the soldiers then leveled their guns and discharged them into the crowd, killing four men instantly. Eight others were wounded, one of whom died a few days later.[29]

Although local concerns were essential to the King Street riot, anti-customs agitation and the colonial nonimportation movement also played a part. Before the Boston Massacre at least twenty customs riots took place, with many of these protesting the Townshend Duties. Typically, the rioters molested an informant or lowly customs official, or interfered with the enforcement of customs duties by protecting contraband items. Violators of colony-wide agreements not to import goods from England were also the object of the mob's wrath.[30]

During the late 1760s colonists developed and elaborated upon ritual humiliation using tar and feathers. Although there may have been one instance of tarring and feathering in Norfolk, Virginia, in 1766, it was only after a tarring and feathering of a minor customs official on September 7, 1768, in Salem, Massachusetts, that the practice spread and became recognized as a specialty of American crowds. Within a few years, rioters employed tar and feathers throughout the colonies. Sometimes crowds varied their routine. One group of Bostonians tarred and feathered the horse of a merchant caught with imported goods in June 1770, and another coated a victim's house with excrement and a dose of feathers. Initially those tarred and feathered tended to be customs guards and others further down on the social scale. In 1775 crowds increasingly used tar and feathers, and once hostilities broke out even high born tories became vulnerable to a fitting for a "New England Jacket."

This ritual was an amalgam of rites of punishment like "riding the stang" or the skimington, official judicial punishments, and ancient sailor custom. "Riding the stang" and skimingtons were a form of charivari in which crowds captured a violator of community morality and held him up to public ridicule. In "riding the stang" the victim was tied to a wooden pole, usually facing backward, and dragged painfully about town. This practice arose in the late colonial era in New England, New York, and New Jersey. Skimingtons might include "riding the stang" and other practices like rough music to publicly ridicule an object of communal scorn. While using a different form of punishment, tar and feathers contained many of the trappings of such rituals, including the infliction of some pain and great mortification upon the victim.

Tar and feathers also resembled judicial punishments. In the eighteenth century officials believed in public punishment. Executions, corporal punishments, brandings, the wearing of letters—like Hester Prynne's embroidered scarlet "A"—and the standing in the town square in stocks contained ritual to sustain the majesty of the law and exhibit for all the fruits of crime. Malefactors also were often carted around town for everyone to see. If the criminal openly confessed his wrongdoing all the better. Thus the public spectacle, with carting, confessions, and the wearing of a special "coat," all mirrored actions taken by the law.

The "coat," however, had a different source. As early as the twelfth century there were references to tarring and feathering as a military punishment. Before the 1760s, there are scattered reports of tar and feathers used by sailors, who always had an ample supply of tar on hand. Moreover, there may be a connection to Pope Day celebrations. Organizers covered their effigies with tar, and there are some parallels between the iconography of devils in the eighteenth century and the sight of an individual when tarred and feathered.

By combining elements of all three components of public ritual outlined above, tarring and feathering had a special appeal to the plebeian crowd. Furthermore, although the practice could be painful, by itself it was not fatal. Like the effigy procession, it was a means to channel crowd rage while not going to any great excess. When someone was hurt seriously by the crowd during a tarring and feathering, as in Philadelphia in November 1770, the injury was sustained by a beating and other physical abuse.[31]

Much to the relief of the whig leadership, not every crowd in the 1760s and 1770s resorted to tar and feathers. For many conservatives, tarring and feathering entailed too much physical abuse and contained the potential for greater violence. Crowds, therefore, continued many practices that first surfaced during the Stamp Act crisis: public confessions, carting through town of the victim or his effigy, parades, and demonstrations. Although fairly persistent, this activity increased during some periods (late 1760s and after 1773), and subsided during others (1771–1773).

Oddly, although the elite struggled to limit the excesses of the mob, a riot they orchestrated provided the incident that drove the English government and their colonies onto a collision course. Whig leaders planned the Boston Tea Party, in which rioters carefully ruined only the tea, and left the vessel and the rest of the cargo unmolested. Indian disguise and blackened faces suggest plebeian influence, and some of the mob may have joined spontaneously, but there can be little doubt that the impulse that lay behind the tea party came from the top down.[32] The idea, however, quickly caught on with tea parties in New York, Philadelphia, Charleston, and elsewhere. Sometimes the mob followed the procedures established in Boston, sometimes there were deviations. New York's "Mohawks" moved to destroy the tea before the local leadership could get organized, but like their Boston cousins, merely tossed the tea into the harbor.[33] In Maryland, after a confession and faced with threats of the "American discipline of tarring and feathering," the owner of a brig that had imported tea burned his own vessel and cargo.[34]

During 1774 and 1775 collective violence became even more pervasive than it had been during the Stamp Act controversy as many Americans joined in opposing the Coercive Acts passed to punish Boston and Massachusetts for the tea party. Court closings, sometimes involving thousands of men, swept through rural New England to stop debt proceedings and to make the Massachusetts Government Act, one of Britain's repressive measures, void. Colonial Americans repeated the effigy parades, demonstrations, public confessions, intimidation, and tar and feathers they had practiced with such frequency for over a decade. Those who continued loyal to the Crown were singled out by the mob. Some of this activity was organized from those on top of society, much of it came simply from those in the street.[35]

Gradually this popular disorder merged imperceptibly with militia organization and outright warfare. In August 1774, New Yorkers headed by Isaac Sears fought a brief engagement with the H.M.S. *Asia* over control of the cannon on the Battery. Fifteen months later Sears entered the city, leading a band of Liberty Boys from Connecticut, and wrecked the press of James Rivington. The armed bands calling themselves Minute Men in rural New England persecuted tories, gathered weapons, and congregated by the hundreds on the slightest whisper of a confrontation with the British. Ultimately, it was a group of these men, organized as a militia but only a short step removed from a mob, that stood on Lexington Green on April 19, 1775.[36]

The war did not end rioting. Americans were far from a united people as they began hostilities with the British. Many wanted to stay loyal to King George III. Dissent was unacceptable for the whigs, and harassment of tories expanded after April 1775. Countless tories were driven from their homes, tarred and feathered, beaten, and sometimes killed. Much of this persecution came under the orders of local committees, but often the crowd went beyond what even whig officials desired. In the near anarchy that accompanied this internecine conflict, whig leaders strove to gain control and provide a new order that sometimes meant disciplining those who participated in a mob, even when that mob acted in the name of the whig cause. The Albany Committee, after a group of whigs had rounded up and whipped some tories and forced them to run the gauntlet, resolved in March 1778 that "the inflicting of any Corporal punishment or the depriving of any of the Subjects of this State of their Property without proper authority is an infringement of the Privileges of the People, contrary to sound Policy and in direct Violation of all Law and Justice."[37]

Rioting also spread to elections. During the colonial era a hotly contested election might include a disturbance. In the new political environment, with the very nature of society at stake, the threshold of violence decreased. Rioting broke out in several Maryland counties over property qualifications for voting in 1776. Some Philadelphians during the same year rioted to exclude Germans from the polls. Political debate in Charleston over the treatment of tories at the end of the war broke out into repeated incidents of street violence.

Mobs even cracked down on dissent within whig ranks. In February 1776 the New York Committee of Mechanics, a body independent of the local committee chosen to oversee resistance, objected to printer Samuel Loudon publishing a response to Thomas Paine's *Common Sense*. When he persisted, believing his good standing in the whig cause would protect him, a crowd broke into his house and destroyed the pamphlet before it was finished. The following year, whig printer William Goddard almost found himself tarred and feathered in Baltimore because he published a satirical comment about the latest British peace offer.[38]

Crowds also rioted over prices. Women, like in bread riots in England and France, dominated many of these disturbances. In July 1777 about one hundred Boston women went to merchant Thomas Boylston's shop demanding coffee at a set price. When he refused, they started to drag him to a wharf for a dunking. Before they could do so, Boylston surrendered the storeroom's keys. The women then left him to get the coffee, which they promised to sell to the poor. Similar disturbances occurred elsewhere. In the state of New York a crowd of twenty-two women and two continental soldiers came to Peter Messier's house in May 1777. Refusing to pay his price for tea, they set a just price and beat him. The same concerns for the good of the local community lay behind some resistance to recruitment during the war. A crowd of approximately one hundred in April 1781 prevented a draft of men in Roxbridge County, Virginia, claiming that they had given enough to the war and feared that they would not be able to get their crops in with a further drain on manpower.[39]

The ideological and political content of these disturbances often went beyond the assertion of an older moral economy and fostered more radical ideas. In May 1777, a Boston mob, headed by Joyce, Jr., persecuted five merchants for adhering to "Tory principles," refusing paper money, and offering discounts for specie. The rioters carted their victims through town, brought them to the outskirts, physically abused them, and told them never to return. This disturbance combined issues of moral economy, since the victims' monetary policies affected the just price of items they sold, and the cause of the revolution, since the merchants' policies accelerated an inflation that hurt the war effort. Perhaps more importantly there was a strain of radical antiauthoritarianism in this plebeian attack on affluent merchants. The title of the mob leader indicates a connection to the radicalism of the English Civil War in the seventeenth century: Coronet George Joyce had led the men who captured Charles I in 1647 and was named one of his executioners.[40]

In Philadelphia the ideological and political crosscurrents were just as complex, entangling the issue of the just price with the larger struggle for political

control of the state. Radicals, espousing a new egalitarianism evident in the
state constitution of 1777, argued for the need for price controls. Conservatives opposed the overly democratic state constitution and supported laissez
faire economics. To complicate things further, the radicals claimed that much
of the price gouging came from known tories and enemies of their country. On
October 4, 1779, this contest came to a head when a few hundred militia, representing the radicals, gathered and captured five men they claimed were
tories. The militia marched four of these men around town, passing the house
of James Wilson, a leading opponent of price fixing. Wilson and several of his
friends were well armed and prepared for a fight. Just as the militia had finished filing by the building a shot rang out. Quickly a full-scale battle broke
out that ended only with the arrival of mounted troops that slashed through
the ranks of militia and dispersed them. The conservatives won. The Fort
Wilson defenders lost one dead, three wounded; the militia numbered five to
seven dead, at least fourteen wounded.[41]

Legacy of the Revolution

Persistent disorder strengthened popular faith in mobs. Rioting had proven
itself a useful tool of resistance against a government that seemed distant,
alien, and intent on usurping the liberty of the people. Moreover, the experience with crowds during the 1760s and 1770s had helped to translate long-
standing plebeian notions of antiauthoritarianism into an egalitarianism that
gave the people preeminence in society and government. Although whig leaders often had opposed excessive rioting, and the people out of doors were
defeated in incidents like those at Fort Wilson, many common folk continued
to believe that the tumultuous crowd held a special place as an expression of
the people's immediate will. Whig leaders accepted the centrality of the
"people" in the novel world order of the 1780s and 1790s. They argued, however, that the new republican forms of government now made politics out of
doors unnecessary. With government theoretically in the hands of the people,
the people no longer needed to riot.

In the years after the Revolutionary War tension between these two contrasting positions can be found in three different areas: riots over community
regulation; agrarian or backcountry rebellions; and a politics of confrontation.
Perhaps the largest riot of the late eighteenth century to regulate communal
morality occurred in April 1788 in New York City. Much of the country was
then all in a hubbub about the Constitution. But in New York, where the issue
of ratification would not be resolved until July, the subject that brought thousands into the street concerned the use at the medical school of cadavers
robbed from graves. When one medical student jokingly told a little boy,
whose mother had just died, that the cadaver he was working on was the boy's
mother, collective violence quickly broke out. A crowd rushed into the medical
school and gutted it of all of its scientific trappings—symbols in the popular

mind of the dissecting of bodies by doctors and their students. The rioters buried all cadavers found and captured several medical students who were later turned over to the custody of city officials. On the next day disturbances continued as a tumultuous crowd insisted on searching the medical school again. Officials placated the rioters, allowing an inspection of the medical school and a search of doctors' houses. Still dissatisfied, a crowd decided to punish the medical students who had been lodged in jail for safekeeping. City officials prepared for the worst. Few militia heeded a call to muster, but enough reported for duty to do battle with the mob. After hurling insults and rocks, the crowd made a rush upon the jail. The defenders opened fire. In the melee at least three rioters were killed and several others wounded.

The doctor's riot was important not only because it was one of the largest and bloodiest urban riots of eighteenth-century America, but also because it illustrated so many of the crosscurrents of the age. Like riots against smallpox inoculation, this disturbance reflected the tension between the enlightened and rational science of the elite and the popular beliefs of the people.[42] The anti-patrician slant to the riot, too, appeared in the confrontation at the jailhouse when a crowd composed of some artisans, laborers, and others of lower standing, insulted and abused magistrates and gentlemen volunteers who saw themselves as the city's elite. The principal aim of the riot, however, was the maintenance of communal morality. Earlier Anglo-American crowds had destroyed bawdy houses or unrigged ships ready to sail with grain. The anti-doctor mob ransacked the medical school, provided proper burial for cadavers, and thereby asserted popular ideas about the sanctity of the grave. Rioters captured some medical students and handled them roughly, but willingly turned them over to civil authorities in the same manner that crowds earlier in the century treated press-gangs. We do not know what the rioters would have done to the medical students on the second day had they succeeded at the jail—perhaps they would have tarred and feathered them, or perhaps, and this was the fear of the authorities, the treatment would have been worse.

The reaction of the authorities was interesting. At first, as in earlier interactions between the crowd and officials where there was a belief that the crowd had a legitimate grievance, the mayor and others tried to work with the mob. As the tumult continued, their attitude changed. Chief Justice Richard Morris declared in his charge to the grand jury investigating the riot that "Though it [the riot] may be palliated in the first stages . . . yet, after every search was made to satisfy the wishes of the people, the attack upon the jail, and the insults to the Magistrates were altogether inexcusable."[43]

During the doctor's riot of 1788 the tolerance for riots to regulate the community was short. Afterward tolerance became even shorter. There were three other large-scale riots in New York City during the 1790s to regulate communal morality: demonstrations against failed speculator William Duer in 1792, and riots attacking bawdy houses in 1793 and 1799. In all three cases magistrates did not hesitate to take action to quell disturbances they believed were unnecessary and violations of the public order. Although this type of riot—especially on a massive scale—decreased in the larger cities after the opening of the nineteenth century, communities across the nation occasionally rioted in the eighteenth-century spirit of regulating community.[44]

Perhaps a more serious threat to both the political and social order, revealing in stark terms the persistence of popular ideas about rioting, was the agrarian unrest that followed the end of the Revolutionary War. In Shays' Rebellion, the Whiskey Rebellion, the decades of rioting on the Maine frontier, and other instances, farmers asserted their right to riot based on the model of the American Revolution and upon older ideas of crowd action. These farmers rioted over issues rooted in their own egalitarian interpretation of the revolution. Most conservative officials reacted to these disturbances with decision, believing that all politics out of doors was now illegitimate.

The Massachusetts farmers that closed courts in August and September of 1786 did not intend to overthrow the government. Hard-pressed by creditors and tax collectors, the farmers clamored for paper money that would ease their financial burdens and allow them to keep the fields and homes that they saw as crucial to maintaining their own independence. They hoped to compel officials to treat them fairly and to offer debtor relief.[45]

The hordes of farmers that marched on Taunton, Worcester, Great Barrington, and Springfield, crowding the courthouses and preventing the judges from hearing any cases, did little more than they had done in 1774 and 1775 to void the Massachusetts Act passed by parliament. There had been many court closings before. New Jersey rioters had done so in their land disputes, as did the Green Mountain boys of Vermont. North Carolina Regulators also had closed courts. More recently, some Massachusetts farmers had shut down the judicial process throughout the 1780s. Similar action took place in Camden, South Carolina; rural Virginia; Maryland; Pennsylvania; and New Jersey. In the same months that Massachusetts farmers marched on courts, their cousins in Vermont and New Hampshire followed suit. In New Hampshire, farmers temporarily surrounded the state capital on September 20, 1786.[46]

There were continuities with the past and with others elsewhere in the United States. Shaysites wore a sprig of evergreen in their hats as a badge of loyalty to their cause, since the pine tree had been a symbol of liberty in Massachusetts. They assumed the name Regulators, believing that they acted in the spirit of the North Carolina backcountry farmers fifteen years earlier. Many Shaysite leaders had military experience in the Revolution, and the Shaysites organized themselves into militia bands that were reminiscent of the Minute Men of 1775.

When the rebellion took on larger proportions during the winter of 1786 and 1787, the pattern paralleled the escalation of events at the beginning of the War for Independence. There was one significant difference, however; the Shaysites failed. In January 1787, Shaysites, following the precedent of the Minute Man and committee persecution of loyalists twelve years earlier, captured several shopkeepers and creditors and appropriated some of their property. To strengthen their hand in the coming confrontation with troops sent to suppress them, and like the revolutionaries who seized arms at Fort Ticonderoga in 1775, the Shaysites attempted to capture the arsenal at Springfield on January 25, 1787. Unfortunately for the rebels, the defenders used artillery and drove them back. The Shaysites lost four dead and at least twenty others wounded. During the next few weeks the Shaysites and the army sent from the east clashed several times, including a decisive surprise attack by the government troops at Petersham in February. Sporadic resistance continued, with occasional harassment of storekeepers and supporters of the government, but the rebellion had been crushed.[47]

When Thomas Jefferson heard of Shays' Rebellion he commented that a little rebellion now and then was a good thing since it would check the power of the governors and guarantee that they acted in the interests of the liberty of the people. He understood that the Shaysites operated in the full spirit of the American Revolution.[48] Most of the major leaders of the country disagreed. Men who once encouraged anti-British mobs, now reversed themselves. Old radicals in Boston, such as Samuel Adams, became frightened by the specter of these backcountry farmers dictating the course of government through extralegal violence.[49] More conservative politicians seized the moment to trumpet their cause. Alexander Hamilton, who at this time was bending his talents toward molding a stronger national government, believed that incidents like Shays' Rebellion, if left unchecked, ultimately would drive the various states apart. He repeatedly referred to the rebellion in the Federalist Papers as proof of the need for a stronger government.[50]

The government under the Constitution of the United States, however, did not suddenly end popular faith in the efficacy of the mob, nor did it prevent the outbreak of other riots and rebellions on the frontier. Whiskey Boys in western Pennsylvania in the early 1790s testified to the resiliency of mob traditions.

Similar to those who had opposed the Stamp Act and other revenue measures, the Whiskey Rebels viewed the excise tax on the produce of their stills as an onerous intrusion of an external power—the federal government—that placed a special burden on frontier farmers while leaving the cosmopolitan east relatively unscathed. Adhering to a rough egalitarianism derived from participation in the Revolution, the frontiersman believed that the money gained from the tax would only enhance the power of the government at the expense of the liberty of the people. The corrupting influence of the law, just as in the Stamp Act, was even more irksome because local men served as collection agents. Again a strain of antiauthoritarianism can be detected in the efforts of some to strike not only at the distant government, but also at all pretensions to distinction. As one tomahawk-wielding frontiersman proclaimed in Pittsburgh, "it is not the excise law only that must go down, [but] your high offices and salaries. A great deal more is to be done; I am but beginning yet."[51]

Resistance to the tax followed well-worn forms of popular disorder. Rioters coerced excise officers into resigning their offices, as mobs had done to stamp distributors almost twenty-five years earlier. The Whiskey Boys also used threats or direct action, again following revolutionary patterns, to convince complying neighbors to join the ranks of resistance. Typical was a disturbance in Pigeon Creek, Pennsylvania, in which a gang of sixteen captured the local excise collector. This small crowd mixed prerevolutionary custom with ritual developed during the Revolution; they donned women's clothing and tarred and feathered their victim. To further humiliate the collector, they took his horse—an important mode of transportation and status symbol—from him. The rioters also cut their victim's hair, an act intended as an insult and perhaps meant to suggest a scalping—a practice that all on the frontier were familiar with and dreaded. Later, government officials referred to the rebels as "White Indians."

The Whiskey Rebels repeated this pattern of behavior in subsequent rioting. Crowds sometimes blackened their faces, another old English riot practice, and selectively smashed the collector's or complier's property. By 1794, as the excise took effect, resistance grew and the number of incidents increased. Distillers paying the excise found themselves visited by "Tom the Tinkerer" and their stills riddled with bullets by "Tom's" men.[52] In one case, when an official decided to resist the rebels, greater violence occurred. Even in this confrontation, the rioters followed eighteenth-century patterns of disorder. After gun battles at excise inspector John Neville's house at Bower Hill on July 16 and 17, 1794, that left two rebels dead, the soldiers defending Neville surrendered. The Whiskey Boys did not exact vengeance with blood. Instead, they gutted, looted, and burned the substantial home of the affluent Neville. The rebels organized committees, held conventions and meetings, and throughout the disaffected areas they raised liberty poles as an emblem of their resistance.

The federal government did not hesitate to quell the disorder. Declaring the Whiskey Boys rebels, the United States government organized a twelve thousand–man army that meandered its way through the Pennsylvania mountains in the fall of 1794. By the time this awesome force arrived in Pittsburgh, chopping liberty poles down as they went, the resistance had evaporated. Many Whiskey Boys accepted amnesty, and the few diehards either surrendered or left western Pennsylvania.[53]

There was a lesson to be learned from the farmers of western Massachusetts and the Whiskey Boys of Pennsylvania; modeling behavior too closely upon the experience of the 1760s and 1770s, and pushing resistance to the point of rebellion, was dangerous and risked bringing forth whatever power the government could wield in suppression.

Frontier settlers in Maine followed a more measured course in disturbances from the 1760s to the 1820s. The sprinkling of people in the region before the Revolutionary War became a flood after 1783 as the poor from coastal New England washed ashore in the hope of a better life. Believing that only widespread and equitably distributed land could ensure the viability of the republic, these settlers held that the American Revolution had opened the Maine woods for anyone with a strong enough back to chop the trees and clear the land. Armed in this belief, these men resisted all claims by those affluent men who had the political connections to have garnered land grants for vast tracks of wilderness. Like the Whiskey Boys, the rioters became known as White Indians. Wearing Indian disguises or blackened faces, they engaged in over one hundred separate crowd incidents, driving surveyors and sheriffs out of their communities, rescuing their comrades who had been captured, and intimidating those who accepted the proprietor's claim as legitimate. Like other crowds of their period, they usually avoided physical violence against people. They attacked property, seized the surveyors' papers or tools, and sometimes stole or killed their horses. In 1808 and 1809, however, greater physical violence took place, and the White Indians injured and even killed a few of their opponents when officials stopped heeding their bluff and bluster. This violence lost the White Indians much of their support and the movement started to crumble.[54]

This agrarian disorder—as well as other incidents among Green Mountain boys in Vermont, tenants in New York, settlers in Wyoming Valley in Pennsylvania, supporters of Fries Rebellion, adherents of the self-proclaimed state of Franklin in the North Carolina mountains, and elsewhere—testifies to the resiliency of the popular faith in rioting to redress grievances despite the best hopes of the political leadership.[55] Rural rioting also demonstrates the persistence of the forms of rioting developed in the revolutionary era. Much of this disorder had something else in common: a political dimension that included an adherence to egalitarian ideals. Most of the Shaysites were against strong government such as established by the Massachusetts Constitution of 1780 and the United States Constitution of 1787. The Whiskey Rebels supported Jeffersonian Republicans fighting the policies of the Federalist administration. Even the contest over land in frontier Maine had a political twist. The proprietors sided with the Federalists and the settlers aligned themselves with the Jeffersonians.[56]

The political orientation to these disturbances should not come as a surprise. Politics after the Revolutionary War was both volatile and violent.[57] The end of the war did not bring relief for all. Many tories discovered when they returned home that passions had not cooled. Mobs persecuted loyalists with tar and feathers, banishment, and even execution, despite the Treaty of Paris that had promised otherwise. The militia in Woodbridge, New Jersey, tarred and feathered two returning tories on a muster day in June 1784. Mobs tormented many tories in Charleston, South Carolina. In the Ninety-Six district of the same state in December 1784 a crowd arrested a returning tory and hauled him before a judge. Though the man was acquitted of all legal charges, a mob waited for the judge to continue his circuit, and, having shown respect for the law, hanged the tory.[58]

Within a few years Americans put aside the whig/tory distinctions and became concerned with other issues. Federalists and anti-federalists clashed in disturbances, showing that neither side could sustain the pretension of being the party of order. In the rioting over the Constitution, violence was more restrained and more in the spirit of the resistance movement than the vengeful passions of the war years. Anti-federalists in Carlisle, Pennsylvania, paraded with effigies of James Wilson and Thomas MacKean in December 1787. Then, like earlier demonstrators, they physically abused the effigies by whipping, hanging, and burning. After news of the state's ratification arrived, New York City Federalists visited the homes of several prominent opponents, screaming and shouting in charivari-like derision. They also demolished equipment in anti-federalist printer Thomas Greenleaf's shop. Fist fights and brawls broke out in Carlisle, Pennsylvania; Baltimore; Dobb County, North Carolina; Albany; and Hudson, New York. Some rioting, too, took place in Rhode Island and South Carolina.[59]

Despite ideological commitment to the ideal of order in politics, the divisions of the 1790s and early 1800s led to clashes in the streets. Initially, these disturbances focused on foreign nationals. But at a time when the most divisive issues revolved around United States policy toward both Britain and France, it was not long before this political rioting became largely an American affair. In Philadelphia, frequent scuffles broke out between various factions among the French refugees who had arrived from Saint Domingue in 1793. In the same year French and British sailors fought in various ports. Given the emotions evoked by the French Revolution, soon Americans joined in. In July 1793 local animosity to a French privateer that had raided American shipping led to a tarring and feathering of an American who invested in the Frenchmen in Savannah. Americans took both sides in the contest. A Boston mob in June 1795 dismantled a Nova Scotia ship believed to be a Bermudian privateer. When the crowd discovered weapons aboard the vessel, it towed the ship into the bay and burned it down to the water.[60]

Although these riots reveal a xenophobic willingness to act against foreigners or their representatives in retaliation for military depredations, the same type of collective violence affected American political debates. On March 15, 1794, a mob in Charleston, South Carolina, paraded with effigies of Fisher Ames, Benedict Arnold, and the devil in reaction to a speech Ames made in congress urging reconciliation with Great Britain during that year's war scare.

To reinforce the partisan message, and joining the domestic issue concerning the chartering of the Bank of the United States to foreign policy, the devil held bank stock in his hands. Supporters of the nascent Democratic-Republicans tarred and feathered opponents in both Norfolk and Baltimore in the same year. Crowds greeted the Jay Treaty in 1795 with demonstrations and effigy parades in Boston, Philadelphia, and New York City, as well as smaller towns like Portsmouth, New Hampshire; and Edgefield, South Carolina. Although there was an antielitist and egalitarian strain to Democratic-Republican crowds, we should not give too much credence to the Federalist propaganda that they were the party of order and their opponents mere mobocrats. Federalist partisans harassed their political opponents during the undeclared war with France. Democratic-Republicans responded by raising liberty poles, like the whiskey and liberty boys before them, only to find them torn down and desecrated as sedition poles by Federalists. Young Federalists and Democratic-Republicans brawled over one such pole in Fisher Ames's own bailiwick of Dedham, Massachusetts. Federalist crowds also assailed Jeffersonian leaders. On May 7, 1798, twelve hundred young men marched to the President's house to offer their services to their country. That night some of these "volunteers" went to newspaper editor Benjamin Bache's house and threatened him. Two days later fights broke out between Federalists and Democratic-Republicans in the state house yard, and another Federalist mob visited Bache's residence and broke windows. In New York City Federalist and Democratic-Republican crowds faced each other several times in informal street singing contests that at times ended in fisticuffs.[61]

Effigy processions, liberty poles, tarring and feathering, and even street battles repeated patterns of behavior practiced during the 1760s and 1770s. Despite the belief that mobs were illegitimate, many political leaders condoned the partisan crowd activity taken for them, while lambasting their opponents for using the mob. With the frightening specter of the French Revolution before them, writers from both sides charged their opponents with Jacobinism and eagerness for the guillotine. This rhetoric, despite the crowd actions of each party, further undercut the legitimacy of the mob.[62]

The American Revolution presents an interesting problem for the student of rioting. Here is a period of social and political turmoil that included a high level of popular disorder. Yet, except for a few extreme cases, the vast majority of mob actions remained in the eighteenth-century mold of minimal collective violence against persons, and action continued to focus on property or symbols of popular discontent. Starting with the reaction to the Stamp Act, American crowds paraded with effigies, demonstrated in the street, and sometimes destroyed property, but seldom physically harmed anyone. Social discontent was widespread during the 1760s and expressed itself in the regulator movements, land rioting on the frontier, as well as urban unrest over

smallpox and labor competition with British soldiers. In a few instances, usually at the instigation of authorities, some of this rioting ended in fatalities.
But like the rioting over the imperial crisis, most of this disorder contained a
low level of violence. During the years of resistance, Americans elaborated on
their ritual of rioting, developing tar and feathers to an art and creating a repertoire of collective behavior that ultimately carried the colonies to revolution.
Crowd action persisted in the forms developed in the preceding years during
the War for Independence, although the passions sometimes released by the
internecine conflict erupted into greater violence. In the aftermath of independence, popular faith in rioting remained in place, as demonstrated in
Shays' Rebellion, more land rioting, occasional urban upheaval, and rioting
accompanying the ratification of the Constitution.

Perhaps we may never fully understand how Americans could remain
committed to a type of rioting that limited violence while experiencing dramatic political and social change. But by the end of the 1790s the situation
had begun to change. Rioters still believed that they acted in the name of the
people and protected the community's interest. Those in government now
claimed that they represented the people and that politics out of doors was no
longer necessary. The logic of democracy was pushing Americans to a new
and different world. The community interest was becoming more difficult to
identify among many separate and competing interests. In the great riots of
communal regulation the crowd might cling to the notion that they acted for
the benefit of all. So, too, might those farmers rebelling against an outside
authority intruding upon their world. But in political disturbances that fiction
became more difficult to maintain. In the new democratic order born out of
the American Revolution, different interests seemed to be struggling against
one another, and, at least in the political arena, those who espoused those
interests were not afraid to bring their conflicts violently into the streets.

DEMOCRACY UNLEASHED | 3

The New Riot

On the night of June 22, 1812, thirty to forty men, encouraged by a much larger crowd of spectators, dismantled the Gay Street newspaper office of the *Federal-Republican* in Baltimore. As far as riots go, it was a standard affair. The *Federal-Republican* had published repeated editorials opposing government policies leading the United States into a war with Great Britain. In heavily Republican Baltimore, these editorials insulted local patriotism and ran counter to popular politics. Mobs had attacked newspaper offices during the Revolutionary War, and the tumultuous crowd had made its presence known in politics for decades. Following eighteenth-century precedents, the rioters proceeded with great "sangfroid" and went about the business "as regularly as if they contracted to perform the job for pay."[1] Republican officials, who were probably happy to see this organ of the opposition driven from town, briefly appeared. Finding their entreaties rebuffed, they withdrew from the scene and allowed the people to have their moment of riot.[2]

One rioter, when confronted by Mayor Edward Johnson, revealed in poignant terms the rationale of the mob as it emerged from the eighteenth century. The man interrupted his work and declared, "Mr. Johnson, I know you very well, no body wants to hurt you; but the laws of the land must sleep, and the laws of nature and reason prevail; that house is the temple of Infamy, it is supported by English gold, and it must and shall come down to the ground!" Seldom has a rioter been more articulate, expressing an unquestioned faith in the legitimacy of the mob to act when legal structures met inadequately the needs of the community. This was not a crime of anonymity. The rioter knew Johnson, and given the mayor's role in popular politics and his strong connections to the city's mechanic community, Johnson probably knew the rioter. This Baltimore crowd associated the Federalist newspaper with the national enemy, and, as such, the *Federal-Republican* violated the "laws of nature and reason" regardless of the stipulations of the "laws of the land."[3]

Had that evening's festivities been the end of the rioting in Baltimore that summer, there would be little more to say about the incident. However, nearly two months of mob rule in Baltimore built to a crescendo of violence. Something had changed in Baltimore, and that change embodied shifting currents elsewhere in the nation. Collective violence soon spread beyond the realm of politics, exposing rifts and fissures within the society. Moreover, when the owner of the *Federal-Republican* foolishly returned to reestablish the paper in the city, a final bloody scene was enacted. In the whirlwind of crowd activity of that summer the lineaments of a new nineteenth-century form of rioting can be discerned.

Baltimore in 1812 was a dynamic city that had risen from a small trading village in the 1770s to being the nation's third largest metropolis. This commercial boomtown contained rich and rising merchants, middling tradesmen, sailors and dockworkers, native-born and immigrant laborers, and both slave and free blacks. Equally important, conflict permeated the city's workshops, as master artisans sought to cut costs by hiring less skilled workers.[4] Although most people in Baltimore basked in the political sunshine of Jeffersonian Republicanism, there were many strains and cleavages hidden in the shadows of social change.

As the Baltimore mob took over the city's streets, racial and ethnic tensions surfaced. James Briscoe, a free black and property owner, saw the war as an opportunity for his race to strike a blow at whites. Rumors spread quickly through Baltimore that Briscoe had declared that "if all the blacks were of his opinion, they would soon put down the whites." Meeting this racial challenge, rioters pulled down two houses owned by Briscoe. Harassment of blacks continued and crowds threatened the African church. Protestant and Catholic Irish began to attack each other in the war fever of that summer. Catholics threatened to tar and feather Alexander Wiley because he was an Orangeman and because they accused him of riding post for the editor of the *Federal-Republican*. Although Mayor Johnson later dismissed these incidents as "inferior disturbances," they presaged more extensive rioting later in the century in Baltimore.[5]

The most serious rioting of the summer focused against Federalist opponents of the war. Even in this instance, however, the political antagonism may have screened some important class and cultural differences. On July 27 the aristocratic and audacious coeditor of the *Federal-Republican*, Alexander Contee Hanson, gathered a small Federalist host at No. 45 Charles Street to set up a distribution center for the paper now published in Georgetown. Most of the men with Hanson came from the state's Federalist elite and included two generals from the Revolutionary War. Hanson believed that he was striking a blow for the freedom of the press.

The Federalist effort to reestablish their newspaper in Baltimore also marked an interesting departure from elite handling of mobs in the previous century. There are two key players in most riot situations: the perpetrators and the victims. In the eighteenth century both sides generally understood their roles within the riot. A good victim either had the sense to get out of the way, or played up to the ritual demands of the mob. In 1812 both sides abandoned

their customary roles. Hanson refused to be a good victim. The Baltimore rioters reacted with a vengeance.

As evening fell on July 27 a large crowd gathered outside No. 45 Charles
Street. Boys shouted insults and curses at the Federalist fortress. The crowd
became more threatening by hurling stones. Hanson and his friends believed
that if they stood firm, a mob composed of riffraff and the dregs of society
would not dare to confront men of their social position. To intimidate the mob
the Federalists fired a volley of blanks. The loud blast briefly cleared the
streets, but the rioters soon rushed the building. As they reached the doorway,
the Federalists again lowered their muskets, this time with real bullets, killing
a shopkeeper. More shots followed as the attackers retreated. Several were
wounded. The Republicans in the street returned the fire and rolled up a
cannon ready to exact retribution upon the Federalist "murderers."

Open warfare had broken out between two opposing political factions from
two different worlds. Artisans, shopkeepers, and laborers filled the crowd in
the street, while the defenders were members of the landed and merchant
elite.[6] When the Republican leaders of the city's militia finally interfered, preventing the firing of that cannon, they abandoned their own aristocratic trappings—such as the insignia of the hereditary military society the Order of
Cincinnati—and appealed to the crowd in the street based on "political"
friendship. The cultural and class chasm between opposing forces can also be
seen after the Republican leaders negotiated the surrender of the Federalists.
Either with an air of unthinking superiority or as a final and purposeful assertion of their social position, the Federalists asked to be escorted from No. 45
Charles Street in carriages—a mode of transportation symbolic of the aristocracy. The shopkeepers, mechanics, and workers of Baltimore refused to allow
this and called for carts—the standard means of transportation of criminals
and victims of the mob. The city's Republican leaders settled on the more
democratic and egalitarian mode of walking and escorted the captives to jail
where the Federalists believed they would be safe, and the crowd thought that
their enemy would be arraigned on charges of murder. This agreement, which
seemed to satisfy both sides in the first rays of light of the morning, set the
stage for even more violence.

That night the Baltimore mob took "justice" into its own hands. A crowd
stormed a jail that was all too lightly guarded and brutally assaulted the
Federalist prisoners. In the dark and confusion, several Federalists escaped.
Using fists and clubs, the rioters beat the remaining Federalists to a pulp.
Worse, some of the crowd took penknives and jabbed them into their victims'
cheeks and then dripped hot candle grease into their eyes. All of the victims
had their clothes torn off. The Federalists believed that this was to secure their
pockets; the mob, however, wanted to strip these members of the elite of their
last emblem of their status—their clothing. Descriptions of the jailhouse after
the riot repeatedly refer to the "foreign clothing," "Montgomery coats," and

"Virginia boots" strewn about. Federalist victims, in their own conceit, later described how they outwitted the mob by pretending to be dead. The Baltimore mob, however, may have been content with this final surrender to the will of the people as a symbolic victory. In the one case where a Federalist, General James Maccubin Lingan, appealed to the crowd because of his social and patriotic stature, the rioters beat him to death.

The Baltimore riots of 1812 became the hallmark of a new type of riot. Rioters in the eighteenth century most often strove to assert an ideal of community unity; now they increasingly revealed the tensions and strains of communities being torn asunder by divisions and enmities. With this shift also came an important shift in action. In the nineteenth century rioters relied upon physical violence on persons with a vehemence almost unknown in the eighteenth century. Even attacks on property became more extensive and all consuming. Rather than rely on workmanlike precision, as in the demolition of the office of the *Federal-Republican*, rioters preferred the quicker method of burning.

This new riot grew out of the democracy and egalitarianism of the age. Corporatism had bound society with ties of deference and paternalism within a system of hierarchy. While there was an undercurrent of opposition to this world view in Anglo-American culture, the myth of the single-interest society had acted as a breakwater, deflecting and limiting the expressions of class resentment. The American Revolution opened the floodgates of change by encouraging more rioting and political participation from a broader base in society. Against the rising tide of egalitarianism the world of corporatism crumbled like a sand castle besieged by pounding waves.

As the ideal of the single-interest society disintegrated, there were three important developments that need to be noted. First, individuals were cut off from the allegiance that the community had offered. Searching for some attachments, individuals associated with one another in political, economic, religious, ethnic, racial, and other areas. On one level new associations provided identity and purpose to the isolated individual. On another level, they also created conflict. It was across these lines of identity that much of the nineteenth-century rioting occurred. Without a common interest binding the components of society together—without a recognition that rioter and victim ought to share values—the level of violence in a riot increased.

Second, nineteenth-century American ideals held the independent and democratic man supreme. Each individual was to act as an isolated economic and political entity, pursuing his own interests. Although this ideology served as a nice antidote for the loss of corporatism, it did not fully reflect the developing social realities. Associations helped the individual to escape the anomie endemic in the new social order but also moderated the extent the individual could act alone. Simultaneous with the emphasis on the common man there arose a mass society that tended to submerge the individual. In an egalitarian world of individuals supposedly standing on equal footing, it became all too easy to get lost in the crowd. These contradictions had important ramifications for rioting. The release and excitement of the moment of the riot allowed each participant to transcend the mundane boundaries of his or her own individuality by not only acting as "Natty Bumppo in crowd" or "Randolph Scott en masse," but also melding into a group identity that added purpose and meaning to life.[7]

Finally, the theoretical role of government now shifted; instead of acting to protect the common good, government was to referee between competing interests. Unfortunately, this lofty principle seldom was extended far enough. Despite the triumph of the new ideal of equality, social change remained incomplete and contradictions abounded. In the grasping and acquisitive America of the nineteenth century some men managed to pursue their interests through influence in the government. Equally important was the exclusion from power and equitable treatment of large sections of American society: blacks, immigrants, the poor, women, and others. Recognition of this fact led to conflict that sometimes erupted into bloodshed.

Ethnic Rioting

Many of the tendencies of the new riot, especially the greater role of personal physical violence, appeared in riots that reflected growing ethnic tensions after 1800. These riots included dramatic attacks against property representative of group identity and virulent assaults on individuals. Ethnic hatreds in the nineteenth century built upon and extended animosities imbedded in Anglo-American culture in the eighteenth century. Although the form and violence of these riots often conformed to the new pattern of nineteenth-century popular disorder, the change was not abrupt and limited to the Jacksonian era.

Americans in the eighteenth century were extremely ethnocentric and strongly anti-Catholic. They shared with the English the belief that the universe revolved around the Anglo-American world and that all other people were civilized only as far as they resembled the English. The Irish, with a religion that many viewed as tinged with paganism, were likened to savages. The French and Spanish, tarred with the same brush of Catholicism, suffered in comparison in the Anglo-American eye. Catholicism became the hallmark not only of superstition, but of absolute monarchies on the European continent and of threats to liberty within England itself. The wars for empire strengthened these prejudices.[8]

Because the American Revolution stripped away trade barriers and created new geopolitical circumstances, increased contact with Catholic nations provided more opportunities for expressing anti-Catholic sentiments. During the 1790s, immigration of Catholics expanded. Long before the famine migration of the 1840s, enough Catholics had entered the country to challenge permanently the Protestant identity of the American nation.

Xenophobic rioting against Catholics occurred frequently in seaports. In Philadelphia American and Spanish sailors rioted in September 1804 and American and French sailors brawled in October 1806. There were fatalities in riots in Charleston (September 2, 1811), Savannah (November 13–15, 1811), New York (June 29, 1812), Norfolk (February 5–6, 1813), and New Orleans (March 17–18, 1817). At times, these ethnic riots did not include any Americans. For instance, on May 19, 1814, Spanish and Greek sailors fought in Boston. American tars, however, more than compensated for their absence in this and other disturbances by rioting in foreign countries. On June 12, 1808, American and Portuguese sailors engaged in a "dreadful affray" in London that left at least two Americans dead.[9]

These disturbances cannot be dismissed as mere sailor rows. American sailors had deeply imbedded prejudices against Hispanics and the French. In the New York riot of 1812 sailors searched the waterfront looking not only for the particular Hispanics involved in an affray during which an American tar had been stabbed—Spaniards and Portuguese were notorious among sailors for the readiness to draw their knives—but anyone whose olive skin and thick accent identified the individual as a "portagues."

Hatred of the Catholic Irish appeared as early as the 1790s. Anglo-Americans believed the Irish could not appreciate ideas about good government and viewed them as an alien and despised people. One of the earliest expressions of American nativism centered on holidays and institutions that emphasized these cultural differences. Starting in the 1790s, American crowds borrowed the English practice of parading with stuffed effigies called "paddies" on Saint Patrick's day to insult Gaelic pride. The Irish took umbrage to these displays. One such "paddie" drew a violent response, leading to one fatality, in a New York waterfront neighborhood in 1799. Twenty years later, the hanging of a "Stuffed Paddy" from the yard arm of the schooner *Appomattox* along a Baltimore wharf elicited another disturbance. Irate Irish boarded the vessel, cut away the rigging, and did other damage, and beat back gentlemen merchants, and even a judge, who tried to interfere.

A nativist gang of apprentices and young mechanics called the Highbinders shouted insults, misbehaved, but did not do any severe injury to a New York Catholic church on Christmas Eve, 1806. All the next day this affront became the talk of "Irishtown" in the Sixth Ward. That evening an Irishman murdered one of the watch in a melee between the police and the Catholics. To seek revenge, Highbinders sacked stores and groceries, fighting any Irish that came in their way.[10]

Several riots also took place concerning the Protestant celebration of William of Orange's seventeenth-century victory at the Battle of the Boyne. Two disturbances broke out on July 12, 1824: in New York City, and in

Lockport. In the first, the contest was between Protestant and Catholic weavers, in the second both sides were canal workers. Philadelphia experienced at
least two such incidents. On a ship packed with immigrants in 1825 the
Protestants beat back any interference by outnumbered Catholics with their
celebration of July 12. Once the vessel touched the Philadelphia wharf, the
odds shifted in favor of the Catholics. In the renewed fight the Catholics
would have triumphed had not the mayor and police arrived and arrested several rioters. The Protestant Gideon Society held a procession in the southern
part of the city in 1831. Catholics intercepted it, but the police drove them off.
During a second affray later, one man was stabbed and several wounded.

To many native born Americans, these riots signified the introduction of
"European politics" into their country. Moreover, from the same perspective,
the Irish were bringing with them a heritage of violence that seemed antithetical to the peaceful interchange between citizens necessary for the smooth
functioning of the republic. One judge lectured Irish rioters in New York that
in the United States they needed to put their ancient conflicts behind them
and recognize that here all were equal before the "protecting influence of the
law." These assertions ignored the fact that officials sided with the Protestants
and did not treat the Catholics equitably.[11]

The mix of Irish traditions and American conditions led to persistent rioting among construction workers along canals and railroads. One of the first of
these disturbances took place at Elkton, Maryland, in September 1804.
Thereafter such riots occurred intermittently, but became more frequent in the
1820s and 1830s. Many immigrants were hired as cheap day laborers on internal improvement projects that dotted the countryside. Often undercapitalized
and built utilizing a contract system that left a shortage of ready cash to pay
employees, these projects experienced repeated labor strife. At first glance
much of this conflict had little to do with economics. Irish laborers fought with
one another based upon county allegiances, molested other workers like
Germans and blacks, abused the contractors, and destroyed work just completed. Battles between different groups of workers, however, were to limit
competition for jobs, and the attacks on the contractors or the construction
itself usually resulted from failure to meet payroll. Beneath all of this violence,
then, was resentment of an exploitative labor system that denied the worker a
living wage.[12]

Constant recourse to violence by Irish workers was a result of their relative
powerlessness within the political process. By the mid 1830s this was changing.
The Irish, and then in the 1840s and 1850s the Germans as well, started to
exert more political influence in several cities. Many opposed this development.

The April 1834 New York City election marked a departure from past
political riots. Upon failing to intimidate voters at the Sixth Ward poll, Whigs
paraded through this heavily Irish and Democratic district with banners and a
mock ship to prove their political dominance. This demonstration led to some

street fighting. After a procession the next day, the Democratic Irish retaliated by besieging Whig headquarters at the Masonic Hall on the border of the Sixth Ward. Thousands fought hand to hand, shots exchanged, and Whigs contemplated raiding an arsenal for more weapons. Fortunately for all involved they were dissuaded from this action at the gate of the arsenal. Brawling and fighting continued in the Sixth Ward and elsewhere, making a mockery of the electoral process.[13]

This riot in New York City was nothing in comparison to the type of disorder of the 1850s. In that decade nativist Americans developed intimidation at the polls into a new art form. In August 1854 eight or ten died when nativists in St. Louis invaded an Irish neighborhood and destroyed between fifty and sixty houses. During the following year there were two election riots in Louisville. The first was relatively innocuous. Fighting broke out in only two wards; besides some property destroyed and a few busted noses, not much damage was done. However, there was a battle royal between nativists and Germans and Irish in August. Knives, muskets, and cannon were used, houses were burned, and at least twenty were killed. Rioting marred Baltimore elections in 1856, 1857, and 1858. Nativist gangs like the "Rip Raps" controlled the polling places, seized would-be Democratic voters, held them captive, and forced them to vote repeatedly for the American or Know-Nothing Party candidates. The most serious of these disturbances was on November 4, 1856, when Know-Nothings fought Democrats all over the city and brought a cannon into play. Estimates of casualties vary, ranging from 8 to 17 dead and 64 to 150 wounded.[14]

Elections, however, reveal only a part of the story of ethnic rioting in the thirty years before the Civil War. Anti-Catholic sentiments led to the burning of the Ursuline Convent in 1834 in Charlestown, Massachusetts. On the night of August 11 a large crowd assembled outside the convent school and watched forty to fifty men burst onto the grounds, drive the nuns and the students before them, and gut and ignite the building. Compared to many riots of this era, this was a tame affair. Yet the totality of the destruction—this was no simple eighteenth-century dismantling—unleashed a fury that seemed to threaten the very fabric of society. Moreover, for the middle class of the time, as well as for historians since then, the irrationality of the destruction of a school dedicated to teaching young girls made this riot peculiar.[15]

One reason for the absence of the physical violence in the Ursuline Convent riot that marred so many disturbances in the antebellum period was that there was no opposition made to the attack. Nativists were not always so lucky. Repeatedly, immigrant groups like the Irish fought back when there were threats to their neighborhoods and institutions. When brute force met brute force not only was there a destruction of property, but as in a few ethnic riots at the beginning of the century, and as in many election riots, there were fatalities.

Two riots in Philadelphia in 1844 reveal just how deep mutual animosities lay. Nativist sentiment ran high in 1844 and Protestant and Catholic became embroiled in a controversy over what Bible to use in the public schools. Catholics believed that the Protestant English version led to interpretations antithetical to their faith; Protestants wanted to sustain their vision of religion in public education. On May 6 nativists organized an outdoor rally in Kensington, but were driven to seek cover during a rainstorm in Nanny Goat Market, in the heart of the Irish District. Rioting, including gun play, soon began between the two forces. Enraged by the death of George Shiffler, a teenage boy, nativists burned two Catholic churches and many Irish houses during three days of rioting before militia and special police were able to reestablish order.

Two months later, the day after the celebration of the fourth of July, there was another riot. Rumors spread that the Catholics had stashed arms in one of their churches. A nativist crowd formed and demanded to search the building. Fearing a repetition of the May riots, officials dispatched militia to guard the building. The precaution failed. The crowd compelled the first unit of militia, composed of Catholics, to leave the area. A second and larger force arrived upon the scene and determined to make a stand. The commanding officer ordered his men to drive back the crowd. Both sides opened fire with guns, and the mob brought up some cannon and blasted away at the militia. A cavalry charge silenced this artillery, and the militia held their ground, quieting the rioting. Casualties were high on both sides; two dead, twenty-three wounded for the militia; ten dead and at least twenty wounded for the mob.[16]

Although multi-day riots like the Philadelphia disturbance in 1844 were exceptional, they occurred against a backdrop of persistent mob violence. Immigrants, especially the Irish, exhibited a penchant for fighting that was only matched by the violent reaction of nativists. Three examples from the 1830s suggest the range of these disturbances. Gun-wielding "Americans and foreigners" (Irish) fought in a tavern in the Five Points district in New York City in late June 1835. Police officers rushed to the scene in the most notorious slum in the nation. During the melee one man was killed and a police justice wounded. A few days later, on July 4, in frontier Detroit thirty to forty Irish laborers grading the town's streets stopped their work and abused passersby, calling them "damned Yankees." A posse of "worthy citizens" quickly formed, but found themselves "bloodied in attempting to arrest the mob, which dispersed of its own accord." In Boston's Broad Street riot of June 11, 1837, as many as 15,000 people were in the street after a fight started when a volunteer fire company ran into an Irish funeral procession. Nativists charged into Irish tenements, dragging the residents into the street and beating them. Eight hundred horsemen helped to quell the riot.[17]

The involvement of a fire company in the Broad Street riot would come as no surprise to Jacksonian police officials. At this time there was a close affiliation between gangs, fire companies, politics, and ethnic identity. The perpetrators of much of the political rioting in Baltimore in the 1850s were nativist gangs associated with fire companies. Democrat and Know-Nothing gangs honed their fighting skills in confrontations to and from fires. These frequent disturbances were more than the roughhouse competition between different adolescent groups typical of traditional society; not all of the participants were adolescents, and as ethnic and political animosities grew, the contests became more lethal. In city after city fire companies ambushed each other and often set fires to attract their opponents. On more than one occasion the combatants used guns.[18]

Ethnic rioting, especially after 1840, involved other groups as well. A picnic of thousands of New York Germans celebrating Pentecost in the Hoboken countryside in 1851 ended in a riot when some nativist rowdies assaulted the Germans headed for the ferry to Manhattan. The Germans retaliated and ransacked a house sheltering the rowdies. The affray continued and in the fighting at least one person was killed. Many others were wounded.[19]

In gold rush California a great deal of nativist activity took place. The victims included a wide spectrum of nationalities—Mexicans, Chileans, Australians, French, and others—whom the nativist prospectors hoped to drive from the mine fields. In Rise Bar, Yankee miners in 1849 attacked a Chilean party, hanging its leader, whipping several others, and cropping the ears of a few of their victims. For a time the nativists managed to get the legislature to pass a special tax on all non-Americans to add legal sanction to their extralegal activities.[20]

The violence of this ethnic rioting matched and perhaps surpassed the violence in any other category of rioting in the antebellum period. A complete tally is impossible, given many sketchy reports, but hundreds of Americans (immigrants and others) lost their lives in this rioting. Thousands of others suffered physical punishment and property losses that amounted to millions of dollars. As the United States groped its way toward becoming a mass egalitarian society, and as independent men were cast off to look for ways of finding a place for themselves in this New World, ethnicity and religion provided a sense of identity and comfort. On the darker side of this development, however, these ties that bound some men together also drove them apart from others, and those cleavages all too often erupted into violence.

Class Conflict and Rowdyism

Ethnicity and religion were important sources of conflict, but they cannot stand alone. Often intertwined with other forms of group identity was an acute awareness of socioeconomic distinctions—class—that set one group off from another. Overlapping ethnic and class tensions can be seen in the chance clash between a column of dirt carts driven by Irishmen that slowly worked its way up New York's Third Avenue, and a series of carriages, driven by self-professed gentlemen, racing downtown on August 5, 1833. When the leading carriage approached dangerously close to the first cart, the Irish cartman proclaimed the democratic rule of the street in a flurry of profanity that the gentleman driver of the carriage believed offensive to the lady he escorted. Two Irishmen nearby grabbed the gentleman's horse by the reins and forced the carriage onto the sidewalk to make way for the carts. The merchants and manufacturers in the other carriages flayed away at the assembled crowd with their whips, only to find themselves overwhelmed by the mass of Irish humanity that poured out of the local groceries and houses. By the time the police arrived, the gentlemen had gotten the worst of the melee. The police had their own bias and arrested only the Irish. Participants in this riot acted upon set assumptions dependent upon group identity. That identity was more than just Irishmen versus non-Irishmen, and included an awareness on both sides of the difference in culture dictated by economic and social background.[21]

Confrontations, like this cart-carriage incident, intertwined ethnic and class differences in a complex web that can never be fully disentangled. Historians like to create categories to organize and to present their vision of the past. Categories such as class and ethnicity can be useful, but we need always to be aware that they are modern constructions that do not necessarily express the way the participants felt. They do usually reflect reality, but not necessarily the entire reality. Class is an important category for analysis only insofar as we can delineate an awareness of distinctions—a consciousness—of social and economic differences.

Elements of class consciousness appeared in rioting in the eighteenth century in the undercurrent of resentment of wealth; in the nineteenth century those elements rose to the surface. Rich and poor always existed, and as we have seen there was a long strain of antiauthoritarianism and tension between social and economic groups in the Anglo-American world. In the United States during the early nineteenth century, as the level of labor unrest grew, awareness of social and economic differences intensified. That awareness built upon plebeian resistance to authority and resentment of wealth, and in many ways was encouraged by the egalitarianism of the age. On the one side was a working-class culture that included customary behavior such as rowdiness, drinking, and defense of the community. This culture also became infused with new concerns over the loss of status as workers and a denial of deference. On the other was a middle-class culture that espoused the virtue of hard work, morality, personal discipline, and order. Although the contrast between these two cultures was stark, they shaded into one another. Many workers came to espouse some middle-class values, and some members of the middle class, especially youths, participated in more rowdy behavior.[22]

Crucial to this developing cultural chasm were changes in the organization of work that dramatically altered the relationship between employer and employee and led to class conflict. In particular, employers sought ways to reduce wages by hiring semiskilled labor, producing larger quantities for a national market, and eventually, introducing machinery into factories. These developments convinced many workers to band together and strike in contests over wages and the control of the workplace. Strikers often avoided violence and garnered community support based upon a call for fairness and equity that found a positive response in the genteel tradition, the Jacksonian emphasis on justice for the individual, and evangelical religion. At times, however, rioting did break out. This violence had many causes, including traditions of collective action among the Irish and "archaic" concerns with revenge and honor.[23] Economic conditions, however, remained central to strikes and the violence they spawned. The less control exerted by workers over the conditions of labor, the more likely it was for strikers to resort to violence. As early as 1802 sailors in New York marched along the docks and dismantled ships to support their labor demands. By the 1820s the violence in strikes expanded. In 1825 and 1828 New York dockworkers turned to extremes, beating all who opposed them. By the late 1820s and 1830s even journeymen used violence.[24]

Economics and class tension were also important in several riots that mixed older corporate concerns, resentment of ill-gotten wealth, and a rough egalitarianism of the streets encouraged by the democratic currents of the nineteenth century. Limited to attacks on property symbolic of specific grievances, these riots often followed eighteenth-century patterns of popular disorder. Yet the political context of the disturbances and its egalitarian rhetoric stressed social and economic distinctions, revealing elements of class antagonism and consciousness.

The flour riot in New York City on February 12, 1837, commenced in the spirit of the Anglo-American bread riots of the eighteenth century. A crowd broke into warehouses and, since the owners asked prices that were too high, rioters took the flour for themselves. While the parallels with the earlier rioting are striking, there was a political dimension absent from most earlier bread riots. This disturbance began with a rally where Locofoco politicians—Democrats who often spoke with class-based rhetoric—spurred the crowd to action.[25]

The crowds preventing completion of a railroad through the Philadelphia suburb of Kensington, populated largely by the working class, might be cast as defenders of a community against intrusion by larger more cosmopolitan forces. These rioters in 1840 and 1841 tore up rails, replaced paving stones, and drove workmen off. Their efforts, however, were seconded by local politicians who, with the crowd activity as testimony of popular sentiment, succeeded in forcing the railroad to change plans. When they celebrated their triumph, the people of Kensington displayed both the political and economic content of their movement on their banners. These declared "NO MONOPOLY," a phrase that every Democrat understood as a challenge to the privilege of wealth, and, linking their cause to the fundamental law of the land, "THE CONSTITUTION PROTECTS THE PEOPLE IN THE USE OF THEIR HIGHWAYS."[26]

Fear of economic inequality, fueled by democratic sentiment and the Jacksonian Bank War, can be seen in riots triggered by bank failures in Baltimore (August 6–9, 1835), Detroit (1841), Cincinnati (January 1842), Louisville (January 1842), and New Orleans (May 1842). The most serious of these disturbances occurred in Baltimore when many in that city suspected that the major investors in the Bank of Maryland had carefully protected their own holdings at the expense of depositors and small investors. This sort of favoritism among the wealthy was unacceptable to the crowds that gathered on the night of August 6, and they expressed their rage by breaking windows in some houses belonging to the rich. This mild tumult was repeated on the next night, but more serious rioting broke out on the evening of the eighth. Discovering that it was useless to combat the mob with their clubs, the mayor's guard fired their guns, killing five and wounding many more. The rioting, however, continued. The guard, hearing the calls for revenge, left the city. By the end of the next day the mob had gutted the unprotected homes of four major investors of the Bank of Maryland and the mayor's house. Although the rioters exhibited some discretion in the selection of targets, the challenge to property holders was clear, and Samuel Smith, an aged politician and war hero, organized a volunteer corps to restore order.[27]

Class consciousness before the Civil War involved more than labor unrest and economics; it included expressions of strident egalitarianism born out of older notions of antiauthoritarianism and resentment of wealth that were evident in the cart and carriage clash in 1833. This conflict appeared in the most unlikely of places.

Two contrasting visions of order can be seen in a riot at a balloon ascension in Philadelphia in September 1819. Tens of thousands gathered to see the balloon, but only the wealthy could pay the one dollar admission to get a closer look. After several delays, a restless crowd became angered when a watchman injured a boy who tried to climb over a fence. Ready to believe the worst of a watchman protecting the inner sanctum of the wealthy, the crowd spread a rumor that the boy had been killed. Soon the fences came crashing down as the human horde poured into the garden, driving the paying customers off. The crowd quickly asserted its egalitarian spirit, destroying the vestiges of privilege. With sticks and stones the crowd tore the balloon to pieces, ransacked the garden, pilfered the bar, and consumed the liquors. After gutting the pavilion, rioters set it afire. To those who comprised the middle class— merchants, lawyers, manufacturers, and businessmen—the action of the crowd was disgraceful and signaled a breach of order that must be controlled. This type of disorder seemed to be on the rise whenever the common people gathered in crowds.[28]

Rowdiness was not new; there had always existed a certain level of disorder, particularly on holidays. In the eighteenth-century Anglo-American world this plebeian rowdiness had been accepted as part of the price the patrician paid for limited government and local dominance in politics. The egalitarian currents swirling through the American landscape in the early nineteenth century, however, appeared to be changing the content and context of this popular disorder. With individuals cut loose from the guidance once offered by the community, the middle class demanded that each person exert an internal discipline. Because of this concern for order, reportage of disorder increased.

Simultaneously, great changes affected the world of the working class. The shattering of the ideal of community corporatism led to intergroup conflict that was often expressed as rowdyism. Moreover, the consumption of alcohol grew as a function of greater availability and of the anxiety and malaise born of a rapidly changing social environment. Groceries, grogshops, and bars sprung up everywhere and became the scene of much brawling and misbehavior. Frequenting these establishments were workers who were now freed from paternalistic supervision because their middle-class employers, releasing themselves from long-term associations that might cost them money, abdicated their responsibilities beyond the immediate confines of the workplace.[29]

This last development had a strong effect on youths. One of the most important cost-cutting measures employed by master craftsmen was to only half train apprentices and hire them by the day. This practice provided young men with an opportunity to earn a wage and live independently from the oversight of both their parents and masters. Reinforcing this new independence was the revolt against patriarchy and deference that grew out of the American Revolution. Young men in traditional society had formed special bonds with each other and occupied a peculiar and awkward niche in society dictated by their dependent status. Usually under the control of their betters and elders, they were allowed occasional liberty to misbehave. Building on these traditions, yet released from customary restraints, there developed a distinct youth cult that found expression in gang warfare, fire company riots, and rowdy misbehavior that was often fueled by alcohol and that could break out on any night.[30]

These changes even reached to the world of academia. Although student rebellion had occurred before, the fluid social boundaries of the nineteenth century wreaked havoc on American campuses. This conflict ranged from traditional town and gown disturbances and brawls among students, to the serious and frequent outbreaks of violence between students and faculty, including brutal physical assault. During this period the number of colleges multiplied, and many poorer students sought higher education as a means to social mobility. Because these students often needed to work before entering college, the average age of the student body was higher. The older "parental" system of control in the residential collegiate community, geared to affluent youths in their teens, was ill suited to these young men in their twenties who revolted against restraints on their lives and who objected to instructors who were young and autocratic.[31]

Student rebellions and juvenile delinquency may have added to the disorder in the first half of the nineteenth century, but it was the specter of the unruly masses that haunted the middle class. The balloon ascension riot in Philadelphia in 1819 was not an isolated affair; any time a crowd gathered there was the potential for disorder. A disappointing display of fireworks, as in New York City in 1826, triggered a riot. During the 1830s a husking frolic turned into a brawl and riot in Maysville, Kentucky, in which one man was stabbed to death and three others seriously wounded. When a crowded pleasure steamer from Baltimore put in at Annapolis on July 5, 1847, young men from the rival cities started to fight. Soon the Annapolis men pelted the steamer with stones. The Baltimore men broke into a rifle cabinet and commenced shooting those on shore, wounding five. Officials interceded as the Annapolis supporters brought up two cannons and the steamer made a hasty departure.[32]

Wherever there were theaters, tumult soon followed. Common folk viewed stage productions aggressively: if pleased they applauded, hooted, and hollered; if displeased they booed, hissed, threw objects, and sometimes rioted. Before the 1820s and 1830s all social levels attended the same theaters so that everyone had to watch the antics of the rowdiest elements in the audience. By the 1830s, however, the middle class began to articulate a code of theater-going decorum, and in the larger cities patronized establishments geared to their more exclusive tastes. These distinctions sometimes exacerbated rather than eased the tensions between the classes.

On May 10, 1849, one of the bloodiest riots before the Civil War took place at the Astor Place Opera House in New York City. Supposedly caused by a dispute between a British and an American actor, class conflict was at the heart of the disturbance. As one contemporary account explained: "it was the rich against the poor—the aristocracy against the people . . . ."[33] The combination of anti-British and class resentment was not unusual in riots. Many a "Bowery B'hoy" viewed the preference of the "Codfish Aristocracy" for British actors as pretentious, and quickly reacted to the smallest slight offered by foreign thespians. In the Astor Place riot, the feud between the American Edwin Forrest and British William C. Macready came to epitomize these antagonisms. On May 7, 1849, Forrest supporters disrupted Macready's performance and drove him from the stage of the opera house. Distressed at this violation of decorum in their own bastion, "a number of influential citizens, men of wealth and standing," threw down the gauntlet and published a notice declaring their support for Macready at his next performance.

The Bowery rose to the challenge and greeted the performance on the night of the tenth with a riot. Thousands gathered outside the opera house, while rowdies disrupted Macready inside. After suffering through this discord

for the first act, police officials interceded and quieted the uproar in the theater. By that time the tumult had reached more serious proportions in the street.
Rioters tossed large paving stones at the windows and battled with the police.
The militia was ordered in. The hail of stones, however, became so fierce that
it disoriented the cavalry at the head of the troops and forced the mounted soldiers to flee. That left the infantry to confront the mob. They, too, came under
heavy bombardment, sustaining injuries before firing over the head of the
crowd. The officers, some of whom had been knocked down by the stones,
decided to assert their control of the streets and strike a blow for order; they
issued the command to fire. In the dark of the night the clamor of the mob
turned to shrieks as the bullets scattered into the crowd and beyond. Blood-
stained rioters fell to the ground as did innocent bystanders who were as far as
two blocks away. By the time the riot was over, twenty-two people had died, at
least forty-eight were wounded.

Riots such as the Astor Place disturbance caused many in the antebellum
period to pause and think where American society was going. One author
believed that the "hatred of wealth and privilege is increasing over the world,
and ready to burst out whenever there is the slightest occasion." The same
writer recognized that imbedded in this antagonism was a consciousness of
class on both sides: "The rich and well-bred are too apt to despise the poor and
ignorant, and they must not think it strange if they are hated in return."[34]

Agrarian Rebellions

The economic and social upheaval that rocked urban areas sent seismic waves
through the nation. Populations shifted, depleting a few areas, but infusing
others with tremendous demographic growth. As Americans moved west,
south, and north they brought their problems with them. Many wanted to
cling tenaciously to the older ideals of community, and even proclaimed that
they had succeeded in doing so, but frequently found themselves surrounded
by strangers and mired in controversies that belied their ideals. The effects of
ethnicity and class were more diffuse in rural America. Cities were like a cauldron, with these elements intermixed, constantly agitated, and boiling to the
surface in repeated eruptions of popular disorder. In the countryside, the various ingredients were often in isolation—in one community ethnic animosities
might violently burst out, and in others strife between rich and poor might
mar the public peace.

Property became the centerpiece of many contests in the countryside,
leading at times to rioting and even rebellion. Groups contested property
claims or competed for local dominance and control of the legal apparatus that
granted deeds. Like earlier land rioters, these nineteenth-century crowds sometimes relied upon ritual and limited their activity to the destruction of property.
Yet the threshold of extreme violence seemed reduced. Moreover, when cultural

distinctions aggravated the situation, personal violence could be expressed with a vehemence that led to some of the bloodiest conflicts of the era.

The Anti-Rent War of 1839 to 1845 in the upper Hudson and Delaware valleys of New York showed the persistence of eighteenth-century patterns of rioting in rural America as well as some of the movement toward greater violence. After the uprisings of the revolutionary period, tenants at times rioted in New York. In 1813 mobs opposed the collection of rents in Columbia County and in one confrontation a sheriff was killed. Land rioting in 1825 culminated in the death of a landowner. Rioters also raided two land offices in western New York in 1836. The largest disorder took place after the death of Stephen Van Rensselaer (the "old Patroon") in 1839, when his heirs tried to collect back rents to help settle a complicated estate riddled with debt.

The anti-renters commenced their resistance with limited collective action. They believed the occupation and improvement of the property gave them a proprietary interest that superseded the legal hold of the landlord, whose claim relied upon the feudal tenure of colonial patroonships. In September 1839 a group of Berne farmers captured a deputy sheriff, and burned in a tar barrel writs that he had not served to farmers who refused to pay rents. The crowd then compelled him to collect and destroy the writs that he had served. The anti-renters good-naturedly forced the peace officer to treat them to drinks until his money ran out and then released him to walk back the twelve miles to Albany. This movement quickly gained support; on December 2, 1839, the gathered strength of as many as 1,500 anti-rent farmers convinced Sheriff Michael Artcher and 500 men to return to Albany without issuing any writs.

Crowds, with techniques developed during the American Revolution, repeated this type of action many times. Intrepid peace officers, like deputy sheriff Jacob Lewis in Rensselaer County, sometimes found themselves tarred and feathered. In March 1841 anti-renters donned a peculiar Indian costume, in mimesis of Bostonians in 1773 and other rioters, that soon became so elaborate a disguise as to appear almost preposterous. These Calico "Indians" wore masks, developed their own ritual and hierarchy of "chiefs," and became the mainstay of the anti-rent movement. Any who opposed them or were willing to pay rent also became a target of crowd action; more than a few "Indian" raids, announced with "tin horns," pulled down a house and ritually humiliated an "up-renter."

The disturbances became more frequent and sometimes more violent in 1844 and 1845. "Indians" killed two men in separate incidents.[35] One was a deputy sheriff. By that time large militia units were in the field and hundreds of arrests made. The insurgency was crushed militarily, but carried the day politically. The tenants turned out to be an important voting block. A newly elected governor soon pardoned the anti-renters who were in prison, and, with a sympathetic legislature sitting in the state capital, many landlords allowed their tenants to obtain title to the contested property.[36]

Settlement on the frontier was not an orderly process. In the early nineteenth century people streamed into newly opened territories, defying rational regulation by the government. Confrontations over land sometimes assumed the proportions of a comic opera. Even in these instances the potential for direct popular action was real. At least one tarring and feathering occurred during the maneuvering of the respective forces of Michigan and Ohio in the so-called "Toledo War" in 1836, and during a controversy between Iowa and Missouri the Iowa Claims Club in 1839 protected squatters' interests in Johnson County by tearing down the house of a claim jumper. In California squatting became pandemic, with many arguing that it was unjust for men like John A. Sutter to monopolize so much land. On August 14 and 15, 1850, Sacramento squatters and deed holders who had purchased the land from Sutter fought gun battles that killed four, including the city assessor and the sheriff.[37]

The most violent confrontations over land featured salient cultural issues that have obscured their agrarian and property base. The Missouri-Mormon controversy of the 1830s is usually recounted in the context of bigotry and prejudice, and the hemorrhage of "Bleeding Kansas" in the 1850s is ordinarily seen as a contest between slavery and freedom leading to the Civil War. Both episodes, however, contained fundamental questions over the control of property and involved techniques of collective action that fit into the overall developments of rioting in American society. The physical brutality of these agrarian rebellions derived in part from the unusual circumstances that gave them national notoriety. Yet the passions of the participants grew out of the explosive mixture of a contest over property exacerbated by cultural distinctions.

The Mormon troubles in Missouri came in three phases. First in the summer and fall of 1833 the Mormons were forced to leave Jackson County. Then, in 1836, local opposition convinced the Latter Day Saints to abandon Clay County, and finally in the summer and fall of 1838, after a bitter struggle with Missourians, they were driven out of the state altogether.[38] Why did the Mormons evoke all of this hostility?

The peculiar revelation of Joseph Smith offers only part of the answer. Many in antebellum America thought Smith's claims of uncovering additional books of the Bible offensive. Mobs harassed Smith in New York, and in Ohio he and Sidney Rigden were tarred and feathered. The Missourians went beyond this earlier disorder; they burned crops and houses, pillaged, raped, and murdered.

The core of this opposition was the challenge the Mormons posed to frontier cultural values. Missourians gambled, swore, and lived a rough and tumble existence. Mormons led a "Godly" life, avoiding the sins of Mammon. Missourians supported slavery. Many Mormons held anti-slavery views. Missourians were committed to perpetual warfare against the Indians. Joseph Smith looked upon Indians as long lost Israelites, and Mormons sought peaceful relations with local tribes. Missourians prided themselves on their independence of thought and deed. Mormons abdicated their own independence of judgment and followed the dictates of their leadership. This last point of contrast was crucial. Within a democratic society a phalanx of voters could easily swamp an election and propel Mormons into political office. Both Mormons and Missourians understood enough about the frontier to know that whoever controlled the local government also controlled the land.

Throughout the three phases of anti-Mormon activity Missourians repeated the same refrain—the people of Illinois would feel the same about the Mormon city of Nauvoo in 1844—the Mormons had to be driven out before they garnered enough strength to dominate everyone else. As Mormon numbers in Jackson County swelled to over one thousand in 1833, many Missourians believed that they could not compete effectively for land with the collective might of the Latter Day Saints. Ex-Mormon Ezra Booth advised as early as 1831 that "It is conjectured by the inhabitants of Jackson County, that the Mormonites, as a body are wealthy, and many of them entertain fears, that . . . when the lists of lands is exposed for sale, they [the Mormons] will outbid others, and establish themselves as the most powerful body in the county."[39] Following patterns of popular disorder long familiar to Americans, and recognizing that they had no basis for legal recourse, Missourians began to harass Mormons in 1832. In July 1833 a mob destroyed the press of the Mormon newspaper in Independence, Missouri, and tarred and feathered two Mormon leaders. The Mormons refused to heed the warnings, and, showing a penchant to use violence themselves, organized resistance. On November 4, 1833, the two sides engaged in a gun battle that left two Missourians and one Mormon dead and many wounded on both sides. That outbreak brought the militia, who were anti-Mormon, into the controversy. Within days the Missourians had disarmed most Mormons. Then the rampage commenced: Missourians drove the Mormons from their homes, burned fields and houses, demolished furniture, and horsewhipped men.[40]

There was less violence in the 1836 withdrawal of the Mormons from Clay County, where the inhabitants had offered asylum to the Mormons after the Jackson County debacle. The non-Mormons held a public meeting in June and expressed the same feelings that the people of Jackson County had—that the Mormons were buying up the land with the intention of driving the Missourians out. As one settler explained, "we must either submit to a Mormon government or trample under foot the laws of our Country."[41] Fortunately for all concerned there was little collective violence in this confrontation. Conjuring up the spirit of 1776 a band of Missourians met three hundred newly arriving Mormons and convinced them to turn around. Recognizing the potential for repeating the Jackson County purge, Mormon leaders agreed to leave the area, and accepted land the governor of the state offered in the unsettled northwestern corner of Missouri.

Within a year or two, Mormons were not only filling up the territory of the newly formed Caldwell County, but were spilling into neighboring counties as well. The same suspicions arose, aggravated by the creation of a Mormon paramilitary organization called the Danites. The 1838 pogrom of Mormons in the state started with a contested election in Gallatin, Davies County, in which the Mormons, led by the Danites, won control over the polls. Although this disturbance was like election riots elsewhere in the country, greater conflict was to follow. In a series of raids and counterraids, farms of Mormon and Missourian alike came under attack. Again the Missouri militia was called upon, but it quickly sided with the anti-Mormons. In late October a force of Mormons occupied, looted, and burned the abandoned town of Gallatin. On October 30, over two hundred Missourians besieged the Mormon community of Haun's Mill, killing at least seventeen men and boys. Many of these were put to death after their capture. The campaign ended in more Mormon disaster with the surrender of their communities at Far West and Adam-ond-Ahman. The Mormons were driven into exile and went to Illinois, where they established the city of Nauvoo. Five years later, anti-Mormons destroyed that community after lynching Joseph Smith.[42]

Like the anti-Mormon agitation, the Kansas fighting broke out in a manner almost indistinguishable from other rioting in the period, and then, with the issue of property looming larger and larger, and with the cultural gulf between northern and southern settlers becoming ever more apparent, the level of brutality and violence on both sides quickly escalated. One of the first incidents was in March 1855. After editor Jeb Patterson complained that the border-crossing voters from Missouri would hurt the southern cause, a mob dumped the type of his *Parkville Luminary* into a river and threatened to hang him. Despite the threats, the destruction of a press fit a long-standing pattern of crowd behavior. Two months later a Leavenworth mob combined several different types of crowd ritual in punishing anti-slave advocate William Phillips for failure to heed a warning to leave the territory. Pro-slavery members of the Squatters Claim Association—the organization's name suggests the importance of real estate—seized Phillips, stripped him, shaved one side of his head, gave him a coat of tar and feathers, and rode him on a rail. After publicly humiliating him with a series of traditional crowd punishments, the pro-slave men turned to another form of popular street theater—role reversal—and sold him at an auction held "by a big buck nigger." Purchasing him for "the enormous sum of one cent and a half," his new "owner," in an act of irony surely not lost on the crowd, then granted Phillips his freedom.[43]

Had all of the Kansas rioting continued in this pattern, the contest would not have attracted much national attention. But as more anti-slave settlers entered the territory, and the contrast between their free state values and those of the pro-slave forces grew, the level of violence rose. Both sides quickly recognized that they were competing for control over the future state government, and with it the land itself. Raid followed raid, and murder followed murder in two years of violence reminiscent of the Mormon Wars. John Brown's massacre of five pro-slavery men (two were boys) at Pottawatomie Creek was only one in a series of such actions. A pro-slavery attack on Osawatomie on August 30, 1856 left at least seven dead. Pro-slavery forces sacked the free state capital of Lawrence, and only federal troops, and the delay in admission of the territory as a state, managed to decrease the murder and mayhem.[44]

The farmer proved himself every bit as capable of rioting as his urban counterpart. Although popular disorder in the countryside often appeared, especially in the early stages of a conflict, to mimic eighteenth-century patterns of rioting, the would-be yeoman seldom sustained the single-interest corporate ideal of his grandfather. Contests over land, like the anti-rent war in New York, had a tendency to escalate. If the lines of cleavage shattering the pastoral landscape cut along deep cultural boundaries, then the violence could be extreme.

Vigilantism

Vigilantism—the practice of quasi-organized crowds taking the law into their own hands—was closely connected to the contest over property represented by the agrarian rebellions. Occurring most frequently in the countryside, vigilantism also took place in urban areas. In most instances vigilantes believed they protected property and upheld the spirit, if not the letter, of the law. Vigilantes articulated a faith in the sovereignty of the people that harked back to older traditions of popular disorder, but, like other rioters, they became increasingly violent during the nineteenth century as their activity reflected divisions within society. Although vigilantism may seem a conservative use of extralegal force to protect property and to assert normal values, all too often vigilantism was a screen behind which one competing group hid to drive away its opponents.[45]

Regardless of their motives, by claiming that they spoke for the "people," vigilantes articulated a crucial component of the ideology that lay behind rioting. In January 1858 the Regulators of northern Indiana declared allegiance to the "*doctrine of popular sovereignty.*" They asserted "that the people of this country are the real sovereigns, and that whenever the laws, made by those to whom they have delegated their authority, are found inadequate to their protection, it is the right of the people to take the protection of their property into their own hands, and deal with these villains according to their just desserts [*sic*]."[46] Thomas J. Dimsdale, in his classic account of the Montana vigilantes, came to the same conclusion. "Leave us the power of the people as a last resort; and, where governments breakdown, the citizens will save the State."[47]

This idea of popular sovereignty drew upon the experience of the American Revolution, eighteenth-century rioting, and English traditions. Defenders of vigilantism understood this heritage. Writing in 1923, decades after the Bald Knobbers terrorized the Missouri Ozarks (1885–1886), A. M. Haswell asserted that "as men of Anglo-Saxon blood have done a thousand times in history, so these pure Anglo-Saxon stock as ever lived [the Bald Knobbers], joined to the end, that, the law having failed them, they would make a law that should not fail."[48] The vigilantes may have added a new twist, but their game was an old one.

In other words, nineteenth-century vigilantism depended upon the idea that the people had a right and a duty to join together outside the normal bounds of law to protect the interests of the community. The rioter who turned to Mayor Johnson in Baltimore in June 1812 and told him that there were times when the law of the land must sleep and the laws of nature and reason prevail offered justification not only for the destruction of a newspaper office, but for a host of crowd activity raised in the name of "justice" and "lynch law."

In the first part of the nineteenth century vigilantes, and other rioters claiming to act in the name of community morals, often relied upon traditional riot ritual. A Bloomfield, New Jersey, temperance mob in 1834 used customary disguises, "with faces blackened, painted with various colors, or veiled," and took an offending tavern owner into a field and beat him severely. Vigilantes in Lexington, Kentucky, pulled down at least one brothel and tarred and feathered some of its male and female occupants. In the winter of 1845 or 1846 a Keokuk County, Iowa, lynch jury convicted two men of preempting land claims. The sentence mixed traditional crowd punishments. First the men were to be tied to a pole and ducked through a hole in the ice in a mill pond. Then they were to be tarred and feathered. Some groups, such as the followers of Captain Slick in northern Alabama during the 1830s, utilized corporal punishment. Frequently vigilantes held an ad hoc court and tried the "suspect" before sentencing. On April 24, 1831, about twenty Alabama slicks rode up to William Hall's house, took him to a swamp, went through the motions of a trial for counterfeiting, and then gave him fifty lashes on his back.[49]

Antiabolition riots can be thought of as a form of vigilantism. If some groups wanted to purge their community of individuals who gambled or who were criminals, others wanted to purge their society of individuals who challenged fundamental notions of property and race. Most of this antiabolitionist activity followed limited forms of popular disorder. During the mid 1830s there were hundreds of crowd outbursts, often led by "gentlemen of property and standing," against advocates of immediate abolition. Many of these disturbances followed a ritual in which the tumultuous crowd and the abolitionist had set roles. Rioters outside a meeting hall shouted charivari-like, screamed, and blew horns and tin trumpets. Borrowing tactics from theater disturbances, the rioters pelted rotten eggs and rocks at the abolitionists, who relished acting as martyrs, and stood bowed but unshaken under this bombardment. After an

1836 anti-slavery meeting in Granville, Ohio, antiabolitionists launched this type of assault upon an abolitionist procession. Some fisticuffs broke out, but the last scene of the riot best typifies the crowd's and victim's behavior in these disturbances. James G. Birney rode his horse—the mob had earlier cropped the tail—slowly and purposefully through a hooting crowd showering him with rotten eggs. After working his way clear, and in an act of defiance, Birney spurred his horse and galloped away, demonstrating that although both his person and his horse may have been ritually violated, his spirit and commitment would prevail.[50]

While traditional ritual and some corporal punishment became mainstays of vigilante movements throughout the country by mid century, paralleling developments in other riots, more and more groups relied on greater violence. In Vicksburg, Mississippi, on July 4, 1835, a crowd seized a gambler, tied him to a tree, and whipped him. After applying a coat of tar and feathers, they banished him. This spontaneous activity could have taken place anywhere in the United States. The incident convinced locals to organize against all gamblers in town. On July 6 the rioters visited the town's gambling houses, and, like good Anglo-American crowds from the previous century, focused their rage on property by destroying faro tables and furnishings. More violence, however, could not be avoided. Some gamblers defended one house, and a gunfight followed in which a citizen was killed. In retaliation the crowd captured and hanged five of the gamblers.[51]

Even antiabolitionist mobs might turn violent. When Elijah Lovejoy decided to defend his printing press, after crowds had destroyed four other presses, he was rewarded with bullets and true martyrdom. By the mid 1830s, some antiabolitionist riots went beyond the limited patterns of ritual and ended in virulent onslaughts against the black community as in New York City in July 1834, in Cincinnati in 1836, in Philadelphia in 1838, and elsewhere.[52]

Vigilantes west of the Mississippi and after mid century were more likely to kill their victims than those east of the Mississippi and before 1850. The California gold fields were sprinkled with corpses as lynch mobs asserted their idea of order against "undesirables"—criminals, misfits, and non–Anglo-Americans. There were also many deaths in Texas, Wyoming, and Idaho. The most lethal vigilante movements were in Montana. During the 1863–1864 purge of Henry Plummer and his gang around Bannock and Virginia City, twenty-five men were killed, and stockman Granville Stuart's Montana vigilantes contributed thirty-five deaths in 1884.[53]

The rough and tumble nature of the frontier and cultural strains of violence offer only part of the explanation for this sanguine record. Absence of regular courts and lack of police probably encouraged those on the frontier to seek justice on their own. In the South the legacy of slavery and racism, along with a heritage of violence, helped to produce an atmosphere conducive to lynch law.

But no region was immune to crowd action in the name of a higher "justice." Anti–horse thief societies in the northeast worked in tandem with officials, but in essence comprised the largest extralegal movement in American history. Scattered lynchings occurred throughout the region and many northerners eagerly participated in vigilante movements when they moved west. Theodore Roosevelt, for instance, desperately wanted to join Montana vigilantes, but was turned away because he already had a reputation of talking too much.[54]

Social change affecting all of the United States may offer a better explanation for extremes in vigilante violence. Many vigilante movements pitted would-be elites allied with the middling elements of society against ne'er-do-wells who often had the support of those on the bottom of society. In the San Francisco vigilante movement of 1856 there was an important cultural chasm between the vigilantes and their opponents. After the murder of a popular newspaper editor, William T. Coleman organized 6,000 men, mainly Protestants, into a committee of vigilance to defend business interests. Based at Fort Gunnybags, the vigilantes smashed the Irish-American political machine, dispatching the editor's murderer and a man who had slain a U.S. marshal. During its three-month reign (from May 15 to August 18), the committee executed two others, and drove out of town twenty-eight Democratic political henchmen. The San Francisco vigilance committee of 1856 may have led to greater "social stability," but that stability was for one social group—Protestants—at the expense of another—Irish Catholics.[55]

This type of popular disorder appeared elsewhere. The New Orleans Committee of Vigilance, composed of creoles and immigrants, in June 1858 opposed the tactics of intimidation practiced by the nativist Know Nothings. Backed by one thousand men, the committee seized an arsenal and, with cannon at hand, sought to insure an orderly election. Some street battles ensued during which eleven people died. Vigilantes, like those of San Francisco, were more likely to focus their rage on non–Anglo-Americans. Many vigilante movements in the California gold fields had an antiforeigner component. Ethnicity was also an issue in Texas and New Mexico. Vigilantes, especially in the South, repeatedly singled out blacks for crowd violence after the Civil War, including gruesome torture, before killing their victim. Other vigilantes strove to control labor unrest and radical politics. Tampa, Florida, vigilantes had several different targets: they hanged and castrated a black charged with child molestation, kidnaped immigrant cigar workers organizing strikes, and beat political agitators accused of being communists.[56]

Social, economic, and cultural tensions were important in many frontier vigilante movements. Land was contested throughout the West. Regulators in Iowa and elsewhere used vigilante methods to assert their particular claim over others. Stockmen had only just moved into Montana a few years before their vigilante sweep of horse thieves in 1884. There have been some suggestions that men like Granville Stuart wanted to drive small landholders and older settlers away. The Johnson County War in Wyoming pitted big ranchers against small ranchers in 1892. The full panoply of motives for the Missouri Bald Knobbers may never be known, but they were reacting to the effects of intrusions from the outside world; the railroad brought strangers, who set up "blind tigers" (gambling and drinking establishments), while government policies led to an influx of new homesteaders.[57]

Vigilantism, either before or after the Civil War, thus represented many of the major trends of the new rioting of the nineteenth century. The mob taking justice into its own hands became increasingly violent as the century wore on and often reflected important social, economic, and cultural divisions.

Persistent Patterns of Disorder

The Civil War did not mark a major break with the past in popular disorder. During that conflict riots followed the patterns established in the antebellum era. Americans persisted in fighting over ethnic divisions, economic strife, and politics. Rowdiness continued in many cities, and rival gangs and fire companies brawled with one another.

As was true throughout the period some riots occurred that repeated older forms of collective action. Food riots in several southern communities avoided extremes of violence. During the Civil War, women marched on the governor's mansion in Richmond, Virginia, to petition for relief. When that did not succeed, the women stormed the markets, pilfering a variety of items that had become too expensive during the wartime profiteering. Officials ordered the militia to break up the riot, arresting several people. Food riots also took place in North Carolina, Alabama, and Texas. In one incident in Galveston, Confederate soldiers took their meager rations and burned them in the street in protest.[58]

Northerners did not experience the same type of food shortages. However, pro-Union crowds did resort to limited collective action to intimidate their opposition. Several mobs smashed into newspaper offices to quiet criticism of the Republican administration and the war. On March 5, 1863, a party of one hundred soldiers sacked the office of Samuel Medary's *Crisis* in Columbus, Ohio, because of the paper's position on the war. Pro-Union mobs intimidated Copperheads and southern supporters in other ways. Sometimes this disorder was limited to jostling and harassment. In La Crosse, Wisconsin, a crowd seized a man who would not blame the war on the South. They led him through town with a rope around his neck and told him to leave the area. At other times crowds relied upon greater violence. One Illinois mob gave their victim twenty-nine lashes and forced him to take a loyalty oath, and in Ogle County, Illinois, a mob hanged a suspected arsonist who they believed had Confederate sympathies.[59]

Political intimidation could swing both ways. After federal officials arrested Clement L. Vallandigham for his antiwar sentiments, his outraged supporters besieged the Republican newspaper office in Dayton, tossing "turpentine balls" into the windows, setting the building ablaze. The Democrats attacked the fire companies that arrived to put out the conflagration and dispersed only after soldiers arrived and shot a rioter who was cutting a fire hose.[60]

Political riots also occurred in the Confederacy. In Raleigh, North Carolina, troops from Georgia tried to capture a Unionist editor. When they could not find him, they raided the office of his newspaper and threw the type and some papers into the street. In retaliation, two hundred of the editor's supporters attacked the office of the *State Journal*, the Confederate paper, and demolished its office.[61]

The drafting of men for the army led to rioting in both the North and the South. In Port Washington, Wisconsin, draft rioters on November 10, 1862, stormed the courthouse, destroyed enrollment records, physically beat local officials, and drove the draft commissioner away. More than the draft was at stake in this community, as most of the rioters were Catholics from the Belgian province of Luxembourg. These "Luxemburgers" resented the control exerted over their lives by Protestant Germans and Anglo-Americans who dominated local business and politics. The rioters thus extended their activity to vandalizing several homes of the affluent and sacking a warehouse. Officials dispatched six hundred troops to the area to restore law and order.[62]

Southerners also resisted the draft. In December 1862 opponents of the war in Industry, Texas, forced the recruiting officer to flee and beat one of his friends with sticks and iron bars. A month later more serious violence broke out in Madison County, North Carolina. About a dozen Confederate loyalists fought twice their number who were resisting the draft. Two men on each side were killed in the gun battle.[63]

The violence in Madison County shows that, like pre-war rioting, Civil War popular disorder could lead to the loss of lives. An even larger disturbance, including extremes of violence that had the potential to affect operations on the battlefield, rocked Baltimore in the opening days of the war. On April 19–21, 1861, pro-secessionist mobs attacked Union troops being rushed to the defense of Washington, disrupted train service and communications, and created havoc in a strategic border state. Seven soldiers and twelve civilians were killed.[64]

This type of violence even broke out after the war was well on its way. On March 28, 1864, Charleston, Illinois, Copperhead opponents of the war launched a vicious onslaught against soldiers returning from leave. The Copperheads were armed and prepared for trouble, while the soldiers stashed their weapons by the railroad as they waited in transit. An argument between a Copperhead and a soldier quickly led to a general gun battle. Getting the worst of the fight, the Union men lost six soldiers and one Republican dead.

Only two Copperheads were killed. Subsequently, soldiers combed the area, arresting many local Democrats they believed were involved in the riot.[65]

Although there were many examples of mobs relying on more traditional and generally limited forms of collective action, rioting in the nineteenth century entailed more physical violence as the century wore on. Rioting also reflected the tensions of competing groups struggling to assert themselves in the new egalitarian and capitalist society that grew out of the American Revolution. Cast adrift by the ideals of individualism and equality, Americans sought group identity in many ways, dividing themselves against one another and then striving to limit democratic access to others. Cultural and ethnic differences often came into play in violent attack and counterattack in a period when the number of immigrants reached into the millions. Likewise as major transformations altered the workplace and changed the relationship between employer and employee, class antagonism, often mixed with other factors, drove Americans apart. Expanding urban areas made the working class more difficult to control on a day to day basis, leading to disturbances triggered by the slightest provocation. In the countryside farmers contended with each other and with landlords over the control of property. While many of these disturbances may not have been that violent, when cultural differences entered the equation, as they did in the Mormon War in Missouri or the contest over the future of Kansas, the violence could be extreme. Americans as vigilantes also asserted a special role for the mob, claiming a need to set aside the normal channels of the law to maintain the sanctity of property and a higher sense of common justice, while they, too, reflected crucial divisions within society. These trends in rioting continued through the Civil War.

Embedded in this popular disorder was an important paradox. Those who held to the ideology of "popular sovereignty"—and particularly those who proclaimed themselves the vigilant protectors of property, law, and order—claimed an exclusive democratic heritage that transcended the confines of the ordinary processes of government. Yet, and herein lies the contradiction, these individuals acted in the name of the people to deny others full participation in the American republic. As they did so, they provided tragic testimony to the unraveling logic of a democracy unleashed.

THE TRAGEDY OF RACE | 4

The Rise of the Race Riot

Race starkly exposed the social contradictions in the egalitarian ideals in nineteenth-century America. Apparent before 1860 through the continuance of slavery in the South and the race riots of the North, this denial of democracy persisted from the War for Independence, past the 1860s and into the years of tragedy that ensued.

The American Revolution transformed race relations in the United States. Throughout most of the eighteenth century all but a handful of blacks were slaves. The experience of the war, with its upheaval and the British recruitment of slaves, helped to free many blacks. More important, egalitarian ideals brought the very institution of slavery into question. White Americans started to believe that this denial of the ideal of liberty was doomed. One state after another took action against slavery. By the opening of the nineteenth century almost every state north of Maryland had set the legal machinery into motion to end slavery, and even states below the Mason-Dixon line had liberalized manumission laws and many had considered ending slavery.

This challenge to slavery did not end racism. White fear, hatred, and dislike for blacks continued. In fact, during the early nineteenth century the liberalizing trend of the eighteenth century was reversed. Southerners became more committed to slavery and expanded upon a racist doctrine justifying the peculiar institution. Racism in the North also intensified, though it assumed a different form as conflict between the races now was on a more equal (but not entirely equal) footing. Free blacks, despite discrimination and repression, expressed their own ideas about freedom and equality, and, in a nation of divided slave jurisdictions, rioted to protect themselves from reenslavement. African Americans also built their own institutions and developed a separate community identity that became the target of northern white mobs.[1]

During the Civil War, as massive armies contested each other on the battlefield, neither southern nor northern racial violence changed. After the war, with the Confederacy defeated and the institution of slavery crushed, white southerners turned to racial violence to assert racial supremacy. No longer able to rely upon slavery and a system of legal repression, white southerners gained control of their state governments and combined legal and illegal race violence. The lynching party of the late nineteenth and early twentieth centuries was the ultimate expression of this development. Northern and southern whites continued to riot against blacks when political, economic, and class tensions came to a boil. Blacks, despite repression, occasionally struck back. When the winds of change gathered strength in the early twentieth century, as a great migration brought blacks to the North and as young African-American men experienced the trauma and exhilaration of war, blacks began to fight white racism in earnest.

In the first half of the nineteenth century, there were two types of race riots involving free blacks in the North. The first was marked by efforts by African Americans to protect themselves and members of their community from slavery. Information on these disturbances prior to the rise of abolitionism in the 1830s is so hard to come by that it almost seems as if news of these incidents was suppressed. White Americans preferred not to discuss action taken by blacks in the name of freedom. The second form of rioting, which became the predominant form during the Jacksonian period, was violent onslaughts by whites against blacks.

One of the earliest examples of free northern African Americans rioting against slavery occurred in 1801 when approximately 250 New York blacks besieged the property of an emigre from the French West Indies who planned to ship her slaves out of the city because their status as slaves was in question. During the 1820s and 1830s, as the North eradicated the last remnants of slavery, and as the South committed itself entirely to the peculiar institution, at least a dozen more such riots took place in New York, Boston, Philadelphia, Detroit, and elsewhere.[2]

These riots reveal the collective identity developed by blacks in both urban and rural areas and show black willingness to defend their own liberty. In Boston on December 28, 1819, a crowd of sixty blacks, armed with "clubs, knives and hatchets," confronted a combined force of the city's watch and white volunteers in an attempt to rescue a captured runaway slave. The whites dispersed the rioters, but only after at least one watchman was wounded and the arrest of fifteen or twenty blacks. Twenty-five blacks captured one of two blacks sent from Maryland in pursuit of runaway slaves, and severely whipped him in York, Pennsylvania, on June 14, 1825. Ten years later, in Philadelphia on June 16, northern blacks broke into a house and beat an elderly black women and her daughter for providing false testimony in a fugitive slave case.[3]

Rarely before 1850 did whites participate in these disturbances. On August 1, 1836, some abolitionists joined a crowd of blacks in their rescue of two women in a Boston courthouse. After 1850 whites and blacks acted together in several instances, including the famous case of Anthony Burns on May 26, 1854, in Boston. Yet the most noteworthy and dramatic gesture to protect runaways was when William Parker and his followers killed a slaveholder and drove off a U.S. marshal and his posse at a Christiana, Pennsylvania, farmhouse on the morning of September 11, 1851. This riot culminated a series of aggressive actions by blacks in southeastern Pennsylvania against slave catchers. The assertive leadership of William Parker combined with a vision of an alarmed rural black citizenry offering armed resistance to the Fugitive Slave Act helped to galvanize public attention in both the North and the South.[4]

In the years before the Civil War, white mobs assaulting blacks characterized most race riots. These disturbances increased in the 1830s as abolitionists trumpeted the cause of immediate emancipation and exposed the raw nerve ends of a racist society. The race riots of the 1830s, however, need to be viewed as part of a continuum of disorder that began with the emergence of free black communities, and that persisted into the 1840s, 1850s, 1860s, and beyond.

Racial rioting before 1830 was relatively small scale and involved the destruction of some property and the rough handling of a few individuals. For example, during the celebration of Independence Day in 1819 a white crowd knocked over food stands and assaulted the black proprietors in New York City. Institutions created by blacks, especially the independent African churches, often came under attack. In 1815 a band of Northern Liberties whites, claiming to be bothered by the noise of emotional religious services in their Philadelphia neighborhood, wrecked an African-American house of worship.[5]

Before the 1830s, larger anti-black rioting might take place. On October 17 and 18, 1824, a riot in Providence, Rhode Island, broke out. After blacks had refused to make way for whites on the sidewalk, a white mob besieged the Hardscrabble section of the city where many blacks lived and where there were many taverns and houses of prostitution. The mob demolished approximately twenty houses, and, despite the shooting of one white, drove the blacks out of the neighborhood. During a pogrom in Cincinnati, August 16–22, 1829, in which one white was killed, the invasion of the African-American district forced hundreds of blacks from their homes.[6]

Amid the hate, fear, and rage that intensified with immediate abolitionism in the 1830s, large-scale assaults on the black community increased. New Yorkers went on a rampage that lasted several days (July 7–11, 1834). Rioters targeted some abolitionists during the riot, but they were most concerned with terrorizing blacks. White mobs wrecked African-American churches and schools, ransacked dozens of houses, and beat many blacks. A month later (August 12–14, 1834) in three nights of disorder in Philadelphia whites destroyed, damaged or looted two churches and over thirty houses. In this riot two people died and hundreds fled their homes.[7]

Countless smaller disturbances broke out through the 1840s and 1850s. In Boston on August 27, 1843, sailors beat four blacks. When the victims defended themselves, a larger crowd gathered and assaulted every black person in sight. During a New York strike in January 1855 Irish longshoremen beat blacks hired to replace them. In Philadelphia's California House riot (Oct. 9–10, 1849) at least four persons were killed. This trend of racial rioting continued into and beyond the Civil War.[8]

Several serious antebellum race riots included active and effective black resistance to whites. The Providence riot of September 21–24, 1831, began when a black man beat five whites in a fight. The brawl soon expanded as black and white sailors battled in the Snowtown neighborhood. On the first night of rioting the blacks triumphed. On the second night, rioting whites invaded the neighborhood and tore down two houses. Blacks continued to resist, and a black man shot and killed a white. The third night belonged to the white mob, which beat back a force of militia and wreaked havoc in Snowtown. On the last night of rioting the militia interceded more success-fully, firing into a crowd of white rioters, killing four, and ending the dis-turbance. Black gunmen on August 29, 1841, greeted white rioters in Cincinnati with a hail of bullets when they invaded "Bucktown" where many blacks lived. Armed only with sticks and stones, the whites retreated. After several unsuccessful sallies they returned with more lethal weapons; some whites even dragged up a cannon and raked the street with chains, slugs, and boiler punchings. The next day the mayor and the militia convinced about 250-300 blacks to surrender for protection. That night, despite assurances to the contrary, mobs assailed several black homes, an African church, as well as some abolition targets. Casualty figures are uncertain, but at least one person, a white, died, with many more seriously wounded.[9]

Antebellum race riots usually occurred in the free northern states. Yet, pre-saging developments in the second half of the century, there were several instances when southerners executed blacks who challenged slavery and racial assumptions. The most famous of these cases was the lynching of Francis McIntosh on April 28, 1836, in St. Louis. McIntosh, a black steamboat worker from Pittsburgh, killed a deputy sheriff and wounded another peace officer while resisting arrest. A mob took McIntosh from jail, dragged him to the edge of town, and then burned him alive. A mob also hanged a black for stabbing a white in a fight in Helena, Arkansas, in August 1836, and during a June 1835 slave insurrection scare in Mississippi, whites strung up at least four blacks.[10]

Both southerners and northerners reacted to a black assertiveness rooted in a revolutionary ideology of equality that had an Atlantic as well as an American context. In particular black and white Americans cast their eyes toward the West Indies with hope and fear. Blacks found hope in the example of a free black nation, and in emancipation in French (1794) and British (1833) colonies; whites feared the bitter racial warfare in Haiti and the end of slavery. The impact of this Atlantic context sometimes can be seen in racial rioting. Many arrested in the New York riot of 1801 to prevent the exportation of slaves from the city had French names—suggesting that these individuals were recent arrivals from the West Indies. During a Philadelphia riot in July 1804, a group of blacks marched through the streets, knocking down whites, and proclaimed that they would "show them San Domingo." Officials blamed "French Negroes" when a crowd of African Americans tried to rescue a black arrested by a constable in Philadelphia on July 24, 1819. The same Atlantic connection arose over twenty years later when, on August 1, 1842, Philadelphia's blacks marched to celebrate emancipation in the British West Indies. Although the black celebrants did not initiate any violence, they became subject to a two-day attack on their persons and property simply because they had planned to commemorate a day that was important to their African-American consciousness.[11]

Racial disturbances were a central part of the violent rioting that marked the nineteenth century. Whites repeatedly focused their rage on property that symbolized the black associational activity that asserted a separate African-American identity, and whites beat, shot, and even fired cannon at blacks with total disregard for life and limb. Despite a racist legal and social system, African Americans often stood their ground firmly and fought back violently against reenslavement and against white incursions into their African-American world.

The Civil War

During the Civil War there were several race riots that followed the form of popular disturbances established in the Jacksonian period. The Civil War exacerbated racial fears that had long agitated northern whites. Workers believed that emancipation would bring a flood of black migrants, who would drive down their wages, take their jobs, and realize all their worst apprehensions of racial amalgamation. In June 1861 fighting between Irish and black stevedores in Cincinnati lasted two days. The rioting started over the supposed "favors" of an Irish girl, but also derived from the stiff competition for work along the levee in a period of depressed river traffic. In July 1862 fights between the same two parties continued for almost a week, with Irish laborers burning black homes. Blacks retaliated by invading an Irish neighborhood and torching some houses. Disturbances concerning labor issues broke out in Toledo, Buffalo, Troy, Brooklyn, and New York City. Even the countryside was not immune. An Indiana mob surrounded the house of a farmer who had hired a contraband—a newly freed slave from the South—captured the black and ordered him out of the community.[12]

These riots often combined several issues. In March 1863 the trial of a black man for molesting a white and a black girl brought large crowds into the streets of Detroit. Jobs, the sexual threat, and the draft all agitated the city's whites. After the man's conviction, the crowd wanted its own immediate justice. The provost marshal's guard fired into the crowd, killing one man. Angered, whites later charged into a black neighborhood, burning houses and assaulting blacks of both sexes.[13]

In Detroit the rioters had expressed some concern about the draft. The joining of the race issue with the draft was not unusual. Several draft riots in

1863 involved some attack on blacks. Many white Americans believed that they were being drafted into a war to free slaves who would then steal their livelihood and possibly sexually assault the women of their family. Distressed by this specter, they struck out at the nearest racial target. The most significant of these disturbances, and perhaps the most violent riot in American history, took place in New York City, July 13–17, 1863.[14]

If personal and physical assaults had become the hallmark of nineteenth-century popular disorder, the draft riots reached a new level of violence; comparisons have often been drawn to the Parisian uprising of 1871, rather than to other American disturbances.[15] Yet the riot was an *American* affair that developed from conditions within the United States that were only exacerbated by the Civil War.

In the early phases of the rioting two separate trends can be discerned: a limited demonstration against the draft; and a violent purge of the city of all emblems of Republican government, including a pogrom of the city's blacks. The first trend had a broad base of support among Democrats—the majority in New York—and included many artisans, laborers, and industrial workers ranging from native Protestants to Irish Catholic immigrants. The second trend recruited its base from Irish Catholic laborers and industrial workers. As the rioting progressed, the more limited trend gave way to the more violent, and New York found itself immersed in an all-out war on its streets.[16]

The riot opened with a semi-organized work stoppage, suggesting some planning, to protest the draft in the city. Hundreds, if not thousands, did not go to work on the morning of the thirteenth. People filled the Eighth and Ninth Avenues uptown, closing those businesses that had opened and convincing more workers to join them. This tactic derived from earlier work stoppages and expressed political opposition to the draft. At the Ninth District Office, where the draft was to be drawn at 10:30 a.m., a crowd collected. After the lottery began, volunteer firefighters of the Black Joke Engine Company Thirty-three broke into the building, disrupted the selection process, and set the building on fire. Despite the limited targets, disorder quickly fed on itself, releasing passions not so easily confined.

As early as the morning of the thirteenth some crowds went beyond draft protest, cutting down telegraph lines and pulling up railroad track to disrupt any government interference. During the day a mob brutally beat Police Superintendent John A. Kennedy until his face and body were a mass of gore. Other police officers were attacked. These men were singled out because Democratic workers saw the city police as an extended arm of the Republican government that had ferreted out thousands of deserters. The fire at the Ninth District office spread to other buildings, and although the Black Jokes wanted to aid in putting out the blaze, the people in the street interfered. More fires broke out. Rioters turned their attention to new targets by the evening. Several homes of the rich were gutted on Lexington Avenue, expressing both class resentment and animus to the Republicans who lived there. Rioters also beat blacks and burned the Colored Orphan Asylum on Fifth Avenue.

By Tuesday the protest movement against the draft had been overwhelmed by rioting that challenged Republican government and threatened the annihilation of all blacks. Many of those who had joined in the first phases of the rioting now stood opposed to it. Fire companies like the Black Jokes patrolled their neighborhoods and struggled to keep the disorder at bay. Although rioters might be excluded from some areas, other sections of the city fell under the sway of the mobs that numbered into the thousands.

The rioting over the next several days was very brutal. Mobs sacked black homes and perpetrated barbarities on black persons. Wednesday morning a crowd attacked black shoemaker James Costello on West Thirty-second Street. Costello ran, firing a shot at his pursuers. He was captured anyway, and the whites beat, kicked, and stoned him. With his body pulverized, the rioters then hanged him. Later that day, another crowd hanged Abraham Franklin from a lamppost. The military arrived and cut the body down. When the soldiers moved on, a crowd strung up the corpse again. Shortly after that the crowd hurrahed for Jefferson Davis. Someone cut Franklin's corpse down, and a sixteen-year-old boy dragged the body through the streets by its genitals to the cheers of the crowd. Brutalities like these were repeated many times.

While blacks were singled out for special atrocities, rioters looted homes and stores, burned houses and police stations, raided armories, and sacked factories. Any police officer who was so unlucky as to fall into the hands of a mob was beaten and sometimes killed.

Quelling the disturbance was no easy matter. There was no single center of rioting; no one mob. The police recorded thousands of telegrams reporting new outbreaks of violence. As soon as reinforcements were dispatched to one section of the city, they were needed in another. Even on the first day of rioting local officials called upon the military for assistance. Despite problems establishing the line of command, the military responded quickly. By Thursday troops arrived fresh from the victory at Gettysburg. Pitched battles were fought between the rioters, often armed with looted rifles, and the forces of law and order. Cannon had to be brought to bear, and by Thursday and Friday, the rioters started to lose ground as the number of military on hand swelled to six thousand.

After the rioting, reports suggested that well over one thousand persons were killed during these days of terror. More recently, a count of the actual bodies found in the historical record indicates that the number was likely under 120. At least eleven of these were blacks. Eight soldiers, two policemen, and two volunteers aiding the police were also killed. The rest were largely rioters. Hundreds more were wounded, and the property destruction ran into the millions.[17] Perhaps even more significant than the casualty figures and the cost of the draft riots was their symbolic importance. For decades after July

1863 these riots were cited as the fulfillment of the urban and industrial nightmare. The draft riots bore witness to the "volcano under the city" that middle- and upper-class Americans had come to dread. Within the larger history of rioting in America, however, they have a different import. These riots stand as a symbol and manifestation of the major trends in popular disorder during the nineteenth century. They illustrate the twisted and conflicted animosities that had emerged between different groups within American society. The grievances of the draft rioters were many and diverse. Yet these frustrations and hatreds became projected onto the issue of race—an area in which howling and raging crowds would continue to express their greatest brutality.

Reconstruction

After the Civil War the effort by white southerners to limit the effects of emancipation created the most violent and nastiest rioting in American history. There is no way to relate the full dimensions of this rioting, nor can we ever comprehend the mixture of emotions that marked the Reconstruction experience of black Americans. Freedom brought great expectations smashed by a reign of white terror. A survey of Reconstruction riots suggests at least four major categories of disturbances. First, there were some riots initiated by blacks. Second, there were a few major outbreaks of urban popular disorder, two of which—Memphis and New Orleans in 1866—had a significant impact on Reconstruction history. Third, there were several rural disturbances that were so bloody and so infamous that they stand out on their own. Finally, there were the countless acts of terror and intimidation practiced by the Ku Klux Klan and other groups of whites. All four areas of rioting reflect the violence and divisions that had come to mark nineteenth-century popular disorder.[18]

Southerners had built their society upon a myth of a corporate identity whose foundation lay in black slavery. Blacks were not invisible in the antebellum South; they were merely property and did not count as human beings. The Union victory threatened southern assumptions by abolishing slavery. White southerners, asserting their racist vision of a united community, struggled to prevent black participation in politics and refute equitable social and economic arrangements. In a flurry of activity—often joining traditional techniques of collective action with extreme violence—southern whites strove to deny the results of the Civil War.

White southerners viewed their resort to violence as a necessary means to save their civilization. One editor deplored mobs, but explained that a lynching in Texas "had become . . . an unavoidable necessity. The sanctity of home, the peace and safety of society, the prosperity of the country, and the security of life itself demanded . . ." action.[19] In this scenario, repeated by scholars even in the middle of the twentieth century, the freedmen, inspired by northern carpetbaggers and supported by southern scalawags, plotted to overthrow republican institutions and install themselves as the dominant force.[20] In every shadow and whisper southern whites saw the beginnings of black conspiracy and race genocide.

Did whites have any real basis for these fears? African Americans, fueled by the promise of freedom and exhilarated by the defeat of white masters, initiated some riots. These disturbances presaged the fulfillment of the southern whites' worst nightmares. For more than a week in June 1866 in Charleston, South Carolina, black gangs, shouting phrases like "Kill the rebel son of a bitch," sporadically attacked whites. Despite participation of Republican whites in Union Leagues, these political clubs that allowed blacks to discuss issues and learn more about their rights aggravated race relations. The presence of armed guards at some meetings sent a shudder down many a white spine. At times, the Union League provided a vehicle to mobilize blacks against their racist opponents. In the fall of 1867 at Hunnicutt's Crossing, South Carolina, Union League blacks fought with whites from a local debating club, killing one and arresting others.[21]

If African-American assertiveness offered a shred of evidence to rationalize—not substantiate—white fears, the response often was out of all proportion to the stimulus. Blacks ordinarily paid a very high price for any sign of aggression. Near Columbia, Tennessee, on the night of July 4, 1868, about twenty to thirty blacks ambushed a Ku Klux Klan gathering, killing one, and wounding three or four others before retreating to the protection of the army. Within a few weeks the Klan, in parties as large as two hundred, hunted down three of the blacks who had participated in the attack and lynched them. In the fall of 1868 an Arkansas trader shot at a black at Shady Grove, Louisiana. Outraged blacks captured the man, roughed him up and tied him to a tree before some whites, after a struggle that saw loss of life on both sides, rescued him. Word spread that the blacks were in a state of rebellion. Seventy-five whites crossed over from Arkansas and killed blacks indiscriminately. Another armed party of whites came from Shreveport, and although they turned back before reaching Shady Grove, they killed nine blacks along the way. This incident set off a series of white attacks on blacks in the area that left as many as from 150 to 200 dead.[22]

The explosiveness of southern race relations and black combativeness is further illustrated by an incident in Cross Plains, Alabama, in July 1870. After several whites beat a freedman, ten armed blacks returned to town seeking vengeance. A short gun battle ensued in which no one was injured. But the whites were now convinced that a black uprising had occurred. Whites scoured the countryside, captured all but a few of those involved in the shooting, and arrested a white teacher who had been preaching racial equality to the blacks. An ad hoc court under a magistrate commenced its investigation. When the proceedings took longer than a day, the Klan stepped in and hanged the white teacher and six blacks.[23]

Black assertiveness also contributed to the larger urban riots that took place. Memphis and New Orleans each were marred by bloody riots in 1866. In both instances the rioting opened with blacks aggressively advancing their claims to equality in the face of opposition by local officials and the white citizenry. Despite the presence of Union troops, southern whites, led by the city police, murderously lashed out at blacks. Together these two riots helped to convince northerners of the intransigence of the South, swept the radicals into power in the congressional elections of that year, and led to the initiation of a new program of Reconstruction.

The Memphis riot began as a street brawl between black Union soldiers and Irish policemen. Animosity between the two groups had been building for some time. Ever since the Union had conquered the city, hundreds of blacks seeking their freedom had collected there. Memphis swarmed with black soldiers, many of whom were then being discharged in the months after Appomattox. Most of these African Americans congregated in the southside of the city, an area whose residents—including Irish policemen—had been struggling toward respectability. On May 1 a minor confrontation between the police and blacks escalated into a riot. White residents of the area joined the police, while black soldiers from a nearby base came to the aid of their comrades. By nightfall military officers had convinced the soldiers to return to the local fort. With serious opposition removed, whites went wild. By the time the military interfered—the civil authorities encouraged the rioting—the damage had been done. In three days of rioting (May 1–3), forty-six African Americans were killed, over seventy people wounded, five African-American women raped, and four African-American churches, twelve schools, and ninety-one homes destroyed.[24]

If the blacks in Memphis had contested white control of the streets with their fists and pistols, blacks in New Orleans took a less bellicose tack; they merely displayed their support for equal rights. The political background of the riot was complex. A state constitutional convention had reorganized Louisiana in 1864 along conservative lines that allowed white domination. By the beginning of 1866 the state's Unionists and Republicans feared that they were about to lose control of the state to ex-confederates in the Democratic Party. The Unionists used a constitutional loophole to reconvene the 1864 convention in July to draw up provisions to enfranchise African Americans and bolster their electoral strength. On July 30, under dubious legality, the convention met at the Mechanic's Institute.

The city's blacks, with banners and music blaring, paraded in support of the convention. New Orleans whites and the city police, many of whom had served in the Confederate army, could not abide this affront to their racial prejudices. Fights and small arms fire marred the progress of the parade. Near the Mechanic's Institute, the harassment turned into an onslaught and the blacks ran for cover among the conventioneers. This was a tactical mistake.

The police surrounded the building and fired their weapons into it. Surrender met with encouragement and then a hale of bullets. The attackers launched several assaults, forcing the Unionists and blacks out of the Mechanic's Institute. Whites then randomly beat blacks throughout the city. Before the military restored order, between 40 and 50 blacks and 3 white Unionists were murdered, and over 150 others injured.[25]

Besides the two great riots of 1866 there were other examples of urban disorder during Reconstruction. New Orleans, with a large and articulate African-American population, experienced a tumultuous Reconstruction history. Whites battled with blacks frequently. The election in the fall of 1868 included several violent episodes. On September 22 white and black political processions became entangled and clashed. Blacks charged a building containing a heckler and fired guns. A white Democratic club counterattacked with rocks, knives, and pistols. One African American was killed and men on both sides were injured. A month later the political conflict also contained an ethnic edge. A Democratic club called the Innocents—composed of Sicilians, Italians, Spanish, Maltese, Latin Americans and Creoles—raided black Republican clubs. Both sides exchanged gunfire. The Innocents also ransacked many black homes over the course of several days. At least twelve African Americans were killed; some estimates suggest that as many as one hundred blacks perished. Contests over the control of the state government brought rival forces into strife in 1873, 1874, and 1877. The attempted coup by the white league on September 14, 1874, was the most violent of these disturbances. White Democrats fought the black militia and Metropolitan (Republican) police and briefly took over the reins of power. The Metropolitans lost eleven killed and sixty wounded. White league casualties were twenty-one killed and nineteen wounded. Federal troops restored the government to the Republicans a couple of days later.[26]

Other urban areas did not accumulate the record of New Orleans. Charleston, with an African-American majority, experienced some outbursts, but they usually entailed fewer casualties. Blacks in Charleston, aware of their numbers, were often the aggressors. In most cities, like elsewhere in the South, African-American assertiveness had its costs. Outraged by the ouster of the Republican sheriff, three columns of armed blacks approached Vicksburg in December 1874. Whites managed either to persuade the invading hordes to turn back, or after short gun battles, to force them to return to the countryside. That night, however, white mobs destroyed the homes of Vicksburg blacks. Twelve blacks and one white were killed that day; many more were wounded.[27]

The most serious rioting remained in the small towns and countryside of the South where emancipation created divided communities ready to erupt into violence. In places like Camilla, Georgia; Meridian, Mississippi; and the Louisiana towns of Opelousas and Colfax, the tragic outlines of Reconstruction history can be traced. For each location the basic plot was the same: African Americans organized to protect themselves only to be over-whelmed by whites who did not hesitate to resort to extremes of violence.

During the fall elections in 1868 Georgia Republicans planned a series of demonstrations throughout the state to encourage African-American voting, including a rally at Camilla on September 19. Soon after 200–300 blacks arrived in town a scuffle broke out that triggered an assault by whites. Coming under a scathing fire, some blacks defended themselves, but most broke and ran. Whites, however, pursued their quarry, hunting down and shooting blacks in the nearby woods. Estimates vary, but from eight to twelve African Americans were killed, and over thirty wounded. Only six whites were injured in the "battle." The riot quickly became a celebrated controversy. Democrats claimed that the blacks had attacked first and that the whites had defeated a racial uprising. Republicans saw the riot as blatant political intimidation and used the incident, along with a host of other violent episodes that accompa-nied the election, to negate Democratic successes.[28]

Compared to later riots the Camilla incident was a tame affair. In Meri-dian, Mississippi, on March 6, 1871, white Democrats staged a virtual coup d'etat after they had two local African-American leaders arrested on trumped up charges. During the court hearing white gunmen opened fire, killing the Republican judge and two black bystanders. They also wounded and later murdered the two black leaders. A pogrom followed that left at least thirty dead, drove all Republicans from political office, and placed white suprema-cists firmly in charge.[29]

In two rural Louisiana riots African-American militancy met with even greater white violence. Racial tension increased in September 1868, after two whites caned a white Republican carpetbagger in St. Landry Parish. Each side armed and prepared for action at Opelousas. When the fighting broke out, better armed and better organized whites quickly gained victory and captured twenty-nine blacks. That night a crowd of whites took the prisoners out of the jail and executed twenty-seven of them. The killing did not stop. Republicans reported that the violence that followed claimed two hundred lives. Even Democrats admitted to some excesses, but asserted that only between twenty-five and thirty died.[30]

Perhaps the worst single-day massacre during Reconstruction was at Colfax, Louisiana, on April 13, 1873—Easter Sunday. Like the other major rural riots, the contest was for control of the local government. White Democrats struggled to purge the community of white Republicans dependant upon African-American votes. Fearing a white onslaught, blacks gathered in Colfax at the end of March. On April 13, 150 whites warned the blacks to remove their women and children by noon. The battle was not an even match. The whites, armed with rifles and a cannon, stayed out of shotgun range—the main African-American weapon—until they had decimated their opponents. A cavalry charge sent the blacks scurrying into a stable that also served as the local courthouse. This proved to be a death trap. The whites peppered the building with gunfire and then had the building set ablaze. When groups of blacks tried to surrender, the whites promised safe passage and then mowed them down. Eventually whites captured about forty prisoners, but summarily shot them that night. No final tally can be accurately made, but an army investigation documented the deaths of at least 105 blacks and three whites (two of the whites probably were shot accidentally by their own partisans).[31]

Although the events that marred Easter Sunday in Colfax in 1873, and the other rural riots with large casualties, stand out because of their individual impact, each of these riots arose against a backdrop of repeated acts of collective violence. The extent of this violence is staggering. We will never know the full number of riots.[32] So extreme was the terror, and so successful, that many incidents were never reported. Congressional and state committees probed the South and provided some tally. The death toll runs into the thousands. In Louisiana an investigation into the political violence between the state election in April and the national election in November 1868 revealed that 1,081 persons were killed, 135 shot, and 507 harassed in some form or another. Most of these victims were African Americans. The Freedman's Bureau surveyed the level of racial violence in Texas between 1865 and 1868; there were at least 2,225 offenses against blacks and somewhere between 400 and 500 murders.[33]

These numbers are from two states for only short segments of the entire period of Reconstruction (1865–1877). They also include total casualties from both individual and group violence. Although there were many incidents of a single white murdering a black, groups perpetrated much of this violence. Bands of nightriders crisscrossed the countryside, beating and murdering blacks repeatedly. From November 1870 to September 1871, Ku Klux Klan raiders sallied forth virtually every evening in York County, South Carolina, committing at least eleven murders and tallying approximately six hundred cases of whipping and assault.[34]

Beyond the extent of the violence was its sheer brutality. Visiting a cabin in the middle of the night and hauling a black into the woods for a lashing—an act intended to remind the victim of the days of slavery—was vicious enough. Often, southern whites did more than that. The Klan castrated black Republican Henry Lowther in Wilkinson County, Georgia, in the summer of 1871. Sometime during the same year, about thirty Klansmen raided a plantation in Fayette County, Alabama, chased away the men and raped the women. Murder, however, remained the ultimate threat to every African American. These killings ranged from isolated ambushes on individuals to gruesome massacres. In August 1874 the whites of Trenton, Tennessee, feared a black conspiracy. In expectation they hatched their own plot. Officials arrested several blacks. A mob of 75 to 150 whites took sixteen men from jail, marched them to a bridge about 400 yards away, and started shooting. When the smoke cleared, four blacks were dead, two others lay writhing from their wounds, and the rest somehow escaped in the confusion. On the night of February 12,

1871, about five hundred Klansmen rode into Union, South Carolina, and took from jail ten black men charged with murdering a white. The next morning two blacks were discovered hanging from a rope, six others were tied to trees, their bodies riddled with bullets, and two had miraculously escaped.[35]

Motivation for the Reconstruction rioting was complex. Many disturbances, as suggested in the examples above, revolved around politics. Yet other issues were also important. Whites who grew up with the specter of slave rebellion before them feared armed black militias and often strove to disarm blacks in a preemptive move to save—so they believed—the white race. Whites also used collective action to control labor at a time when the end of slavery left the status of labor ambiguous. Many riots also regulated social behavior. Although the vast majority of victims were black, mobs sometimes punished whites for being carpetbaggers, scalawags, or just morally deficient.[36]

The savagery, frequency, and variety of this violence make it difficult to study. On one level the repeated letting of blood appears irrational. Yet, despite the extremes, there are similarities between Reconstruction rioting and earlier forms of collective violence. The costume of the Ku Klux Klan was reminiscent of other disguises worn by Euro-American rioters for centuries. The long robes may have suggested the female garb that rioters had previously donned to humiliate moral offenders. Ritual and bizarre clothing had marked the antirent movement in New York State in the 1840s, and many American rioters had worn various disguises. Although most Reconstruction collective violence had a racist edge to it, the Klan also regulated morals. Even the effort to control blacks could reflect the southern sense of order as well as racial and economic concerns. The shattering of the white moral order meant that instead of the customary corporate world, whites would be compelled to compete with blacks.[37] Ex-Confederate general Martin Witherspoon Gary explained that if blacks were allowed to vote "you have consented to make this a mongrel government—to make the children of your former slaves the successful competitors of your children for the honors of the state. . . ."[38] To maintain the old moral order, with its corporate identity and mythical unity of interests, a separate and distinct interest group had to be suppressed. Whites thus turned to what almost might be seen as a traditional extralegal activity to sustain their world order.

There was, however, a difference between Reconstruction rioting and older forms of collective action. That difference can be seen in the blood and mayhem caused by white southerners. Racial hatred intensified southern white actions, and that racial hatred, in turn, was exacerbated by a pattern of violence that predates the Civil War and that was aggravated by the legacy of defeat.

White Terror

Redemption did not end the white terror. By 1877 Reconstruction was over and white southerners felt safely ensconced in their own state governments.

The scalawags, carpetbaggers, and their dark-skinned allies had been beaten back. Federal troops were withdrawn, and the national administration looked askance at the political conditions in the South. Caught up in their own economic problems and the specter of a disordered labor market, worn down by the intransigence of southern Democrats, and tired of aiding southern blacks, white northerners abandoned their interference in state affairs in the South. With white supremacists in power, race relations, according to the southern mythology, should have assumed the benign patterns of the antebellum era. Violence, however, had always underpinned southern race relations, and now that blacks were no longer slaves, violence continued as the centerpiece of white domination.

The white terror after 1877 took many forms, covering both rural and urban areas, and spreading north and south, east and west. This terror was an extension of rioting during Reconstruction and fits the pattern of violent nineteenth-century collective action. Whites continued to intimidate blacks, threatening them with punishments ranging from whipping to murder. Despite the overwhelming power of this white terror, and despite the failure of the national government to continue its role as protector, African Americans did not simply abdicate all power. Occasionally, despite the odds, blacks confronted the system of racial oppression head on. Invariably they lost. Yet the fortitude expressed at these times stands as testimony to the power and persistence of the idea of liberty and freedom among African Americans.

The most virulent form of the white terror became the lynching-bee. In this quasi-legal brutal and sanguine practice southerners—joined eventually by Americans from other parts of the country—took public terror to new levels. Lynching was a refinement of vigilantism. It involved a crowd or a group of persons seizing an individual who had been accused of a crime or had supposedly violated moral sensibilities, and inflicting discipline extraneous to the normal judicial process. Sometimes the lynchers held an ad hoc peoples court. More often, especially when it came to the treatment of blacks in the South, the crowd assumed guilt and went straight to the punishment.

As with the Reconstruction violence, the complete dimensions of lynching will never be known. A record of lynching only began in 1882 when the *Chicago Tribune* started to list all major disasters and crimes, and included a tally of lynching. Blacks were not the only targets of lynching, although they did comprise over 70 percent of the victims. Between 1882 and 1937 there were 5,112 persons lynched in the United States. Of this total 3,657 were blacks. We cannot be sure how many separate riot instances these numbers represent. Lynching ranged from violence perpetrated by less than a half dozen individuals to massive actions that brought together crowds of ten thousand or more. Regardless of the absolute accuracy or inaccuracy of these figures for a total of riots, the impression is clear. Thousands of riotous lynchings occurred. The vast majority of these were in the South, and, as you move toward and into the twentieth century the proportion of African-American victims increased.[39]

The savagery of lynching also stands out. There is no pleasant way to murder an individual, but there are varying degrees of pain that can be inflicted in the process. A well-placed bullet is faster than hanging, and hanging less gruesome than being burned alive. All these tactics, in combination or alone, were used. In the late nineteenth and early twentieth centuries, torture and burning became more frequent. Before 1890, burning was rare. Mobs burned almost 15 percent of the 416 blacks lynched between 1919 and 1929. The extent of the brutality sometimes defies the imagination. The mob that executed Sam Hose, a black charged with killing a white farmer and raping the farmer's wife, in Newman, Georgia, on April 23, 1899, exhibited incredible sadism. Whites tortured Hose, burned him alive and, after he had died, chopped slices out of his heart and liver. A crowd of one thousand gathered at Vicksburg, Mississippi, on February 13, 1904 to lynch Luther Hubert and his wife. Hubert, too, had been charged with murdering a white man. His wife's crime was that she was married to Luther Hubert. Whites tied the Huberts to a tree, chopped off their fingers, poked out an eyeball with a stick, and inserted a large corkscrew into their bodies that tore out "big pieces of raw, quivering flesh." Then the rioters lit a fire and burned the couple. On May 15, 1916, a mob took seventeen-year-old Jesse Washington out of a Waco, Texas, courtroom soon after he was convicted of murder and sentenced to death. He was dragged through the streets by a chain, hanged, stabbed, pelted with rocks, and finally burned. Souvenir hunters cut off parts of his body for keepsakes. After a black man killed a white farmer and wounded the farmer's wife in rural Georgia in 1918, whites reacted with ferocity. They did not know the identity of the murderer, so they sought all of the likely suspects. At least eleven blacks died in the bloodbath. When one woman protested the innocence of her husband in the hands of the mob, she, too, became a victim. The lynchers "tied her upside down by her ankles to a tree, poured petrol on her clothing, and burned her to death." This story of horror continued: "White American women will perhaps take note that this coloured sister of theirs was in her eighth month with child. The mob around her was not angry or insensate, but hysterical with brutal pleasure. The clothes burned off her body. Her child, prematurely born, was kicked to and fro by the mob."[40]

Southern whites claimed that the reason for all of this carnage was simple: black men were mere animals whose sexual drive had been unleashed by emancipation and the false idea of racial equality. White women therefore needed to be protected by the noble sons of the Confederacy from the insatiable lust of freedmen. One defender of southern lynching proclaimed as late as 1918 that "As the world is to be made safe for democracy, so ought the South to be made free for white women."[41] Violating a white woman was so horrendous, and blacks so incorrigible, that only immediate and unrelenting retribution could save the purity of southern womanhood. After hanging a black man accused of assaulting a white girl—"assault" was a southern euphemism for attempted rape—a Tarboro, North Carolina, mob in 1887 left a placard on the victim that read: "We hang this man, not in passion, but calmly and deliberately, with a due sense of the responsibility we assume. We take executive power in this case and hang this man in accordance with the unwritten law of the land, because the written law provides no penalty adequate to the crime. And be it understood, we who have done this act will repeat it under similar circumstances."[42]

Even many individuals who opposed lynching around the turn of the century tended to blame black lust as encouraging white "social insanity." John Carlisle Kilgo wrote in 1902 that in the South a woman "is a social deity upon whom men are expected to bestow high honor and all possible luxuries." If a black man violates a white woman, Kilgo believed, southern sensitivities, reaching back to a supposed cavalier and chivalric past, were exercised and the entire community went crazy with rage.[43] A retired associate justice in the state of Alabama traced the problem of lynching to racial prejudice—a prejudice exacerbated by politically active blacks. Encouraging blacks to vote made them socially uppity, which in turn led to their raping white women, which in turn led to lynching. The judge's solution was inescapable; remove all political rights for blacks and you end "uppityness," race prejudice, and lynching all in one blow.[44]

Interracial rape and sexual relations did take place. Some black males, just as some white males, committed rape across race lines. Whites, however, allowed their imaginations to run wild and overstated the case; the slightest misstep or misplaced glance was blown into the "unspeakable crime"—another euphemism for sexual assault. Sex by mutual consent between a black man and a white woman often brought dire consequences. If a black man lived with a white woman, or if an illicit liaison developed, both violated the law. But it was the black man who would be lynched.[45]

Rape was not even the most frequently stated cause of lynching blacks—that distinction belongs to the charge of murder. The National Association for the Advancement of Colored People (NAACP) study of lynching reported that between 1889 and 1919, the heaviest period of lynching, 35.8 percent of African-American victims had been charged with murder and only 19 percent had been charged with rape.[46]

Beyond sexual offenses and murder, all types of crimes and offenses to white sensibilities could bring on the wrath of a mob. In September 1891 a Whitfield County mob of white Georgians whipped a black man for allegedly stealing a gun. Whites took a young black, charged with the theft of some cattle, out of the custody of the deputy sheriff and lynched him in Vicksburg, Mississippi, in January 1915. An "impudent" sleeping car porter in the same year was dragged off a train and flogged in Lake, Mississippi, for having sassed a white telegraph operator. On June 8, 1895, black lawyer Thomas A. Harris sought vainly for safety with Booker T. Washington from a mob that had already shot him in the leg because he had allowed a traveling white evangelical to stay at his house.[47]

Ida B. Wells cut through the veneer of white explanations when she declared that lynching was "An excuse to get rid of Negroes who were acquiring wealth and property and thus keep the race terrorized and 'keep the nigger down.'" In 1892, a mob killed one of her friends in Memphis because he and his partners had the effrontery to defend their property against white competitors who were breaking into their store to drive them out of business. Wells soon found herself a victim of the mob. Having concluded that rape was not the cause of lynching, she wrote editorials for her paper *Free Speech* lambasting the rape myth, attacking lynching, and suggesting that white men were attracted to black women. On May 27, 1892, a mob demolished her press and office. Wells, in New York at the time, did not soon return to Memphis.[48]

The charge of rape was thus a bugbear that veiled deeper and more complicated roots. The Alabama associate justice, imbedded in his own racial bias, had admitted to the political causes. In several instances they became obvious. On an August day in 1882 the white citizens of Choctaw, Alabama, organized themselves into a "committee of safety of the whole people" and voted 998 to 2 to hang Jack Turner, a leader of the black community. Although local Democrats used this extralegal tribunal based on the legacy of the Sons of Liberty because of an alleged fear of a black conspiracy, the real motive was race politics. Turner ran the Republican political machine that had marshaled black voters in elections. With Turner eliminated the white Democrats could rule supreme.[49]

The handful of black Republican political appointees were liable to mob action. Whites lynched the black city collector of Yazoo City, Mississippi, in 1883. When Frazier B. Baker obtained an appointment as the postmaster of Lake City, South Carolina—the Republican national government distributed some patronage among blacks in the South in repayment for support in the nominating process—the white community was outraged. On the night of February 21, 1898, several hundred whites gathered at the postmaster's house. After Baker refused to come out, they set fire to the building. Frazier Baker was shot dead in the house. Then, as the Baker family ran from the flames, the crowd took aim at them. His wife and three children were wounded; a bullet also struck and killed an infant cradled in the mother's arms as she tried to escape.[50]

Political and economic motives remained entangled in these incidents, since politics was one form of economic mobility for African Americans. Other blacks found themselves facing a lynch mob for more explicit economic reasons. In Mississippi, in June 1910, Jim Brady questioned his sharecropping account with his landlord. Whites flogged Brady for his insolence. A short time later a mob sought to lynch him. Brady and a group of black friends defended themselves in a shoot-out that left three blacks and one white killed. Anthony Crawford, an affluent black farmer worth $20,000 in assets, argued with a white merchant over the price of cotton seed. For this "impudence" he was beaten and jailed. Apparently many whites in the community believed Crawford had become too "uppity." Within hours of his incarceration a mob broke into the jail and lynched him. A mob also slowly burned to death a black sharecropper in Estill Springs, Tennessee, in 1918 for defending himself and beating an employer.[51]

Competition between whites and blacks for scarce resources often led to lynch-like activity. Night riders, conjuring up images of the Ku Klux Klan, intimidated black farmers and property holders to convince them to leave the district. The most notorious of these movements were the whitecappers of Mississippi in 1892–1893 and 1902–1904. Whitecappers toured the country-side posting notices, illegally evicting blacks from their own property, whipping some individuals, and even killing others. In late 1903, for instance, night riders murdered two African-American property owners in Lincoln County, Mississippi. Similar incidents occurred in Tennessee in 1892, central Texas in 1898, Oklahoma in 1911 and 1912, and Georgia in 1912.[52]

African Americans responded to this terror in a variety of ways. Some almost blithely accepted their fate. When taken from his jail cell in Greensboro, Georgia, in April 1894, William Denham said, "I reckon I'm the buck you're hunting for." The twenty-one-year-old black, charged with rape, was brought a short distance, hanged from a tree, and his body was pumped full of bullets.[53]

There can be little doubt that the white terror of lynching was effective in intimidating blacks and sustaining white domination. Fear was instilled at an early age. Richard Wright later remembered that as a youth he fantasized about killing as many whites as he could before being killed himself. He also admitted, however, that he "felt completely helpless in the face of this threat that might come upon me at any time . . . because there did not exist to my knowledge any possible course of action which could save me if I had ever been confronted with a white mob."[54] No matter their inner feelings, many southern African Americans recognized that to survive they had to bend with the system of oppression. Often lynching induced a retreat of blacks to within their own community, and for fear that the slightest misstep might trigger the rage of a white mob, many retained a low, almost invisible, profile. This system of intimidation lasted well into the twentieth century. When the St. Louis *Post-Dispatch* reporter John Rogers, along with armed state officials, investigated the 1922 murder of two white men by the Klan in Morehouse Parish, Louisiana, they asked for the assistance of some local blacks. In every instance, the sight of cars full of armed whites met the same response—plenty of excuses and a quick exit.[55]

Despite the odds, blacks sometimes "successfully" contested lynching. In August 1899 African Americans in Darien, Georgia, repeatedly refused to allow officials to move an affluent black, Henry Delegale, from the local jail. Such a transfer, Delegale and his supporters feared, left him vulnerable to lynching while in transit. Armed and threatening blacks, however, were not to be tolerated in Georgia, and officials sent word to the governor that there was a black insurrection taking place. The state's chief executive ordered in the militia. When they arrived, the blacks disbanded on the promise that the militia would protect Delegale during his transfer to Savannah. A price, however, had to be paid for this black audacity. The sheriff sent deputies to the Delegale home to arrest his sons for participating in the riot. A gun battle broke out and one deputy was killed and another wounded. The final resolution of this crisis was in the courtroom. Delegale was acquitted of the spurious charge of rape. Several of his supporters, on the other hand, served prison terms for rioting, and because of the shooting, two of Delegale's sons were given life sentences.[56]

The Darien episode was not an isolated incident. In Matagorada County, Texas, in 1887, seventy-five armed blacks set out in search of a white man who had murdered a black constable. Whites retaliated and ambushed some blacks, killing at least two. On July 11, 1892, a group of Paducah, Kentucky, blacks defended another black held in jail on charges of rape. When some white lynchers showed up, the blacks opened fire, killing one. This set off a "race war" panic and state troops were sent in to reestablish order.[57]

The aggressiveness exhibited by blacks in these cases was important. It not only showed that some African Americans were willing to lay down their lives in fighting the system of oppression that confronted them, it also indicated that lynching sometimes expanded to include general rioting as well. On Christmas Eve, 1906, whites in Wahalak, Mississippi, lynched a black man and then invaded the black section of the town. Blacks fought back for two days, and one white and sixteen blacks were killed. Blacks and whites also squared off in Wilmington, Delaware, in July 1903 when the whites, celebrating the release of a member of an earlier lynching party, invaded an African-American neighborhood. Armed black residents defended themselves. No one was killed, but people were wounded on both sides.[58]

An alternative to overt resistance was to vote with your feet. A succession of lynchings and other acts of terror contributed to an out-migration of blacks that left whites distraught over the loss of a cheap labor supply.[59] Migration out of the South, however, did not mean a complete escape from the white terror and Judge Lynch. As the number of blacks grew in the North, so, too, did the possibility of a lynching-bee. Lynching of blacks, however, was largely a southern phenomenon and needs to be understood within the southern context.

Two essential questions remain about lynching: who participated, and why this penchant for brutal violence? To answer these questions we must recognize that we are dealing with thousands of incidents. Each lynching may conform to a pattern, yet each was also unique. Even southerners admitted that there were good lynchings—when a black "rapist" was the target—and bad lynchings—when the crowd acted too precipitously. The type of people in the crowd might differ from case to case. Given that variance, however, the southern white lynch mob was not limited to the "poor white trash" as some apologists argued. Plenty of poor whites participated. So, too, did some affluent individuals. Lawyers, merchants, and politicos were not above leading a mob if it suited their purposes. Even women and children gathered, encouraged, and at times took an active role in lynch mobs.[60] Until the 1920s, most whites in the South supported lynching. In the summer of 1897 Rebecca Latimer Felton, an outspoken journalist and later United States Senator, called upon southern men to do their duty to stop black rapists. Her appeal struck a responsive chord as she proclaimed that ". . . if it takes lynching to protect woman's dearest possession from drunken, ravening human beasts, then I say lynch a thousand a week if it becomes necessary."[61]

If there was consensus in the South, why the extralegal procedure of lynching? The parallels with Reconstruction rioting are instructive. Both before and after 1877 whites used collective violence to maintain a world order challenged by emancipation and rapidly changing social and economic circumstances. Yet after redemption of the southern state governments, whites controlled the legal system and, as the chain gangs that dotted the landscape attested, could confine and punish African Americans at will. Why then the persistence of savage lynching? Scholars have offered many answers, including a southern heritage of violence and a peculiar code of honor.[62] Some sociologists and psychologists have striven to draw connections between lynching and economic and political developments.[63] There is no one answer. Ultimately, however, we must return to the insight of Ida B. Wells: lynching was a form of terror used to keep black Americans down.

That terror included an important psychosexual component. The charge of interracial rape—chimera that it often was—may have reflected the racial and sexual tensions of a society that had practiced forced miscegenation between white men and black women for generations. Slavery was a power relationship with a sexual content. Loss of that power was a form of emasculation that may have been projected upon the fear of interracial intercourse between black men and white women. Repeatedly, defenders of lynching argued that black sexual assault was almost unheard of in the slave South and that it was a *new* crime that came with emancipation. The frequent references to black men as "uppity" and demanding equality in politics and the economy suggests that southerners connected the empowerment in these areas with empowerment in sexual matters as well.

Although lynching varied in brutality, the nature of the tortures used by the most extreme crowds suggests this sexual context. Victims sometimes had their penises chopped off. Souvenir hunters satisfied themselves with fingers—a phallic representation—as keepsakes. Penetrating the flesh with a stick or pole also had phallic symbolism, as might the pulverizing of a body beyond recognition with bullets.[64]

Torture and lynching of blacks also was a way of denying the humanity of African Americans. The callousness of the collective action is more reminiscent of the treatment of animals than of other human beings. Racism persisted as a largely unquestioned doctrine in the late nineteenth and early twentieth centuries, and even Darwin's science might be cited as testimony to faith in the supremacy of the white race.[65] Such beliefs made the supposed threat of rape by black men even more frightening and liable to a punishment that went beyond the capabilities of government. Within this context there could be no room for racial ambiguities. Burning the victim not only resuscitated earlier practices of ritual bonfires, but also may have been a way to clarify racial identity. Frequent mixing of white and black blood in slavery left many a light-skinned Negro. Charred corpses turned black reasserted the supposed culprit's race in a most gruesome way. Burned bodies were often left hanging for days for crowds to see, and in a few instances, for photographers to take pictures.

Much more can be read into the particular actions of the southern lynch mob. All is admittedly speculative. In the final analysis, however, we are left with the thousands of deaths and a level of racial terror unparalleled in American history. While the terror of lynching was brutal to extremes, it also represented the type of collective disorder prevalent in the period, demarking a divided community venting itself in violence. This white terror went beyond lynching and included racial rioting as well.

Race War

By the end of the nineteenth century, racial antagonism was reaching new heights. Jim Crow laws segregating blacks from whites dominated the South, and the beginnings of a great migration brought more African Americans into the North. The industrialization and urbanization of the United States provided opportunities for a generation of black Americans, born out of slavery, that wanted to assert its equality in ways unacceptable to most whites. This combination of factors provided a recipe for disaster; riots broke out in American cities that bordered upon race war.[66]

The earliest of these confrontations were in southern cities and were an extension of the sexual fears and race supremacy imbedded in the white terror typical of that region. In the opening decades of the twentieth century these ideas spread to northern cities as well. The great race riots of these years, however, were complex affairs that centered as much upon competition between whites and blacks over jobs and housing as they did upon southern racial concerns. Regardless of their cause, race riots were characterized by extensive personal physical violence that epitomized the popular disorder of the nineteenth and early twentieth centuries.

These disturbances followed a pattern. Grievances between blacks and whites accumulated over a variety of issues—sexual anxiety, housing, and jobs. African Americans exhibited an assertiveness that brought those mutual grievances into focus. An incident took place, usually but not always an affront to white sensibilities. Whites then launched attacks on blacks in areas of the city where the two groups often interacted. Frequently this took place in a downtown business district. Emboldened by their success, whites then invaded black areas, beating, looting, killing, and burning. Pockets of black resistance might appear, creating casualties on both sides. Blacks might even counterattack into white areas. Local officials countenanced and even encouraged the violence against blacks. Forces from outside the community, such as the national guard, were brought in and peace eventually was restored. Black Americans by then had sustained the heaviest casualties.[67]

The first of these massive urban race wars was in Wilmington, North Carolina, on November 9–10, 1898. This riot revealed a close connection between white concerns with black sexuality and the desire for white supremacy in politics. The ostensible cause of the disturbance was an editorial in the local African-American press written by Alexander Manly that flayed out against lynching and claimed that white women were attracted to black men. White southerners considered this assertion heresy and decided to defend their honor by destroying Manly's press. The sons of the Confederacy also had larger goals. North Carolina politics had been in a state of upheaval during the 1890s as Populists and Republicans joined forces to overthrow the Democrats. This fusionist politics had allowed blacks in some areas to gain political prominence not enjoyed since the end of Reconstruction. Wilmington became a center of these fusionists, and whites in the months before the riot complained about the threat to southern womanhood and honor posed by "uppity" blacks encouraged by a sympathetic and corrupt Republican administration.

When the heavily armed crowd of whites invaded the black neighborhood of Brooklyn to smash Manly's vitriolic press, they also intended to purge the city of their black nemesis and seize control of the local government. Soon after dismantling the press, the arrogant white mob attacked a group of angry blacks. Whites then engaged in a pogrom, firing upon blacks indiscriminately, massacring at least eleven—although some claimed that the number reached over one hundred—and driving African Americans from the city. Many of these refugees never returned. Encouraged by their success, the white supremacists then coerced the mayor and other local fusionist officials to resign, held an ad hoc election that placed their leaders in power, and with Democratic big shots once more ensconced in city hall, declared an end to the disorder that they had created.[68]

Eight years later a major disturbance broke out in Atlanta—the queen city of the new South. Although this riot lacked the overt political content of Wilmington, the pattern was the same. First came charges connected to white sexual anxiety, then civil discord. In this instance, however, despite the white success, some blacks struck back with effectiveness.

On September 22 reports circulated through the city of four separate incidents of black men "assaulting" white women. By evening crowds of whites gathered on the streets of downtown Atlanta talking excitedly about these latest affronts to white womanhood and a supposed "Negro uprising." Fights soon broke out with nearby blacks. Whites then commenced assailing any black that crossed their path. Black-owned businesses were gutted, their proprietors beaten and killed. The crowds stopped street cars, dragged black passengers off and beat them mercilessly. White mobs swelled, and as many as ten thousand people took to the streets. The body count began to mount. On the next day the rioting spread to black neighborhoods as whites looted and wrecked homes as well as beat their opponents. Some blacks armed themselves and fought back. Walter White, later a leading NAACP official, was thirteen at the time. Yet his father handed him a rifle, and the two of them lay on their living room floor ready to kill the first rioter to approach their house. A volley from neighbors across the street drove the mob away before the father and son had to shoot.

Local police opposed this form of resistance. When the black residents of Brownsville, an Atlanta suburb, armed themselves for protection, the police attempted to confiscate their weapons. Seeing that the police allowed whites to stay armed, the blacks resisted. This gun battle left one policeman and several blacks dead. The next day the police, supported by the military, swept through the area, arrested sixty blacks, and disarmed the neighborhood.

The presence of troops eventually brought an end to the disorder. The message to black Americans, however, was clear. Local authorities were not going to protect them, and the power of the state, as well as the rage of the mob, would be wielded to keep them in place. Twenty-five African Americans were reported dead and countless others were wounded, lost property, or were driven from their homes.[69]

Exacerbating race relations, and acting as an important backdrop to the race war of the early twentieth century, was a new black aggressiveness. Examples of blacks resisting racial prejudice and white mobs can be found throughout American history. In the early twentieth century, however, the sense of identity and purpose among African Americans expanded. Some blacks heeded the call to go back to Africa. Others abandoned the accommodationist doctrines of Booker T. Washington, and joined the Niagara movement led by W. E. B. DuBois that gave birth to the NAACP. What this meant in the street was that more and more African Americans became less willing to accept the daily abuse, threats, and insults. This new attitude contributed to violence in rioting and could lead to spectacular acts of resistance.[70]

Robert Charles made headlines in New Orleans in July 1900, becoming an important symbol for both races. Whites saw Charles as everything that was wrong with the urban black; African Americans viewed him as a hero. Charles lived on the edges of society and steeped himself in the pro-Negro literature of the day. He also reacted strongly to lynching and resolved to fight to the end if confronted by a white mob. When two policemen clubbed him during a chance encounter on a New Orleans street, Charles drew his revolver and fired. He killed both of them. Later that evening, during the manhunt, Charles slew two other officers. He then hid for three days. Raging whites beat blacks, gutted a school, and murdered at least twelve. When Charles was discovered on July 27, he shot down another two officers. Trapped in a house by thousands of whites he fought with deadly accuracy, killing three more whites and wounding twenty during the two-hour siege before the assembled host shot his body full of bullets.[71]

Black assertiveness leading to collective violence also occurred in 1917. Black soldiers of the Twenty-fourth Infantry Regiment defied Houston's codified Jim Crow restrictions by mutinying after local police beat a popular corporal. One hundred fifty men, about a quarter of the regiment, marched out of camp under the leadership of Sergeant Vida Henry to wreak vengeance on the police and the city's whites. By the time that night was over, the soldiers had killed sixteen whites and wounded seriously eleven more. Only four blacks died that night, including Henry by suicide. Military tribunals, however, more than evened the score. Based on flimsy evidence—the cover of darkness and the confusion of the mutiny made it difficult to identify exactly who participated and who remained on duty—110 out of 118 men charged were found guilty of some degree of misbehavior. Ultimately nineteen soldiers were executed and fifty-three others sentenced to life in prison.[72]

The same forces that erupted into violence in the South also set afoot a migration of African Americans from the rural South to the urban and industrial North, leading to more bloodshed and rioting. The causes of this rioting varied as competition over jobs and housing became as important as, if not more important than, racial prejudice in the violent rioting of the North.[73]

Sexual fears played a prominent role in many northern lynchings that occurred more frequently with the growing racial tension that came with the migrations that began in the 1890s. Having failed to remove a black held in jail on charges of rape, a Danville, Illinois mob of six hundred in the summer of 1903 hanged and burned another black man who had killed a white while defending himself from the crowd. On March 7, 1904, a white mob in Springfield, Ohio, hanged Richard Dixon, a black charged with murdering a policeman. The whites followed this action with a rampage through the black section of town. In Cairo, Illinois, in 1908 a large mob took a black man accused of killing a white woman from the sheriff, fired over five hundred bullets into him, and abused and then burned the body.[74]

Competition for jobs and housing, however, lay behind much of northern race rioting. The crowd that watched the brutal slaying of Zachariah Walker in the small Pennsylvania industrial town of Coatseville on August 13, 1911, acted in large part from resentment against southern blacks taking jobs held by whites. There was a riot during the 1880s at the Elba steel works near Pittsburgh because the company had hired black strikebreakers. In 1898 coal mine operators in Virden and Pana, Illinois, brought in armed black miners to break a strike. Nine miners and ten guards were killed during the ensuing gun battles. Similar riots erupted the next year in other Illinois towns. Violence accompanied the use of black strikebreakers in several Chicago labor confrontations in 1894, 1895, 1904, and 1905. In 1905 the riots continued for five days and included intermittent mob attacks on blacks throughout Chicago.[75]

Housing, too, could be a central concern in northern rioting. Many antagonisms separated whites and blacks in New York's tenderloin district in 1900, but competition for housing was crucial to the outbreak of the riot in August of that year. When a black man stabbed and killed a plainclothesman, whites—led by the police—vented their rage in sporadic harassment of blacks that injured at least seventy-nine. This riot helped to convince blacks to move uptown to Harlem, an area that within twenty years would become almost completely black.[76]

Northern race riots often combined the standard fear of the black sexual challenge and the reaction to black assertiveness with competition for jobs and housing. The riot that marred the hometown of Abraham Lincoln (Springfield, Illinois) almost on the centennial of his birth represented all of these concerns. Rumors that a black man assaulted a white woman led to calls for a lynching. Local officials, however, acted quickly and whisked the two men intended as victims of the mob out of town and out of harm's way. They could not do the same for the city's other blacks. The angered mob first vandalized the car and property of the white man who had provided transportation for the two suspects. For two days, August 14–15, 1908, white mobs invaded the black sections, beating, burning, and killing. Although some blacks valiantly defended their homes, most fled the onslaught. Before the state militia could restore order six people were dead—a seventh, an infant, died of exposure during the exodus—and a great deal of black-owned property was ruined. Despite the fear of black sexuality, white working-class hostility to black achievement was a significant factor in the Springfield riot.[77]

The First World War—an event that had a profound impact on black Americans—intensified conditions leading to race riots. Opportunities for employment in urban industrial areas expanded, and northern cities became even more swamped with African Americans arriving from the South. With the entrance of the United States into the war, under Woodrow Wilson's insistence that Americans were going to make the world safe for democracy, many blacks demanded that white Americans needed first to make the United States safe for democracy. The use of African-American troops encouraged black assertiveness by proving their equality on the battlefield. White Americans did not accept these developments willingly.[78]

In a wave of brutal rioting that embodied the violent trends of collective disorder that had been in place for almost a century, dozens of racial disturbances broke out from 1917 to 1921 in which whites and blacks battled each other. While each riot had its own unique blend of causes, they all fit a general pattern. Focusing on a few of the largest moments of popular disorder reveals the outlines and extent of this bloodshed.

Two days of rioting engulfed East St. Louis, Illinois, on July 1–2, 1917, leaving at least nine whites and thirty-nine blacks dead. (The NAACP estimated that one hundred fifty blacks were killed).[79] Here, the competition for both jobs and housing was the salient issue. In the weeks and months before the outbreak, tension grew between blacks and whites as white unions agitated against the importation of black laborers who took industrial jobs from whites. The influx of blacks also aggravated a housing shortage. This tension led to repeated beatings and drive-by shootings by whites against blacks. On the night of July 1 some blacks retaliated. Unfortunately, the next vehicle driven by whites in the black neighborhood was an unmarked police car. As the automobile cruised down the street as many as two hundred blacks opened fire. Two policemen died in the ambuscade. Following this murder, which was probably a case of mistaken identity, roving mobs of whites struck back by dragging blacks off trolleys, stoning, clubbing, and kicking them. Thousands filled the streets and then invaded black areas. They burned houses and shot any black that tried to escape. Some victims were consumed by the flames. Several blacks were lynched while officials looked the other way. A few African Americans fought back, but the odds were overwhelming. Most sought safety by fleeing. Eventually the presence of the Illinois National Guard quelled the disturbance, although hours of beatings and killings were allowed to glide by, during which both the police and the national guard were largely inactive. These forces of law and order shared a race prejudice with the rioters and were just as happy to see this Illinois community purged of blacks.[80]

Many Americans were shocked by the East St. Louis riot, and some compared it to the atrocities believed to be perpetrated by the German "barbarians" in Europe. This reaction, which included a congressional investigation, did not prevent the eruption of other race riots with extremes of violence. In the next few years disturbances broke out in many localities.[81]

Chicago in the summer of 1919 was a divided city. Between 1910 and 1920 the black population swelled from 44,103 to 109,594. This gain of nearly 150 percent strained black neighborhoods and frightened white workers. The decade was punctuated with a flurry of smaller interracial conflicts that peaked in 1919. Nor were African Americans placid and complacent; they often insisted on equality before the law. The riot started when a small group of blacks wanted to use a white section of a lakeside beach. This confrontation led to the stoning and drowning of Eugene Williams, a black teenager who had drifted on a raft into the white zone. Blacks demanded justice, but the white officer on duty refused to make any arrests. Tempers flared. White and black crowds exchanged volleys of bricks and stones, and when a black man shot a policeman, bullets whizzed all across the beach. The rioting spilled over to other sections of the city and continued for five days. Whites beat any black they came across, stopping streetcars, driving through black sections and shooting wildly. Blacks also fired back at the invaders and struck at any white target that came their way. Gangs of white toughs, however, inflicted the most serious damage and, as in East St. Louis, black-owned and -occupied property was destroyed. Before the national guard could restore order twenty-three blacks and fifteen whites had been killed and over five hundred were injured.[82]

The upheaval that accompanied World War I also had an impact on the rural and urban South. In the backwater of Phillips County, Arkansas, African Americans asserted themselves anew and joined the Progressive Farmers and Household Union of America to lift themselves out of the bondage of share-cropping. On the night of September 30, 1919, police officers shot into a church at Elaine where blacks were holding an organizational meeting. The black sharecroppers fired back, killing one officer and wounding another. The next day all hell broke loose in the county as whites and blacks blasted away at one another. Outgunned and outmanned by white troops called in to put down the uprising, black members of the Progressive Farmers were killed, arrested, or driven into hiding. The final casualty list of this episode of America's race war was five whites and over twenty-five blacks killed.[83]

The May 30–June 2, 1921, riot in the oil boom town of Tulsa, Oklahoma, combined all of the worst features of the racial strife of this era. The disturbance began after the arrest of a black youth for allegedly molesting a white female elevator operator (later the charges were dropped). Threats of a lynching brought armed black men to the police station. This angered the gathering white mob. Police managed to defuse the situation once, but on a second appearance of the armed blacks, the shooting commenced. African Americans got the better of this contest; one black was wounded and one white killed. The battle, however, had just begun. Whites invaded the black neighborhood to the north of the city for three days. This house to house combat included the use of machine guns, and, according to some reports, aircraft. Blacks, with no support from officials, fought in vain. Rioters devastated the entire African-American section, and some reports estimate that fifty whites and two hundred blacks died in the fighting.[84]

The murderous and vicious assaults on people in the race rioting of the opening decades of the twentieth century represented an extension and refinement of the type of rioting that had emerged in the Jacksonian period. Starting in the first half of the nineteenth century, cultural rifts led to personal physical violence in many forms of popular disorder. With Americans refusing to identify with each other, it had become relatively easy for crowds to flail out at their victims, often with lethal effect. An outgrowth of the ideal of freedom, emancipation of black slaves aggravated the divisions in society that created this violence. The centuries of prejudice could not be easily erased as African Americans and European Americans now competed in a free society. Whites reacted to this new social order by striving to limit African American equal participation through lynching and rioting that left thousands dead.

Although there was continuity in racial rioting from the 1820s to the 1920s, some changes had occurred. In the earlier period extralegal collective action against blacks had been limited largely to the North. Freedom for slaves in the South led to an extensive use of white terror during Reconstruction and after. Raising the bugbear of racial purity, southerners engaged in an orgy of violence and brutality. By the end of the nineteenth century, as blacks moved to cities and to the North, the level of rioting intensified throughout the nation. Lynching of blacks persisted throughout the South, but appeared with increased frequency in the North. By the 1910s blacks and whites battled each other in cities throughout the United States. The sources of this violence were complex, intertwining popular beliefs about race and competition for jobs and housing. Racial antagonisms allowed one race to deny the humanity of another, and interpersonal violence followed along the lines of race hatred. Government forces often sided with the whites; seldom were they neutral. The tragedy of race had deep roots in American history and bore bitter fruit in the nineteenth and twentieth centuries. The spread of race rioting, from the antebellum mobs in the North, to the white terror of the South, to the race warfare of the early twentieth century, threatened to tear American society asunder and helped bring the United States to the brink of anarchy.

BRINK OF ANARCHY | 5

Strike

Although there is no matching the brutality of white against black after the Civil War, hatred, animosity, and collective action concerning labor, ethnicity, and politics remained bitterly violent. The greatest conflict was between workers and employers. Before 1865 laborers had struck for wages, battled strikebreakers, and destroyed property. After the Civil War labor organization increased dramatically. Most strikes were peaceful. However, when workers began to feel desperate and when employers became intransigent, the potential for an explosion of violence increased. Strikers might thus resort to forceful collective action, confronting police and strikebreakers who were equally capable of flailing out in turn. There were enough confrontations that led to the spilling of blood to color the entire relationship between capital and labor.[1]

The causes for the sanguinary record in violent strikes lay in the growing distance between the forces of labor and capital. Bristling at any effort by workers to dictate terms of employment, capitalists used every weapon at their disposal to maintain control of the means of production. Thus businessmen pushed for profits by exploiting labor to the utmost—minimizing wages and maintaining difficult working conditions—while refusing to recognize the legitimacy of the right of labor to organize. Wielding money, influence, and power, employers hired private guards, imported swarms of new laborers, and often garnered the support of government to protect property rights. The lives of many workers were far different from the businessman's. Frequently compelled to labor under atrocious conditions for a wage that barely sustained existence, workers became desperate. Moreover, there was seldom a united front; skilled workers gravitated to the world of the middle class while an influx of immigrants, comprising dozens of nationalities, and black migrants from the South, drove wedges between different elements of the workforce. To maintain solidarity, coercion often was necessary. With both capital and labor so far apart, neither identified with the other and both were capable of escalating any contest into violence.

Government at the local, state, and federal levels had an important and complex role in the development and extent of labor's collective violence. The position of the local government varied depending on circumstances. Some-

times local officials supported labor, and violence was reduced. State governments, more easily influenced by businessmen, tended to rush to the defense of
corporate property, leading to some of the most explosive confrontations in
American labor history. The position of the federal government changed over
time. Initially, federal officials sided with capital and became involved after
state governments failed to quell labor unrest. However, in the opening
decades of the twentieth century, and in part as a result of the rise of the
Progressive and labor movements, the federal government became more neutral. The president might dispatch the army to disrupted areas to protect property and maintain order, but when he did so, it was to rein in both sides of the
dispute. By the 1920s laborers still struggled for recognition and could still
find themselves enmeshed in violence, but government officials, and ultimately
businessmen, were starting to respond with greater flexibility.

These patterns of conflict can be traced in the famous and not-so-famous
labor-capital contests of the period. The history of this upheaval is punctuated
with stories of well-known confrontations: in the railroad strike of 1877; in the
battle at Homestead in 1892; in the turmoil that began at Pullman in 1894; in
the massacre at Ludlow in 1914; and in the mine war in West Virginia in
1921. The saga of these epochal struggles barely scratches the surface of the
violent strike activity. Railway workers often resorted to sabotage and collective action. Miners fought for their rights in Colorado, Alabama, Tennessee,
West Virginia, Pennsylvania, Idaho, and elsewhere. Industrial workers repeatedly beat and sometimes murdered those whom they believed stole their
jobs—strikebreaking scabs—and fought forces of law and order that stood in
their way. Even farmers rioted to obtain a redress of economic grievances. To
list all labor riots would be almost impossible; it would entail cataloguing every
cracked head found along countless miles of picket lines. A review of the better
known strikes and some representative examples of lesser known disturbances
demonstrates the persistence of physical violence in rioting.

In 1877, the most spectacular and widespread strike in American history
revealed labor and capital animosity, and the varying responses of different
levels of government. Forced to reduce costs during an economic downturn,
the nation's railroads cut wages on July 1. Besieged by hard times, the
Baltimore and Ohio workers decided to resist. Company officials dismissed
the strikers and found eager replacements among the unemployed. Beginning
at Martinsburg, West Virginia, and then spreading all along the line, strikers
intent on keeping jobs and maintaining wages prevented the rolling of freight
stock.

Quelling the strike proved difficult. In many communities the strikers
found encouragement and support. Railroad executives turned to their allies in
the state and federal governments. State troops were ordered in and, reinforced
by federal forces, the soldiers managed to gain control—without too much
bloodshed—of Martinsburg and a few other localities. Facing a vast flood of

labor discontent that was about to sweep the land, no sooner had the military plugged one breach in the levee of law and order, than leaks opened elsewhere. The great strike was just beginning.

A call for reenforcements from Baltimore brought terrible rioting. Thousands of laborers, angered by officials who ignored their economic distress, packed the streets on the night of July 20. When the militia units moved from the armory to the railroad depot, crowds greeted them with brickbats, stones, and pistol shots. Soldiers fired rifles point blank into the crowd and killed ten civilians. Officials dispatched troops to Baltimore, and only minor disturbances followed the next day, as the locus of action shifted again.

By July 20 the strike spread to other railroads. Trainmen in Horneville, New York, stopped working, as did the men at Newark, Ohio, and other cities. National attention, however, focused on Pittsburgh, the heart of industrial America, where radicals proclaimed open warfare between capital and labor. When the local militia sympathized with the strikers, state officials ordered in fresh units from Philadelphia. These troops arrived on the twenty-first. Regional animosities now compounded economic grievances, and both sides eyed each other with suspicion and distrust. Taunted by a crowd of thousands determined not to allow any freight trains to move, the Philadelphians opened fire. Surrounded by masses enraged at the sight of the blood of their compatriots, the militia retreated to a round house. That night the rioters laid siege to the Philadelphians, setting ablaze car after car and sending them down the tracks into the militia ranks. Eventually the roundhouse caught flame and the Philadelphians were compelled to withdraw from the city. Pittsburgh was in the hands of a mob—by the time the upheaval was over, at least twenty-four were dead (five were Philadelphia militia), and five million dollars of Pennsylvania Railroad property was destroyed. This total included 104 locomotives and 2,152 railroad cars. Officials sent three thousand federal troops and thousands more militia to restore peace to the city.

Still the disorder spread. In Pennsylvania riots broke out at Altoona, Reading, Harrisburg, Scranton, and even Philadelphia. Beyond that state, strikers fought police in Chicago, St. Louis, San Francisco, and locations between. Soldiers and warships were deployed to defend Washington, D.C., as federal and state troops scurried to one location after another to deny "the right to seize other people's property and to prevent other men from selling their labor on terms satisfactory to themselves. . . ."[2] By the end of the month property rights as defined by business and government had been secured, and the strike and rioting ended.

The magnitude of the 1877 strike startled contemporaries. The strike was not organized by any union, and the contagion spread extemporaneously along the nation's rail lines. Class distinctions played a major role in the conflict. Workers united from a variety of occupations and battled government forces in the streets of many cities. Yet at times, the appeal of the strikers transcended economic boundaries and evoked sympathy from other elements of the community. Unfortunately, little of that sympathy came from the businessmen who controlled the rail lines. Encouraged and supported by these capitalists, the state and federal governments stepped in and transformed the strike into a violent defense of property rights that left a swath of casualties strewn across the nation.[3]

By the time of the labor war at the Pennsylvania steel town of Homestead in 1892, capitalists and workers had developed two different interpretations of their relationship with the workplace. Many laborers believed that they had a proprietary right to their jobs. Living in the mill town, breathing the belching smoke and sweating before the blast furnace, they viewed the factory as an extension of their lives. They did not deny that Carnegie, or another distant millionaire, had invested his capital in the enterprise; they only asserted that they, too, had invested a different type of capital. The owners of the means of production looked at a factory as private property for them to do whatever they wanted. They claimed to have full control over who worked and who did not. Andrew Carnegie and his supervisor, Henry Clay Frick, decided to break the Homestead union and reduce wages by locking out their employees. On the night of July 6, 1892, two barges loaded with three hundred Pinkerton agents sailed up the Monongahela River to occupy the Homestead plant for the company. Workers guarding access to the plant called their brethren to action. Thousands of steelworkers commenced firing into the barges. Both sides sustained casualties; seven workers and three Pinkertons were killed. Their barge grounded and with no avenue of escape, the Pinkertons surrendered. The workers compelled the Pinkertons to run a gauntlet—where many sustained more injuries—and then expelled them from Homestead in humiliation. Victory for the laborers was short-lived. An army of eight thousand state national guardsmen occupied the city and ultimately crushed resistance by protecting replacement workers.[4]

Two years later another great strike took place that also revealed the violence that accompanied the growing distance between labor and capital. The Pullman Railroad Car Company, which had prided itself on its paternalistic relationship with its employees, cut wages to retrench its finances. When workers struck, Pullman retaliated by evicting families from company housing and hiring scabs. Flushed with success in a recent strike, Eugene V. Debs, president of the American Railway Union, ordered workers not to move any trains with Pullman cars. Nationwide trains came to a screeching halt.

The railroad managers responded adroitly, tagging United States Mail carriers to trains with Pullman cars, providing the rationale for federal intervention. From California to the midwest, state and federal troops occupied rail yards and escorted trains. Dozens of riots broke out in cities like Chicago, St. Louis, and San Francisco, as well as whistle stops such as Raton, New Mexico; Ogden, Utah; and Hammond, Indiana. The most severe rioting was close to the center of the strike at Chicago. On July 7, 1894, several thousand laborers confronted the Illinois national guard at the rail yards and bombarded them with stones and other objects. The guard fought back, firing into the crowd, killing four, and wounding at least twenty others. In over a week of rioting in the windy city 13 were killed, 53 seriously wounded, and 515 arrested. In total the strike paralyzed rail communications in twenty-seven states and territories and led to at least twenty-five deaths. As July wore on, the strike faltered, Debs and other leaders were arrested, the American Railway Union disintegrated, and the businessmen—with the army at their back—triumphed.[5]

During the opening decades of the early twentieth century the physical violence continued, but capitalists could no longer count on the unflinching support of the federal government. The Colorado mine fields broke out in warfare between labor and capital in 1913 and 1914. Thousands of immigrant miners joined a strike protesting the horrendous living and working conditions in southern Colorado. On October 17, 1913, at least one person was killed in a shoot-out between strikers and mine guards in the town of Forbes. A week later a two-day battle erupted at Walsenburg during which three strikers and one mine guard were killed. State militia, siding with the mine operators, fought with a crowd of women and children in a protest march in Trinidad, January 21, 1914.

On April 20 the miners and the militia clashed at Ludlow. Trigger-happy guardsmen poured a devastating fire into a tent city of strikers and their families. Strikers fought back, but were driven from the field. When the militia arrested strike leader Louis Tikas, they summarily executed him. The militia also burned the tent city, trapping and affixiating eleven children and two women in an underground shelter beneath a tent. Despite capturing ground, the militia was far from victorious. Angered miners struck back and fought a series of engagements at Delugua, Walsenburg, and Forbes. Only the arrival of federal troops defused the situation. The United States officers demanded that both the miners and the militia withdraw from the field.

The Ludlow Massacre shocked the United States. The tragedy of the loss of innocent lives and the violence of the strike affected public opinion. As many as two hundred persons died in this labor war. Following the federal intervention, the Commission on Industrial Relations issued a report that dwelt on the conditions of labor and the grievances of the strikers. The report portrayed the mine companies as insensitive and inflexible, and described the state militia as biased and unprofessional. The real blame, and the Commission did not mince words on the issue, was placed at the doorstep of John D. Rockefeller, Jr., who owned the lion's share of stock in the mining companies. For Rockefeller this was a public relations disaster. He moved to meet some strike demands, conducted his own experiment in labor-management relations with company unions, and even visited the miners' camps.[6]

Labor and capital antagonism, as well as the emerging role of the federal government as referee, can also be seen in the largest single engagement fought by American labor. A force of fifteen to twenty thousand miners invaded Logan County, West Virginia, to gain recognition for the United Mine Workers of America. As in the fighting in Colorado, state officials sided with mine operators, and the federal government entered the fray to separate the protagonists. The march on Logan County commenced on August 26, 1921, and lasted until September 3. Meanwhile the miners and about 2,500 guards and deputies from Logan County fought along the crest of Blair Mountain. War veterans on both sides shot at each other, and at least fifteen miners and seven guards were killed. The United States Army, aided by a detachment of airplanes, arrived on the scene and, with the help of union leaders, convinced the union men to put down their guns and to return home. Thus, like at Ludlow, and unlike in the 1890s, the federal troops had a calming effect on the situation.[7]

The antagonism between labor and capital that led to violence in these labor battles was echoed in countless other strikes. The great southwestern railroad strike of 1886 almost rivaled the strikes of 1877 and 1894 in size and bloodshed. Riots broke out in Illinois, Missouri, Texas, and elsewhere. In one clash in East St. Louis, nine people were killed, and strikers set fire to the railroad yards, shops, and some private homes. In the Colorado and West Virginia mine fields, both sides murdered and assaulted one another in struggles that lasted years. The anthracite coal region of eastern Pennsylvania remained unstable for decades starting with the rise of the Molly Maguires in the 1860s and 1870s and continuing through the early twentieth century. Tennessee miners in 1891 marched on coal fields worked by convict labor, released the prisoners, and destroyed company buildings in protest. Trouble broke out in Idaho in 1892 and 1894. In 1892 workers killed three and blew up a mine in Cour d'Alene. Forty masked men in 1894 murdered a witness from the first case, kidnaped a superintendent, and tried to blow up another mine. During the same year iron miners in Minnesota drove workers off the job, and coal miners in Alabama engaged in several gun battles with guards and dynamited company property. Miners attacked white and black scabs imported into the coal fields of south central Illinois and committed depredations to property in 1894, 1898, and 1922. During a gun fight on June 21, 1922, near Herrin, Illinois, two strikers were killed and a third was fatally wounded. After the defenders surrendered the next day, strikers murdered nineteen scabs and guards, wounding several others.[8]

This sad litany of violence was not limited to miners and railroad workers. Striking streetcar workers in the 1890s and early 1900s, joined by working classes who depended on public transportation, disrupted urban transit companies that exploited their labor force and hired scabs to run trolleys. These companies alienated many city dwellers by watering stocks, utilizing holding companies, and creating fortunes for a few, while minimizing services. The bloodshed accompanying the transit strike in January and February 1895 in Brooklyn, New York, paralyzed that city. Seven thousand troops occupied Brooklyn and guarded trolleys as crowds beat strikebreakers, destroyed the cars, tore down electrical lines, and fought police and the military. At least two people died. In February and March 1910 crowds as large as ten thousand fought with the police in Philadelphia. Rioters burned streetcars and killed at least one strikebreaking motorman. The contagion of collective action spread, and many other workers walked off their jobs at industrial plants to join the crowds in the streets, threatening a general strike.[9]

Factory workers also resorted to rioting. During the summer of 1909 plant officials at the Pressed Steel Car Company in McKees Rock, Pennsylvania, hired a strikebreaking firm to provide both replacement workers and private guards. On July 14 the strikers beat back strikebreakers arriving along the Ohio River and at the factory gates. Over the next few weeks the company smuggled scabs into the plant, much to the chagrin of workers. Strikers scoured the city and searched trolleys for possible scabs. On August 22 a group of strikers caught a notorious private detective hired by the company and murdered him. This act led to an orgy of violence on both sides. The state police retaliated by shooting into crowds. The strikers returned the fire, smashed stores, and demolished streetcars. By the time peace was restored seven strikers and four police officers were dead.[10]

If desperation could drive industrial workers to violence, the same alienation and loss of control over their work could affect farmers as well. Repeated acts of terrorism from 1906 to 1909 rocked Kentucky and Tennessee as tobacco farmers organized their own association to sell their crops in opposition to trust domination of warehouses and marketing. Using night raids to intimidate others, members of the association burned barns, dynamited trust property, and whipped and even murdered opponents. On a successful raid the night of December 1, 1906, 250 masked men rode into Princeton, Kentucky. They occupied the town for two hours and dynamited two factories operated by the Tobacco Trust, destroying 400,000 pounds of tobacco. Eventually officials sent state troops into the rebellious areas to protect the trust and those who sold to them. With the help of informers and some federal prosecutions, order was restored late in 1909.[11]

These examples of labor violence can be multiplied many times. Not every strike, nor every labor riot, led to fatalities. In most strikes the laborers limited themselves to walking off the job and establishing picket lines. Problems arose when employers hired replacements for the often unskilled and therefore vulnerable workers. Then, needing a more dramatic gesture, strikers might intimidate and possibly beat the scabs. If the employer used special police or relied on local authorities to protect the strikebreakers, the violence might become more serious. Once this threshold was crossed, however, the workers were likely to sustain the greatest casualties and alienate a public opinion that was ready, because of class differences, to believe the worst. The pervasiveness of violence in labor agitation therefore cannot be ignored. Both sides not only threw brickbats, but, often viewing each other as almost alien beings, shot guns at each other. The position of government in all of this violence varied, but all too often it was on the side of business and capital—especially at the state level. Only gradually, and then in the most extreme cases and toward the later part of the era, did the federal government assume a more neutral position. As long as there continued a lack of an identity of interest between the various forces contesting the workplace, the level of violence would persist, and the nation would be subject to the paroxysms of disorder.

The Immigrants

Ethnicity and cultural diversity remained important areas of distinction after the Civil War, preventing groups from identifying with each other and leading to violence. Sometimes this conflict was related to labor strife, and other times it was not. Immigrants contested the workplace with other ethnic groups, with African Americans, and with more established nonimmigrants. While these various groups clashed with each other as strikers and strikebreakers, the relationship between ethnic and cultural conflict and labor issues often was less direct. Long-standing competition for jobs might operate as an undercurrent, creating mutual animosities that exploded into outbreaks of rioting unconnected to a strike. In still other ethnic rioting, labor competition played a small role, and it was the cultural differences alone that led to collective action. Whatever the circumstances, Americans of all stripes used ethnicity and culture as a way of dividing society and engaging in intergroup conflict.

The Irish participated in riots during this period, and as in the antebellum era, were often identified as prone to violence. Two major Orange-Irish clashes occurred in New York City. Three people were killed and seventeen injured in an Irish Catholic attack, that included gun play, on a Protestant Orange celebration on July 12, 1870. With the threat of more violence the next year, parade organizers and city officials decided to cancel the celebration. The governor, however, promised that the state militia would protect the Protestant marchers. Irish Catholics were not intimidated and assaulted the small band of Orangemen protected by twelve regiments of militia. After one soldier was hit by a bullet the combat began in earnest. By the time the smoke cleared, three soldiers were dead, seven wounded. Twenty-three police and two Orangemen were injured. The Catholics sustained even more damage: 41 killed and at least 56 wounded.[12]

Most commentators failed to recognize the American roots of this violence and blamed the Irish Catholics, labeling them "desperate" and un-American for denying religious freedom and bringing ancient feuds to this country.[13] A similar analysis lay behind much of the coverage of the secret organization of Irish miners called the Molly Maguires that disrupted the Pennsylvania anthracite coalfields in the 1870s. Ethnic slurs portrayed the Mollys as self-seeking opportunists who used violence for individual ends. Although the Molly Maguires threatened, intimidated, and murdered to gain some control over the workplace, theirs was a mass movement typical of American labor. The riot at Mahony City and Hazelton on June 3, 1875, when as many as one thousand strikers fought police and besieged operating mines, was typical of both labor and ethnic collective action.[14]

After the 1870s, Irish workers continued to fight for control over their labor. Irish ore-trimming crews on Michigan's upper peninsula battled inter-lopers from other ethnic groups in the 1880s and 1890s. During a Brooklyn longshoreman's strike in August 1893, the Irish fought both Italian and black strikebreakers.[15]

The Irish also rioted in nonlabor disturbances. They played a major role in the 1900 New York City race riot. On November 10, 1920, a crowd of five hundred Irish fought police outside New York's Capitol Theater because they objected to the flying of the British flag. In the same city fifteen days later, five thousand supporters of Irish hunger striker Terence MacSwiny, angered by a British flag atop the Union Club, rioted after leaving St. Patrick's Cathedral.[16]

If the Irish were accused of being violent and riot-prone, so, too, were many of the new immigrants of the late nineteenth century. Before 1880 there were hardly any immigrants from the multiethnic empires of Russia and Austria-Hungary and only a few thousand from Italy. After 1880 not only did the total immigration increase, but these nations and other eastern and southern European states contributed over half the total. Thus, between 1880 and 1920 approximately 23,500,000 immigrants arrived in the United States. More than 12,000,000 came from these new sources. Unlike the northern Europeans of earlier immigration, whose cultures were more alike, but who also found a great deal to fight over, these new immigrants represented vastly different cul-tures from earlier Americans and from each other. They spoke a multitude of dialects and languages, and practiced a variety of religions. With their arrival, and the arrival of several hundred thousand Asians, the ethnic diversity of America took a quantum leap. With that diversity came even more room for bloodshed.[17]

Unable to draw ethnic distinctions among these alien nationalities, Anglo-Americans often lumped together many eastern Europeans as "Hungarians." In 1886 *Harper's Weekly* described striking coke shovellers in Pennsylvania as "Hungarians" who "are the most difficult class of laborers to manage when they are peaceful, or to pacify when they are enraged." Not only did few of them speak English, but "they live here in the same squalid fashion as in Hungary." Moreover, they knew "nothing of American life or manners, or of the courts, or of working-men's rights." Instead they relied on carrying a point with physical violence. Since many of them had been in the army they knew how to fight, eagerly resisted authority, and viewed police officers as "an enemy in war."[18]

Harper's Weekly was right; many immigrants did resort to violence. But it was American conditions that drove them to it. When Slavic workers replaced the Irish in the anthracite mines of eastern Pennsylvania after 1880, the change in ethnicity did not alter the basis for conflict; exploitation, poor pay, and harsh working conditions persisted. Eastern Europeans responded to these conditions with violent opposition to the private coal and mine police and strikebreakers of any kind. During the 1894 strike Slavic workers beat scabs and a mine superintendent. In 1897 several violent confrontations culminated in the Lattimer Massacre when, faced by a massive demonstration of Polish, Hungarian, and Italian strikers, a sheriff and his posse of eighty-five panicked and fired into the crowd, murdering nineteen. During the 1900 strike, eastern European workers, led by "Hungarian women," had the audacity to assail English-speaking miners willing to return to work. In this melee the guards fired into the crowd of five hundred, wounding several. Subsequently the strikers captured two policemen, killed one, and severely beat the other. A riot broke out in Shenandoah during the 1902 strike when a sheriff fired into a crowd that threatened the strikebreakers he was escorting. Fifteen hundred state troops had to be sent to restore order.[19]

Immigrants, especially from eastern and southern Europe, played a crucial role in many other violent labor strikes. Three hundred armed immigrant iron miners marched through the town of Iron Mountain, Minnesota, in May 1894, forcing the closing of the local mines. Italian dam workers in Marmaroneck, New York battled with police and nonstrikers in April 1900. One person was killed. Italian garbage collectors fought scabs and police in New York City in June and July 1907. Immigrant garment workers, including many women, fought hostile authorities, company thugs, and strikebreakers in New York City, Cleveland, and Chicago in 1910 and 1911. Some violence also accompanied the famous textile strikes in Lawrence, Massachusetts in 1912 and Paterson, New Jersey in 1913. In both strikes, immigrants comprised the overwhelming majority of the labor force. Moreover, the mainstay of the strikers in the southern Colorado mine fields in 1914 was immigrants.[20]

The intensity of all of this rioting varied greatly. Immigrant strikers seldom, contrary to the 1886 *Harper's* report, resorted to violence simply because they believed that was the only way to carry a point. Although some immigrants came from cultures that had certain traditions of violence, they acted more in desperation born out of the situation in the United States than any ethnic tendency. Suffering under horrendous conditions at work and home, and with a political system that was unresponsive, some immigrants were willing to use their fists, clubs, and guns to gain control over their work and lives. Casualties mounted when authorities denied the legitimacy of their claims and met the strikers' force with force of their own. With both sides viewing each other with suspicion and incapable of identifying with the other, the violence always had the potential to escalate.

Many of these immigrant labor disturbances are also noteworthy for the level of involvement of women. Rioting for most Anglo-Americans was male dominated. Officials were shocked and outraged by the participation of Irish women in disturbances before the Civil War and in the New York City draft riot. After 1865, with the livelihood of their families threatened, immigrant women not only encouraged their spouses and sons, but threw stones, hurled epithets, and asserted leadership at a time when their Anglo-American counterparts could not even vote. A week after the Lattimer Massacre several Slavic women, arming themselves with rolling pins and pokers, headed a group of over one hundred men and boys in driving scabs from the mines near Hazelton, Pennsylvania. On January 21, 1914, a large crowd of immigrant women protesting the arrest of labor organizer Mother Jones confronted the state militia in Trinidad during the mine war in southern Colorado. Flustered by this crowd, and embarrassed when a militia officer fell off his horse, the soldiers charged into the marchers with drawn sabers.[21]

Although immigrants helped in the development of an American labor movement, ethnicity also divided the working class. During the 1880s the employees of the Cleveland Rolling Mills were split between the skilled and unionized who had English background, and the unskilled Poles and Czechs. In an 1882 strike the English-speaking workers fought with the immigrants who stayed on the job. By 1885, however, the unskilled immigrants struck and rioted when new immigrants were brought in to replace them. During the Telluride mine strike in Colorado in 1901 union workers had to beat back Mexican strikebreakers.[22]

Not only were there struggles between Anglo-Americans and immigrants and between one ethnic group and another, but there were intraethnic conflicts as well. Striking Japanese and Mexican sugar beet workers at Oxnard, California, in 1903 shot at a wagon load of Japanese strikebreakers. One Mexican striker was killed, and two Japanese and two Mexican strikers were wounded. In the fall of 1887 Hungarian strikers fought other Hungarians used as scabs during a coal strike in Hazelton, Pennsylvania. Latin cigar workers— mainly Cubans and Spaniards—in Tampa, Florida, squared off against one another several times in the 1890s and early 1900s. In August 1892 striking cigar workers threw rocks and exchanged shots with Spaniards who continued to work. In November 1900 two competing cigar maker unions fought a gun battle when one union refused to join the strike with the other.[23]

Some of the most serious ethnic disturbances occurred in efforts to drive a particular group from a community. The social and cultural divisions represented by these pogroms were reflected in the burning glow of intensified violence against both people and property.

The Chinese, whose culture was even more different from the Anglo-American than was that of eastern and southern Europeans, were singled out for special ill treatment during the late nineteenth century. Chinese immigration began in the 1840s, peaked during the 1870s, and, due to legal restrictions, decreased after that. Fear of labor competition from an alien group that many Anglo-Americans believed were willing to work for next to nothing contributed to the anti-Asian hostility. But only some violence against the Chinese was related to strikes. Because Chinese Americans formed insular communities, heavily dependent upon menial work with some involvement in illicit activities like running opium dens or prostitution rings, Anglo-Americans believed that there was a great cultural chasm between themselves and the Asian foreigners. During the 1850s the Chinese had been one of several foreign groups expelled from California mining camps.[24] Starting in the 1870s, they increasingly became the targets of American xenophobia in the West.

On October 24, 1871, a major riot broke out in Los Angeles that revealed the depth of Anglo-American hostility to the Chinese and demonstrated the violence endemic in American society. Two rival Chinese gangs had a gunfight over a prostitute. After an Anglo-American, who attempted to interfere, was killed and a policeman was shot, the city's whites launched a general assault on the Chinese. Chinatown was gutted, the houses were looted, and fifteen Chinese were hanged. Several others were also killed during the pogrom. The ethnic hatred evident in the Los Angeles riot of 1871 came close to matching the race hatred of the South.[25]

Denver experienced a less violent riot on October 31, 1880. Denver's Chinese population, which numbered at most a few hundred, did not threaten the Anglo-American. However, local Democratic politicians featured anti-Chinese propaganda in a parade on the thirtieth and in their newspapers. After an Anglo-American beat a Chinese American in a saloon on the thirty-first, a crowd of thousands gathered in the street. City officials decided to disperse the crowd with a fire hose. Instead of extinguishing the crowd's ire, this act triggered an attack on the city's Chinese-American community. Rioters beat dozens of Chinese, destroyed their property, and killed one man before the police restored order.[26]

Anti-Chinese rioting spread elsewhere in the West. Angered by rival Chinese gangs fighting in February 1885, the white citizens of Eureka, California, rounded up every Chinese American they could find, robbed them, burned their homes, and banished them from town. Twenty-five other California communities followed this precedent and purged their towns of Chinese.[27]

Several anti-Chinese riots were more directly connected to labor competition. In February 1867 a crowd of four hundred whites attacked Chinese railway workers in San Francisco. The assailants injured at least twelve persons, destroyed or burned several shanties and sheds at the work site, and threatened to attack the Mission Woolen Mills because they employed Chinese workers. In July 1877, as part of the great railroad strike, white workers spent three evenings destroying Chinese wash houses, assaulting Chinese-American workers, and battling with police in San Francisco.[28] The largest and most violent labor-related anti-Chinese riot, however, was on September 2, 1885, in Rock Springs, Wyoming.

The Union Pacific Railroad operated a huge coal mining facility at Rock Springs and imported Chinese workers as early as 1875 to forestall union organizing among the white miners. By September 1885 there were close to one thousand Chinese in Rock Springs. White miners claimed that the company gave the Chinese preference in work stations, allowing them to mine more coal and depriving the whites of higher wages. Several hours after a fist fight between Chinese and Anglo-American miners, 100 to 150 whites armed themselves and invaded Chinatown. Sweeping through the area, the whites killed and wounded as many Chinese as they could. They looted and burned the Chinese housing and drove all Chinese out. By the time they were finished at least fifty-one Chinese Americans were dead. The government ordered federal troops to secure the area, and eventually the Union Pacific reopened the mines with more Chinese labor. Government soldiers, however, were stationed at the scene for thirteen years.[29]

The tragedy did not end at Rock Springs. Word of the miners' action spread through the West. In Squeak Valley, Washington, on September 7, a mob set upon thirty-five Chinese hop pickers, killed three, and looted and burned their tents. During the same month whites in Douglas Island, Alaska, rounded up one hundred Chinese, hurled them on a boat, and then set them adrift in the Pacific. White miners drove the Chinese from a coal mine, injuring nine, in Black Diamond, Washington. Early in November, whites in Tacoma, Washington, purged the city of all Chinese. Similar action was taken in Seattle on February 7, where a shooting confrontation between whites and the military left one person killed.[30]

The combination of labor competition and cultural differences led to purges of other ethnic groups. On September 5, 1907, five hundred whites raided mills where Hindus worked in Bellingham, Washington, invaded their lodging, and escorted them to the city limits. Greek immigrants also found themselves the objects of the mob. In the early twentieth century the Greek-American community was comprised largely of adult males who roomed together in groups, worked hard and cheaply, and insulated themselves from the mainstream culture. Newspapers often reported that Greek men insulted American women on the streets. After a Greek murdered an Irish-American policeman in South Omaha, Nebraska, while the officer was arresting the Greek on a charge concerning his relationship with an Anglo-American woman, rioting started on February 21, 1909. Between 500 and 1,000 people stormed into the Greek community, killing one person, beating several others, looting and burning property, and driving away the city's 2,000–3,000 Greek-American residents. Less extreme disturbances took place in Kansas City, Kansas, and Dayton, Ohio, in the same month.[31]

Although labor competition played a role in the anti-Greek and the anti-Chinese pogroms, these incidents were based on animosity over cultural differences. Most nonimmigrant Americans looked upon the clannishness of these groups with suspicion. The fact that some immigrant individuals participated in activities the nonimmigrants identified as unseemly or illicit only accentuated the ethnic animosities. Italian Americans confronted many of the same problems. Often denied the opportunity of achieving success through legitimate means, some Italian Americans turned to illicit means. Occasionally, this activity led to anti-Italian rioting.

A mob of self-proclaimed vigilantes lynched eleven Italian Americans in a New Orleans prison on March 14, 1891. The victims, who were reputedly members of a Mafia crime family, had been tried for the murder of the police chief, but the jury ruled that some were not guilty and could not come to a decision on the others. Many in New Orleans believed that bribes had been paid and that justice had not been served. City leaders therefore called a mass meeting, decried the verdict, and led a mob to the jail, where, with hardly any resistance, they captured and quickly dispatched their victims. On one level, this action was just another example of the American vigilante tradition. An editorial in a New Orleans paper declared to the lynchers that "you have in one righteous upheaval, in one fateful gust of mighty wrath, vindicated your laws," and that "your vengeance is consecrated in the forfeited blood of the assassins." Like the lynching of African Americans, the racial or ethnic slant to this action transcended the boundaries of maintaining law and order and involved deeply ingrained prejudices that presumed guilt.[32]

The New Orleans riot was not an isolated incident. Between August 5 and 7, 1920, a huge crowd took over the town of West Frankfort, Illinois. The rioters blamed the death of two local boys on an Italian-American criminal gang. The rioters commandeered the telegraph and telephone lines, disarmed police, and set fire to large sections of Frankfort Heights, an immigrant neighborhood. One person was killed and over forty injured before state troops arrived and restored order.[33]

Immigrant groups might also riot against the mainstream society and, striving to maintain or define cultural identity, fight among themselves. These riots ordinarily were less violent than interethnic disturbances. The Jewish community in New York City expanded rapidly in the late nineteenth century, but found itself challenged from the outside and divided within. On August 4, 1898, over two thousand participated in a disturbance in Brownsville, Brooklyn, that began because many Jews believed that a school teacher had tried to convert their children to Christianity. A little more than a month later riots broke out on Manhattan's Lower East Side when one group of

Jews protested the secular practices of other Jews who ate and drank on Yom Kippur.[34]

Cultural divisions could also set nonimmigrant groups against each other. The Mormons developed their own identity that stood in contrast to the rest of society. This distinction had led to conflict in the 1830s and 1840s and ultimately compelled the Mormons to seek their promised land in the far West. Once the Mormons established themselves by the Great Salt Lake their problems did not end. In 1857 the Mormons virtually waged war against the United States government, resisting the invasion of a federal force sent to subdue them. In the process a group of fifty Mormons joined some Indians in a massacre of 120 non-Mormon members of a wagon train at Mountain Meadows on September 7, 1857. After the Civil War hostile feelings persisted, and Mormon missionaries were attacked and even murdered. In one incident at Cave Creek, Tennessee, a mob killed four Mormons who were there teaching the gospel according to the Church of Latter-day Saints.[35]

Ethnic and cultural divisions sliced American society in a variety of directions and created a host of warring factions. With many of these groups denying that they had much in common with the others, it became all too easy to lift up a cudgel, or raise a gun, and engage in extreme violence. The competition for jobs and the need to maintain one's identity in this mixture of cultures and animosities only enhanced the anarchy and disorder.

Politics Left and Right

Politics offered another arena where stark divisions led to conflict. To understand this intergroup violence we need to look beyond party contests in the late nineteenth and early twentieth century and focus on the politics of the left and the right. The struggle of labor and capital, the rise of immigration, and the growth of socialist and anarchist ideas made for political tension that often broke out into violence. On the left much of this violence was not collective; the throwing of the bomb at Haymarket, the assassination of William McKinley, and the dynamiting of the *Los Angeles Times* building are examples of acts committed by an individual or a small group of individuals. Radicals on the left, however, often used rhetoric that condoned collective violence, and their supporters participated in enough riots to sustain the left's reputation as a seedbed for disorder. Collective violence on the right was more extensive and ranged from limited acts of intimidation reminiscent of early traditions of rioting to more brutal attacks on persons akin to the racial, labor, and ethnic rioting.

Although most political collective violence occurred among extremists, Republicans and Democrats still clashed at the polls or harassed one another's processions. In 1900 a mob in Victor, Colorado, pelted Teddy Roosevelt with eggs. In the same year a crowd of men carrying bricks and clubs assaulted the tail end of a Republican parade in Chicago, and three hundred Columbia

University students, shouting for William Jennings Bryan, brawled with young Republicans in New York's Broadway. Two persons died in a riot in Denver at a polling place in the same year. Local contests also led to bitter conflict. In April 1905 in Huntington, West Virginia, three men were shot and several beaten by police after an election left the town council with a 6–6 split between two factions.[36] Yet it was the violence committed by those on the left and right that grabbed most headlines.

Many strikes by workers in this period were inspired or supported by radical ideas derived from Karl Marx, and the rioting related to such actions became linked with leftist politics. Although the great railway strike in 1877 spread extemporaneously, strike leaders in Pittsburgh, Chicago, and St. Louis used anticapitalist rhetoric that conjured up fears of a red menace and images of the Paris commune in 1871. The attempted assassination and shooting of Henry Clay Frick by anarchist Alexander Berkman also cast a red tint to the Homestead strike in 1892. This trend of guilt by association continued into the twentieth century.

Labeling a labor movement as anarchist, socialist, or even communist often enabled officials to take preemptive action that, while legal or quasi-legal, often set off popular disorder. On January 13, 1874, about seven thousand workers, their wives, and children crowded Tompkins Square in New York City to demonstrate for public works projects that would employ them and prevent starvation. Police charged into the crowd to disperse this "communist" threat. Amid the stampede some workers attacked police and both sides sustained injuries.[37]

Twelve years later the Haymarket Riot in Chicago was also started by police. Throughout the nation the labor movement gained momentum as the Knights of Labor and other groups pushed for an eight-hour day. Workers struck in support of this measure in several cities. In Chicago strikers at the McCormick factory fought against scabs and police on May 3, 1886. The police fired into the strikers, killing two and wounding many others. Anarchists who had joined in the eight-hour movement called a meeting at Haymarket for May 4, to protest the McCormick shootings. Thousands packed the public square. The police allowed the meeting to go on unmolested until near the end, when, during the last speech, they approached in force and demanded that the crowd disperse. At this point someone—the individual's identity remains a mystery—hurled a bomb into the police ranks. The explosion, which killed several officers, brought an all-out assault by the police, who fired wildly into the crowd. Some protestors fought back. Most, however, headed for cover. By the time the street was cleared seven policemen were dead, sixty injured. Four civilians are known to have been killed and countless injured. More telling, however, was the repression that followed, including the end of the eight-hour movement, and the show trials of the anarchists responsible for organizing the Haymarket meeting.[38]

In the early twentieth century the Wobblies replaced the anarchists as the lightning rod attracting political collective violence from on the right and on the left. The Wobblies—members of the Industrial Workers of the World (IWW)—began their movement in the mine fields and timber forests of the American West in 1905 and called for the formation of "one big union." Abandoning the craft orientation and exclusionist policies of the American Federation of Labor, the IWW strove to organize both skilled and unskilled, Anglo-Americans and immigrants, and even reached out to African Americans and Asian Americans. They preached the end of the capitalist system and government and found their greatest successes among the dispossessed. Although their leaders might lapse into a rhetoric that seemed to encourage violence, in most instances they counseled passive nonviolent means to carry their message.[39]

If the Wobblies cautioned for the need to keep one's hands in one's pockets during a strike, they were often perceived as encouraging violence. When the steel workers at McKees Rock went on strike in 1909 and fought repeatedly with scabs and private detectives, the Wobblies were there to organize them. When Lawrence textile workers charged through the mills and marched in the street, the Wobblies quickly arrived to lead the strike. Conservatives also blamed the limited violence in the Paterson silk weaver strike of 1913 on the Wobbly organizers despite the IWW's pacifist approach. And when hop pickers battled with officials over their horrendous working and living conditions in Wheatland, California, on August 3, 1913, the resulting bloodshed was blamed on the IWW even though there were only about thirty or forty Wobblies present—out of thousands—and they had not organized the protest.[40]

Occasionally the radical left, including the IWW, continued the revolutionary tradition and inspired open resistance and violence. In August 1917, central Oklahoma farmers, spurred on by socialists and the Working Class Union (affiliated with the IWW), organized to oppose the draft. Arming themselves, a few hundred men met on the banks of the South Canadian River and prepared to march on Washington. Local townsfolk took the Green Corn Rebellion seriously, marshalled their own forces, and fought a brief battle with the rebels before the farmers scattered. Subsequently 266 men were arrested; 150 were convicted and 75 sent to jail.[41]

Radicals also strove to interpret some apparent customary forms of rioting within their own analytical framework. In February 1917, as prices soared on the eve of the American entry in the great war, thousands of immigrant women in New York City, Philadelphia, and Boston rioted over the cost of onions, potatoes, and other items, knocking down pushcarts, raiding shops, and fighting police. Although the riots expressed an older spirit of moral economy, they also had a more modern context. The Philadelphia disturbances took place in conjunction with a strike at Franklin Sugar Refinery. In New

York several hundred East Side women marched on City Hall to demand action by the mayor, and expressed class resentment in a demonstration outside the Waldorf-Astoria Hotel. They also beat at least one wealthy motorist driving by. Socialist congressman Meyer London, representing Manhattan's Lower East Side, defended the rioters and derided the market system in the halls of the United States Congress.[42]

Whatever the role of leftist organizers in encouraging or condoning disorder, they managed to inspire conservatives to attack them with extralegal violence. This activity ranged from mild harassment to extremes of physical violence. During the free speech fight in San Diego in 1912 hundreds of Wobblies were taken, beaten, forced to run a gauntlet, and sometimes tarred and feathered for simply trying to enter the city and speak at a street corner. Four years later a patina of legality covered the action of the sheriff in Everett, Washington. On October 30, the Commercial Club, as the city's vigilantes called themselves, took their cue from San Diego and stripped and clubbed about forty Wobblies and forced them to run a gauntlet. The Wobblies were not easily intimidated and on November 5, they shipped over two hundred fifty men on the Seattle ferry to inundate the city with street corner speakers. This decision set the stage for greater violence. The sheriff prepared for the invasion and ordered his deputies to meet the ferry at the dock. Before the passengers could land, a shot rang out. The sheriff claimed the Wobblies started the battle. Four Wobblies and two deputies were killed (some reports indicate that the deputies were shot accidently by their own men), and many others were wounded.[43]

Right-wing violence intensified from 1917 to 1920 against the backdrop of the strident patriotism that accompanied America's entry into war. While the IWW was a major target of this violence, anyone who opposed the war, people of German heritage, and other ethnics might be the subject of attack. State and local government often eagerly supported extralegal intimidation. The federal government's reaction was more mixed. Some government officials understood that right-wing mobs violated civil rights, but believed that "reds" and German "agents" had to be curtailed to fight the war effectively. Other officials, who by the end of the war appeared most influential, experienced less ambiguous feelings and encouraged vigilantism by super patriots.

Reaction to the Wobbly-inspired copper strike in Arizona and Montana reveals some of these trends. Sheriff Harry Wheeler organized 2,000 vigilantes in Bisbee, Arizona, to deport about 1,300 striking copper miners in July 1917. Only about a third of the victims were members of the IWW, but Wheeler and company believed that the Wobblies were foreign agents bent on destroying America's ability to fight a war. His extralegal posse scoured the town, and any man unwilling to work on company terms was roughly handled, herded onto a cattle car, and shipped to New Mexico. Local businesses and companies applauded and supported the action. The state governor objected, but did little to countermand the deportations. The federal government also mouthed objections and eventually initiated prosecutions against Wheeler and others. But these halfhearted efforts were not rigorously pursued. The deportation, and a similar action at Jerome, Arizona, effectively broke the strike in the area.[44]

As outrageous a violation of civil rights as the Bisbee deportation was, at least the violence was kept to a minimum. Only one miner was shot when he resisted the vigilantes. The right wing was capable of greater brutality. In August 1917, vigilantes lynched Frank Little, a Wobbly veteran of many a strike and free speech campaign. August 1917 found Little in Butte, Montana, to help with the copper strike and to preach against the American involvement in the First World War. A group of gunmen burst into his hotel room, dragged him through the street, tied him to the back of a car, and then hanged him from a bridge. Montana Senator H. L. Myers excused the murderers, and offered an explanation for mob action that recalled older notions of rioting. Myers explained that had Little "been arrested and put in jail for seditious and incendiary" speeches "he would not have been lynched."[45]

Almost as if it was heeding the senator's advice, and in some measure sanctioning the anti-Wobbly violence, the federal government took official action against the IWW in September 1917. Federal agents raided Wobbly offices, seized papers, and arrested the organization's leaders. The outcome of the trials that followed was predictable; the courts convicted the IWW leadership of hindering the war effort and sentenced them to long prison terms. These actions removed the IWW from serious contention as a labor organization and limited, but did not eliminate, mob action against this group.[46]

Other Americans fell victims to "patriotic" mobs. Like the anti-Wobbly action, these disturbances ranged from rituals of humiliation and intimidation to more serious destruction of property and life. They also brought little government intervention and were reinforced by anti-treason laws.

Anti-pacifist mobs often relied upon symbolic gestures intended to humiliate victims. A crowd in Audubon, Iowa, in December 1917, grabbed two men who opposed the war, tied ropes around their necks, and dragged them through town until one of them agreed to buy a $1000 Liberty Bond. Then both were released. In March 1918 a mob took O. F. Westbrook from his farmhouse near Altus, Oklahoma, forced him to kiss the flag, whipped him, and tarred and feathered him because of his supposed disloyalty. Another group in Buffalo, New York, doused Jacob W. Oswald with yellow paint and rode him on a rail in June 1918 for not contributing to the Red Cross.[47]

Germans and other ethnics received plenty of attention from patriotic mobs. Minnesotans gave E. H. Stratemeyer, a naturalized German, a coat of tar and feathers in Osakis in November 1917 for alleged disloyal statements. Two months later a mob in Connecticut punished Maximilian Von Hoegen for his pro-German comments by beating him and forcing him to kiss the flag and sing the "Star-Spangled Banner." Four hundred members of the "Volunteer Vigilance Committee" in Delphos, Ohio, compelled five German businessmen to march down a street and to kiss the flag in March 1918. A pro-German Polish Catholic priest and three others were tarred and feathered in Christopher, Illinois, and the Benton, Illinois, Liberty League rode a Bohemian woman on a rail and made her retract her anti-Wilson statements. Similar actions occurred throughout the country with various degrees of personal violence.[48]

Members of the Socialist Party and the Nonpartisan League—a reformist group that wanted the state to control marketing and shipping of agricultural products—were often victims of this type of violence because of their opposition to the war. Soldiers in Boston broke up a socialist parade on July 1, 1917, forced socialists to kiss the flag, and gutted the local Socialist Party headquarters. A Philadelphia mob beat socialists distributing antiwar pamphlets in August 1917. Sailors raided the Seattle-based Piggot Printing, upset type cases, and destroyed presses because it published the Socialist *Daily Call* and the *Industrial Worker* in January 1918. Four months later, students at Rutgers University tarred (with molasses) and feathered Samuel H. Chovenson, an antiwar socialist, when he refused to speak at a Liberty Loan rally.[49]

In the great plains and the far West mobs harassed members of the Nonpartisan League. In Haxtun, Colorado, a mob painted Nonpartisan C. T. Raywalt's car yellow, drove him out of town, and threatened to destroy the local newspaper office that had supported the Nonpartisan League and opposed the war. Several Nonpartisan leaders were tarred and feathered in the state of Washington in late April 1918. Texas patriots kidnaped three Nonpartisan League organizers in Mineola, declared that they were German spies, took them out of town, stripped their backs, whipped them, and poured salt on their wounds.[50]

Although many of these riots emphasized ritual humiliation, as suggested by the Mineola incident, greater physical violence was possible. Speaking out against American involvement in the war could be dangerous. Even before hostilities, a Baltimore mob of thousands harassed an antiwar rally that featured David Jordan, President of Stanford University. Over twenty people were injured. A mob in Gregory, South Dakota, beat antiwar Nonpartisan League organizers and forced them to march to the next town, where they were put on a train to Nebraska.[51]

One of the most violent incidents took place in Collinsville, Illinois, on April 4, 1918, when a mob hanged Robert Paul Prager merely because he was German by birth. Prager had not even uttered a pro-German statement, although he may have had socialist leanings. A crowd of four to five hundred stripped him naked, wrapped him in an American flag, and marched him through town. The police interceded and placed Prager in their custody. There was no safety in jail. The mob took Prager away from the officials, dragged him to the edge of town and, after allowing him a minute or two for prayer, they hanged him.[52]

Until the Prager incident, President Woodrow Wilson had made no strong public statement against the vigilantes. Even with the loss of life Wilson hesitated, but when a local jury refused to convict the men involved in the Prager murder, Wilson declared that "every American who takes part in the action of a mob . . . is no true son of this great democracy. . . ." He went on to assert that "every mob contributes to German lies about the United States" and offers grist for the German propaganda mill.[53]

These powerful words had little impact. Mobs stayed active, and many state officials condoned extralegal collective action and called upon the federal government to step up its anti-sedition program. After the Prager murder, Governor Frank Orren Lowden of Illinois declared that mobs "assembled and righted wrongs which neither the local nor the federal authorities have dealt with." Testifying to its own superpatriotism, and almost ratifying the mob persecution of the so-called disloyal, Congress passed a new Sedition Act in April 1918 that strengthened the federal government's hand in dealing with the antiwar movement.[54]

Renewed labor unrest, a postwar recession, and the Bolshevik Revolution in Russia convinced many Americans that after the armistice the United States was on the brink of revolution. Attorney General A. Mitchell Palmer took this opportunity to launch raids on radical organizations, make hundreds of arrests, and preemptively deport foreign-born leftists. Official action, however, was but one component of the larger repression of the "Red Scare." On May 1, 1919, antisocialist riots took place in several cities. Local authorities, supported by the military, broke up socialist-sponsored May Day activities in Cleveland. Quarrels over red flags occurred in at least four places, and one person was killed and over forty seriously injured in the fighting. In New York City soldiers stormed the Russian People's House on East 15th Street, confiscating books and compelling socialists there to sing the national anthem. Later that day about four hundred soldiers raided the offices of a socialist newspaper, breaking up a reception and forcing the seven hundred guests into the street. At least seventeen were injured. A disturbance in Boston began when fifteen hundred members of the Lettish Workmen's Association continued their parade even though they had no permit and the police ordered them to disperse. The police, joined by soldiers and patriotic bystanders, attempted to capture the marchers' red flags. Three police officers and one civilian were seriously injured in the fighting. News of the riot spread throughout the city, and other anti-red mobs beat supposed socialists. One group sacked the Socialist Party headquarters on Wenonah Street.[55]

Throughout 1919 patriotic mobs, often composed of members of the newly formed veterans association called the American Legion, assailed "red" targets. In November 1919 the sheriff of Ortonville, Minnesota, who was the head of the local American Legion post, led a mob that prevented former congressman Ernest Lundeen from speaking. They grabbed Lundeen and brought him to the railroad where they locked him in a refrigerator car headed for Appleton. The American Legion saw action in many antisocialist and antilabor union disturbances.[56]

Legionnaires also played a prominent role in the violence at Centralia, Washington, on Nov. 11, 1919. An Armistice parade, featuring the legion, passed a newly opened IWW hall. Fearing an attack, local Wobblies prepared themselves for battle. When the marchers returned, bent on the destruction of the hall, both sides started shooting. The Wobblies managed to kill three legionnaires before succumbing to the overwhelming odds. All but Wesley Everest surrendered and were turned over to local authorities. The legionnaires pursued Everest and trapped him by the Skookumchuck River. There, Everest fired his gun at his assailants until it was empty. Another legionnaire fell dead. The crowd captured Everest, severely beat him, and placed him in official custody. That night a mob broke into the jail and took Wesley Everest, whom they tortured, castrated, and hanged from a bridge.[57]

For many, 1919 was a year of chaos and hysteria. The "Red Scare" formed only one component of the unraveling order. The same year witnessed race riots and a great steel strike that included countless incidents of labor-capital violence. After 1920 sanity and normalcy appeared to be returning. Yet the decade that followed also brought one of the most extensive right-wing movements in American history.

The second Ku Klux Klan began in Georgia in 1915, but it was not until the 1920s, when modern marketing techniques were used to gain membership, that it expanded to three million members nationwide. Such large numbers meant that its membership was diverse and that reasons for entering the Klan were varied. The revived Klan, however, was more than the vehicle of racial repression that the earlier Klan had been. While in some areas blacks continued as its victims, in other areas the Klan cast its net more broadly to include Catholics, Jews, immigrants, criminals, corrupt politicians, violators of morality, and anyone else who might be deemed less than one hundred percent American by Klan leaders. In the words of one commentator in 1927, the Klan was popular because "the people were frightened" by the social changes that seemed to engulf them, and joining the KKK offered them an opportunity "to cling to one's neighbor." By the late 1920s, however, the Klan, due to government and popular opposition, corrupt leadership, and high dues had begun its decline.[58]

The KKK spawned two types of popular disorder. First, the Klan itself committed many depredations. The Klan's techniques of collective violence included ritual humiliation like tar and feathers and more extreme measures like kidnaping and murder. Thus in 1921 in Fort Worth, Texas, the Klan provided Benny Pinto a coat of tar and feathers for his gambling activities, and in Teneha, Texas, Klansmen not only tarred and feathered a woman supposed to be guilty of bigamy, but also clipped her hair. In Morehouse Parish, Louisiana, the Klan had a more lethal effect. On August 24, 1922, Klansmen stopped a vehicle between Bastrop and Mer Rouge to punish Watt Daniels for a reported offense to a Klan leader. When Daniels and Tom Richards recognized their tormentors, the two were separated from their companions and murdered. The other three were merely whipped. Violence arose almost everywhere the Klan reared its hooded head, but was especially prevalent in the South and Southwest during the early 1920s. By the middle of the decade, as the Klan vied for legitimate political power in several states, the extralegal violence became less frequent.[59]

The second type of collective action involving the Klan developed when the KKK found itself opposed by strong segments of the population. That opposition might lead to concerted violence like the ethnic and other intergroup violence of the era. Although this type of disorder might surface anywhere the Klan was active, the largest disturbances took place in the mid to late 1920s in the Midwest and Northeast, where there were many Catholic ethnics who saw themselves as potential targets of the Klan. Ten thousand members of the Klan met on a hill overlooking Carnegie, Pennsylvania, on August 25, 1923, as an insult to the heavily Catholic community. Although the mayor refused permission for the KKK to march into the town, five thousand white-robed Klansmen started into Carnegie anyway, pushing aside cars placed in their path. The locals greeted the Klan with a hail of stones. Confusion in the Klan ranks followed. A shot rang out, killing one Klansman, and the rest retreated from town. The Irish and Italian citizens of Niles, Ohio, fought off Klansmen intent on rallying in their town on November 1, 1924. Eventually the national guard had to restore order. Disturbances arose in places as disparate as McKinney, Texas; Brooklyn, Maryland; Perth Amboy, New Jersey; Memphis, Tennessee; Lilly, Pennsylvania; Worcester, Massachusetts; Detroit, Michigan; and Queens, New York. Virtual warfare erupted in and around Herrin, Illinois, between the Klan, which used brutal methods to assert its own morality, and its opponents. In one gun battle on August 30, 1924, six men were killed, and fighting during an election in April 1926 left another six dead.[60]

Political rioting on the left and the right thus ran the gamut from extreme personal physical violence to more ritualized crowd activity reminiscent of the eighteenth century. Despite the many less violent episodes, the full range of these disturbances represented the deep divisions in society that pitted one group against another and that seemed to threaten American democracy with mob rule.

A Search for Order

Government forces did not stand idle during the flirtation with anarchy. Confronted with violence and a nation that was tearing itself apart along racial, economic, ethnic, and political lines, officials struggled to meet the challenge. Initially, however, the federal, state, and local governments took sides. This bias tended to aggravate the problem rather than alleviate it. Gradually, new enforcement mechanisms emerged, sometimes taking one step backward for every two steps forward, that dealt with the problem of order more effectively.[61]

First came the development of the local police. The nineteenth century opened without police and closed with cities and many towns having swarms of police officers to deal with crime and disorder. In the eighteenth century officials assumed that the combined weight of their official position as magistrates and their unofficial position as economic and social leaders was enough to maintain order. They believed that all they had to do to suppress a disturbance was to confront a mob—the members of which they would know personally—and demand that the individuals go about their own business.[62] The rise of egalitarian ideals, as well as the expansion and fluidity of American communities, made it difficult to continue this method of riot control. Officials thus came to rely on special agents of local government to interfere and break up disturbances. Initially these were an ad hoc collection of constables, sheriffs, and watchmen, but starting in Boston in 1829, and modeled after police practices in England, one community after another organized police departments.[63]

The establishment of these police forces did not always meet the full needs of society to maintain order. Despite professionalization and the wearing of uniforms, the police were often tied to local political machinery. After the Republican state government overhauled Democratic New York City's police department in 1857, political appointees from both sides battled outside City Hall. Only the intercession of the militia restored peace.[64] Most police forces were mired in local politics until well into the twentieth century.[65]

When it came to riots, therefore, the police frequently took sides. Sometimes they supported the forces in the streets that had the greatest number of voters—including immigrants and labor. Sid Hatfield was a local sheriff whose shoot-out with Baldwin-Felts private detectives during the West Virginia miners' strike in 1920 helped to provoke the war between miners and the companies in Logan County. More often, peace officers merely followed the trail of the greatest money—capital and business. Policemen interceded in many strikes, attacking demonstrators in New York's Tompkins Square on January 13, 1874, and at Chicago's Haymarket on May 4, 1886. Police officers might also allow their own prejudices to dictate their action. During the New York City race riot of 1900 the police not only stood by and allowed whites to vent their rage in assaults on blacks, but they also helped in the beatings.[66]

The police, however, could be unbiased and effective in maintaining order. Sometimes police officers could draw fine distinctions about what was and what was not acceptable crowd behavior. During a strike against the Kellogg

Switchboard Company in July 1903 teamsters blocked the street with their wagons while other strikers threw rocks at working employees. Chicago police dispersed the mobs and cleared the street, but then allowed the union to organize picket lines. The police sometimes looked past their own bias and protected blacks from lynching and minorities from mobs. This more professional approach to policing disorder became more prevalent as the nation moved from the nineteenth to the twentieth century.[67]

Combating rioters was only one component of police work: policemen had many duties, including serving in the trenches against crime and disorder. They dealt with a full complement of thieves and murderers, areas of crime beyond the purview of this study, and confronted a persistent level of rowdy violence that defies facile categorization. The type of street brawl and tavern disruption noted with such frequency in the court records at the beginning of the nineteenth century persisted. A few examples from New York City suggest the range of this activity. On July 10, 1870 a gang of street toughs started three fights. Two occurred at bars after they refused to pay for their drinks. In the third disturbance the rowdies attacked a group of Germans. The night's frolic left one dead and two severely wounded. Thirty years later college students started a riot over a baseball game and attempted to steal guns to use against their opponents. On May 29, 1920, a crowd assaulted a watchman at the New York Leather Manufacturing Company because he had thrown away a ball some youths had been playing with. In this confrontation the watchman shot one young man who threatened him, only to find himself besieged by a crowd of four hundred. In facing this day-to-day disorder the police were relatively successful and provided a veneer of law and order.[68]

Failure to control the streets could be disastrous. Just how important the police were to a well-regulated society became apparent during the Boston police strike of September 9–12, 1919. Political conflict between the Democratic city government and Republican state government precipitated the crisis as the local Democrats strove to arbitrate the police grievances, while the Republican-appointed police commissioner stood intransigent. No matter the cause, the city's police felt underpaid and unappreciated. The officers walked off the job. Within hours the city erupted into violence, looting, and lawbreaking. Crowds numbering into the thousands roamed the streets, breaking into stores, stealing, and destroying property. On the second day of the strike the national guard had to be called in. To disperse the crowds the troops used their guns. Before the rioting was over nine persons had been killed and fifty-eight wounded.[69]

Those who sought greater social order in the late nineteenth and early twentieth centuries tried to augment and even replace local police. Businessmen hired private detective agencies as a bulwark against the rising demands of the worker. The Pinkerton agency created a national sensation, and guaranteed decades of business, when its labor spies broke the grip of the

Molly Maguires on the Pennsylvania anthracite coalfields in 1876 and 1877. Groups like the Pinkertons and the Pennsylvania Coal and Iron Police sometimes took over the regular functions of local government to ensure labor discipline. In turn, the private police forces developed a nasty reputation among workers.[70]

Beginning with Pennsylvania in 1905, several states addressed the shortcomings of both private and public police by organizing a state constabulary or state police. This force provided law enforcement in rural areas and a body of police that could be concentrated at any hot spot in a given state. One pro-business commentator described the state troopers assigned to quell the Philadelphia transit strike of 1910 as "sinewy, athletic fellows, clear of eye and lean of jaw, bent simply but with terrible intentness upon their single business of keeping peace," who differed dramatically from the fat political appointees who filled Philadelphia's "debauched police force."[71] Although this reform strengthened the hand of the governor in dealing with a crisis, workers often saw the state police as mounted "cossacks" brought in to brutalize strikers.[72]

Viewed together, the local, private, and state police represented a complex weave of differing forces for law and order that sometimes worked in concert and sometimes worked at cross purposes. Yet even if the three spoke in one voice against a disturbance there was no guarantee that peace would ensue. As any survey of American history reveals, greater power was often needed to bolster these forces. In the second half of the nineteenth century that power came from the state and federal armed services.

Starting in the 1870s state governments reorganized their own ability to step into the breach with state militia and the national guard. The militia as an institution had been on decline since early in the century. The railroad riots of 1877 marked the nadir of this development. During this massive uprising of American workers the militia was either ineffective or too tainted with sympathy for the rioters. Thus in Pittsburgh, local troops hesitated to battle their neighbors and relatives, while the Philadelphia militia too eagerly waged bloody war on citizens of a competing city. The solution for state officials was to transform the militia into the national guard, whose professed purpose would be "to aid the civil officers, to suppress or prevent riot or insurrections. . . ."[73] Businessmen chipped in financial support to help underwrite the national guard, whose numbers were to be limited, but who would undergo more training and stricter discipline. State after state followed this procedure to control its unruly masses. As one riot duty manual later explained, the idea was to follow the rule that "A soldier is effective in riot duty not as an individual but as a soldier."[74] To further support this process states constructed new armories with a combination of private and public funds. Architects designed the armories to look and be defended like medieval castles to intimidate the working classes. Businessmen and the national guard were quite intimate. After the bloody Pullman riots in Chicago, local capitalists donated land and subscribed to the building of a new armory on the edge of the city to facilitate the dispatch of troops in the next round of industrial warfare. The national guard thus tended to support big business and was seldom neutral in a dispute. The results could be disastrous, as attested to by the massacre at Ludlow and the near civil war in West Virginia, 1920–1921.[75]

At the same time the federal government assumed a more active role in quelling rioting. Granted power by the United States Constitution to suppress insurrections, the federal government had intervened in its first one hundred years to put down several revolts—from the Whiskey Rebels to the contending forces of bleeding Kansas. In the second half of the nineteenth century the federal government interceded in the South during Reconstruction to combat racial disorder and after 1877 frequently entered labor disputes as well. Initially, as in the coalfields of Wyoming and in the Pullman confrontation, federal troops supported business. By the early twentieth century that position started to change. Federal troops in Ludlow and West Virginia intervened in the coalfields with impartiality.[76]

The shift in the attitude of officials toward rioting eventually reached all levels of government and reflected both Progressive distrust of business and an expanding understanding of democracy. It was now becoming possible for officials to admit that the striking worker struggled for human rights and bread and butter issues. There was also an increased awareness of racial injustice.[77] Authors of riot control manuals started to portray the mob less as an undifferentiated mass of aliens inspired by communistic revolt, and more as misguided American citizens. Military men still advocated force and stern measures when confronted by howling rioters, but instead of offering plans that strove to annihilate the enemy, they advised measures that would drive the crowd back and allow them to escape from the maddening scene to return to normal lives. Officers no longer ordered soldiers to shoot to kill, but told their men to aim low to inflict wounds and create panic.[78]

Surveyed as a whole, it is often hard to distinguish between labor, ethnic, and political strife. Each category overlapped with the other. While workers sometimes battled strikebreakers, police, and military solely over economic issues, their contests often reflected ethnic tensions and confrontations between the political left and right.

The Cincinnati riot of March 1884 suggests how complicated these various crosscurrents can be. In this disturbance at least thirty-five people died as crowds, composed largely of German-American workers, stormed the jail and burned the courthouse in objection to a corrupt political system that had failed adequately to punish two murderers—one a German, the other a black. The crowds were also labeled as communists by commentators. On one level this riot appeared to be a manifestation of vigilante justice. But it can also be seen as an effort to lynch a black, an expression of ethnic resentment, and an attempt to assert political ideas from the radical left by members of the working class.[79]

However difficult it is to unravel this jumble in each specific incident, we can still examine each category of analysis on its own terms. Labor riots included great cataclysms like the railroad strike of 1877 and the conflicts at Homestead, Pullman, Ludlow, and West Virginia, as well as countless disturbances along picket lines across the nation. Collective violence continued with and against immigrant groups like the Irish, and expanded as waves of new arrivals from eastern and southern Europe, Asia, and Latin America surged into the United States, churning the ethnic cauldron with ever increasing diversity. Although rioting decreased in mainstream politics between Democrats and Republicans (except in the racially charged atmosphere of the South), popular disorder occurred with great frequency revolving around groups like socialists, Wobblies, and the second Ku Klux Klan.

Collective action in all these areas could range from the peaceful demonstration to the most violent and bitter bloodshed. Despite the variety of crowd behavior, physical violence remained the hallmark of rioting throughout the nineteenth and into the beginning of the twentieth century, representing a nation that was divided into several hostile camps.

Government struggled to deal with the resulting upheaval. At first all levels of government took sides. Usually, but not always, local, state, and federal officials supported capital against labor, Anglo-Americans against ethnic Americans, and the right against the left. Gradually, especially with the rise of the Progressive movement, the federal government emerged as a mediator between groups in conflict and asserted an increased power and control over state and local governments. This change was glacial; the mountain of ice sometimes edged forward toward a new world, and at other times receded backward, as it did in 1919–1920, revealing the older landscape of hostility and violence. Yet as government assumed a new neutrality, it gained in effectiveness, and set the stage for greater transformations in the 1930s.

DEMOCRACY ENTRENCHED | 6

Transition

During the mid twentieth century the nature of rioting changed. Instead of flailing out at each other and committing acts of physical brutality, rioters attacked property that symbolized their grievances. Violent labor confrontations gave way to the sit-down and the sanctity of the picket line. Lynching and racial warfare gave way to crowds of angry demonstrators shouting at each other and the looters and arsonists of ghetto riots. Mob bloodshed on the right and the left gave way to political extremists defying the law by occupying buildings or disrupting traffic. Rioting became a form of ritualized rebellion that minimized violence against persons. This shift was not sudden and by no means complete. In any given period there are many different types of collective violence. There were moments when people called upon the heritage of the American Revolution and rioted following age-old patterns. There were also moments of brutal violence in lynching and bloody confrontations at the workplace. Yet by the 1950s a pattern emerged that marked a shift away from the type of rioting that had dominated the American scene for over a century.

The reasons for this shift are complex. American society altered dramatically: a larger United States government actively sustained the ideal of equality, information and news traveled faster to end isolation and insulation, and Americans increasingly became alike and shared the same values.

During the Progressive era officials saw themselves as representing more and more Americans. Supporters of the New Deal in the 1930s, faced with the possible collapse of capitalism in the Great Depression, expanded further the definition of democracy to include previously excluded groups. Typical of this development was section 7a of the National Industrial Recovery Act and the Wagner Act that legitimized the labor movement. Instead of siding with the businessmen, New Deal Democrats now openly claimed a neutrality that insisted on the right of the worker to organize and to strike.

The rise and power of the national state reinforced these developments. To combat the Depression, the federal government expanded rapidly in the 1930s. The new gospel of social welfare meant an enlarged bureaucracy. The Second World War and the global power that followed sustained these trends. The scale of government gave federal officials the ability to back up the democratic agenda and intrude on local politics to an extent unimaginable a decade or two earlier. During the 1950s and 1960s this power was not only wielded for the benefit of workers, but also in the interests of civil rights.

Changes in communications ended the isolation of regions. First radio, and then newsreels and television created instant and highly evocative news reportage. A lynching in a southern town was no longer an obscure happening in an isolated hamlet. A police assault on a parade of strikers no longer could be hidden behind the black and white prose of print journalism. The sounds and images were brought vividly into the homes of millions of Americans. By the last decade of the twentieth century the roving television news crew, supplemented by the amateur video cam, could trace the unraveling of civil order with such rapidity that it was almost impossible for any one individual to keep up.

Ethnic animosities became less severe within American society with the decline of immigration. The xenophobia that followed the First World War led to naturalization acts that limited the flow of arrivals from overseas. These immigration restrictions were aimed at freezing the ethnic composition of America at a ratio that existed before the great migration from southern and eastern Europe. Whatever the ethnic percentages, the effect was to make Euro-Americans more like each other as the second and third generations abandoned the culture of their parents and grandparents, intermarried, and merged their identities.

The growth of government intrusion into everyday lives, combined with the development of a mass communications market, contributed to the homogenization of American society and culture. Not all Americans shared equally in this new American order; African Americans, Latin Americans, Asian Americans, and Native Americans were excluded in various degrees from the mainstream. Yet this process helped to limit violent physical conflict and enabled government to deal more effectively with civil disorder.

During the 1930s and 1940s the decline in physical violence in rioting could be seen in labor relations, extremist politics, and ethnic conflict. Of these areas, the change was most dramatic in the labor movement, which lost its pariah status to become a bulwark of American politics. This shift was not easy, nor was it without some upheaval. Union efforts to organize workers met with stiff opposition in the opening years of the 1930s.

The initial difficulties of the labor movement during this period can be seen in the violence of 1934. Minneapolis, Toledo, and San Francisco each experienced strikes that led to the spilling of blood and revealed the militancy and the aggressiveness of both workers and agents of capital. To participants, America appeared on the brink of class warfare. In Minneapolis truckers went on strike in May and July, preventing all deliveries in the city. Initially union organizers maintained effective leadership and discipline over their cadres. On May 21 and 22, 1934, strikers routed a combined force of police and Citizen Alliance volunteers—businessmen who opposed the strike—in a succession of contests that left scores of wounded and at least two dead. Only a few of the truckers were hurt. The tables were turned in July when the police ambushed a group of pickets preventing a truck from rolling. In this bloodbath sixty-seven pickets were wounded, two fatally, and only one policeman injured. The same determination surfaced in the Autolite strike in Toledo. On May 23, company men and strikebreakers threw gas bombs and iron bits at six thousand strikers outside the plant. The pickets retaliated, hurled bricks, and broke into the factory at least twice during the seven-hour struggle. Arriving at dawn the next day to lift the siege, the national guard found themselves victims of the crowd's wrath. The rioters drove the guard back into the factory. Still hounded by the strikers, the guard fired, killing two and wounding others. That day, ten national guardsmen were treated for wounds inflicted by the rioters. Violence broke out repeatedly during the longshoremen's strike in San Francisco. Efforts to open selected sites on the waterfront met concerted resistance. On July 3, police attacked one area, killing a striker and wounding twenty others. On the fifth, 2 persons were killed and 115 wounded in a battle at Rincon Hill, and, as in several other strikes that year, the national guard had to be sent in.[1]

Although these violent strikes show continued conflict between officials and workers, and suggest that the situation had not changed from earlier years, there were some key differences. Minnesota Governor Floyd B. Olson sided with the strikers and ordered in state troops only to separate the combatants.[2] Authorities may have been less sympathetic in Ohio and California, but there were signs that the climate of opinion was changing. The militancy of the strikers showed the seriousness with which workers took their plight. The discipline and organization of the strikers were outstanding and accounted for some victories in the streets, even if their opponents continued to wield greater firepower. This combination of government acquiescence and labor discipline allowed strikers to alter strategies and pursue a less bellicose tactic—the sit-down.

Sit-downs are a mild form of rioting. Although strikers ideally strove not to physically harm any one, their action should be seen as an effort to assert their collective will immediately through the use of force outside the normal bounds of law. Any doubts about the coercive component of the sit-down disappear when we consider the violence that erupted when sit-downers were opposed by strikebreakers or the forces of law and order.

The temporary seizure of the means of production by workers was not a new technique in the 1930s. Steel workers at Homestead had occupied their plant during and immediately after their melee with the Pinkertons, and many other strikes in the intervening years included action similar to the sit-down. During the 1930s the sit-down increased in frequency and profile. The sit-down was useful because it allowed workers to focus their protest on property rather than physical violence and effectively stopped work by would-be scabs or replacements. Since officials refused to intercede on behalf of business, and with labor unions striving to maintain discipline and prevent the destruction of property, sit-downs became dramatic forums for union organizers to elicit public support. The first Depression-era sit-down was at the Austin, Minnesota, Hormel meatpacking factory in 1933. During the next few years there was a flutter of sporadic and short occupations of plants in the Midwest. Between 1936 and 1938 came the great age of sit-downs: 48 in 1936 involving 87,817 workers, 477 in 1937 involving 398,117 workers, and 52 in 1938 involving 28,749 workers.[3]

The most famous sit-down occurred at the General Motors (GM) plant in Flint, Michigan. The strike started on December 30, 1936, as a spinoff of labor disputes in Atlanta, Kansas City, and Cleveland. Although United Auto Worker (UAW) organizers had been planning for a strike in Michigan, and had evolved a strategy to concentrate on key installations that would cripple GM production, the strike at Flint almost caught them by surprise. Local conditions dictated the timing, but the union readily jumped into the fray and organized the one thousand or so workers that occupied Fisher Body No. 1 plant.

With UAW leaders maintaining sanitation and guaranteeing the safety of factory equipment, the situation was peaceful for almost two weeks. The company then decided to provoke a confrontation to bring the state in on its side. The strike had spread to a few other plants including the small Fisher No. 2. On January 11, 1937, company guards, who had hitherto stood passively at the gates, prevented the delivery of food, shut off the heat, and closed all contact between the men inside the plant and those outside. The union retaliated by taking control of the entrance. Twenty union men chased the guards into a washroom. When more police arrived they fired tear gas at the strikers and drove them into the factory. As luck would have it, the wind blew the gas back into the police ranks and, along with a fire hose manned by strikers, forced the police to retreat. A second assault followed that the union men met with brickbats and other projectiles. Although the police fired shots into the crowd, wounding about fourteen, the workers held their ground and the officers again withdrew, leaving the union to claim victory in the "Battle of the Running Bulls."

The violence persuaded Governor Frank Murphy he had to order the national guardsmen to Flint. Murphy, a New Deal Democrat, struggled to maintain a careful balancing act representative of government reaction to sit-downs in the 1930s. He wanted the strike settled, but not at the expense of the workers. He instructed the troops to do everything they could to avoid force and declared, "The state authorities will not take sides. They are here only to protect public peace . . . and for no other reason at all."[4]

Mob violence flared in Saginaw and Bay City, Michigan, when company thugs terrorized union organizers, and in Anderson, Indiana, pro-GM vigilantes beat unionists, drove off pickets at the Guide Lamp plant, and ransacked the local union headquarters. Fearing that they were losing the initiative, union leaders planned to occupy the strategic Chevrolet No. 4 plant in Flint. On February 1, union men stormed Chevrolet No. 9, drawing most of the company's guards into a fray. Then, after the workers in Chevrolet No. 6 joined the strike, the union men marched almost unopposed into Chevrolet No. 4. Capture of that engine factory ground GM production to a halt.[5]

The UAW strikers behaved in a manner that was to be typical of mid-twentieth-century rioting. They combined concerted and well-planned violence with the symbolic gesture of the sit-down. Although GM managed to obtain an injunction ordering the workers out of the plants, the governor refused to use the troops to enforce it. He did not want to go down in history as "bloody Murphy," and confessed to one friend that if he sent "those soldiers right in on the men ther'd be no telling how many would be killed." He added that such an action "would be inconsistent with everything I have stood for in my whole political life." The workers' determination, and the continued neutrality of government officials, ultimately convinced the company to give in, and an agreement was reached February 11.[6]

Sit-down strikes raised complicated issues concerning property rights. The sit-down was a violation of the law. When workers took over a factory and stopped the machinery they were denying the property rights of those capitalists who had invested their money in the plant. The strikers viewed the situation differently. They asserted, as their forebears had for generations, that they had property rights to the job in the factory, and insisted that they had to protect those rights through the formation of unions of their own choosing.

As important as the sit-down was in the developing legitimacy of the labor movement, the Supreme Court outlawed the practice, and reliance on it declined. Of more long-term significance was the ratification of the right to strike and to establish picket lines. This right was not obtained without bloodshed. In the Memorial Day massacre of 1937 Chicago police fired point blank into the crowd of pickets approaching a Republic Steel plant, and brutally clubbed individuals who fell. Ten died and scores were wounded. So outrageous was the police behavior that a newsreel that captured the atrocities was banned as too provocative until after a congressional investigation compelled its release. That newsreel did little to help the steel strikers in 1937, but stands today as a reminder of how ideas about collective action were changing.[7] In 1921 the Supreme Court had ruled that any picket was innately intimidating and therefore illegal. The court reversed this decision in 1940 in an opinion written by Supreme Court Justice and former Michigan governor Frank Murphy, who asserted that picketing was an expression of the right to freedom of speech and that any abridgement of that right was a violation of the First Amendment. This guarantee removed one of the areas of greatest contention and potential violence in labor and management relations. Combined with other developments, it helped to defuse an important arena of bloodletting among Americans.[8]

The decline of violence to persons that marked the labor movement occurred in other areas as well. During the 1930s and 1940s extremist politics still brought rioting crowds into action. The dire economic conditions of the Great Depression encouraged some Americans to ally with and join the communists, and red-baiting continued as an effective brush with which to tar an opponent. Yet the rioting associated with these conflicts now more often entailed symbolic gestures and rarely led to extensive physical violence.

In the countryside the political right and left were both busy during the 1930s. In the Midwest, farmers turned to rioting, with occasional flashes of personal physical violence. Wreaking havoc in the farm belt, the Depression drove prices down and threatened the tenuous hold farmers had on their land. Rising to that challenge, farmers opposed additional government intervention in livestock tuberculosis testing in 1931 and 1932. On September 21, 1931, 450 farmers at Wilton Junction, Iowa, drove off deputies trying to enforce a tuberculosis test on a dairy herd. In Iowa, Nebraska, Wisconsin, and other states, farmers, in order to raise prices, set up blockades to stop delivery trucks from bringing milk to the cities. Recalling the heritage of the American Revolution, some farmers asserted that they were reenacting the Boston Tea Party as they spilt the milk out on the highway. If opposed, however, they were willing to turn to blows. In May 1933 Wisconsin dairy men fought several pitched battles with the national guard, who arrested hundreds. The Farm Holiday Association, with some communist influence, encouraged and helped organize these milk strikes to drive up prices. Farmers also gathered at foreclosures to intimidate auctioneers and bank agents, either to prevent the sale or to guarantee an appropriate price. Most of these "Sears and Roebuck" sales went off with only threats, or with some ritualistic intimidation of an official. One crowd took a judge out of town, stripped him of his pants, and dumped a hubcap full of grease on his head. Although farmers avoided extremes of violence, they were not averse to some fighting. On April 27, 1933, six hundred farmers armed with clubs battled deputies to halt one bank sale. Despite serious bruises, no one appears to have been killed in these disturbances.[9]

Farmworkers in the South and West, influenced by leftists, often found themselves the victims of right-wing violence. Where political differences exacerbated already tense race relations, physical violence similar to earlier rioting might occur. In Arkansas, whites shot African-American sharecroppers in the Southern Tenants Farmers' Union and burned their homes and meeting places. Elsewhere, rioters acted with more care, centering their attacks on property. In California, vigilantes claimed to be purging the countryside of reds when they harassed union organizers, but they were also striving to keep wages down. Their tactics were simple: they warned newcomers, and if ignored they beat them. A crowd attacked Wilmer Breedon, an attorney defending union men, and two organizers near the courthouse in Brawley on May 14, 1934. They also slashed his tires, poured meal into the gas tank, and pushed his car out of the town.[10]

During the Great Depression many industrial workers had been attracted to radical politics, admired the Soviet Union, and joined the Communist Party. In San Francisco, Minneapolis, and Flint, opponents of union organization claimed to be protecting the American way of life against a communist threat. During the Little Steel strike of 1937 newspapers defended the Memorial Day massacre as an action against communists who planned to take over the country.[11]

Anticommunism became more virulent after the Second World War. But popular disturbances associated with red-baiting also were relatively nonviolent. The Communist Party planned an interracial concert for Peekskill, New York, in August 1949 featuring Paul Robeson. An anticommunist mob, burning a cross and using brass knuckles and clubs, assailed some early arrivals on August 27. Police intervened, escorted the victims out of the area, and canceled the performance. A few days later, on September 4, the communists held a second concert attended by twenty thousand blacks and whites. Although guards protected the picnic grounds, local police, legionnaires, and others clubbed and stoned cars and busses in a gauntlet, shouting racial, anti-Semitic, and anti-radical slurs and epithets. As vicious as these attacks seemed to concertgoers, the rioters, though they damaged property and injured a few people, killed no one.[12]

Cries that "the Jews are all Reds . . . and now they're getting what's coming to them" marked the Peekskill rioting, but during these same decades ethnicity became a less important reason for strife.[13] Ethnic rioting did not entirely disappear. During the 1930s gangs of Irish and German youths expressed their anti-Semitism in vandalism and harassment of Jews in the New York City neighborhoods of Washington Heights, the South Bronx, and Flatbush. The extent of violence of these attacks was nowhere near earlier ethnic conflicts.[14]

The most notable ethnic conflict of the mid century was the zoot suit riot of the Second World War in southern California, June 3 to 7, 1943. Off-duty servicemen claimed that they had been the victims of Mexican-American gangs and objected to the flagrant waste of wartime resources and rejection of mainstream values in the extravagant use of cloth in the zoot suit. Although over one hundred persons were injured, like many other disturbances in the period, violence was less than in previous rioting. The servicemen usually limited themselves to beating and then, in an act that highlighted their grievances, stripping the zoot suiters. In one case the symbolic and dramaturgical aspects of this rioting became manifest when the Mexican-American victim, shorn of his finery, was thrust onto a stage in a theater in his underwear.[15]

By the beginning of the 1950s, labor, political, and ethnic rioting had changed. The American servicemen assaulting zoot suiters in 1943 channeled most of their rage away from murder and mayhem. Instead, they often inflicted some bodily harm and removed the symbol of their grievances—the zoot suit. As intense as the rioters at Peekskill had been, they did not use firearms, nor did they murder. The victims viewed the behavior of the raging mob as horrifying and a break with civilization as well as a violation of civil liberties. Yet, in comparison with earlier incidents, the rioters were restrained. Labor rioters had begun to rely more on the picket line and courtroom than on physical coercion. Violence continued intermittently, but with the legitimization of the labor movement, and with the presence of a more benign and cooperative government, it now played a less significant role. Similar developments, on a different time schedule, can be seen in American race relations.

Black Revolt

On September 4, 1957, Elizabeth Eckford attempted to enroll at Central High School in Little Rock, Arkansas. With an air of unassuming dignity this young African-American woman walked through a huge crowd of heckling whites and was turned back by unsympathetic national guardsmen. This event, while only a small part of a larger movement for civil rights, signifies a major change in American history. The crowd outside Central High School called Elizabeth all kinds of names, spat on her, and threatened to lynch her. Yet they did not physically assault her. Here was a black person shattering the sacred southern color line. In years gone by the mere suggestion of such an act might bring down the most heinous retribution. By the 1950s the lynch mob, although not completely gone from the scene, was no longer quickly roused.

We will never know what prevented further violence. Amid the hundreds at the scene only a Jewish reporter from New York and an elderly white woman showed any sympathy for Elizabeth's plight. The presence of the Arkansas National Guard might have held the mob back. In other instances in other times, officials benignly looked in a different direction when it came to mob action in defense of southern racial honor. Moreover, no guardsmen so much as twitched a muscle to aid Elizabeth during her ordeal.

The drama, however, was played out before a national, even a world, audience. The affair at Little Rock was not an isolated event in a provincial backwater. News cameras and reporters captured every move of both Elizabeth and the segregationists. In the contest for this larger audience, although greatly outnumbered, Elizabeth won. For months afterward Elizabeth received letters of support from all over the globe. When Elizabeth, joined by eight other black students, reenrolled at Central later that month the reporters were again there. This time the crowd beat four reporters—a sign that racist whites understood the implications of the presence of the media—and officials withdrew the students for their own safety. Again, however, isolation was not possible. On the next day President Eisenhower federalized the national guard and sent paratroopers to guarantee that the nine African-American youths could proceed with their education.[16]

Something had changed in America to allow Little Rock to happen. The students knew all about racial repression. Elizabeth's mother vividly recalled that when she was young whites chased her off the street during a lynching and compelled her to hide in a friend's house. She remembered that she was close enough to the scene of the murder to "hear the screams of the mob" and "close enough to smell the sickening odor of burning flesh."[17] Yet in 1957 the students persisted in the face of intimidation and threats during the rest of the school year. Other blacks took similar action. African Americans challenged segregation across the South throughout the 1950s and into the 1960s. Rosa Parks refused to give up her seat on a bus in Montgomery, Alabama. And young blacks sat at lunch counters, made "freedom rides," and joined marches to force social change.[18]

Although catapulting onto the national scene in the late 1950s, this black revolt against segregation and discrimination had been going on for most of the twentieth century. The new identity and purpose among African Americans that came from the great migration and their participation in World War I, and that helped to spawn the race riots of the early twentieth century, also led to the Niagara Movement and the creation of the National Association for the Advancement of Colored People (NAACP). The NAACP took it upon itself to be the watchdog of American race relations, pointing out white hypocrisy and the glaring racist contradiction with democracy. That contradiction became even more trenchant during the Second World War when Americans confronted the racist doctrine of Nazi Germany and called upon African Americans to fight in the crusade against fascism.[19] In 1944 Swedish sociologist Gunnar Myrdal published his study of American race relations that highlighted the American dilemma of unequal treatment based upon race and an ideology based upon equality. Myrdal optimistically predicted a major alteration in American race relations. In the short run he was absolutely wrong; as the book worked its way to press the country experienced several brutal race riots. Over the long haul, however, he may have been correct, as America moved toward a world that allowed Elizabeth Eckford to attend a white school.[20]

This seismic shift in American society had an impact on rioting; as American race relations altered, the nature of collective violence changed. Two types of racial disturbance replaced vicious interracial warfare. The decline of the political terror of lynching allowed the rise of the civil rights movement. Blacks asserted and ultimately obtained a political voice of their own. Many racial disturbances now centered on political demonstrations in which the level of physical violence was lessened. The second type of racial disturbance has been called the ghetto riot. During World War II some race wars like those that had marred the early twentieth century took place. But this kind of violence was on the wane. Instead African Americans now rioted in their urban neighborhoods, expressing their resentment and rage by looting and destroying property.

Lynching had been a main instrument of racial repression in the United States. In 1911 the fledgling NAACP began studying mob violence, compiling statistics, sponsoring meetings, and engaging in public education concerning the cause of lynching. Repeatedly the NAACP sent investigators like Walter White into regions where lynching took place and then printed their findings in a national forum. Others joined this movement, including Ida B. Wells and Jesse Daniel Ames. The latter headed the Association of Southern Women for the Prevention of Lynching, an organization of white women that exploded the myth that lynching was to protect southern womanhood and that sought to influence law enforcement agents to intervene against lynching.[21]

Lynching declined after a high of 226 in 1892, and dropped precipitously after 1920. During the 1890s there was an average of 155 lynchings per year. In the opening decade of the twentieth century that average dropped to about 90, during the 1910s it was just under 70, and during the 1920s it reached under 30. In 1925 the *Literary Digest* announced the passing of Judge Lynch. The obituary was premature; some lynchings continued through the 1930s and 1940s and even into the 1960s. During the 1920s more lynchings were prevented every year than were allowed to occur.[22] Keeping the peace against lynchers could turn violent. In February 1920, Governor Edwin P. Morrow ordered the military to protect a black man in Lexington, Kentucky, accused of murder and possible sexual assault. The military fired upon the threatening crowd, killing five and wounding twenty others. Ironically the prisoner was soon tried, convicted, and executed to forestall further disorder. Despite the over-hasty legal process, the governor had made a strong statement for law and order, and against lynching.[23]

Change in official reactions to lynching was slow but steady, as southern politicians decided that it was necessary to maintain the sanctity of the law over ad hoc mob justice. During the 1930s several efforts to pass a federal anti-lynching bill were stymied by southern filibuster. The contest for public opinion, however, even in the South, was going the other way; polls suggested that southerners wanted an end to lynch law, and states passed their own legislation against Judge Lynch.[24]

A few spectacular cases helped to highlight public concern over lynching. The 1934 gruesome extralegal execution of Claude Neal brought national attention to the subject. Neal was taken from a jail in Alabama and whisked into Florida where a Committee of Six issued a schedule for the lynching. Newspapers printed and radios announced its timetable. The committee's statement declared that "All white folks are invited to the party." The crowd that attended the lynching numbered between 3,000 and 7,000, representing eleven southern states. The Florida governor was conveniently out of the capital, and the federal government refused to intervene. The lynching went off as advertised, fully reported by newsmen. The nation stood aghast as the descriptions of the brutality of the mob became public. "First they cut off his penis. He was made to eat it. Then they cut off his testicles and made him eat them. . . . Then they sliced his sides and stomach with knives and every now and then somebody would cut off a finger or a toe." He was burned with red-hot irons, hanged by the neck until he almost choked to death, and treated to other tortures. The lynchers dragged his body from an automobile to the front of his alleged victim's house. There, a woman came out and plunged a knife into his heart. His body was left hanging in the courthouse square of Marianna. Photographs of the victim went on sale, and parts of his body were put on display.[25]

Amid such reportage, lynching had a hard time justifying itself. Southerners seeking racial retribution still might turn to violence, but they had to move underground. There had long been some lynchings by small groups; starting in the 1930s whites resorted more frequently to lynching parties of only a half dozen and strove to maintain anonymity and avoid publicity. The secret nature of the murder of Emmet Till in 1955 illustrates the change. Till, a young African American from Chicago visiting relatives in Mississippi, made some inappropriate remarks to a white storekeeper's wife and gave a wolf-whistle. For this offense a handful of white men kidnaped and drowned him in a nearby river. The lynchers did not brag of the deed, and avoided prosecution.[26] The days of brazenly standing next to a lynched corpse for the photograph were over. Whites no longer held a monopoly of power. Lynching had become a crime that dictated anonymity. Crimes of anonymity indicated growing powerlessness.

Judge Lynch may have been gasping for his last breath, but he was not dead. On June 21, 1964, officials in Philadelphia, Mississippi, arrested three civil rights workers, two of them white, for speeding. The prisoners were later released to a waiting gang, who murdered and buried them in a nearby dam. Local whites resisted the investigation of this crime. Ultimately the federal government assigned 150 agents to the case and convicted seven members of the revived Ku Klux Klan on civil rights violations. While the Philadelphia murders were part of the racist violence that summer, the lynch-like quality of the action was unusual.[27]

The decline of lynching allowed the civil rights movement to expand in the 1950s and 1960s as black Americans asserted themselves into the segregated spheres of Jim Crow. This crusade confronted state-sanctioned violence in the guise of club-wielding policemen and individual violence from bombings. But the crowd activity associated with the civil rights movement was not as physically violent as earlier race conflicts.

Whites typically confined their actions to heckling, rock and bottle throwing, and the hurling of epithets. In February 1956, one thousand University of

Alabama students assembled outside a classroom attended by Autherine J. Lucy, a black graduate student. They taunted "Hey, hey, ho, ho, Autherine gotta go!" and tossed rocks and eggs at her car and the president's house until the president suspended her for her protection and the safety of the university. White mobs in 1960 assaulted blacks who sat down at segregated lunch counters across the South. Rioting broke out on February 23 and 24, in Chattanooga, Tennessee, at the S. H. Kress store. There were fights in Nashville a couple of days later, and within a few months disorder took place in Portsmouth, Virginia; Jacksonville, Florida; Biloxi, Mississippi; Greenville, South Carolina; and elsewhere. When the freedom riders toured the South in 1961 to desegregate busses and terminals, white mobs rioted in several locations but especially at Montgomery, Alabama on May 20 and 21. These mobs physically assaulted their targets, who sometimes sustained serious injury. Yet the violence was relatively mild when compared to the brutality perpetrated against Claude Neal.[28]

By the 1960s a new form of interracial conflict had emerged, similar to other political disturbances and labor confrontations, in which pickets, protestors, and marchers espousing one cause would confront opponents. Each might carry signs to advocate their cause. More often than not, they merely exchanged heated words, slurs, or obscenities. At times, they came to blows. Seldom would greater violence, leading to serious injuries or death, erupt.

If these political disturbances represent one kind of racial unrest in the mid twentieth century, the ghetto riot represents another. In the 1940s racial violence similar to the riots of World War I surfaced. At the same time a new type of rioting appeared within urban ghettos that emphasized the destruction of property rather than personal physical violence.

The Second World War was another watershed in American race relations. The experience and rhetoric of fighting for democracy had a major impact on African Americans. Blacks from the North were shuttled to military camps in the South for training. They were unaccustomed to Jim Crow ordinances and had an elevated self-esteem derived from donning an army uniform, so the situation was fraught with tension. Scores of confrontations and several older style race riots that led to fatalities broke out in and around military encampments.[29] On August 6, 1941, black soldiers compelled to ride on a Jim Crow bus in Fayetteville, North Carolina, fought with white military policemen. During the melee, one black and one white were killed, and a few others injured. In the spring of 1943 at least one person was killed when white and black soldiers battled in El Paso, Texas. Rumors at Camp Stewart, Georgia, that a white had raped a black woman, led to a riot among African-American soldiers that took two white battalions to quell in June 1943. On August 16, 1944, black soldiers at Camp Claibourne, Louisiana, mutinied, pinning down their white officers with gunfire, after word spread that a white mob had killed four blacks.[30]

Racial strife reached into the civilian world. The Social Science Institute at Fisk University reported 242 outbreaks of racial violence in 1943. This disorder included fights between ethnic groups and blacks in cities like Chicago, Philadelphia, and Buffalo and more serious disturbances with whites launching pogroms similar to the actions in Tulsa, Chicago, and East St. Louis two decades earlier. On May 25, 1943, white workers rioted when the Alabama Dry Dock and Shipbuilding Company in Mobile complied with federal regulations and gave twelve blacks skilled positions in the shipyard. The whites beat every black they could find and drove them off the job. Not quite a month later, allegations that a black raped a white woman set off a riot in Beaumont, Texas. Whites invaded the black section. Three people were killed in the fighting and hundreds injured, while as many as twenty-five hundred black workers fled the city.[31]

The most severe rioting, and the last of the classic race riots with extreme personal physical violence, took place in Detroit June 20–22, 1943. Youth groups from both races harassed one another on a Sunday afternoon on Belle Island, an amusement park contested by blacks and whites. Each side spread rumors about atrocities committed by the other. The combat escalated as roving bands assaulted any passerby of a different race. Streetcars were searched and passengers beaten and killed. Whites invaded black neighborhoods. Blacks fought back. By the time the police, eventually aided by the military, managed to quell the disturbance, 34 people, 25 of whom were black, were dead.

The Detroit riot of 1943, and the other racial disturbances of the period, had deeper causes than simply the rising expectations of African Americans during the Second World War. Detroit, like many northern cities, was a terminus of the great black exodus from the South. Blacks and working-class whites were thrown together competing for limited housing and for jobs. Wartime conditions only exacerbated preexisting tensions by bringing more whites and blacks to the city and offering the prospects of greater economic security for those who could obtain war production jobs. Identification of the Detroit rioters confirms these observations. As in any major riot, participants were recruited from a broad spectrum of society, including criminal and noncriminal elements. However, the typical Detroit rioter was a long-time resident—whether black or white—from the lower working class who acted from real and perceived grievances. African Americans resented daily repression in the face of promises offered by wartime economic and political opportunity. Whites resented the incursion into their lives of blacks who competed for housing and jobs.[32]

Even if by the 1940s these accumulated tensions could flare out in a violent riot reminiscent of early racial conflagrations, they already fostered less violent disturbances. Starting in the 1920s controversies over housing led to rioting in which the crowd was more restrained, often concentrating on property rather than on persons. White mobs in Detroit harassed Dr. Ossian Sweet, a black dentist, after he bought a house in a white neighborhood in 1925. The crowds threw stones and bottles, but never got more violent even though Sweet's brother shot one white threatening the property. Another Detroit disturbance broke out along a picket line to prevent blacks from moving into the federally funded Sojourner Truth Housing Project on February 28, 1942. In this case police acted as a restraining force, despite their own prejudice reflected in the arrest of more than two hundred blacks while leaving most whites unmolested. Although this riot included some street fighting there was little blood spilt. After the Second World War, rioting over housing took place in a few cities. Chicago and its suburbs experienced several disturbances to protect all-white enclaves, culminating in the Cicero riot of July 1951, when crowds ranging up to six thousand objected to the renting of an apartment to Harvey E. Clark, a black war veteran. Eventually they drove Clark off, invaded and wrecked the building, hauled his furniture into the street, and consumed it in a bonfire. The behavior of these rioters, like those who opposed civil rights, illustrated a crucial change in the nature of popular disorder. Mobs increasingly limited their sanguinary impulses and centered their action on the destruction of property.[33]

This change had even begun to appear among the African American rioters in Detroit in 1943. Although this disturbance fits the mold of earlier racial unrest, it also included a large amount of looting. Angered and frustrated by racial oppression, and eager to seek advantage in the moment of disorder, blacks destroyed and confiscated white property in black neighborhoods. This focus on property reflected the new trend in ghetto rioting first evident in the Harlem riots of 1935 and 1943.[34]

The parallels between the two Harlem riots, the urban rioting of the 1960s, and many ghetto disturbances since then is striking. Both the 1935 and 1943 riots started with a confrontation between blacks and the police. In 1935 Lino Rivera, a young black teenager, had been caught shoplifting in a five-and-dime department store. The police arrived on the scene, and, after a stern warning, let Rivera go. Rumors rapidly spread, however, that the police had killed the boy. When the police failed to dispel that story, Harlemites sought vengeance on the store and then demolished other white-owned stores. The riot lasted two days, during which one black died. Rioters destroyed two hundred shops and damaged two million dollars in property.[35] In 1943 a clash in a hotel lobby between Robert Bandy, a black soldier, and a policeman precipitated a riot. During the altercation the officer shot and wounded Bandy. Again the truth quickly became distorted and people said that Bandy, while in uniform, had been killed by the police. The streets became total confusion, with glass shattering, fires breaking out, and police struggling to gain control. Mayor Fiorello La Guardia, aware of the mistakes made by officials in the Detroit outbreak a few weeks before, ordered the police to minimize their use of violence, concentrated the officers in key areas, and isolated the district. With the help of several black leaders and a disciplined police force, La Guardia was able to quash the rioting by the next morning. However, almost 1,500 stores were looted and damaged, six persons were killed, and 550 persons were arrested.[36]

The riots of the ghetto revolt of the 1960s followed the same general pattern. Ordinarily there was some confrontation between blacks and the police, mutual misunderstandings escalated the conflict, and soon ghetto residents unleashed pent-up rage by looting and destroying property. The Los Angeles riot in Watts, August 11–16, 1965, began when a white state highway patrolman stopped a car on the suspicion that the driver was drunk. A crowd gathered and became unruly, and the rioting started. The Newark outbreak, July 12–17, 1967, commenced after the police arrested a black taxicab driver in the Central Ward. The driver scuffled with officers outside the police station. Witnesses reported, falsely as it turned out, that the cab driver had been killed. A crowd outside the police station threw rocks and soon the riot was on. In Detroit, July 23–30, 1967, a police raid on an after-hours club in the black section led to rumors of police brutality. Another crowd collected that soon smashed windows and looted stores. Several days of tumult followed.[37]

The Watts, Newark, and Detroit riots were only the most lethal of a series of disturbances. The sheer size of this disorder was outstanding. Between June 1963 and May 1968 the National Commission on the Causes and Prevention of Violence identified 239 separate urban riots involving at least 200,000 participants that led to 8,000 injuries and 190 deaths.[38] This rioting included the flurry of rage after the assassination of Martin Luther King on April 4, 1968, when there were disturbances in 125 cities across 28 states that led to 46 deaths. During this outbreak in Washington, D.C., there was rioting almost within the shadow of the White House.[39]

There can be little question that there was a contagion of disorder, just as in the 1760s and 1770s and the 1830s and 1840s, spreading across the land. Participants in these riots, largely African Americans but also including some Hispanics and others, had the added benefit of watching each other on television. The effectiveness of news coverage helped to spread knowledge not only of the disturbances, but also the methods of rioting.[40]

This wave of disorder distressed many Americans at the time since it seemed to shatter the consensus that so many believed held the society together. At first, these observers wanted to dismiss the rioting as the product of hoodlums and criminals who sought any advantage they could. More careful analysis indicates a link between the growing civil rights movement and the ghetto riots. Having observed the assault on institutional segregation in the South, the rioters in urban areas throughout the nation reminded whites of the de facto segregation that predominated elsewhere in America and that seemed to be preventing African Americans from escaping the inner city.[41]

The significance of police and civilian confrontations in the ghetto rioting only confirms the relationship between these disturbances and the civil rights movement. On one level the mutual antagonism between law officers and residents of the inner city revolved around day to day interaction. Both the largely white police force and the African-American urban dweller greeted each other with fear, suspicion, and hatred. The police struck out with acts of brutality and arbitrary law enforcement. Blacks in the cities responded with resistance and ultimately civil disorder. On a deeper level, however, the conflict centered on issues of social justice concerning equal treatment before the laws. African Americans believed that the police could abuse them because of the racism that infused American society and because full legal recourse was denied to them.

Several commissions established to investigate the root of all of this rioting went even further. The Kerner Commission proclaimed that the source of urban disorder was in the unequal treatment of blacks that created two societies: one suburban and white, the other urban and black. The bulk of this report examined education, housing, and job opportunities. From this perspective preventing riots was not a matter of more police, but of the need to correct racial injustice.[42]

For our understanding of rioting in American history we need to go beyond this liberal interpretation of social unrest and explore the various meanings of the riot activity. We can divide the behavior of participants in these ghetto riots into three categories—looting, arson, and physical assaults.

Looting became almost a ritualized affair in riots. It was more than mere opportunism—although that was a component. During the twentieth century America became a consumer-oriented society where the possession of "things" marked status and prestige. Looting took place in popular disorder before the Harlem riots of 1935, 1943, and the tumult of the 1960s. But the nature of looting assumed a different direction in these disturbances. Previously mobs might gut the home of a political enemy, or whites might sack houses of a black neighborhood. Now rioters looted stores. Rioters grabbed the chance to play at some supermarket game show to fill their shopping carts before the clock—the restoration of civil order—ran out. The resulting surreal atmosphere—a summertime Christmas to which some women brought their children—was more a statement about the nature of our consumer society than an expression of the lack of morality.[43]

Arson is an ancient crime perpetrated by the dispossessed. In the eighteenth and the early nineteenth centuries English laborers set fire to machinery that threatened their jobs. Enslaved African Americans utilized the torch to resist oppressive masters.[44] Arson, like looting, became common in mid twentieth-century popular disorder. During the 1960s middle-class whites sat agog as they watched television and wondered about those in the ghetto who set stores and apartments aflame. From the comfort of their living rooms such actions seemed self-defeating; the fires consumed businesses and homes that should be the life blood of the city. Many ghetto residents agreed. The fires, however, also represented a rejection of middle-class values that poor urbanites found constantly denied to them. The destruction of property was not the destruction of *their* property. Instead it was the destruction of property of some individual who lived outside the ghetto. The helplessness of civil authorities to deal with the repeated fires further fueled the message. The inadequacy of the fire department to quell the conflagrations empowered the powerless. Arson may have been a pathetic and misguided blow at a system of oppression; but it was a blow nonetheless.[45]

Despite the death toll in several larger disturbances, these ghetto riots were marked by a relative absence of violence committed by rioters against people. Careful examination of the casualty lists shows that the police and military inflicted the vast majority of fatalities and injuries on blacks in the riot areas. In Watts, 28 out of 34 killed were black; in Newark 24 out of 26 killed were black; and in Detroit 36 out of 43 killed were black. Most of those who died in the rioting after Martin Luther King was assassinated were also black. A more detailed breakdown is revealing. A little over a month after the Detroit outbreak, the *Detroit Free Press* provided a summary of the fatalities. Eighteen had been shot by the police, six had been killed by the national guard, and five had been slain by gunfire from either the police or national guard. Store owners shot two, private citizens (maybe some rioters) killed three, two looters died in a fire, two persons were electrocuted by fallen power lines, a paratrooper accidentally killed one, a policeman was shot while a fellow officer struggled with a prisoner, and three died of uncertain causes—either stray bullets, sniper fire, or another source. In other words, there were no verifiable deaths definitely attributed to the rioters themselves.[46]

Rioters inflicted personal physical violence in many of these disturbances. Blacks in Watts stopped some white motorists, beat them and burned their cars. No injury is to be dismissed lightly, yet, in these instances, whites were seldom killed. Crowds also interfered with firefighters, throwing rocks and preventing them from putting out fires lit by arsonists. There were also many confrontations between rioters and the police in which the crowd would throw bottles and rocks. In a few situations, a rioter fired shots. Sniping was reported in several disturbances, most notably in Newark and Detroit. *Life* magazine even interviewed a group that claimed to be organizing the sniping in Newark, and published a photograph of a sniper posing at a window.[47] During the Detroit riot officials reported that there were over one hundred active snipers. Yet in these disturbances, and others with supposed snipers, all of their gunfire had little net effect. Investigations after the fact suggest that the report of sniping was more the product of overactive imaginations by police and guardsmen, and a rationale for them to bring overwhelming firepower into play, than a reality.[48] Militant black groups, like the Black Panthers, were organized at the time and preaching black revolution. But they tended to practice what they preached in situations that did not include general collective action. In the final analysis, there may have been some sniping, but it was never a major component of rioting.

It is important to distinguish between perceptions at the time and later judgment. As city after city erupted into rioting, with flames destroying entire blocks, with airline schedules altered for fear a stray bullet might bring down a plane, and with looting pandemic, government looked powerless. The power of the state, however, was not in doubt. Repeatedly during the 1960s whenever anarchy threatened, the state or federal government stepped in. If there was a report of snipers, then in rolled the armored vehicles that peppered buildings with machine guns, ripping into apartments and striking innocents huddled in the security of their homes. In Newark over 1,500 persons—mostly black— were injured. If the looting was out of control for a few days, the state soon garnered the manpower and brought thousands into custody. The total of arrests was staggering. Between 1963 and 1968 at least 50,000 persons were arrested. Watts, Newark, and Detroit accounted for about one sixth of this total. A government that could arrest, hold, and process that army of individuals—even temporarily—over such a broad geographic landscape was not in jeopardy of disintegrating. Moreover, the greater the threat, the greater the response, as each level of government, local, state, and federal, came into play. During the uproar following King's assassination untold thousands of police were supplemented by 21,000 federal troops and 34,000 national guardsmen.[49]

By the late 1960s, then, two new patterns of rioting concerning race had become firmly entrenched. Within the inner city, the ghetto riot predominated, featuring looting, arson, and some physical violence. By the 1970s there was almost a set of rules that dictated behavior on the part of rioters and police officials. When a blackout struck New York City on July 13, 1977, a "party atmosphere" permeated the streets in a "shopping spree" where items were snatched from stores with broken windows. The police had orders to minimize violence and not to confront crowds when outnumbered. They often merely persuaded the rioters to go home, even allowing them to leave with their new possessions in hand.[50]

The second pattern of rioting also had ritualized aspects and at times overlapped with the first. Derived from the practices of the civil rights and labor movement, minorities had developed specialized tactics. These included picket lines, marches, and sit-ins. Usually such protests took place without any violence or threat of violence and were thus not riots. At times, however, when opposed by authorities, or by other groups, an exchange of punches, throwing rocks, shoving and pushing might follow. These two types of popular disorder persisted beyond the 1960s. Rituals of protest percolated into other areas of American society, and the rituals of ghetto rebellion continued sporadically to appear and reappear.

Movement on the Left

The new pattern of rioting belies the image of turmoil and violence of the 1960s. To understand the reality behind this image we need to distinguish between collective action in riots and other types of social conflict. In some areas of American society the violent image holds true. Political leaders were assassinated. Radicals employed terrorism in wild acts of sabotage and random shootings. The streets of American cities seemed to be more unsafe, and even a rural farmstead became the scene of murder and mayhem. Against this back-drop the pandemic of social protest, reflected in the glow of burning cities and amid the din of disrupted institutions, appeared as just another manifestation of a world unraveling at the seams.[51] Yet, despite the violence in other areas, most collective action at this time deemphasized personal physical harm and focused on the gesture symbolic of group discontent.

In the 1960s this trend held true for campus disorder and the antiwar crusade. Although the two movements were not identical, they became conflated in the second half of the decade and can therefore be considered together. There were several different sources of the student rebellion. Youths caught between adolescence and full adulthood, such as those who attended college, had a long tradition of challenging authority. There had been student riots in the colonial era, the Jacksonian era, and intermittently after that. Flooded by children born in the post–World War II baby boom and the affluence of the 1950s, it might almost be expected that students crowded into the newly expanded institutions of higher learning would rebel against something. The stultifying and moribund nature of American politics, locked into a Cold War mentality, provided an almost irresistible target.

Young radicals borrowed tools of collective resistance from both the labor and the civil rights movement. The Students for a Democratic Society (SDS) drew up their initial platform at the Port Huron, Michigan, retreat owned by the AFL-CIO, and student rebels consciously adopted the tactic of the sit-down from the labor unionists of the 1930s and the civil rights activists of the 1960s. Many student protestors in the early 1960s received their initiation into politics during the freedom summer of 1964 in the South.[52]

Popular disorder began innocently enough on college campuses with limited forms of collective action. In the fall of 1964 the administration of the University of California, Berkeley, decided to limit political agitation on Sproul Plaza. Student activists contested the prohibition of political discourse—especially concerning civil rights. During a protest over the ruling on October 1, police arrested Jack Weinberg, a former student working at a civil rights information table. Several hundred outraged students surrounded the police car holding Weinberg, and refused to allow it to leave. Student organizers, showing respect for law and order, removed their shoes, climbed to the top of the vehicle, and rallied supporters with speeches delivered with a megaphone. The sit-down lasted for thirty-two hours before administration officials and student leaders reached a compromise.

Two months later the free speech debate still raged on. Berkeley students decided that more direct nonviolent action was necessary. On December 2, over one thousand occupied Sproul Hall. Believing that the protestors were damaging offices, the police moved in at 3:00 a.m. Since the students passively resisted and had to be carried out, it took until after daylight, with some very rough handling, before a total of 773 were arrested. Publicity from the arrests helped to galvanize support, leading to a student strike and eventual capitulation by the university on the issue of free speech.[53]

The Berkeley battle became a benchmark for later student activists and established an important pattern. Students had succeeded in enforcing their will immediately through the seizure of property and the breaking of law. The crowd, whether surrounding a squad car or occupying a building, centered on the symbolic gesture. There was little physical violence here. What opened with civility, almost politeness, did not stay that way. In 1965 the war in Vietnam escalated dramatically, and SDS organized a march on Washington in April that drew 20,000 participants.[54] Protest became more frequent as the war raised the stakes for students and their opponents. Passions became inflamed. The level of violence also increased, but almost always within certain bounds—rioters continued to organize their behavior around property or actions that symbolically represented their grievances.

Starting in 1966, the pace of serious confrontations picked up when the army decided to remove deferments for some students and initiated tests to determine who would be drafted. Following well-worn patterns of limited collective action, one campus after another experienced disruption. Five hundred students at the University of Chicago took control of the administration building for three and one half days, closing it down. With student riots at the University of Wisconsin, City College of New York, Oberlin College, and elsewhere, like an uncontrollable epidemic, the "Berkeley situation" seemed to be spreading.[55]

Students discovered that the institutions of higher education provided support for the American war machine. Armed forces recruiters found themselves besieged by student activists who surrounded them and distributed pacifist literature and, at times, resorted to acts of intimidation. Dow Chemical Company also became a target since it produced napalm, the incendiary fluid dropped on Vietnamese villages. Sit-ins and protests objected to the presence of the Central Intelligence Agency, ROTC, and every government contract that might contribute to the development of weaponry.[56]

Antiwar organizers called for nationwide protests in October 1967. Rioting broke out in several locations, but the action remained largely confined to symbolic gestures. Protestors barred draftees from entering the Oakland, California, induction center on the sixteenth. On the next day a police force of four hundred routed up to three thousand marchers with clubs and chemical sprays, arresting twenty and injuring many more. On October 20, ten thousand Berkeley and Oakland activists took over the streets surrounding the induction center, blocking intersections by pushing parked cars into the street, slashing tires, strewing nails all over, and covering everything with slogans and graffiti. The rioters skirmished with over one thousand police for hours before being dispersed. Affrays on October 18 between police and a crowd of one thousand at the University of Wisconsin left seventy persons injured—mostly students—and several buildings damaged. On October 19, students clashed with police and occupied Brooklyn College's Boylan Hall to protest the presence of two navy recruiters. Police met about one hundred students from the University of Chicago, who tried to break into the windy city's induction center, arresting eighteen. Bottles and rocks might be thrown, but the overall level of violence remained low.[57]

The largest rally took place in the nation's capital, where as many as 150,000 peace advocates gathered on October 21 and 22. Both officials and organizers understood the basic ground rules of ritualized rebellion. Norman Mailer, who wrote the classic account of the event, described the respective positions as a compromise: "We, the government, wage the war in Vietnam for our security, but will permit your protest provided that it is only a little disorderly. The demonstrators: we still consider the war outrageous and will therefore break the law, but not very much."[58] Most participants sought to avoid violent confrontations. Their intention was to register their protest and show the extent of their opposition to the war. At least 30,000–35,000 joined in a march on the Pentagon. Again, most of those who crossed over the Arlington Bridge were not intent on breaking the law. Just standing outside the corridors of the heart of America's war machine, or sticking flowers into the barrel of a gun, was enough for them. Theirs was a symbolic act. So, too, was the behavior of the minority who sought to break the law in civil disobedience. Several thousand purposely crossed the lines demarcating the restricted areas despite the presence of federal marshals and soldiers. A few of these individuals exchanged blows with the guards. All were either driven back or arrested. By the end of the day 681 had been taken into custody; 13 marshals, 10 soldiers, and at least 24 demonstrators were wounded. That night, after the media had left, officials ordered the exterior of the Pentagon cleared and many more protestors suffered injuries.[59]

The march on Washington did not change anything. By the beginning of 1968 the chasm between college youths and their left allies on the one side and those in power and their centrist and right supporters on the other was getting wider. The 1968 Tet offensive in Vietnam may have ended with an American victory after weeks of bitter fighting, but the extent of the offensive, the capture of Hue, and the fighting outside the American embassy in Saigon indicated that the United States was not going to win the war. Student radicals were ready for another step away from the civility of Berkeley in 1964.

That step came at Columbia University where a group bent on more direct action took over the leadership of SDS in the spring of 1968. But even these radicals avoided extremes of violence. The protest joined domestic and foreign policy issues; the SDS and radical black students opposed the construction of a gymnasium near Harlem that seemed to ignore the needs of blacks in the area, and they denounced the university ties with the Institute for Defense Analysis. On April 23, after being rebuffed at the construction site by police, the students occupied university buildings. Over one thousand students encamped in five buildings, trashed some offices, held a dean hostage, and set up self-governing communes. Officials suspended classes and then decided to allow the New York City police to clear the buildings on the night of April 29. The police did so with billy clubs swinging, injuring 132 students and four faculty. In the melee twelve police were also hurt. After more clashes on May 1, the faculty voted on May 5 to end classes for the year. The students thought that the "revolution" had begun, but as in earlier confrontations they had merely occupied property and destroyed symbols of what they perceived as a reactionary institution—symbols that included the notes of one history professor's unwritten book. Yet SDS had succeeded in closing the university, and soon other radicals called for "two, three, many Columbias."[60]

At Columbia, it was the forces of law and order that had inflicted the greatest personal physical damage. By 1968 this violence had assumed a definite pattern that revealed the relative strength of officials and protestors. Observers felt impotent at the inability of administrators to stop the occupation of buildings and to control protest, but ultimately government wielded the greater power. Nowhere was this fact in more evidence than during the Democratic National Convention in August 1968.

Faith in the normal political channels ebbed in 1968 in the wake of the assassinations of Robert Kennedy and Martin Luther King and the failed nomination bid of Eugene McCarthy. Although Lyndon Johnson was stepping down, in the weeks before the convention the Democratic Party seemed committed to Hubert Humphrey and a continuation of administration policy. Radicals on the left hoped at least to proclaim their opposition to this trend by a call for demonstrations during the Democratic Convention in Chicago. Mayor Richard Daley made it clear that he was not going to tolerate a hippie takeover of public spaces and threatened to meet protestors with force. This promised confrontation caused many to shy away from Chicago. Others came prepared to take on the "pigs" of Chicago's police force.

The so-called Chicago riots were a bizarre combination of police excess and radicals engaging in the theater of the absurd. Some groups, like the Yippies, had decided to provoke the police, rehearsed tactics, and even donned football helmets, coated themselves with vaseline, and sported athletic cups for special protection. The battles that followed—if the overwhelming use of police force against crowds pelting rocks, bottles, and bags of urine and feces can be called a battle—were a disaster for all involved. The fighting began on August 25 when the police ordered the crowd out of Lincoln Park at 10:30 p.m. during the Yippie "Festival of Life." The police met the obscenities and objects thrown at them with unleashed fury, smashing into the assembled masses with a covering of tear gas, clubs swinging and mace spraying. The police also broke up an intended march toward the loop.

What had happened the first day, with slight variations, continued the rest of the week. Police, sometimes aided by the national guard, charged protestors when they desecrated a statue, flag, or another symbol, or attempted an unlicensed march. Late at night the police might also sweep through Lincoln or Grant Park, or other public space, to clear it of protestors. Demonstrators fought in a disorganized and ineffective fashion. A total of 192 police reported injuries—mostly minor—from August 25 to August 30. Rioters damaged 81 police vehicles; 24 windshields were shattered, 17 cars were dented from stones thrown, some side windows were broken, aerials snapped, and paint splattered on cars. No vehicle was put out of commission. As Todd Gitlin, an SDS leader who wrote a history of the sixties, put it: "Viewed on a revolutionary scale, of course, this was penny-ante stuff."[61]

For participants at the time, however, Chicago was high drama. Tom Hayden, after being arrested twice, started to wear disguises, shuttling from group to group encouraging resistance. Many of those in the crowd watching and experiencing the police beatings—over one hundred civilian victims were hospitalized—became convinced that the United States was a police state. When a police charge drove a retreating mass of protestors, onlookers, and passersby through a large plate glass window of a fashionable bar in the Hilton Hotel, the crowd chanted "The Whole World Is Watching! The Whole World Is Watching! The Whole World Is Watching!" To many it seemed that America was at the brink of revolution.[62]

Over the next two years the student and antiwar movement radicalized even further. The SDS splintered and one group, the Weathermen, started to advocate greater violence. In October 1969 they staged a brief comeback in Chicago in "Days of Rage." They garnered little support. Three hundred Weathermen destroyed property and fought police. Despite the Weathermen's added pads and protection, the police were able to strike back with fervor, shooting six, beating most of the rest, and arresting about two hundred fifty. The revolutionaries were no match for the government. Extremists went underground to plot the overthrow of their enemies, turning away from collective action, and engaged in terrorism. Typical of the politically impotent, the bomb became the weapon of choice. Radicals had a lethal reminder of the dangers of pursuing this path when in March 1970 three Weathermen accidentally blew themselves up in an apartment in Greenwich Village.[63]

Campuses meanwhile continued in turmoil. All across the nation one college and university after another was disrupted by demonstrations, sit-ins, and even bombings. A few examples, out of hundreds, reveal the nature of this activity. On March 19, 1969, students at the State University of New York, Buffalo, attacked the construction site of the Project Themis research facility, identified as military connected. They demolished sheds, shattered windows, and then occupied Hayes Hall. In October on the same campus, a hundred SDS and other radicals ransacked the Air Force ROTC office, burning files, books, and equipment in a giant bonfire. Harvard students seized University Hall on April 9, 1969, forcibly ejecting nine university deans, in protest of the presence of ROTC on campus. About a hundred African-American students took over the student union building at Cornell University on April 19, 1969. When a group of fraternity boys tried to eject them, the blacks armed themselves with rifles. After thirty-six hours of occupation officials negotiated a settlement, and the black students emerged to a chilled national audience with their weapons in hand.[64]

If students intensified their assault on property and became more antagonistic to authority, the forces of law and order reacted accordingly. Most of the collective action continued to follow the pattern of behavior of limited attacks on property, although both sides seemed to threaten greater physical violence. On May 15, 1969, Berkeley officials ordered a fence built around an open area proclaimed by students and local residents as a "People's Park." Two to six thousand marched in protest, but were intercepted by police. When the crowd threw various missiles, the officers retaliated with tear gas, then bird shot, and then buck shot. At least 110 persons were injured and one died of his wounds. One student was killed during an exchange of gunfire between black students and police and national guardsmen at North Carolina Agricultural and Technical University in Greensboro on May 22, 1969. Students from the University of California, Santa Barbara, burned a Bank of America branch on February 25, 1970, as a symbol of capitalist society. More disorder broke out near the campus on April 18, 1970, and a student was slain by a stray bullet fired by a policeman.[65]

Then came May 1970. On April 30 President Nixon announced that American forces had invaded Cambodia. Antiwar protest broke out across the country and students firebombed ROTC offices at Maryland, Michigan State, Washington, Wisconsin, and Yale.[66] Thousands of national guardsmen were ordered to contain the protest and destruction of property. On one obscure campus the guardsmen struck with unexpected fury. Students at Kent State University, Ohio, had rampaged the local downtown area, set fire to the ROTC building, and obstructed town traffic with a sit-in at a major intersection. On May 4 student leaders called an antiwar rally despite the occupying troops. Firing tear gas and brandishing bayonets, the guardsmen broke up the meeting, but could not disperse all of the crowds milling about. A few student activists hurled stones, shouted names and obscenities, and even heaved some canisters of tear gas back at the guard. In response to these taunts, Troop G of the Ohio National Guard turned and fired into the crowd of students. After they had expended sixty-one rounds, four students were dead and nine wounded.[67]

Kent State led to a paroxysm of disorder that makes all that had gone before pale in comparison. One estimate claims that protest occurred at 1,350 institutions of higher learning and included 4,350,000 participants.[68] Rather than face further disruptions over four hundred schools simply shut down for the rest of the year. The president may have believed that "When dissent turns to violence, it invites tragedy," but many students held that the response of the officials was out of proportion to the stimuli. As if to ratify that judgment, police opened fire on a dormitory at Jackson State College on the night of May 14, killing two black students, and two other youths were killed in a disturbance in Lawrence, Kansas, in July.[69]

Despite the emotion of the spring of 1970, the basic patterns of the student rebellion remained largely the same. Students continued to occupy property or express themselves with symbolic gestures even when confronted by the violence of the agents of law and order. In one photograph of the shooting at Kent State a student can be seen displaying his middle finger as the guardsmen kneeled down, aimed, and fired. Pictures taken at Kent State fully document the day's disorder; nowhere are students doing anything more threatening than hurling a few stones and canisters of tear gas.[70] The casualty figures revealed the relative ability to inflict physical harm by the guard and the students.

The outrage felt on other campuses made many believe that they stood at a unique and important crossroads of history. Kent State was not unique. Although workers, as revealed in an assault by hard hats on protestors on Wall Street on May 8, may have been hostile to the new left, the union movement itself had experienced the wrath of unbridled police at the Memorial Day Massacre in 1937, at Haymarket in 1886, and at Tompkins Square in 1874.[71] The historical parallels go back further than that to the harassed parcel of British redcoats who fired on a body of youths and others hurling ice and rocks in the King Street riot of March 5, 1770. If the moment was not unique, it was also not at the crossroads that many believed. After 1770 the British had made the mistake of not fully incorporating the dissidents into the political system. American officials made the same mistake with labor organizers until the 1930s. By 1970 the government was already accommodating the student rebellion and peace movement. While progress was slow, the United States by that time was committed to pulling out of Vietnam. President Nixon soon inaugurated a lottery system to make the draft more equitable and moved toward its total abolition in the 1970s. In 1972 the Democratic Party proclaimed its allegiance to those on the left with the nomination of George McGovern and went down in glaring defeat. Following the spring of 1970, students continued to protest and even riot, but after Kent State, all of this activity was anticlimactic.

Ritualized Rebellion

Americans did not stop rioting after 1970. As the decade wore on disturbances became less frequent, and the United States seemed to retreat from the abyss that had been ready to engulf it. Yet riots broke out. The popular disorder of the 1970s, 1980s, and 1990s continued to follow the forms of ritualized rebellion that had surfaced in labor and other areas in the 1930s and 1940s and in the black revolt and the student and antiwar movements in the 1960s. In some cases, the mode of behavior became so regularized that many no longer considered the collective action a riot. Previous generations would have labeled as rioting the occupation of property by members of the antinuclear movement in New Hampshire, but this behavior was now called "nonviolent direct action." Opponents of abortion, generally recruited from white middle America, also created disturbances that if committed by blacks would have been considered rioting. Many groups took to the street to advocate their causes, sometimes leading to civil disorder. The patterns of popular upheaval established by the black revolt persisted in racial strife and intermittent ghetto rioting from the 1970s to the 1990s.

Reminiscent of the student campus unrest of the 1960s, the lunch counter campaign of 1960, and the labor strikes of the 1930s, the Clamshell Alliance of New England on August 1, 1976, occupied the construction site of the Seabrook nuclear power plant in New Hampshire. The first few activists, a total of eighteen, were quickly arrested. On August 22 a larger party of 180 were also arrested. Several months later, after much organization and "training," on the weekend of April 30 and May 1 about 2,400 people marched onto the site with tents and sleeping bags and set up their own village. When the encampment awoke Sunday morning, they found themselves surrounded by national guardsmen. Both sides understood their roles. Officials gave the protestors twenty minutes to leave the property. About one thousand left. The other 1,400 were then herded onto buses and placed under arrest. Although neither side perpetrated any physical violence to persons or property, the members of the Clamshell Alliance had attempted to enforce their will immediately outside the normal channels of law. In October 1979, some more fervent opponents of the power plant even cut down fences.

The example provided by the Clamshell Alliance was picked up by other antinuclear groups, especially on the West Coast. The Abalone Alliance organized antinuclear and antiwar activities, including rallies outside the Diablo nuclear plant in August 1977 where they tried to occupy the building. During two weeks in September 1981 protestors blockaded Diablo and police arrested

1,900. The Livermore Action Group planned to shut down the production of nuclear weapons at the Lawrence Livermore National Laboratory. On Mother's Day 1982, women armed with teddy bears sat down on the highway outside Livermore, preventing traffic from entering or leaving. Four women even chained themselves to the front gate. The group also took action against Vandenberg Air Force Base, and in March 1983, police arrested 777 protestors who hiked through the back country to occupy military property.[72]

Although antiabortion advocates generally came from the opposite end of the political spectrum as the antinuclear advocates, some pro-life supporters practiced many of the same tactics during the 1980s. In particular Operation Rescue, founded by Randall Terry in 1986, blocked abortion clinics and harassed their clients and workers. During the summer of 1988 the organization undertook the "siege" of Atlanta, the site of the Democratic National Convention. Terry called prayer meetings the night before a "rescue," and rendezvoused with his warriors the next morning. His supporters descended upon a clinic, barring entrances and swamping the waiting room. In twenty-four rescues over four months, Atlanta police arrested 1,235. These contests continued across the nation. Operation Rescue targeted Wichita, Kansas, in the summer of 1991, where officials arrested two thousand people at clinics. Few would call any of these demonstrations riots, yet there was a definite parallel to early sit-ins and civil disobedience of students and African Americans considered so threatening in the 1960s.[73]

Assertion of political rights by fringe groups sometimes elicited popular disorder. The gay pride movement made the June 27, 1969, Stonewall riot a symbol of their new public identity, holding annual parades celebrating its anniversary. In the riot about four hundred homosexuals hurled coins, beer bottles, and some bricks at police who had just raided the Stonewall Inn and arrested the bartender, doorman, and three transvestites. Most gay protests were tame affairs, but on a few instances, such as a sit-down at St. Patrick's Cathedral in 1974 or the disruption of a New York meeting of the Association for the Advancement of Behavioral Therapy for using aversion therapy on homosexuals, more forceful but nonviolent action was taken. Moreover, the visibility of the gay pride movement brought greater publicity to incidents of crowd gay bashing.[74]

The women's movement, too, became more assertive. Pro-choice activists confronted pro-life forces at clinic "rescues," exchanging words and sometimes blows. Many women joined the peace campaigns of the 1970s and 1980s. During the summer of 1983 several thousand gathered at Seneca Falls, New York, and some activists sat down at the gate of the local army depot that contained cruise missiles destined for Europe. Local residents, objecting to lesbians at Seneca Falls and disliking the challenge to the army, stopped a "walk for peace" through Waterloo on July 30. The women marchers sat down in the highway and were arrested. Later, townsfolk assaulted another group of women holding a vigil for those placed in custody after the sit-down. On

August 1, the national guard was ordered to protect another march by women.[75]

During the same period labor unions experienced a series of reverses and decline in membership. Workers, who had relied on collective action since the 1930s, continued to do so. Although there were times when guns came into play, such as during a coal strike in West Virginia in the summer of 1989, much of this activity followed the patterns of ritual rebellion. Coal strikers built barricades to prevent nonunion workers from proceeding, and attempted to control mining equipment. In September of the same year a crowd of four hundred protesting the hiring of nonunion labor at a Boise-Cascade paper mill in Minnesota burned temporary housing, overturned cars, and threw stones at guards. Thirty-two persons were arrested as police used tear gas to disperse the rioters. In the 1990s newspaper delivery strikes in New York and Pittsburgh also led to collective violence. During the Pittsburgh strike in late July 1992, union workers and their supporters beat some scab drivers and burned their newspapers.[76]

The largest source of popular disorder in this era remained the issues of race and ethnicity. However, even in this emotion-packed area, the essential patterns of late-twentieth-century rioting were generally maintained. In Boston, for instance, whites and blacks fought over desegregation of schools and bussing from 1974 to 1976. White crowds stoned busses carrying black children into neighborhoods like the Irish-dominated South Boston. At times greater violence flared, as on October 7, 1974, when a crowd of five hundred whites, crying for a lynching, beat but did not kill Haitian-born Andre Yvon Jean-Louis. Whites also fought blacks in the high schools. A more violent incident occurred after whites peppered a black housing project with bullets on April 19, 1976. Young African Americans retaliated by disrupting Amtrak service and severely beating a white driving near the projects. Although these actions included some physical violence and are not to be slighted, they fall shy of the type of murder and slaughter that accompanied disturbances of the earlier twentieth century.[77]

In part as a reaction to the successes of the civil rights movement, white racists organized groups like a resurgent Ku Klux Klan and the American Nazi Party. This development was not unopposed. At Camp Pendleton, California, on December 6, 1976, picketers assaulted David Duke, leader of the renewed Klan. Six were wounded in the disturbance, and fourteen blacks arrested. On July 4, 1977, Klansmen and hecklers clashed in Columbus, Ohio, and Mobile, Alabama, on September 24, 1977. Protestors harassed the American Nazi Party in San Jose, California, on October 8, 1977, in St. Louis, Missouri, on March 11, 1978, and elsewhere. Civil rights supporters also came under attack. Whites harassed black protestors in Chicago's Marquette Park on July 23, 1977, and the KKK assailed civil rights marchers in Decatur, Alabama, on May 26, 1979, wounding four. Although some of these incidents led to arrests and a few injuries, the level of violence was low.[78]

The most bloody of these confrontations, and an exception to the general pattern, took place at Greensboro, North Carolina, on November 3, 1979. Extremes of physical violence occur when either the government fails to step in and mediate between two groups, or when mutual hatreds are so intense that each group denies the legitimacy of the other. Both situations pertained in the Greensboro killings. In late-twentieth-century America it would be hard to find two more mutually antagonistic groups than the forces that met in Greensboro. On the one hand was the Communist Workers Party composed of some whites, many of whom were Jewish and from the urban North, and blacks. On the other were southern crackers who advocated white supremacy in the Klan and American Nazi Party. In a rally at China Grove earlier that year, the communists had faced down their racist opponents. Both sides, however, had brought guns, and only the interposition of the police avoided a bloodbath. There was no such luck on November 3. The communists were marching in a "death to the Klan" rally when a caravan of white supremists pulled up. After both sides exchanged words and then blows, the racists opened fire, killing four and wounding eight (one of the wounded died later).[79]

More typical, and based upon the civil rights activities of the 1960s, was the experience of the blacks who marched through nearly all-white Forsyth County, Georgia, in January 1987. Hundreds of Klan supporters threw rocks, heckled, and threatened about sixty blacks on the seventeenth, compelling them to abandon their march. The next week twenty thousand marchers, protected by sheer numbers and the police, swamped the county in protest. Civil rights workers sued the KKK, won a one million dollar settlement, and forced the Klan to give up the right to its name.[80]

Another legacy of the sixties was the ghetto riot. The ordeal of the long hot summer in which city after city exploded with looting, arson, and some physical violence, had ended, but as the New York City blackout riot of 1977 reminded Americans, rioting could burst onto the urban scene at almost any given moment. Miami experienced several episodes of disorder that fit the ghetto riot pattern. From May 17 to 19, 1980, blacks vandalized and looted stores and assaulted some whites in reaction to an all-white Tampa jury acquitting four policemen charged with shooting a black. The disturbance included some unusually violent action: the rioters beat to death three whites, but officials killed eleven blacks as 3,600 guardsmen were called in and nearly 1,000 blacks arrested. In late December 1982, there were three days of rioting in the black Overtown district after a Hispanic policeman shot a black youth who was working as a messenger. Rioters overturned cars, looted stores, and threw bottles and rocks. One black was killed, twenty-six persons were injured, forty-three were arrested. After an all-white jury acquitted the Hispanic officer from the 1982 case, looting and property destruction broke out in March 1984. In January 1989 a fourth major riot erupted after another Hispanic officer shot and killed a black motorcyclist.[81]

Other ethnic groups might behave in a similar manner. On June 17–19, 1975, Cubans in Elizabeth, New Jersey, fought with police after the arrest of two Cubans in a traffic incident. The rioters destroyed two cars, but only seven people were injured and 143 arrested. On June 4, 1977, police and Puerto Ricans clashed in Humboldt Park, Illinois. One man shot at the police. They returned fire and killed him. Forty-nine people were injured in subsequent rioting. In mid May 1991, rioters burned vehicles, looted stores, and threw molotov cocktails in Washington, D.C., for two nights after a policeman shot a Hispanic. A similar incident caused a riot among Dominican Americans in New York City in July 1992. As many as one thousand people overturned cars, smashed windows, littered the street, set fire to three buildings, and blocked traffic to the George Washington Bridge.[82]

So ingrained did the pattern of looting and the destruction of property become, that there was almost a built-in assumption that in certain situations, like during the New York City blackout, it was permissible to put the normal rules of society aside and enjoy a moment of disorder. Detroit suffered through repeated "nights of the devil" on Halloween, as inner city residents vented their frustration and animosity in a wave of arson-ignited fires. Extensive vandalism occurred in other communities on the same holiday. Celebrants of sports victories trashed downtowns and broke into bouts of looting and arson, as happened in Chicago in June 1992 after the Bulls won the National Basketball Association championship. Any demonstration, such as in Vineland, New Jersey, in August 1989 could lead to looting and vandalism. Even gatherings of youths at the beach might follow the same pattern of rioting. The annual Labor Day black greek fest at Virginia Beach in 1989 was disrupted by rioting that included the looting of one hundred businesses and the calling out of the national guard.[83]

There persisted in these years the potential for greater personal violence, especially in the inner cities. Economic and social change had left many urban areas ravaged as a decline in manufacturing, combined with white flight into suburbia, expanded ghettos populated by the poor and disenfranchised. Crime and violence seemed to increase, and youth gangs turned to drug dealing and fighting over turf. Groups like the "crips" and "bloods" fit into a hazy area between organized crime and popular disorder. At times, urban youths participated in more extemporaneous and senseless behavior like the "wilding" party of April 19, 1989, when thirty teenagers from East Harlem rampaged through Central Park, molesting at least nine persons, and beating and raping a twenty-eight-year-old investment banker as she was jogging.[84]

Within the confines of many cities ethnic and racial friction also intensified. When a Hasidic Jew ran over and killed a black girl in Brooklyn in August 1991, four days of rioting followed, including the stabbing death of one member of the Hasidim. In Howard Beach, Queens, whites chased a black youth on December 20, 1986, onto a highway where he was struck by a car and killed. On August 23, 1989, a mob of white youths ambushed three blacks in Bensonhurst, Brooklyn, shooting and killing one. Almost a year later, mutual antagonism between Korean Americans and African Americans in New York flared into a bloody assault by black youths, armed with bats, knives, and bottles on three Vietnamese men they believed were Korean.[85]

The Los Angeles riot of April 30–May 2, 1992, with a death toll of almost sixty that ranks it as one of the bloodiest upheavals in American history, must be seen against the backdrop of the larger trends of popular disorder in the second half of the twentieth century. On one level the riot fit the pattern of ghetto disorder established in Harlem in the 1930s. On another, it contained elements that suggested the potential for more bloodshed and a return to the violent patterns that had marred so much of the United States past.[86]

The riot opened, not surprisingly, in reaction to perceived injustice and bad police-civilian relations. The acquittal of the four officers who beat Rodney King reminded African Americans of just how vulnerable they were to police abuse. Many believed that if a videotape of the beating did not lead to a conviction in court, justice could not be obtained for blacks. News of the acquittal set the crowds in South Central Los Angeles into motion. The slow response of the police was a signal that a free-for-all could begin. Moreover, just as in the sixties, there was a certain contagious element to the disturbance. Not only did the rioting spread through large sections of Los Angeles, joined by many Hispanics who shared African-American grievances, but across the nation about thirty other disturbances flared. The locations of these other riots ranged from big cities like Atlanta, San Francisco, and Seattle, to small cities and towns like Springfield, Illinois; Ames, Iowa; and New Rochelle, New York.[87]

Most of the action in the Los Angeles riot was confined to the three key elements of almost every ghetto riot: looting, arson, and some physical assaults. The looting allowed participants to obtain goods and strike out at merchants whom they believed sought undue profits. The arson served as a cover for theft and a signal of anarchy, and empowered the powerless by revealing the impotence of government in the face of too many conflagrations. Even the physical assaults contained symbolic meanings. One of the most potent and frightening visual images from the riot was the beating of white trucker Reginald Denny by four blacks. As it was taped from a circling helicopter, Americans watched live, and then in countless news reports, the pummeling that Denny experienced. As frightful as this attack was, it was also oddly reminiscent of the video of the police assault on King. Change the color of the skin on Denny's assailants, put uniforms on them, and it would be difficult to tell the two crimes apart. It was classic role reversal.

The level of physical violence, however, might suggest that the Los Angeles riot deviated from recent patterns where there had been a relative absence of violence against people. Despite fatalities, however, the Los Angeles riot was not that great of an exception. The loss of even one life is a tragedy. So, too, is the assault on any individual. But the actual death toll definitely attributable to the rioters was under twenty. The police killed at least half that many, and probably many more. The cause of the other fatalities is unclear. Some may have been murdered by rioters; others by the police. Several incidental deaths—heart attack victims, individuals who died in a car accident, and a fireman killed while fighting a fire—have been included in the death count. Moreover, although some whites and Korean Americans were killed, the vast majority of fatalities were African Americans and Hispanic Americans who died as bystanders or as rioters opposing civil authorities.[88]

If most rioters damaged property through looting and arson, some did not. There were incidents of greater physical violence such as drive-by shootings, beatings that led to death, and gun battles between police and rioters. In several cases, unlike in many other riots, gangs took an active part. Moreover, rioters expressed severe ethnic animosity against Asians. These confrontations have serious implications; when rioters threatened their property, Korean Americans stood poised to protect their stores and businesses with force of their own. Although this violence was not unprecedented among recent disturbances, it threatened to go beyond earlier levels and bring on interethnic war not seen in the United States since the beginning of the twentieth century.[89]

During the twentieth century rioting underwent a subtle and gradual change. Starting with labor, ethnic, and political conflict in the 1930s and 1940s, rioters began to emphasize attacks on property or physical assaults that fell short of extremes. Sit-downs and destruction of material goods that represented the grievances of the crowd emerged as the tactics of choice. A victim might be beaten, harassed, or humiliated, but he was now seldom killed. By the 1950s these trends can be detected in race relations. Lynching did not disappear, but it had declined precipitously. African Americans asserted themselves by occupying lunch counters and insisting on equal treatment in public facilities. Some violence broke out when whites opposed these efforts, but these skirmishes generally occurred on picket lines, in the glare of a national audience, and hardly ever led to fatalities. Black and white stopped fighting with one another in racial warfare after the 1940s. Instead, beginning in 1935, and peaking in the 1960s, urban African Americans registered their protest and frustration with the police, the politicians, and the exploitive economic system in a flurry of looting, arson, and some assaults within the ghettos that confined them. The sixties were also marked by a youth rebellion that included antiwar protest and campus unrest. This new politics of the left divided Americans and created a crisis in American society and culture. But the challenge posed by all this upheaval followed the patterns of collective action that marked the second half of the twentieth century—limited physical violence and a preoccupation with seizing, desecrating, or even destroying property.

By the 1970s and 1980s crowds knew all too well the rituals of rebellion established in the middle of the twentieth century. The level of civility dictated a change in vocabulary. Most individuals involved in collective action that previous generations would have labeled as a riot, were no longer called members of a "mob." Instead they became "protestors" who had a legitimate right to march, picket, and demonstrate. The powers of the state and the members of the crowd understood the rules of the game even when the crowd decided to break the law by occupying property, sitting down to obstruct traffic, or threatening violence. Ghetto riots, too, assumed a standardized pattern in which license was granted to loot stores, while officials combated arson and the threats of assault.

Some riots in this period do not fit the standard mold. As has been true throughout American history, generalizations cannot apply in every case. Riots remained a passionate experience that could explode in unanticipated directions. Ethnic and racial conflict in places like New York City, Miami, and Los Angeles at times seemed ready to come boiling to the surface and threaten a resurgence of greater physical violence.

EPILOGUE

Rioting has been an important part of American history. Not only has there been an ever present level of some popular disorder, but riots have been instrumental in compelling political change and have reflected major social developments. To tell the story of rioting in American history is in large part to rehearse the story of *all* of American history. This task has been daunting. Generalizations do not come easy. No two riots are exactly the same, and each incident is the product of specific circumstances. Shifts in patterns of rioting have been subtle, and it is impossible from any one incident to draw absolute conclusions. Exceptions abound. Yet if we look for patterns over the centuries we can see changes in rioting.

Four distinct phases of rioting can be delineated. A mixture of ritualized and limited rioting with more violent rebellion marked the seventeenth century. This period experienced great political and social unrest that reflected conditions in both the colonies and Great Britain. Challenges to the social order created the background for the English civil wars, the Interregnum, and the Glorious Revolution. This discord in England drifted across the Atlantic to a colonial world that was struggling to establish its own order in a new and sometimes hostile environment. Nearly every colony went through a form of rebellion, varying from the violent upheaval of Bacon's Rebellion and the contests with the proprietor in Maryland, to the more civil mobs that overthrew Governor Andros in Massachusetts. Colonial crowds also acted in more limited ways less challenging to the state. These mobs followed patterns of crowd behavior, established in England, aimed at asserting a community will through ritual and destruction of property that symbolically represented local grievances. Despite the differences between these two types of disorder in both England and the colonies they formed part of a continuum, tied together by a strident popular antiauthoritarianism that harked back to ancient legacies that surfaced briefly during the 1640s and 1650s in Cromwellian England.

In the eighteenth century limited action by crowds came to the fore and predominated even in the midst of a revolution. Mobs seldom threatened greater physical violence and remained focused on destroying some property that represented their grievance, or they demonstrated their ire by parading with effigies and creating public spectacles. This second phase of rioting resulted from increased political and social stability as an Anglo-American aristocracy emerged to lead the colonies. Antiauthoritarianism and resentment of wealth now became confined to more restricted channels as crowds defended communal morality. Normally a paternalistic elite was to ensure the interest of all levels of society. At times, legal restrictions or some other hindrance prevented the elite from acting. Within this context the crowd could assert itself, often led by the high born, to protect the community's corporate interest. Mobs might also be tolerated, such as on Pope Day, as a source of plebeian entertainment and as a social safety valve to allow the lower orders to let off some steam.

While crowds seldom turned to violence against persons, they did not always operate within patrician expectations. The challenge to authority remained just beneath the surface. During the 1760s and 1770s, as mobs became a necessary ingredient in the resistance to imperial restrictions, the people in the street began to assert themselves as never before. Discord appeared in the resistance movement as well as in the host of other disturbances that rocked colonial society. The two areas of popular disorder often overlapped, helped to propel a resistance movement toward revolution, and fueled a call for democracy unexpected by an elite defending liberty and property. As a result of the American Revolution the behavior of the crowd did not immediately change, but the political and social context had altered dramatically.

During the nineteenth century the democratic emergence of an egalitarian ideal unleashed new violent forces that led to rioting centered around attacks on persons and increased bloodshed. The gift of equality cut individuals off from the social identity that had provided so much meaning to their lives. People now asserted new group identities, vied with one another for political power, and strove to deny democratic access to others. The crowd also empowered people in a world where anomie and the feeling of powerlessness grew with equality and the size of the population. A democratic rhetoric further strengthened the mob that claimed, despite the violence of its actions, that it was a special representation of the will of the people.

Americans set themselves off from each other by race, religion, ethnicity, wealth, and a host of other categories. Patterns of violence and rage appeared by the 1820s and 1830s that dominated the American scene for the next century. Ethnic and religious groups squared off against one another, contesting neighborhood, workplace, and elections. More limited riots might occur, especially in the countryside, but whenever cultural differences came into play, the violence increased, as can be seen in the Missouri-Mormon wars and bleeding Kansas. Vigilantes raised the call for popular justice, claiming to act in the spirit of the American Revolution, but also turning, as the century wore on, to more and more physical violence.

Amid all of this violent rioting, race emerged as the area of greatest bloodshed and stood as tragic testimony to the failures of American democracy. After emancipation in the North, whites assaulted blacks who they believed challenged their jobs and threatened racial amalgamation. During the Civil War the pattern of northern race riots persisted and found its greatest expression in the New York riot of July 1863, when the city erupted into several days of turmoil that went beyond a protest of the draft and witnessed brutal murder of African Americans. Emancipation in the South brought on more horrors as whites refused to accept the equality of blacks. Utilizing traditions of collective action whites defended their sense of community with crowd intimidation, torture, and assassination. During Reconstruction thousands of African Americans were killed, and thousands more died at the hands of Judge Lynch after 1877. At the end of the nineteenth and beginning of the twentieth centuries, as blacks moved to the cities in the North and the South, and as blacks began to assert a new pride and identity, race wars broke out across the nation. In these riots whites often invaded black neighborhoods with guns blazing. Blacks retaliated, and the death count of both races soared in places like East St. Louis, Chicago, and Tulsa.

The intensity of racial conflict does not diminish the sanguinary record of rioting in other areas. Labor and capital repeatedly confronted each other over wages and the control of work in the new American industrial giant. Most strikes remained peaceful. But the litany of labor wars, from the railroad strike of 1877 to the great steel strike of 1919, also reflected the violence endemic in collective action in this period. Ethnicity, too, continued to divide Americans, especially with the millions of new immigrants flooding the nation from eastern and southern Europe as well as Asia and Latin America. While the major political parties usually avoided the type of confrontations at the polls that had marked the antebellum period, radicals on the left and the right engaged in violent confrontations typical of the popular disorder of the period.

Gradually and hesitantly the powers of the state began to be mobilized to deal with this popular disorder. During the nineteenth century local authorities created police forces that in part were to counter the violence of the mob. State governments reorganized an inefficient militia into the national guard after the 1877 debacle. But these forces too often took sides in riots. State police forces, created in the early twentieth century, had the same problem, and private guards by definition protected the interests of those who hired them. The federal government also was initially not neutral, but became increasingly so by the early twentieth century. Indeed, after 1900 government officials on all levels began to take more seriously the democratic creed established in 1776. Simultaneously, the federal government started to assert the power necessary to control both mobs and the forces arrayed against them. As these ideas and conditions spread, changes in rioting began to occur.

By the mid twentieth century the democratic process was opened to more and more Americans and popular disorder became less violent and again—for different reasons—centered on the destruction of property. We can see this development in the labor movement of the 1930s. Violent strikes, like those that took place in 1934, might still erupt. But with government officials increasingly accepting the legitimacy of the labor movement, strikers concentrated on less violent crowd tactics like the sit-down, in which workers occupied factories until management came to an agreement with the union. Similar trends can be detected in ethnic and political disturbances in the 1940s.

Even in the most explosive area of American conflict—race relations—rioting changed. Lynching declined precipitously, while battles between blacks and whites, typical of early-twentieth-century rioting, became rare. Racial strife, however, continued. Only now it took different forms. Whites and blacks still confronted one another in the street, especially as the civil rights movement gained momentum in the 1950s. Blacks practiced sit-ins, marches, and boycotts. Crowds of both races might strike out at each other during these activities. But the crowds limited themselves to shouting obscenities, shoving, pushing, and maybe even throwing rocks and bottles. Seldom did gunfire and deaths result from these confrontations.[1] Another form of racial rioting emerged in urban ghettos in which blacks would vent pent up rage at an unresponsive justice and political system as well as economic exploitation in looting, arson, and some assaults. The ghetto riot first took shape in Harlem disturbances in 1935 and 1943 and was repeated with great frequency in the 1960s and occasionally in the 1970s, 1980s and 1990s.

During the 1960s and early 1970s a resurgent political left swept across campuses preaching free speech, opposition to war, and even revolution. Collective action by this rebellion of youth, however, followed the new patterns of popular disorder. Students marched, occupied buildings and campuses, obstructed traffic, and concentrated on the symbolic gesture. Occasionally they battled police and even the military with rocks and bottles. A few radicals went underground and engaged in bombings and political terrorism, but the student crowd did not pick up guns and participate in more lethal violence even after shots were fired by the military at Kent State in 1972.

Ritualized rebellion became a hallmark of crowd action in the closing decades of the twentieth century. Protestors against nuclear power followed the lead of labor, African Americans, and students by occupying construction sites, sitting down on roadways, and obstructing traffic. Antiabortion forces besieged clinics in a similar manner. Protestors for and against integration grabbed their signs, walked picket lines, and sometimes clashed. Only rarely did these incidents involve serious bloodshed. Ghetto riots sporadically erupted, but they, too, mirrored similar actions of the 1960s. Occasionally greater violence threatened in racial and ethnic hotbeds like New York, Miami, and Los Angeles.

On a superficial level it might seem as if the emphasis on property and the symbolic gesture of the late-twentieth-century rioters were merely a cyclic return to eighteenth-century patterns of mob behavior. Such a conclusion obscures the unique historical conditions that molded the forms of crowd behavior. Eighteenth-century popular disorder was the product of a society that insisted on a single corporate interest that needed to be cared for first by the elite in a social hierarchy, and then, if the patricians failed, by the people in the street who could act to protect the community. When the crowd acted, it limited violence so as not to threaten the social system. More often than not, the crowd and victim knew each other and intended to sustain contact beyond the excited moment of disorder. In the late twentieth century the corporate image was long gone. The rise of democracy after American independence had created interest group politics. Demographic growth compounded this change by expanding distances between individuals. Rioters no longer knew or identified with their victims. More often than not the mob wanted to strike out and destroy the people—whoever they might be—who opposed them in the street. Only gradually did a democratic state emerge that had the will and power to check the fury of the mob. During the twentieth century the federal government in particular began to work to ensure that all Americans could participate in democratic politics. Aiding this process was the homogenization of the American people through the creation of a national media, limits on immigration, and the economic uplifting of the working class. By mid century these developments had created a less violent form of rioting.

Where, then, do we go from here? Democracy remains a fragile experiment. Several recent riots, especially the disturbance in Los Angeles in 1992, threaten the gains that Americans have made. Cities confront problems that need to be addressed. Violence by individuals continues to disrupt social peace. Americans—including those far from the inner city—face a changing world. New immigration and new demographics have made the United States far more ethnically diverse than thirty years ago. The waning power of unions and the growing disparities between rich and poor threaten to undo the gains of previous generations. We need to be careful to extend democracy to all and not draw lines dividing the American people. The possibility remains of new and more physically violent patterns of popular disorder in which different races and ethnic groups engage in armed conflict. That violent future may or may not come about. Yet it remains something to be guarded against.

APPENDIX: COUNTING RIOTS

How many riots were there in American history? For this study I examined over four thousand riots. That number, however, does not come close to the total of all rioting. It merely represents the riots I included in my files. My method of research was to note each riot described in the various books and articles I read that fit my working definition of rioting (outlined in the Introduction). In some areas the gaps in my counting are glaring. As noted in Chapter 4 there were 5,112 persons lynched between 1882 and 1937. Since I only included lynchings where I read the details and confirmed that they were riots that fit my definition, my count contains only a few hundred of these. Thousands more probably fit the definition but were not explicitly described in the literature I read. Therefore they did not make it into my file. Similarly, while I read the major sources on labor history, many case studies not perused contain descriptions of riots that are also not part of my file. If I strove to list every riot I could probably research ad infinitum.

I have relied heavily on secondary sources for my list of riots. But even turning to the primary sources leads to difficulties. A classic case in point concerns antebellum rioting. Leonard Richards provides us with an excellent study of the antiabolitionist movement and the riots that accompanied it. He unearthed 209 examples of northern mobs attacking abolitionists. Most contained little violence against persons. Given the numbers of riots Richards discerned for the 1830s, indeed even given the numbers of riots David Grimsted has found for the entire 1828 to 1861 period (totalling 1040 incidents), these disturbances would appear to comprise a significant proportion of total rioting.[1]

Our knowledge of quantity, however, is a function of sources and can be misleading. The abolitionists relished counting as a riot any crowd that even hinted at behaving like a mob. The result was that they filled their letters, reports, and newspapers with incidents that the historian can now read and count—or that editor Hezakiah Niles might cull and occasionally include in his weekly national newspaper.[2] If the compilers of this information operated from a different set of assumptions, then they would provide information that would lead to different conclusions. Given the nature of theatergoing in the early nineteenth century, which included throwing at the stage and audience nuts, fruit, and other items almost nightly, had someone kept a scorecard on each incident in the theater, we would be left with statistics that would indicate that theater riots were the most frequent and significant form of rioting in the first half of the nineteenth century. Such a conclusion would miss the point. Theater riots were important not only because of the frequency of rowdy behavior, but even more so because they occasionally broke out into more serious disturbances, and as in the case of the Astor Place riot of New York City in 1849, came to represent significant class and cultural differences.[3]

Another danger with counting riots is that increased apprehensions over rioting can lead to underestimating the level of violent conflict at other times. There is no question that the years of 1834 and 1835 were unusual in the number of riots that occurred. Like the years preceding independence from Great Britain, and more recently, the mid to late 1960s, there appeared to be a contagion of rioting in the mid 1830s.[4] But that intensification in the number of incidents should not lead us to think that other periods lacked a great deal of rioting. No doubt word of one riot encouraged the occurrence of another riot in these special years. But the frequency in disturbances suddenly made all rioting seem more important to contemporaries. The result was that people began to take note of incidents that they might otherwise not even mention. My own counting of riots in the antebellum period, which is by no means comprehensive, suggests that there were almost as many occurrences of rioting in 1828 and 1829 as there were in 1834 and 1835.[5]

Throughout this study, while occasionally referring to the numbers of riots, I have stressed the overall context of the popular disorder and the significance of the most extreme and noted examples of rioting.

Notes

Abbreviations

Introduction

1. For citations on these riots and others mentioned in the introduction, see the relevant sections of the book.

2. The English Riot Act of 1715 used the distinction of twelve or more persons. See Danby Pickering, ed., *The Statutes at Large from the Twelfth Year of Queen Anne, to the Fifth Year of George I*, vol. XIII (Cambridge, 1764), 142–46. Americans in the

eighteenth and nineteenth centuries followed this practice as indicated in the indictments in the District Attorney Papers, Court of General Sessions, 1791–1835, Municipal Archives and Records Center of the City of New York.

3. For the importance of rioting to sociology see James B. Rule, *Theories of Civil Violence* (Berkeley, 1988).

4. My understanding of the rationality of the crowd derives from reading scholars like Charles Tilly, E. P. Thompson, George Rudé, and Georges Lefebvre. For the most noted works see Georges Lefebvre, "Revolutionary Crowds," in Jeffry Kaplow, ed., *New Perspectives on the French Revolution: Readings in Historical Sociology* (New York, 1965), 173–90; George Rudé, *The Crowd in History: A Study of Popular Disturbances in France and England, 1730-1848* (New York, 1964); E. P. Thompson, "The Moral Economy of the English Crowd in the Eighteenth Century," *PP,* 50 (1971), 76–136; Natalie Zemon Davis, "The Reasons of Misrule: Youth Groups and Charivaris in Sixteenth-Century France," ibid., 41–75; and Charles Tilly, "Collective Violence in European Perspective," in Hugh Davis Graham and Ted Robert Gurr, eds., *Violence in America: Historical and Comparative Perspective* (Beverly Hills, 1979), 4–45. For a sociological perspective see Neil J. Smelser, *Theory of Collective Behavior* (New York, 1962).

5. While outdated and highly criticized, there remains a germ of truth to Gustave Le Bon's analysis of the irrationality of the crowd. See his *The Crowd: A Study of the Popular Mind,* intro. by Robert K. Merton (New York, 1960); and *The French Revolution and the Psychology of Revolution,* Robert A. Nye, ed. (New Brunswick, 1980). Le Bon's work always needs to be measured against its criticism, especially the work of Georges Lefebvre. See Lefebvre, *The Great Fear of 1789: Rural Panic in Revolutionary France,* trans. by Joan White (New York, 1973).

6. Kai T. Erikson, *Wayward Puritans: A Study in the Sociology of Deviance* (New York, 1966); Emile Durkheim, *The Rules of Sociological Method* (Chicago, Ill., 1938), 47–75; Lewis A. Coser, *The Functions of Social Conflict* (Glencoe, Ill., 1956); and Georg Simmel, *Conflict and the Web of Group-Affiliations,* trans. by Kurt H. Wolff and Reinhard Bendix (Glencoe, Ill., 1955).

7. Charles Tilly, Louise Tilly, and Richard H. Tilly, *The Rebellious Century, 1830-1930* (Cambridge, Mass., 1975).

1. Disorder and Order in Colonial America

1. Alfred Young, "English Plebeian Culture and Eighteenth-Century American Radicalism," in Margaret Jacob and James Jacob, eds., *The Origins of Anglo-American Radicalism* (London, 1984), 185–212.

2. Although not all white colonists were from the British Isles, the other Europeans in British North America shared many similarities, and British culture dominated the colonial scene. The following discussion therefore centers on English society and traditions.

3. This discussion of English society relies upon Peter Laslett, *The World We Have Lost: Further Explored,* 3rd ed. (New York, 1984); Carl Bridenbaugh, *Vexed and Troubled Englishmen, 1590-1642* (New York, 1967); Wallace Notestein, *The English People on the Eve of Colonization, 1603–1640* (New York, 1954); R. H. Tawney, *The Agrarian Problem in the Sixteenth Century* (New York, 1967; orig. pub. 1912); David Underdown, *Revel, Riot, and Rebellion: Popular Politics and Culture in England, 1603–1660* (Oxford, 1985), 9–43.

4. Roger B. Manning, *Village Revolts: Social Protest and Popular Disturbances in England, 1509–1640* (Oxford, 1988), 319.

5. This discussion relies upon Barrett L. Beer, *Rebellion and Riot: Popular Disorder in England during the Reign of Edward VI* (n.p., 1982); Buchanan Sharp, *In Contempt of All Authority: Rural Artisans and Riot in the West of England, 1586–1660* (Berkeley, 1980); D. G. C. Allan, "The Rising in the West, 1628–1631," *Economic History Review,* 2nd ser., 5 (1952), 76–85; John Walter, "Grain Riots and Popular Attitudes to the Law: Malden and the Crisis of 1629," in John Brewer and John Styles, eds., *An Ungovernable People: The English and Their Law in the Seventeenth and Eighteenth Centuries* (New Brunswick, 1980), 47–84; Walter and Keith Wrightson, "Dearth and the Social Order in Early Modern England," *PP,* 71 (1976), 22–42.

6. The best surveys of Tudor-Stuart disorder are Anthony Fletcher, *Tudor Rebellions,* 2nd ed. (London, 1973); and Christopher Hill, *The Century of Revolution, 1603–1714* (New York, 1966; orig. pub. 1961).

7. Roger B. Manning, "Violence and Social Conflict in Mid-Tudor Rebellions," *Journal of British Studies,* 16 (1977), 18–40; Manning, "Patterns of Violence in Early Tudor Enclosure Riots," *Albion,* 5 (1974), 120–33; Manning, *Village Revolts,* 50; M. E. James, "Obedience and Dissent in Henrician England: The Lincolnshire Rebellion 1536," *PP,* 48 (1970), 3–78; Allan, "Rising in the West," *Economic History Review,* 2nd ser., 5 (1952), 76–85.

8. Manning, *Village Revolts,* 284–305. See also E. P. Thompson, *Whigs and Hunters: The Origins of the Black Act* (New York, 1975); and Douglas Hay, "Poaching and the Game Laws on Cannock Chase," in Douglas Hay et al., eds., *Albion's Fatal Tree: Crime and Society in Eighteenth-Century England* (New York, 1975), 189–253.

9. Christopher Hill, "The Norman Yoke," in Hill, *Puritanism and Revolution: Studies in Interpretation of the English Revolution of the Seventeenth Century* (New York, 1964), 50–122; Rodney Hilton, *Bond Men Made Free: Medieval Peasant Movements and the English Rising of 1381* (New York, 1973).

10. John Walter, "A 'Rising of the People'? The Oxfordshire Rising of 1596," *PP,* 107 (1985), 90–143.

11. The best discussions on the popular component in the English Civil War are Brian Manning, *The English People and the English Revolution, 1640-1649* (London, 1976); and Christopher Hill, *The World Turned Upside Down: Radical Ideas during the English Revolution* (New York, 1972). On London apprentices see Bernard Capp, "English Youth Groups and *The Pinder of Wakefield,*" *PP,* 76 (1977), 127-33; and Steven R. Smith, "The London Apprentices as Seventeenth-Century Adolescents," ibid., 61 (1973), 149–61. See also Sharp, *In Contempt of All Authority.* On Restoration crowds see Tim Harris, *London Crowds in the Reign of Charles II: Propaganda and Politics from the Restoration until the Exclusion Crisis* (Cambridge, 1987).

12. Underdown, *Revel, Riot, and Rebellion.*

13. The best discussions of the political content of eighteenth-century crowds are George Rudé, *The Crowd in History, 1730-1848: A Study of Popular Disturbances in France and England* (New York, 1964); Rudé, *Paris and London in the Eighteenth Century: Studies of Popular Protest* (New York, 1971); Rudé, *Wilkes and Liberty: A Social Study in 1763 to 1774* (Oxford, 1962); John Brewer, *Party Ideology and Popular Politics at the Accession of George III* (Cambridge, 1976); E. P. Thompson, *The Making of the English Working Class* (New York, 1963). See also Geoffrey Holmes, "The Sacheverell Riots: The Crowd and the Church in Early Eighteenth-Century London," *PP,* 72

(1976), 55–85; Max Beloff, *Public Order and Popular Disturbances, 1660–1714* (London, 1938); Nicholas Rogers, "Popular Protest in Early Hanoverian London," in Paul Slack, ed., *Rebellion, Popular Protest and the Social Order in Early Modern England* (Cambridge, 1984), 263–93.

14. The best discussions of the traditional content of eighteenth-century English crowds are E. P. Thompson, "The Moral Economy of the English Crowd in the Eighteenth Century," *PP,* 50 (1971), 76–136; and Thompson, "'Rough Music': Le Charivari anglais," *Annales: Economies, sociétés, civilisations,* 27 (1972), 285–312. For labor riots see E. J. Hobsbawm, "The Machine Breakers," *PP,* 1 (1952), 57–70. See also the works cited in note 16 below. For a critique of this approach see Mark Harrison, *Crowds and History: Mass Phenomena in English Towns, 1790–1835* (Cambridge, 1988); Robert J. Holton, "The Crowd in History: Some Problems of Theory and Method," *Social History,* 3 (1978), 219–33; Dale Edward Williams, "Morals, Markets and the English Crowd in 1766," *PP,* 104 (1984), 56–73. See also John Bohstedt, *Riots and Community Politics in England and Wales, 1790–1810* (Cambridge, Mass., 1983); Walter J. Shelton, *English Hunger and Industrial Disorders: A Study of Social Conflict during the First Decade of George III's Reign* (Toronto, 1973); John Stevenson, *Popular Disturbances in England, 1700–1870* (London, 1979).

15. J. H. Plumb, *The Origins of Political Stability: England, 1675–1725* (Boston, 1967).

16. E. P. Thompson, "Patrician Society, Plebeian Culture," *JSH,* 7 (1974), 382–405; Thompson, "Eighteenth-century English Society: Class Struggle without Class?" *Social History,* 3 (1978), 133–65; Thompson, "The Crime of Anonymity," in Hay et al., eds., *Albion's Fatal Tree,* 255–308. Thompson elaborated on his ideas in these articles in *Customs in Common* (New York, 1991). See also John Brewer, "Theater and Counter-Theater in Georgian Politics: The Mock Elections at Garret," *Radical History Review,* 22 (1979–1980), 7–40; Brewer, *Party Ideology and Popular Politics;* Robert W. Malcolmson, "'A Set of Ungovernable People': The Kingswood Colliers in the Eighteenth Century," in Brewer and Styles, eds., *An Ungovernable People,* 85–127; John G. Rule, "Wrecking and Coastal Plunder," in Hay et al., eds., *Albion's Fatal Tree,* 167–88.

17. The best analysis of the social upheaval of the seventeenth century is Bernard Bailyn, "Politics and Social Structure in Virginia," in James Morton Smith, ed., *Seventeenth-Century America: Essays in Colonial History* (Chapel Hill, 1959), 90–115. See also Bailyn, *The New England Merchants in the Seventeenth Century* (New York, 1955); Warren M. Billings, *The Old Dominion in the Seventeenth Century: A Documentary History of Virginia, 1606–1689* (Chapel Hill, 1975), 236–87; Lois Green Carr and David William Jordan, *Maryland's Revolution of Government, 1689–1692* (Ithaca, 1974); Russell R. Menard, "Maryland's 'Time of Troubles': Sources of Political Disorder in Early St. Mary's," *MHM,* 76 (1981), 124–40; Hugh F. Rankin, *Upheaval in Albemarle: The Story of Culpepper's Rebellion, 1675–1689* (Raleigh, 1962); Robert C. Ritchie, *The Duke's Province: A Study of New York Politics and Society, 1664–1691* (Chapel Hill, 1977).

18. Edmund S. Morgan, *American Slavery, American Freedom: The Ordeal of Colonial Virginia* (New York, 1975), 215–70; Thomas Archdeacon, *New York City, 1664–1710: Conquest and Change* (Ithaca, 1976); Charles M. Andrews, ed., *Narratives of the Insurrections, 1675–1690* (New York, 1915); Beverly McAnear, ed., "Marilands Grevances Wiy The Have Taken Op Arms," *JSoH,* 8 (1942), 392–409.

19. The best analysis of Virginia is Morgan, *American Slavery, American Freedom*. For the battle at Jamestown see ibid., 268. See also Andrews, *Narratives of the Insurrections*, 9–141.

20. A good narrative of Maryland in this period is Bernard C. Steiner, "Maryland during the English Civil Wars, Part I," *Johns Hopkins University Studies in Historical and Political Science* (Baltimore, 1906), ser. 24, nos. 11–12, 751–813; and Steiner, "Maryland during the English Civil Wars, Part II," ibid., (Baltimore, 1907), ser. 25, nos. 4–5, 153–268. See also Menard, "Maryland's 'Time of Troubles,'" *MHM*, 76 (1981), 124–40; Richard Hofstadter and Michael Wallace, eds., *American Violence: A Documentary History* (New York, 1970), 48–51; Aubrey C. Land, *Colonial Maryland: A History* (Millwood, N.Y., 1981), 45–53.

21. Andrews, *Narratives of the Insurrections*, 165–296, 299–314, 315–401.

22. Rankin, *Upheaval in Albemarle*.

23. Morgan, *American Slavery, American Freedom*, 286–87; Billings, ed., *Old Dominion*, 247–49, 282–87; William H. Gaines, Jr., "Some Called It Treason: A Narrative of the Tobacco Riots in the York-Rappahannock Counties of the Virginia Colony during the Spring and Summer of 1682," *Virginia Cavalcade*, 1 (1951), 39–43.

24. James Axtell, "The Vengeful Women of Marblehead: Robert Roule's Deposition of 1677," *WMQ*, 3rd ser., 31 (1974), 647–52.

25. Morgan, *American Slavery, American Freedom*, 246–47; Ritchie, *Duke's Province*, 50; Jerome R. Reich, *Leisler's Rebellion: A Study of Democracy in New York, 1664–1720* (Chicago, 1953), 30, 107; Billings, ed., *Old Dominion*, 243–44, 263–66; Daniel Vickers, "Competency and Competition: Economic Culture in Early America," *WMQ*, 3rd ser., 47 (1990), 22.

26. Leon DeValinger, Jr., "The Burning of the Whorekill, 1673," *PMHB*, 74 (1950), 473–87; Harry C. W. Melick, "The Fordham 'Ryott' of July 16, 1688," *New-York Historical Society Quarterly*, 36 (1952), 210–20; John E. Pomfret, *The Province of East New Jersey, 1609–1702: The Rebellious Proprietary* (Princeton, 1962), 332; Charles M. Andrews, *The Colonial Period of American History: The Settlements*, III (New Haven, 1937), 177.

27. Reich, *Leisler's Rebellion*, 6; Ritchie, *Duke's Province*, 71–74; Andrews, *Colonial Period*, III, 108.

28. There are exceptions. In the West Indies colony of Montserrat in 1666 ethnic conflict and prejudice led to a rebellion among Irish Catholic indentured servants. In Rhode Island in 1691 a mob attacked and dispersed a Huguenot settlement. Riva Berleant-Schiller, "Free Labor and the Economy in Seventeenth-Century Montserrat," *WMQ*, 3rd ser., 46 (1989), 539–64; Thomas J. Curran, *Xenophopia and Immigration, 1820-1930* (Boston, 1975), 15.

29. The literature on this ideology is huge. For the roots of these ideas see Caroline Robbins, *The Eighteenth-Century Commonwealthmen: Studies in the Transmission, Development, and Circumstance of English Liberal Thought from the Restoration of Charles II until the War with the Thirteen Colonies* (Cambridge, Mass., 1959); Bernard Bailyn, *The Ideological Origins of the American Revolution* (New York, 1967). See also Robert E. Shalhope, "Toward a Republican Synthesis: The Emergence of an Understanding of Republicanism in American Historiography," *WMQ*, 3rd ser., 29 (1972), 49–80.

30. For quotations see [John Trenchard and Thomas Gordon], *Cato's Letters; or, Essays on Liberty, Civil and Religious, and Other Important Subjects*, 3rd ed. (London,

1733), IV, 247–54; Thomas Gordon, trans., *The Works of Tacitus,* II (London, 1731), 61. See discussion in Paul A. Gilje, *The Road to Mobocracy: Popular Disorder in New York City, 1763–1834* (Chapel Hill, 1987), 6–9; and Pauline Maier, *From Resistance to Revolution: Colonial Radicals and the Development of American Opposition to Britain, 1765–1776* (New York, 1972), 3–48.

31. Rhys Isaac, "Preachers and Patriots: Popular Culture and the Revolution in Virginia," in Alfred F. Young, ed., *The American Revolution: Explorations in the History of American Radicalism* (DeKalb, Ill., 1976), 125–56; Isaac, *The Transformation of Virginia: 1740–1790* (Chapel Hill, 1982), 88–114, 121–34, 194–98, 248–55; A. G. Roeber, "Authority, Law, and Custom: The Rituals of Court Day in Tidewater Virginia, 1720 to 1750," *WMQ,* 3rd ser., 37 (1980), 29–52.

32. Quotations from Young, "English Plebeian Culture and Eighteenth-Century American Radicalism," in Jacob and Jacob, eds., *Origins of Anglo-American Radicalism,* 198–99. See also Gilje, *Road to Mobocracy,* 25–30.

33. For further analysis see Gilje, *Road to Mobocracy,* 16–30. For a general anthropological discussion of ritual and symbolic action see Max Gluckman, ed., *Essays on the Ritual of Social Relations* (Manchester, 1962); Gluckman, *Order and Rebellion in Tribal Africa: Collected Essays, with an Autobiographical Introduction* (London, 1963); Victor W. Turner, *The Ritual Process: Structure and Anti-Structure* (Chicago, 1969); Turner, *Dramas, Fields and Metaphors: Symbolic Action in Human Society* (Ithaca, 1974); Turner, "Symbols in Ndembu Ritual," in Max Gluckman, ed., *Closed Systems and Open Minds: The Limits of Naivety in Social Anthropology* (Edinburgh, 1964), 20–51; and Clifford Geertz, *The Interpretation of Cultures: Selected Essays* (New York, 1973).

34. A. J. Williams-Myers, "Pinkster Carnival: Africanisms in the Hudson River Valley," *Afro-Americans in New York Life and History,* 9 (1985), 7–17; Joseph P. Reidy, "'Negro Election Day' and Black Community Life in New England, 1750–1860," *Marxist Perspectives,* 1 (1978), 102–17.

35. Thompson, "Moral Economy of the English Crowd," *PP,* 50 (1971), 76–136.

36. The best overviews on social and economic conditions in the colonial period include James A. Henretta and Gregory H. Nobles, *Evolution and Revolution: American Society, 1600–1820* (Lexington, Mass., 1987); John J. McCusker and Russell R. Menard, *The Economy of British America, 1607–1789* (Chapel Hill, 1985); and Gary B. Nash, *The Urban Crucible: Social Change, Political Consciousness, and the Origins of the American Revolution* (Cambridge, Mass., 1979).

37. The best discussions of colonial rioting include Pauline Maier, "Popular Uprisings and Civil Authority in Eighteenth-Century America," *WMQ,* 3rd ser., 27 (1970), 3–35; Dirk Hoerder, *Crowd Action in Revolutionary Massachusetts, 1765–1780* (New York, 1977); and Nash, *Urban Crucible.* See also Gilje, *Road to Mobocracy;* and Thomas P. Slaughter, "Crowds in Eighteenth-Century America: Reflections and New Directions," *PMHB,* 115 (1991), 3–34. For a detailed survey of colonial rioting see John Kern, "The Politics of Violence: Colonial American Rebellions, Protest, and Riots, 1676–1747" (Ph.D. diss., University of Wisconsin, Madison, 1976). In the following discussion, unless it is the most significant source for a riot, I do not cite this dissertation for each specific incident.

38. Donald L. Kemmerer, *Path to Freedom: The Struggle for Self-Government in Colonial New Jersey, 1703–1776* (Princeton, 1940), 199; E. B. O'Callaghan, ed., *Documents relative to the Colonial History of the State of New York; Procured in Holland,*

England, and France, VI (Albany, 1855), 471; Gilje, Road to Mobocracy, 15–16, 30–35; Carl Bridenbaugh, Cities in the Wilderness: The First Century of Urban Life in America, 1625–1742 (New York, 1938), 224; Gregory H. Nobles, Divisions throughout the Whole: Politics and Society in Hampshire County, Massachusetts, 1740–1775 (Cambridge, 1983), 122.

39. Rudé, The Crowd in History, 255–57.

40. Bridenbaugh, Cities in the Wilderness, 223–24; Bridenbaugh, Cities in Revolt: Urban Life in America, 1743–1776 (London, 1955), 115, 311; [New York] Mercury, Aug. 11, 1760.

41. Charles Desmond Dutrizac, "Local Identity and Authority in a Disputed Hinterland: The Pennsylvania-Maryland Border in the 1730s," PMHB, 115 (1991), 35–61; Irving Mark, Agrarian Conflicts in Colonial New York, 1711–1775, 2nd ed. (Port Washington, N.Y., 1965; orig. pub. 1940), 128–29; Sung Bok Kim, Landlord and Tenant in Colonial New York: Manorial Society, 1664–1775 (Chapel Hill, 1978), 328, 338–40.

42. [New York] Evening Post, Nov. 21, 1748; J. Thomas Scharf, History of Baltimore City and County from the Earliest Period to the Present Day: Including Biographical Sketches of their Representative Men (Philadelphia, 1881), 778.

43. Philip L. White, The Beekmans of New York: In Politics and Commerce, 1647–1877 (New York, 1956), 151–52; Hoerder, Crowd Action, 65; Norman S. Cohen, "The Philadelphia Election Riot of 1742," PMHB, 92 (1968), 306–19; William T. Parsons, "The Bloody Election Riot of 1742," PH, 36 (1969), 290–306.

44. Bridenbaugh, Cities in the Wilderness, 383; [New York] Gazette and Weekly Post-Boy, Oct. 3, 1748, Dec. 23, 1751, Feb. 3, Mar. 2, 1752; [New York] Weekly Journal, Oct. 31, 1743.

45. The best analysis of land riots is Edward Countryman, "'Out of the Bounds of the Law': Northern Land Rioters in the Eighteenth Century," in Young, ed., The American Revolution, 37–69. For incidents mentioned in text see Pomfret, Province of East New Jersey, 338–40; Kemmerer, Path to Freedom, 197–204, 216–17; Kern, "Politics of Violence" (Ph.D. diss., University of Wisconsin, Madison, 1976), 148–72; James M. Poteet, "Unrest in the 'Land of Steady Habits': The Hartford Riot of 1722," Proceedings of the American Philosophical Society, 119 (1975), 223–32; Hoerder, Crowd Action, 60; Mark, Agrarian Conflicts, 122–26; Kim, Landlord and Tenant, 311, 323–38; Alan Taylor, "'A Kind of Warr': The Conflict for Land on the Northeastern Frontier, 1750–1820," WMQ, 3rd ser., 46 (1989), 18–19. See also Thomas L. Purvis, Proprietors, Patronage, and Paper Money: Legislative Politics in New Jersey, 1703–1776 (New Brunswick, 1986).

46. Bridenbaugh, Cities in the Wilderness, 196, 383; Maier, Resistance to Revolution, 4–5; Hoerder, Crowd Action, 55–56; G. B. Warden, Boston, 1689–1776 (Boston, 1970), 115–24.

47. Charles Albro Barker, The Background of the Revolution in Maryland (New Haven, 1940), 91; Steven J. Rosswurm, "'That They Were Grown Unruly': The Crowd and Lower-Classes in Philadelphia, 1765–1780 (M.A. thesis, Northern Illinois University, 1974), 18–19; Bridenbaugh, Cities in the Wilderness, 383; [New York] Evening Post, Nov. 21, 1748; Bernard Knollenberg, Origin of the American Revolution 1759–1766 (New York, 1960), 130–32; Robert G. Albion, Forests and Sea Power (Cambridge, Mass., 1926), 262–65. On English rioters' disguises see Thompson, Whigs and Hunters, 55–115.

48. Hoerder, *Crowd Action*, 51.

49. James Elbert Cutler, *Lynch-Law: An Investigation into the History of Lynching in the United States* (Montclair, N.J., 1969; orig. pub. 1905), 46–47; *New York Gazette*, Dec. 31, 1752; *New York Gazette and Weekly Post-Boy*, Feb, 12, 1753. See also Natalie Zemon Davis, "Women on Top," in Davis, *Society and Culture in Early Modern France* (Stanford, 1975), 124–51, and 315, n45.

50. Bridenbaugh, *Cities in the Wilderness*, 388–89; *New York Gazette and Weekly Post-Boy*, July 23, 1753.

51. Bridenbaugh, *Cities in Revolt*, 117; Rosswurm, "'That They Were Grown Unruly'" (M.A. thesis, Northern Illinois University, 1974), 21; John Smith, *Hannah Logan's Courtship, a True Narrative: The Wooing of the Daughter of James Logan . . . as Related in the Diary of Her Lover, the Honorable John Smith . . .*, Albert Cook Myers, ed. (Philadelphia, [1904]), 69–70.

52. Thomas C. Barrow, *Trade and Empire: The British Customs Service in Colonial America, 1660–1775* (Cambridge, Mass., 1967), 91; Edmund S. Morgan and Helen M. Morgan, *The Stamp Act Crisis: Prologue to Revolution*, rev. ed. (New York, 1962; orig. pub. 1953), 59–67.

53. Barrow, *Trade and Empire*, 89–90; John Lax and William Pencak, "The Knowles Riot and the Crisis of the 1740s in Massachusetts," *Perspectives in American History*, 10 (1976), 166; Nash, *Urban Crucible*, 237–38.

54. Jesse Lemisch, "Jack Tar in the Streets: Merchant Seamen in the Politics of Revolutionary America," *WMQ*, 3rd ser., 25 (1968), 381–95; Lax and Pencak, "Knowles Riot," *Per. in Amer. Hist.*, 10 (1976); *New York Gazette and Weekly Post-Boy*, July 12, 1764.

55. Stanley McCrory Pargellis, *Lord Loudon in North America* (New Haven, 1933), 128–29; Hoerder, *Crowd Action*, 58; *Newport Mercury*, July 9, 16, 23, 1764; Douglas Greenberg, *Crime and Law Enforcement in the Colony of New York, 1691–1776* (Ithaca, 1974), 122.

2. Rioting in the Revolution

1. For a general discussion of themes developed in this and the next five paragraphs see James A. Henretta and Gregory H. Nobles, *Evolution and Revolution: American Society, 1600–1820* (Lexington, Mass., 1987); John J. McCusker and Russell R. Menard, *The Economy of British America, 1607–1789* (Chapel Hill, 1985); Gary B. Nash, *The Urban Crucible: Social Change, Political Consciousness, and the Origins of the American Revolution* (Cambridge, Mass., 1979); Kenneth A. Lockridge, *Settlement and Unsettlement in Early America: The Crisis of Political Legitimacy before the Revolution* (Cambridge, 1981); Lockridge, "Land, Population and the Evolution of New England Society, 1630–1790," *PP*, 39 (1968), 62–80.

2. The best analysis of revolutionary rioting includes Pauline Maier, *From Resistance to Revolution: Colonial Radicals and the Development of American Opposition to Britain, 1765–1776* (New York, 1972); Gordon S. Wood, "A Note on Mobs in the American Revolution," *WMQ*, 3rd ser., 23 (1966), 635–42; Nash, *Urban Crucible*; Jesse Lemisch, "Jack Tar in the Streets: Merchant Seamen in the Politics of Revolutionary America," *WMQ*, 3rd ser., 25 (1968), 371–407; Dirk Hoerder, *Crowd Action in Revolutionary*

Massachusetts, 1765–1780 (New York, 1977); and Alfred F. Young, "English Plebeian Culture and Eighteenth-Century American Radicalism," in Margaret Jacob and James Jacob, eds., *The Origins of Anglo-American Radicalism* (London, 1984), 185–212. See also Paul A. Gilje, *The Road to Mobocracy: Popular Disorder in New York City, 1763–1834* (Chapel Hill, 1987).

3. Paul A. Gilje, "Republican Rioting," in William Pencak and Conrad Edick Wright, eds., *Authority and Resistance in Early New York* (New York, 1988), 202–25.

4. Peter Force, *American Archives,* 4th ser., I (Washington, D.C., 1837–1853), 342–43.

5. This analysis of the Stamp Act riots relies heavily on Edmund S. Morgan and Helen M. Morgan, *The Stamp Act Crisis: Prologue to Revolution,* rev. ed. (New York, 1962; orig. pub. 1953), 157–262, passim. See also Maier, *From Resistance to Revolution,* 51–76; Hoerder, *Crowd Action,* 85–143; Gilje, *Road to Mobocracy,* 44–52; Nash, *Urban Crucible,* 292–311. In the following discussion of all revolutionary rioting, unless one of these sources is the most significant source for a riot I do not cite it for the specific incident. For instances of Stamp Act rioting see Carl Bridenbaugh, *Cities in Revolt: Urban Life in America, 1743–1776* (London, 1955), 305–11; Edward Countryman, *A People in Revolution: The American Revolution and Political Society in New York, 1760–1790* (Baltimore, 1981), 37–39; Donald L. Kemmerer, *Path to Freedom: The Struggle for Self-Government in Colonial New Jersey, 1703–1776* (Princeton, 1940), 283–92; Benjamin W. Labaree, *Patriots and Partisans: The Merchants of Newburyport, 1764–1815* (New York, 1962), 17–19; Lawrence Lee, "Days of Defiance: Resistance to the Stamp Act in the Lower Cape Fear," *NCHR,* 43 (1966), 186–202; Steven Rosswurm, *Arms, Country, and Class: The Philadelphia Militia and "Lower Sort" during the American Revolution, 1775–1783* (New Brunswick, 1987), 30–31; Donna J. Spindel, "Law and Disorder: The North Carolina Stamp Act Crisis," *NCHR,* 57 (1980), 1–16; Richard Walsh and William Lloyd Fox, eds., *Maryland: A History, 1632–1974* (Baltimore, 1974), 64, 70; Richard Walsh, *Charleston's Sons of Liberty: A Study of the Artisans, 1763–1789* (Columbia, S.C., 1959), 36–40.

6. Young, "English Plebeian Culture and Eighteenth-Century American Radicalism," in Jacob and Jacob, eds., *Origins of Anglo-American Radicalism,* 185–212; Peter Shaw, *American Patriots and the Rituals of the Revolution* (Cambridge, Mass., 1981), 16–18, 71–73, 177–223. See also George P. Anderson, "Ebenezer Mackintosh: Stamp Act Rioter and Patriot," *PCSMT,* 26 (1924–1926), 15–64, 348–61.

7. Walsh, *Charleston's Sons of Liberty,* 36–38; Labaree, *Patriots and Partisans,* 17; Rosswurm, *Arms, Country, and Class,* 30; Spindel, "Law and Disorder," *NCHR,* 57 (1980), 1–16.

8. Gilje, *Road to Mobocracy,* 45; Morgan and Morgan, *Stamp Act Crisis,* 247–48; Walsh, *Charleston's Sons of Liberty,* 36–38; Spindel, "Law and Disorder," *NCHR,* 57 (1980), 1–16.

9. Bernard Bailyn, *The Ordeal of Thomas Hutchinson* (Cambridge, Mass., 1974), 35–69.

10. Morgan and Morgan, *Stamp Act Crisis,* 187–204; Countryman, *People in Revolution,* 39.

11. Morgan and Morgan, *Stamp Act Crisis,* 245–49.

12. Quoted in Maier, *From Resistance to Revolution,* 60.

13. Gilje, *Road to Mobocracy,* 44–52; Morgan and Morgan, *Stamp Act Crisis,* 301–24; James H. Hutson, "An Investigation of the Inarticulate: Philadelphia's White Oaks," *WMQ,* 3rd ser., 28 (1971), 3–25; Jesse Lemisch and John K. Alexander, "The White Oaks, Jack Tar, and the Concept of the 'Inarticulate': A Note on the Economic Position of Philadelphia's White Oaks," *WMQ,* 3rd ser., 29 (1972), 109–42.

14. Philip G. Davidson, "Sons of Liberty and Stamp Men," *NCHR,* 9 (1932), 38–56.

15. For a general discussion of land rioting see Edward Countryman, "'Out of the Bounds of the Law': Northern Land Rioters in the Eighteenth Century," in Alfred F. Young, ed., *The American Revolution: Explorations in the History of American Radicalism* (DeKalb, Ill., 1976), 37–69; Richard Maxwell Brown, "Back Country Rebellions and the Homestead Ethic in America, 1740–1799," in Brown and Don E. Fehrenbacher, eds., *Tradition, Conflict, and Modernization: Perspectives on the American Revolution* (New York, 1977), 73–99; Gregory H. Nobles, "Breaking into the Backcountry: New Approaches to the Early American Frontier," *WMQ,* 3rd ser., 46 (1989), 641–70; and Alan Taylor, "Agrarian Independence: Northern Land Rioters after the Revolution," in Alfred F. Young, ed., *Beyond the American Revolution: Explorations in the History of American Radicalism* (DeKalb, Ill., 1993), 221–45.

16. Oscar Handlin, "The Eastern Frontier of New York," *NYH,* 18 (1937), 50–75; Sung Bok Kim, *Landlord and Tenant in Colonial New York: Manorial Society, 1664–1775* (Chapel Hill, 1978), 346–415; Staughton Lynd, "The Revolution and the Common Man: Farm Tenants and Artisans in New York Politics" (Ph.D. diss., Columbia University, 1962); Lynd, "The Tenant Rising at Livingston Manor, May 1777," *New-York Historical Society Quarterly,* 48 (1964), 163–77.

17. The best discussions of the North Carolina Regulator movement are A. Roger Ekirch, "The North Carolina Regulators on Liberty and Corruption, 1766–1771," *Perspectives in American History,* 11 (1977–1978), 197–256; James P. Whittenburg, "Planters, Merchants, and Lawyers: Social Change and the Origins of the North Carolina Regulation," *WMQ,* 3rd ser., 34 (1977), 215–38; L. Marvin Michael Kay, "The North Carolina Regulation, 1766–1776: A Class Conflict," in Young, ed., *The American Revolution,* 71–123; John S. Bassett, "The Regulators of North Carolina (1765–1771)," *Annual Report of the American Historical Association* (1894), 141–212; Hugh T. Lefler and William S. Powell, *Colonial North Carolina: A History* (New York, 1973), 217–39. See also George R. Adams, "The Carolina Regulators: A Note on Changing Interpretations," *NCHR,* 49 (1972), 345–52; A. Roger Ekirch, *"Poor Carolina": Politics and Society in Colonial North Carolina, 1729–1776* (Chapel Hill, 1981); and William S. Powell, *The War of the Regulation and the Battle of Alamance, May 16, 1771* (Raleigh, 1962; orig. pub. 1949).

18. The best discussions of the South Carolina Regulator movement are Richard Maxwell Brown, *The South Carolina Regulators* (Cambridge, Mass., 1963); Rachel N. Klein, "Ordering the Backcountry: The South Carolina Regulation," *WMQ,* 3rd ser., 38 (1981), 661–80; and Klein, *Unification of a Slave State: The Rise of the Planter Class in the South Carolina Backcountry, 1760–1808* (Chapel Hill, 1990), 9–77.

19. James Edward Brady, "Wyoming: A Study of John Franklin and the Connecticut Settlement into Pennsylvania" (Ph.D. diss., Syracuse University, 1973); Allan Nevins, *The American States during and after the Revolution, 1775–1789* (New York, 1969; orig.

pub. 1924), 583–90; Oscar Zeichner, *Connecticut's Years of Controversy, 1750–1776* (Chapel Hill, 1949), 143–58; George D. Peck, *Wyoming: Its History, Stirring Incidents, and Romantic Adventures* (New York, 1858), 20–26; Carl Carmer, *The Susquehanna* (New York, 1955), 107–18, 184–97.

20. On Vermont see Matt Bushnell Jones, *Vermont in the Making, 1750–1777* (Cambridge, Mass., 1939), 255–77; *New York Gazette,* March 27, 1775; *New York Journal* (Holt's), March 23, 1775. On Massachusetts see Hoerder, *Crowd Action,* 134–35, 283–84; Gregory H. Nobles, *Divisions throughout the Whole: Politics and Society in Hampshire County, Massachusetts, 1740–1775* (Cambridge, 1983), 166–69; Force, *American Archives,* 4th ser., I, 724–25, 732–44.

21. Gilje, *Road to Mobocracy,* 47.

22. Patrick Henderson, "Smallpox and Patriotism: The Norfolk Riots, 1768–1769," *VMHB,* 73 (1965), 413–24.

23. George A. Billias, "Pox and Politics in Marblehead, 1773–1774," *Essex Institute Historical Collections,* 92 (1956), 43–58.

24. Many believed that a lawyer was a wolf in sheep's clothing. Goats came to represent lawyers because while they resembled sheep, everyone knew by both behavior and sight that it was a very different animal. *New York Gazette and Weekly Post-Boy,* March 27, 1766.

25. Gilje, *Road to Mobocracy,* 51; Hoerder, *Crowd Action,* 50–52, 58n, 253; Pauline Maier, "Popular Uprisings and Civil Authority in Eighteenth-Century America," *WMQ,* 3rd ser., 27 (1970), 6; Wesley M. Gewehr, *The Great Awakening in Virginia, 1740–1790* (Gloucester, Mass., 1965; orig. pub. 1930), 119–22; Sheldon S. Cohen, "The Turkish Tyranny," *NEQ,* 47 (1974), 564–83; William C. Lane, "The Rebellion of 1766 in Harvard College," *PCSMT,* 10 (1904–1906), 33–59.

26. Arthur M. Schlesinger, "Liberty Tree: A Genealogy," *NEQ,* 25 (1952), 435–58.

27. Gilje, *Road to Mobocracy,* 52–58.

28. *New York Journal,* Aug. 6, 1767.

29. Hoerder, *Crowd Action,* 223–34; Hiller B. Zobel, *The Boston Massacre* (New York, 1970).

30. For customs rioting see Hoerder, *Crowd Action,* 144, 157, 167–70, 188, 189, 206–207, 209; Rosswurm, *Arms, Country, and Class,* 32, 58–61; William Ander Smith, "Anglo-American Society and the Mob" (Ph.D. diss., Claremont Graduate School, 1965), 212–13; Countryman, *A People in Revolution,* 41; *New York Journal,* July 20, 27, Sept 2, 1769.

31. This discussion relies heavily on Young, "English Plebeian Culture and Eighteenth-Century American Radicalism," in Jacob and Jacob, eds., *The Origins of Anglo-American Radicalism,* 185–212. See also Frank W. C. Hersey, "Tar and Feathers: The Adventures of Captain John Malcolm," *PCSMT,* 34 (1941), 429–73; Hoerder, *Crowd Action,* 189, 194, 209, 237, 241, 268–69, 302–303, 340; Smith, "Anglo-American Society and the Mob" (Ph.D. diss., Claremont Graduate School, 1965), 210–13; Rosswurm, *Arms, Country, and Class,* 32–33, 46–48, 64–67; Walsh, *Charleston's Sons of Liberty,* 72. For tarring and feathering sources see Force, *American Archives,* 4th ser., II, 120–21; ibid., III, 823; *New York Journal,* Oct. 19, 1769, Sept. 21, Oct. 26, 1775, Jan. 25, 1776; *New York Gazette,* Aug. 28, 1775; *Boston Gazette,* Oct 5, 16, 1769; Isaac Q. Leake, *Memoir of the Life and Times of John Lamb* . . . (Albany, 1857), 46–47.

32. Hoerder, *Crowd Action*, 257–64; Benjamin Woods Labaree, *The Boston Tea Party* (New York, 1966).

33. Gilje, *Road to Mobocracy*, 58–59.

34. Aubrey C. Land, *Colonial Maryland: A History* (Millwood, N.Y., 1981), 301–303; Ronald Hoffman, *A Spirit of Dissension: Economics, Politics, and the Revolution in Maryland* (Baltimore, 1973), 133–38.

35. For examples of this activity see Hoerder, *Crowd Action*, 274, 282–91, 302–303, 309, 340–42; Smith, "Anglo-American Society and the Mob" (Ph.D. diss., Claremont Graduate School, 1965), 224–27; Nobles, *Divisions throughout the Whole*, 166–76; Rosswurm, *Arms, Country, and Class*, 34, 72–73; Leake, *Memoir of Lamb*, 86–87; Force, *American Archives*, 4th ser., I, 724–25, 732–44, 963, 1070–1072; ibid., II, 120–21, 347–49, 920; *New York Journal*, June 16, 23, Sept. 15, Oct. 13, Nov. 17, 1774, April 13, 1775.

36. Gilje, *Road to Mobocracy*, 58–64; Hoerder, *Crowd Action*, 270–310.

37. Force, *American Archives*, 4th ser., II, 922–23; ibid., III, 823; ibid., VI, 430; *New York Gazette*, Aug. 28, 1775; George Clinton, *Public Papers of George Clinton, First Governor of New York, 1777–1795, 1801–1804*, II (New York, 1900), 854–59, 876–79. See also Rosswurm, *Arms, Country, and Class*, 36, 46–48, 113–17, 155, 246; John A. Munroe, *Federalist Delaware, 1775–1815* (New Brunswick, 1954), 35; Wallace Brown, *The Good Americans: The Loyalists in the American Revolution* (New York, 1969), 131–39; Catherine S. Crary, *The Price of Loyalty: Tory Writings from the Revolutionary Era* (New York, 1973), 55–111.

38. Walsh and Fox, eds., *Maryland: A History*, 96; Rosswurm, *Arms, Country, and Class*, 92–93; Walsh, *Charleston's Sons of Liberty*, 120–21; Force, *American Archives*, 4th ser., V, 438–40, 1389, 1441–42, and VI, 1348, 1363; Charles G. Steffen, *The Mechanics of Baltimore: Workers and Politics in the Age of Revolution, 1763–1812* (Urbana, Ill., 1984), 70–74.

39. Barbara Clark Smith, "Food Rioters and the American Revolution," *WMQ*, 3rd. ser., 51 (1994), 3–38; Hoerder, *Crowd Action*, 360–61; Richard B. Morris, *Government and Labor in Early America* (New York, 1946), 124–25; Charles Royster, *A Revolutionary People at War: The Continental Army and American Character, 1775–1783* (Chapel Hill, 1979), 323.

40. Hoerder, *Crowd Action*, 359–61; Young, "English Plebeian Culture and Eighteenth-Century American Radicalism," in Jacob and Jacob, eds., *Origins of Anglo-American Radicalism*, 185–212; Albert Matthews, "Joyce Junior," *PCSMT*, 8 (1903), 89–104; Matthews, "Joyce Junior Once More," ibid., 11 (1906–1907), 280–94.

41. John K. Alexander, "The Fort Wilson Incident of 1779: A Case Study of the Revolutionary Crowd," *WMQ*, 3rd. ser., 31 (1974), 589–612; Rosswurm, *Arms, Country, and Class*, 205–27.

42. Paul A. Gilje, "The Common People and the Constitution: Popular Culture in New York City in the Late Eighteenth Century," in Gilje and William Pencak, eds., *New York in the Age of the Constitution, 1775–1800* (Rutherford, N.J., 1992), 48–73.

43. Quoted in Gilje, *Road to Mobocracy*, 83.

44. Gilje, *Road to Mobocracy*, 78–92.

45. The best recent account of the background to the rebellion and the activity of the Shaysites is David P. Szatmary, *Shays' Rebellion: The Making of an Agrarian Insurrection* (Amherst, Mass., 1980). See also John L. Brooke, "To the Quiet of the People:

Revolutionary Settlements and Civil Unrest in Western Massachusetts, 1774–1789," *WMQ*, 3rd ser., 46 (1989), 425–62; Richard D. Brown, "Shays's Rebellion and Its Aftermath: A View from Springfield, Massachusetts, 1787," ibid., 3rd ser., 40 (1983), 598–615; Andrew MacFurland Davis, "The Shays Rebellion, A Political Aftermath," *PAAS*, new series, 21 (1911), 57–79; Albert Farnsworth, "Shays's Rebellion," *Massachusetts Law Quarterly*, 12 (1927), 29–42; Barbara Karsky, "Agrarian Radicalism in the Late Revolutionary Period (1780–1795)," in Erich Angerman et al., eds., *New Wine in Old Skins: A Comparative View of Socio-Political Structures and Values Affecting the American Revolution* (Stuttgart, 1976), 87–114; Richard B. Morris, "Insurrection in Massachusetts," in Daniel Aaron, ed., *America in Crisis: Fourteen Crucial Episodes in American History* (New York, 1952), 20–49; Stephen T. Riley, "Dr. William Whiting and Shays' Rebellion," *PAAS*, 66 (1956), 119–66; Jonathan Smith, "The Depression of 1785 and Daniel Shays' Rebellion," *WMQ*, 3rd ser., 5 (1948), 77–94; Marion L. Starkey, *A Little Rebellion* (New York, 1955); Robert J. Taylor, *Western Massachusetts in the Revolution* (Providence, 1954).

46. Robert E. Moody, "Samuel Ely: Forerunner of Shays," *NEQ*, 5 (1932), 105–34; Taylor, *Western Massachusetts*; L. Marx Renzulli, Jr., *Maryland, The Federalist Years* (Rutherford, N.J., 1972), 35–39, 48; Jean Butenhoff Lee, "Maryland's 'Dangerous Insurrection' of 1786," *MHM*, 85 (1990), 329–44; Lynn Warren Turner, *The Ninth State: New Hampshire's Formative Years* (Chapel Hill, 1983), 52–54.

47. In addition to the items cited in note 45 see Robert A. Gross, ed., *In Debt to Shays: The Bicentennial of an Agrarian Rebellion* (Charlottesville, Va., 1993); Szatmary, *Shays' Rebellion*, 56–119; Eric Manders and George A. Snook, "Shays' Regulators, 1786–1787," *Military Collector and Historian*, 15 (1963), 83, 85; John Noble, "A Few Notes on the Shays Rebellion," *PAAS*, 15 (1902), 200–32.

48. Merrill D. Peterson, ed., *The Portable Thomas Jefferson* (New York, 1975), 414–17.

49. Pauline Maier, *The Old Revolutionaries: Political Lives in the Age of Samuel Adams* (New York, 1980), 26–32, 41; Millard Hanson, "The Significance of Shays' Rebellion," *The South Atlantic Quarterly*, 39 (1940), 305–17.

50. Alexander Hamilton et al., Edward Mead Earle, ed., *The Federalist: A Commentary on the Constitution of the United States* (New York, n.d.), 29, 36, 47–62, 156–58, 170–82.

51. Hugh Henry Brackenridge, *Incidents of the Insurrection* (New Haven, 1972), 131.

52. The mythical "Tom the Tinkerer" forms an interesting parallel to English riot leaders "Ned Ludd," "Captain Swing," and "Rebecca" in rural early nineteenth-century England and the "Black Cat" that striking weavers used to threaten their boss in 1828 in New York City. Gilje, *Road to Mobocracy*, 173–76; E. P. Thompson, *The Making of the English Working Class* (New York, 1963), 547–602; E. J. Hobsbawm and George Rudé, *Captain Swing* (New York, 1968).

53. The best accounts of the rebellion are Leland D. Baldwin, *Whiskey Rebels: The Story of a Frontier Uprising*, rev. ed. (Pittsburgh, 1968; orig. pub. 1939); and Thomas P. Slaughter, *The Whiskey Rebellion: Frontier Epilogue to the American Revolution* (New York, 1986). See also the essays and documents in Steven R. Boyd, ed., *The Whiskey Rebellion: Past and Present Perspectives* (Westport, Conn., 1985); Brackenridge, *Incidents of the Insurrection*; H. M. Brackenridge, *History of the Insurrection in Western Pennsylvania Commonly Called the Whiskey Insurrection, 1794* (Pittsburgh, 1859); Jacob

E. Cooke, "The Whiskey Insurrection: A Re-Evaluation," *PH*, 30 (1963), 336–42; and Dorothy E. Fennell, "From Rebelliousness to Insurrection: A Social History of the Whiskey Rebellion, 1765–1802" (Ph.D. diss., University of Pittsburgh, 1991).

54. Alan Taylor, *Liberty Men and Great Proprietors: The Revolutionary Settlement on the Maine Frontier, 1760–1820* (Chapel Hill, 1990).

55. David M. Ludlum, *Social Ferment in Vermont, 1791–1850* (New York, 1939), 13–14; David Maldwyn Ellis, *Landlords and Farmers in the Hudson-Mohawk Region, 1790–1850* (Ithaca, 1946), 32–36; Alfred F. Young, *The Democratic Republicans of New York: The Origins, 1763–1797* (Chapel Hill, 1967), 61, 204–207; William W. H. Davis, *The Fries Rebellion, 1798–1799: An Armed Resistance to the House Tax Law, Passed by Congress, July 9, 1798 in Bucks and Northhampton Counties, Pennsylvania* (Doylestown, Penn., 1899); Peter Levine, "The Fries Rebellion: Social Violence and the Politics of the New Nation," *PH*, 40 (1973), 241–58; Elizabeth K. Henderson, "The Northwestern Lands of Pennsylvania, 1790–1812," *PMHB*, 60 (1936), 156. See also *New York Daily Advertiser*, June 21, 1786, March 4, 1791; *New York Evening Post*, Jan. 15, 1802; *New York Gazetteer*, March 31, 1784, Oct. 12, 1785, Sept. 28, 1791; *New York Independent Journal*, April 23, 1788; *New York Journal*, Feb. 19, 1784, Oct. 12, 1785, Sept. 28, 1791; *New York Packet*, April 22, 1788.

56. Richard D. Brown, "Shays's Rebellion and the Ratification of the Federal Constitution in Massachusetts," in Richard Beeman et al., eds., *Beyond Confederation: Origins of the Constitution and American National Identity* (Chapel Hill, 1987), 113–27; Szatmary, *Shays' Rebellion*, 120–34; Slaughter, *Whiskey Rebellion*, 190–204; Baldwin, *Whiskey Rebels*, 259–72; William Miller, "The Democratic Societies and the Whiskey Insurrection," *PMHB*, 62 (1938), 324–49; Taylor, *Liberty Men*, 209–32; Brown, "Back Country Rebellions," in Brown and Fehrenbacher, eds., *Tradition, Conflict, and Modernization*, 73–99.

57. John R. Howe, Jr., "Republican Thought and the Political Violence of the 1790s," *American Quarterly*, 19 (1967), 147–65.

58. *New York Gazetteer*, June 11, July 9, 14, 1784; *New York Journal*, July 21, 1785; Walsh, *Charleston's Sons of Liberty*, 118–21.

59. Saul Cornell, "Aristocracy Assailed: The Ideology of Backcountry Anti-Federalism," *JAH*, 76 (1990), 1148–72; Gilje, *Road to Mobocracy*, 96–100.

60. Frances Sergeant Childs, *French Refugee Life in the United States, 1790–1800: An American Chapter of the French Revolution* (Baltimore, 1940), 173; *New York Daily Advertiser*, June 1, 3, 5, 1793; Phineas Bond to Lord Grenville, June 8, 1793, "Letters of Phineas Bond," *Annual Report of the American Historical Association* (1897), 529–30; *New York Daily Advertiser*, Aug. 19, 1793; *New York Argus*, June 29, 1795.

61. *New York Journal*, April 16, 1794; Steffen, *Mechanics of Baltimore*, 149–50; James Morton Smith, *Freedom's Fetters: The Alien and Sedition Laws and American Civil Liberties* (Ithaca, 1956), 257–70; Alexander DeConde, *The Quasi-War: The Politics and Diplomacy of the Undeclared War with France, 1797–1801* (New York, 1966), 82–84; Gilje, *Road to Mobocracy*, 107–12.

62. Gilje, *Road to Mobocracy*, 95–119.

3. Democracy Unleashed

1. *Annapolis Maryland Republican*, July 1, 1812.

2. This account of the Baltimore riots relies heavily upon Paul A. Gilje, "The

Baltimore Riots of 1812 and the Breakdown of the Anglo-American Mob Tradition," *JSH*, 13 (1980), 547–64; and Gilje, "'Le Menu Peuple' in America: Identifying the Mob in the Baltimore Riots of 1812," *MHM*, 81 (1986), 50–66. See also Frank A. Cassell, "The Great Baltimore Riot of 1812," *MHM*, 70 (1975), 241–59; Donald R. Hickey, "The Darker Side of Democracy: The Baltimore Riots of 1812," *Maryland Historian*, 7 (1976), 1–20; and Charles G. Steffen, *The Mechanics of Baltimore: Workers and Politics in the Age of Revolution, 1763–1812* (Urbana, Ill., 1984), 243–50.

3. On Mayor Johnson's interaction with the crowd and the quotation above see *Report of the Committee of Grievances . . . on the Subject of the Recent Riots in the City of Baltimore, Together with the Depositions taken for the Committee* (Annapolis, 1813), 242, 160–61, 199, 336, 334–45.

4. Charles G. Steffen, "Changes in the Organization of Artisan Production in Baltimore, 1790 to 1820," *WMQ*, 3rd. ser., 36 (1979), 101–17; Steffen, *The Mechanics of Baltimore.*

5. *Report . . .* , 3, 149, 160, 169, 177, 200, 203.

6. Gilje, "'Le Menu Peuple,'" *MHM*, 81 (1986), 50–66.

7. David Grimsted, "Rioting in its Jacksonian Setting," *AHR*, 77 (1972), 361–97. See also Carl E. Prince, "The Great 'Riot Year': Jacksonian Democracy and Patterns of Violence in 1834," *Journal of the Early Republic*, 5 (1985), 1–20.

8. Nicholas P. Canny, "The Ideology of English Colonization: From Ireland to America," *WMQ*, 3rd ser., 30 (1973), 575–98; Ray Allen Billington, *The Protestant Crusade, 1800–1860: A Study of the Origins of American Nativism* (Chicago, 1964; orig. pub. 1938).

9. J. Thomas Scharf and Thompson Wescott, *History of Philadelphia, 1609–1884*, I (Philadelphia, 1884), 519; *New York Evening Post*, Oct. 21, 1806, August 9, 1808, Sept. 11, Nov. 25–28, Dec. 2, 4, 11, 1811, Feb. 16, 1813, April 23, 1817; *Niles' Weekly Register*, Nov. 30, 1811; [New York] *National Advocate*, April 17, 1817; Paul A. Gilje, *The Road to Mobocracy: Popular Disorder in New York City, 1763–1834* (Chapel Hill, 1987), 123–25; [New York] *Gazette*, May 24, 1814.

10. Gilje, *Road to Mobocracy*, 123–25, 129–33; *New York Evening Post*, March 20, 1819.

11. Gilje, *Road to Mobocracy*, 133–37; [New York] *National Advocate*, July 23, 1824; *New York Evening Post*, August 3, 1825; Sam Bass Warner, Jr., *The Private City: Philadelphia in Three Periods of Its Growth* (Philadelphia, 1968), 126, n. 1.

12. *New York Evening Post*, Oct. 13, 1804; Peter Way, "Shovel and Shamrock: Irish Workers and Labor Violence in the Digging of the Chesapeake and Ohio Canal," *LH*, 30 (1989), 489–517; Way, *Common Labour: Workers and the Digging of North American Canals, 1780–1860* (Cambridge, 1993); W. David Baird, "Violence Along the Chesapeake and Ohio Canal: 1839," *MHM*, 66 (1971), 121–34; David Grimsted, "Ante-Bellum Labor: Violence, Strike, and Communal Arbitration," *JSH*, 19 (1985), 5–28; Richard B. Morris, "Andrew Jackson, Strikebreaker," *AHR*, 55 (1949), 54–68.

13. Gilje, *Road to Mobocracy*, 138–42.

14. The best works on these riots include John C. Schneider, "Riot and Reaction in St. Louis, 1854–1856," *MHR*, 68 (1974), 171–85; and Charles E. Deusner, "The Know Nothing Riots in Louisville," *RKHS*, 61 (1963), 122–47. See also William Barnaby Faherty, "Nativism and Midwestern Education: The Experience of St. Louis University, 1832–1856," *History of Education Quarterly*, 8 (1968), 456; Agnes Geraldine McGann, *Nativism in Kentucky to 1860* (Washington, D.C., 1944); Wallace S.

Hutcheon, Jr., "The Louisville Riots of August 1855," *RKHS*, 69 (1971), 150–72; Betty Carolyn Congleton, "George D. Prentice and Bloody Monday: A Reappraisal," ibid., 63 (1965), 218–39; J. Thomas Scharf, *The Chronicles of Baltimore; Being a Complete History of "Baltimore Town" and Baltimore City from the Earliest Period to the Present Time* (Port Washington, N.Y., 1972; orig. pub. 1874), 549–73; Benjamin Tuska, "Know Nothingism in Baltimore, 1854–1860," *Catholic Historical Review*, new series, 5 (1925), 217–51.

15. Ray Allen Billington, "The Burning of the Charlestown Convent," *NEQ*, 10 (1937), 4–24; Theodore M. Hammett, "Two Mobs of Jacksonian Boston: Ideology and Interest," *JAH*, 62 (1976), 845–68; Wilfred J. Bisson, *Countdown to Violence: The Charlestown Convent Riot of 1834* (New York, 1989). See also the account of one of the students in Louise Goddard Whitney, *The Burning of the Convent* (New York, 1969; orig. pub. Cambridge, Mass., 1877).

16. The best coverage of these riots is Michael Feldberg, *The Philadelphia Riots of 1844: A Study of Ethnic Conflict* (Westport, Conn., 1975). See also Billington, *Protestant Crusade*, 220–37; Warner, *Private City*, 144–52; John C. Schneider, "Community and Order in Philadelphia, 1834–1844," *Maryland Historian*, 5 (1974), 15–26; David Montgomery, "The Shuttle and the Cross: Weavers and Artisans in the Kensington Riots of 1844," *JSH*, 5 (1972), 411–46; and *A Full and Complete Account of the Late Awful Riots in Philadelphia* (Philadelphia, 1844). See also Vincent P. Lannie and Bernard C. Diethorn, "For the Honor and Glory of God: The Philadelphia Bible Riots of 1840," *History of Education Quarterly*, 8 (1968), 44–106.

17. Joel Tyler Headley, *The Great Riots of New York, 1712–1873* (Indianapolis, 1970; orig. pub. New York, 1873), 95; Billington, *Protestant Crusade*, 196; Paul O. Weinbaum, *Mobs and Demagogues: The New York Response to Collective Violence in the Early Nineteenth Century* (Ann Arbor, 1979), 55; John M. Werner, "Race Riots in the United States during the Age of Jackson" (Ph.D. diss., Indiana University, 1973), 38; John C. Schneider, "Urbanization and the Maintenance of Order: Detroit, 1824–1847," *MiH*, 60 (1976), 260–81; Roger Lane, *Policing the City: Boston, 1822–1885* (New York, 1967), 33.

18. The best discussions of rioting fire companies are Bruce Laurie, "Fire Companies and Gangs in Southwark: The 1840s," in Allen F. Davis and Mark H. Haller, eds., *The Peoples of Philadelphia: A History of Ethnic Groups and Lower-Class Life, 1790–1940* (Philadelphia, 1973), 71–87; and David R. Johnson, *Policing the Urban Underworld: The Impact of Crime on the Development of the American Police* (Philadelphia, 1979), 83–89. See also Scharf, *Chronicles of Baltimore*, 549–74; Gilje, *Road to Mobocracy*, 260–64; Augustine E. Costello, *Our Firemen: A History of the New York Fire Departments, Volunteer and Paid* (New York, 1887), 97, 100, 115–18, 134, 162, 168–76; Deusner, "Know Nothing Riots in Louisville," *RKHS*, 61 (1963), 122–47.

19. Richard Hofstadter and Michael Wallace, eds., *American Violence: A Documentary History* (New York, 1970), 309–12.

20. Leonard Pitt, "The Beginnings of Nativism in California," *PHR*, 30 (1961), 23–38.

21. Gilje, *Road to Mobocracy*, 245–46.

22. Ibid., 203–64.

23. Grimsted uses the term "archaic" borrowed from Charles Tilly, who views intra-community conflict involving issues of honor and respect as primitive and pre-political. Grimsted, "Ante-Bellum Labor," *JSH*, 19 (1985), 8–14, n. 30; Charles Tilly, "Collective

Violence in European Perspective," in Hugh Davis Graham and Ted Robert Gurr, eds., *Violence in America: Historical and Comparative Perspectives*, rev. ed. (Beverly Hills, 1979), 83–118.

24. Gilje, *Road to Mobocracy*, 173–202; Grimsted, "Ante-Bellum Labor," *JSH*, 19 (1985), 8–14. See also Way, "Shovel and Shamrock," *LH*, 30 (1989), 489–517.

25. Headley, *Great Riots*, 97–110; Weinbaum, *Mobs and Demagogues*, 85–87.

26. Michael Feldberg, *The Turbulent Era: Riot and Disorder in Jacksonian America* (New York, 1980), 64–65, 67–71.

27. Schneider, "Urbanization and the Maintenance of Order," *MiH*, 60 (1976), 269; John Bach McMaster, *A History of the People of the United States* (New York, 1910), VII, 6–7, 9–10; David Grimsted, "Democratic Rioting: A Case Study of the Baltimore Bank Mob of 1835," in William L. O'Neill, ed., *Insights and Parallels: Problems and Issues of American Social History* (Minneapolis, 1973), 125–91; Scharf, *Chronicles of Baltimore*, 474–78.

28. Scharf and Wescott, *History of Philadelphia*, I, 598.

29. This discussion relies on a large literature. The most relevant works are W. J. Rorabaugh, *The Alcoholic Republic: An American Tradition* (New York, 1979); David J. Saposs, "Part I: Colonial and Federal Beginnings (to 1827)" in John R. Commons et al., *History of Labour in the United States*, I (New York, 1966; orig. pub. 1918), 50–104; Howard B. Rock, *Artisans of the New Republic: The Tradesmen of New York City in the Age of Jefferson* (New York, 1979), 237–63; Sean Wilentz, *Chants Democratic: New York City and the Rise of the American Working Class, 1788–1850* (New York, 1984), 23–48; Paul E. Johnson, *A Shopkeeper's Millennium: Society and Revivals in Rochester, New York, 1815–1837* (New York, 1978).

30. Gilje, *Road to Mobocracy*, 253–64; John R. Gillis, *Youth and History: Tradition and Change in European Age Relations, 1700-Present* (New York, 1974); Elliott J. Gorn, "'Good-Bye Boys, I Die a True American': Homicide, Nativism, and Working-Class Culture in Antebellum New York City," *JAH*, 74 (1987), 388–410; Joseph F. Kett, *Rites of Passage: Adolescence in America, 1790 to the Present* (New York, 1977). See also Susan G. Davis, "'Making Night Hideous': Christmas Revelry and Public Order in Nineteenth-Century Philadelphia," *American Quarterly*, 34 (1982), 185–99; Davis, *Parades and Power: Street Theatre in Nineteenth-Century Philadelphia* (Philadelphia, 1986); Loretta T. Johnson, "Charivari/Shivaree: A European Folk Ritual on the American Plains," *Journal of Interdisciplinary History*, 20 (1990), 371–87; Bryan D. Palmer, "Discordant Music: Charivaris and Whitecapping in Nineteenth-Century North America," *Labour: Le Travailleur*, 1 (1978), 5–62.

31. Lowell H. Harrison, "Rowdies, Riots, and Rebellions," *American History Illustrated*, 7 (1972), 18–29; David F. Allmendinger, Jr., "The Dangers of Ante-Bellum Student Life," *JSH*, 7 (1973), 75–85; Steven J. Novak, *The Rights of Youth: American Colleges and Student Revolt, 1798–1815* (Cambridge, Mass., 1977).

32. Gilje, *Road to Mobocracy*, 252–53; Werner, "Race Riots" (Ph.D. diss., Indiana University, 1973), 32; Scharf, *Chronicles of Baltimore*, 524–25.

33. *Account of the Terrific and Fatal Riot at the New-York Astor Place Opera House, . . .* (New York, 1849), 19.

34. Gilje, *Road to Mobocracy*, 246–53; *Account of the Terrific and Fatal Riot*, 16–19; Moody, *Astor Place Riot*; Peter George Buckley, "'To the Opera House': Culture and Society in New York City" (Ph.D. diss., SUNY Stony Brook, 1986); Bruce A.

McConachie, "'The Theatre and the Mob': Apocalyptic Melodrama and Preindustrial Riots in Antebelllum New York," in McConachie and Daniel Friedman, eds., *Theatre for Working-Class Audiences in the United States, 1830–1980* (Westport, Conn., 1985), 17–46.

35. A third person was killed accidently at an "Indian" meeting. Henry Christman, *Tin Horns and Calico: A Decisive Episode in the Emergence of Democracy* (New York, 1945), 109.

36. The best account is Eldridge Honaker Pendleton, "The New York Anti-Rent Controversy, 1820–1860" (Ph.D. diss., University of Virginia, 1974). For the incidents described in the text see ibid., 29–31, 74–101, 126; David Maldwyn Ellis, *Landlords and Farmers in the Hudson-Mohawk Region 1790–1850* (New York, 1967; orig. pub. Ithaca, 1946), 154–55; Christman, *Tin Horns and Calico*, 22–27, 32–34, 74–101, 126; Edward P. Cheyney, *The Anti-Rent Agitation in the State of New York, 1839–1846* (Philadelphia, 1887); Cheyney, "The Anti-Rent Movement and the Constitution of 1846," in Alexander C. Flick, ed., *History of the State of New York*, VI (New York, 1934), 281–322; David Murray, "The Antirent Episode in the State of New York," *Annual Report of the American Historical Association for the Year 1896*, 1 (1896), 137–73; Arthur Pound, "The Down-Rent War in Olde Ulster," *NYH*, 23 (1942), 410–18; Simon W. Rosendale, "Closing Phases of the Manorial System in Albany," *Proceedings of the New York State Historical Association*, 8 (1909), 234–45.

37. See James Edward Brady, "Wyoming: A Study of John Franklin and the Connecticut Settlement into Pennsylvania" (Ph.D. diss., Syracuse University, 1973); Alan Taylor, *Liberty Men and Great Proprietors: The Revolutionary Settlement on the Maine Frontier, 1760–1820* (Chapel Hill, 1990); Peter S. Onuf, *Statehood and Union: A History of the Northwest Ordinance* (Bloomington, Ind., 1987), 88–108; Carroll J. Kraus, "A Study in Border Confrontation: The Iowa-Missouri Boundary Dispute," *Annals of Iowa*, 3rd. ser., 40 (1969), 81–107; Allan G. Bogue, "The Iowa Claim Clubs: Symbol and Substance," *MVHR*, 45 (1958), 231–53; Theodore H. Hittell, *History of California*, III (San Francisco, 1897), 666–90.

38. The best account is Kenneth H. Winn, *Exiles in a Land of Liberty: Mormons in America, 1830–1846* (Chapel Hill, 1989). See also R. J. Robertson, Jr., "The Mormon Experience in Missouri, 1830–1839, Part I," *MHR*, 68 (1974), 280–98; Robertson, "The Mormon Experience in Missouri, 1830–1839, Part II," ibid., 393–415; Stephen C. LeSueur, *The 1838 Mormon War in Missouri* (Columbia, Mo., 1987); Leonard J. Arrington and Davis Bitton, *The Mormon Experience: A History of the Latter-Day Saints* (New York, 1979); Richard L. Bushman, *Joseph Smith and the Beginnings of Mormonism* (Urbana, Ill., 1984).

39. Quoted in Winn, *Exiles in the Land of Liberty*, 92–93.

40. T. Edgar Lyon, "Independence, Missouri, and the Mormons," *Brigham Young University Studies*, 13 (1972), 10–19; Warren A. Jennings, "Factors in the Destruction of the Mormon Press in Missouri, 1833," *Utah Historical Quarterly*, 35 (1967), 57–76; Jennings, "The Army of Israel Marches into Missouri," *MHR*, 62 (1968), 107–35; Jennings, "The Expulsion of the Mormons from Jackson County, Missouri," ibid., 64 (1969), 41–63.

41. Quoted in Winn, *Exiles in the Land of Liberty*, 102.

42. Robertson, "Mormon Experience . . . , Part I," *MHR*, 68 (1974), 280–98; Winn, *Exiles in the Land of Liberty*, 102–105, 208–38; Reed C. Durham, "The Election Day

Battle at Gallatin," *Brigham Young University Studies*, 13 (1972), 36–61. On Nauvoo see Robert Bruce Flanders, *Nauvoo: Kingdom on the Mississippi* (Urbana, Ill., 1965); David E. Miller and Della S. Miller, *Nauvoo: The City of Joseph* (Santa Barbara, Cal., 1974); Dallin H. Oaks and Marvin S. Hill, *Carthage Conspiracy: The Trial of the Accused Assassins of Joseph Smith* (Urbana, Ill., 1975).

43. William Phillips, *The Conquest of Kansas, by Missouri and Her Allies: A History of the Troubles in Kansas, from the Passage of the Organic Act until the Close of July, 1856* (Boston, 1856), 86–87; Alice Nichols, *Bleeding Kansas* (New York, 1954), 27, 30.

44. For a discussion of the cultural clash see David Thelan, *Paths of Resistance: Tradition and Dignity in Industrializing Missouri* (New York, 1986); and Michael Fellman, *Inside War: The Guerilla Conflict in Missouri during the American Civil War* (New York, 1989). See also Phillips, *Conquest of Kansas*; Nichols, *Bleeding Kansas*; Samuel A. Johnson, *The Battle Cry of Freedom: The New England Emigrant Aid Company in the Kansas Crusade* (Lawrence, Kan., 1954); Allan Nevins, *Ordeal of the Union: A House Dividing, 1852–1857*, II (New York, 1947), 380–486; James A. Rawley, *Race and Politics: "Bleeding Kansas" and the Coming of the Civil War* (Philadelphia, 1969); James C. Malin, *John Brown and the Legend of Fifty-Six* (Philadelphia, 1942), esp. 560–628; Charles Robinson, *The Kansas Conflict* (New York, 1892). For a discussion of the land problem see ibid., 66–90; Paul Wallace Gates, *Fifty Million Acres: Conflicts Over Kansas Land Policy, 1854–1890* (Ithaca, 1954).

45. The most noted analysis of vigilantism is Richard Maxwell Brown, *Strain of Violence: Historical Studies of American Violence and Vigilantism* (New York, 1975). For other general surveys of vigilantism see William E. Burrows, *Vigilante!* (New York, 1976); Wayne Gard, *Frontier Justice* (Norman, Ok., 1949); Arnold Madison, *Vigilantism in America* (New York, 1973); C. C. Rister, "Outlaws and Vigilantes of the Southern Plains, 1865–1885," *MVHR*, 19 (1932), 537–54; H. Jon Rosenbaum and Peter C. Sederberg, eds., *Vigilante Politics* (Philadelphia, 1976). For a discussion of the relationship between the frontier and violence see also Joe B. Frantz, "The Frontier Tradition: An Invitation to Violence," in Hugh Davis Graham and Ted Robert Gurr, eds., *Violence in America: Historical and Comparative Perspectives* (New York, 1969), 119–43; W. Eugene Hollon, *Frontier Violence: Another Look* (New York, 1974); Richard Slotkin, *Regeneration through Violence: The Mythology of the American Frontier, 1600–1860* (Middletown, Conn., 1973).

46. Quoted in Brown, *Strain of Violence*, 117.

47. Thomas J. Dimsdale, *The Vigilantes of Montana or Popular Justice in the Rocky Mountains*, 4th printing (Virginia City, Mon., 1921), 275.

48. A. M. Haswell, "The Story of the Bald Knobbers," *MHR*, 18 (1923), 29.

49. *New York Evening Post*, Aug. 1, Nov. 14, 1825, Aug. 21, 1834; Hofstadter and Wallace, ed., *American Violence*, 447–50; Lane, *Policing the City*, 24–25; Werner, "Race Riots" (Ph.D. diss., Indiana University, 1973), 42–43; [New York] *Commercial Advertiser*, May 2, 1834; Herbert Asbury, *The French Quarter: An Informal History of the New Orleans Underworld* (New York, 1936), 247–52; Paul Walton Black, "Lynchings in Iowa," *Iowa Journal of History and Politics*, 10 (1912), 178; James W. Bragg, "Captain Slick, Arbiter of Early Alabama Morals," *Alabama Review*, 11 (1958), 125–34.

50. The most noted work on antiabolitionist mobs is Leonard L. Richards, *"Gentlemen of Property and Standing": Anti-Abolition Mobs in Jacksonian America* (New York, 1970). For further discussion and coverage of incidents described above see also Gilje,

Road to Mobocracy, 162–70; Werner, "Race Riots" (Ph.D. diss., Indiana University, 1973), 101–106; Carter G. Woodson, "The Negroes of Cincinnati prior to the Civil War," *JNH*, 1 (1916), 8–9; John L. Meyers, "Antislavery Activities of Five Lane Seminary Boys in 1835–36," *Bulletin of the Historical and Philosophical Society of Ohio*, 21 (1963), 95–111; Robert Price, "The Ohio Anti-Slavery Convention of 1836," *OSAHQ*, 45 (1936), 173–88; Samuel T. Pickard, *Life and Letters of John Greenleaf Whittier* (New York, 1894), I, 146–53; Henry Howe, "Granville Riot," *Historical Collections of Ohio*, II (Cincinnati, 1888), 80–81.

51. *New York Evening Post*, December 14, 1819; Hofstadter and Wallace, ed., *American Violence*, 450–53.

52. Richards, *"Gentlemen of Property and Standing,"* 92–111; Werner, "Race Riots" (Ph.D. diss., Indiana University, 1973), 206–18; Joseph C. and Owen Lovejoy, *Memoir of the Rev. Elijah P. Lovejoy; Who Was Murdered in Defense of the Liberty of the Press at Alton, Illinois, Nov. 7, 1837* (Freeport, N.Y., 1970; orig. pub. 1838); Edward Beecher, *Narrative of Riots at Alton: In Connection With the Death of the Rev. Elijah P. Lovejoy* (Alton, Ill., 1838; reprt. 1969); Robert Merideth, "A Conservative Abolitionist at Alton: Edward Beecher's *Narrative,*" *Journal of Presbyterian History*, 42 (1964), 39–53, 92–103; Scharf and Wescott, *History of Philadelphia*, I, 651–65.

53. See Brown, *Strain of Violence*, Appendix 3, 305–19. On California see Hittell, *History* III; Mary Floyd Williams, *History of the San Francisco Committee of Vigilance of 1851: A Study of Social Control on the California Frontier in the Days of the Gold Rush* (Berkeley, 1921); Roger D. McGrath, *Gunfighters, Highwaymen, and Vigilantes: Violence on the Frontier* (Berkeley, 1984); and Robert W. Blew, "Vigilantism in Los Angeles, 1835–1874," *Southern California Quarterly*, 54 (1972), 11–30. On California, Wyoming, Montana, and Idaho see Hubert Howe Bancroft, *The Works of Hubert Howe Bancroft: Popular Tribunals, vol. 1*, XXXVI (San Francisco, 1887). On Montana see Granville Stuart, *Forty Years on the Frontier: As Seen in the Journals and Reminiscences of Granville Stuart, Gold-Miner, Trader, Merchant, Rancher and Politician*, II, Paul C. Phillips, ed. (Cleveland, 1925); Hoffman Birney, *Vigilantes* (Philadelphia, 1929); Christopher P. Connolly, *The Devil Learns to Vote: The Story of Montana* (New York, 1938); Dimsdale, *Vigilantes*; Helen Fitzgerald Sanders, ed., *X. Beidler: Vigilante* (Norman, Ok., 1957); Oscar O. Mueller, "The Central Montana Vigilante Raids of 1884," *Montana Magazine of History*, 1 (1951), 23–35. On Montana and Idaho see Nathaniel Pitt Langford, *Vigilante Days and Ways: The Pioneers of the Rockies: The Makers and Making of Montana and Idaho* (New York, 1912; orig. pub. 1890). On Texas see C. L. Sonnichsen, *I'll Die before I'll Run: The Story of the Great Feuds of Texas* (New York, 1951); Sonnichsen, *Ten Texas Feuds* (Albuquerque, 1957); Rister, "Outlaws and Vigilantes," *MVHR*, 19 (1932), 537–54.

54. Sheldon Hackney, "Southern Violence," *AHR*, 74 (1969), 906–25; Arthur F. Howington, "Violence in Alabama: A Study of Late Ante-bellum Montgomery," *Alabama Review*, 27 (1974), 213–31; Anthony S. Nicolosi, "The Rise and Fall of the New Jersey Vigilant Societies," *New Jersey History*, 86 (1968), 29–53; Brown, *Strain of Violence*, 3–36, 144–79.

55. Brown, *Strain of Violence*, 134–43; Hubert Howe Bancroft, *The Works of Hubert Howe Bancroft: Popular Tribunals, vol. 2*, XXXVII (San Francisco, 1887); Robert M. Senkewicz, *Vigilantes in Gold Rush San Francisco* (Stanford, Cal., 1988).

56. Asbury, *The French Quarter*, 298–314; Bancroft, *Works*, XXXVI, 142–78; Hittell, *History*, III, 272–309; Sonnichsen, *Ten Texas Feuds*, 87–156; Chester D. Potter, "Reminiscences of the Socorro Vigilantes," Paige W. Christiansen, ed., *New Mexico Historical Review*, 40 (1965), 23–54; William F. Holmes, "Whitecapping: Agrarian Violence in Mississippi, 1902–1906," *JSoH*, 35 (1969), 165–85; Lawrence C. Goodwyn, "Populist Dreams and Negro Rights: East Texas as a Case Study," *AHR*, 76 (1971), 1435–56; James Elbert Cutler, *Lynch-Law: An Investigation into the History of Lynching in the United States* (Montclair, N.J., 1969; orig. pub. New York, 1905); Robert P. Ingalls, *Urban Vigilantes in the New South: Tampa, 1882–1936* (Knoxville, Tenn., 1988); Ingalls, "Lynching and Establishment Violence in Tampa, 1858–1935," *JSoH*, 53 (1987), 613–44.

57. Black, "Lynchings," *Iowa J. of His. and Pol.*, 10 (1912), 151–254; Bogue, "The Iowa Claim Clubs," *MVHR*, 45 (1958), 231–53; John Ely Briggs, "Pioneer Gangsters," *Palimpsest*, 21 (1940), 73–90; Orville F. Grahame, "The Vigilance Committees," ibid., 6 (1925), 359–70; Patrick B. Nolan, *Vigilantes of the Middle Border: A Study of Self-Appointed Law Enforcement in the States of the Upper Mississippi from 1840 to 1880* (New York, 1986); John C. Parish, "White Beans for Hanging," *Palimpsest*, 1 (1920), 9–28; Eliphalet Price, "The Trial and Execution of Patrick O'Conner at the Dubuque Mines, 1834," ibid., 1 (1920), 86–97. For other movements see Harold E. Briggs, "Lawlessness in Cairo, Illinois, 1848–1858," *Mid-America*, new ser., 22 (1951), 67–88; Calvin W. Gower, "Vigilantes," *Colorado Magazine*, 41 (1964), 93–104; H[arry] L. Griffin, "The Vigilance Committees of the Attakapas Country; or Early Louisiana Justice," *Proceedings of the Mississippi Valley Historical Association*, 8 (1914–1915), 146–59; Robert Huhn Jones, "Three Days of Violence, the Regulators of Rock River Valley," *JISHS*, 59 (1966), 131–42; Charles W. Shull, ed., "Minutes of Vigilance Committee, Florence, Nebraska, May 29-July 30, 1857," *NH*, 58 (1977), 73–87; J. W. Vincent, "The 'Slicker War' and Its Consequences," *MHR*, 7 (1912–1913), 138–45; Genevieve Yost, "History of Lynchings in Kansas," *Kansas Historical Quarterly*, 2 (1933), 182–219; Mueller, "The Central Montana Vigilante Raids," *Montana Magazine of History*, 1 (1951), 25–35; Helena Huntington Smith, *The War on Powder River* (New York, 1966); Gard, *Frontier Justice*, 121–45; Mary Hartman and Elmo Ingenthron, *Bald Knobbers: Vigilantes on the Ozarks Frontier* (Gretna, La., 1988); Lucile Morris, *Bald Knobbers* (Caldwell, Id., 1939); Thelan, *Paths of Resistance*, 86–99.

58. Douglas O. Tice, "'Bread or Blood!': The Richmond Bread Riot," *Civil War Times, Illustrated*, 12 (Feb. 1974), 12–19; William J. Kimball, "The Bread Riot in Richmond, 1863," *Civil War History*, 7 (1961), 149–54; Georgia Lee Tatum, *Disloyalty in the Confederacy* (Chapel Hill, 1934), 22, 52.

59. Eugene H. Roseboom, "The Mobbing of the *Crisis*," *OSAHQ*, 59 (1950), 150–53; Frank L. Klement, *The Copperheads in the Middle West* (Chicago, 1960), 88, 122, 162, 221. Republicans harassed opponents to the war in Canton, Ohio (Aug. 1861), Terre Haute, Indiana (Oct. 1861), Bloomington, Illinois (summer 1862), Lebanon, Ohio (summer 1862), Keokuk, Iowa (Feb. 1863), and other places. Wood Gray, *The Hidden Civil War: The Story of the Copperheads* (New York, 1964; orig. pub. 1942), 68, 89, 142; Nolan, *Vigilantes of the Middle Border*, 105.

60. Klement, *Copperheads*, 92.

61. Tatum, *Disloyalty*, 122.

62. Lawrence H. Larsen, "Draft Riot in Wisconsin, 1862," *Civil War History,* 7 (1961), 421–27; Gray, *Hidden Civil War,* 111; Klement, *Copperheads,* 27, 79. For other draft riots see Gray, *Hidden Civil War,* 110–11; Robert E. Sterling, "Civil War Draft Resistance in Illinois," *JISHS,* 64 (1971), 244–66; Lane, *Policing the City* (New York, 1967), 133–34; William Frederic Reekstin, "The Draft Riots of July, 1863 on Staten Island," *Staten Island Historian,* 19 (1958), 27–30; Williston H. Lofton, "Northern Labor and the Negro during the Civil War," *JNH,* 34 (1949), 272; William F. Hanna, "The Boston Draft Riot," *Civil War History,* 36 (1990), 262–73.

63. Tatum, *Disloyalty,* 46–47, 115.

64. Edward G. Everett, "The Baltimore Riots, April, 1861," *PH,* 24 (1957), 331–42; Scharf, *Chronicles of Baltimore,* 587–614; Matthew Page Andrews, *History of Maryland: Province and State* (New York, 1929), 511–25; Charles B. Clark, "Baltimore and the Attack on the Sixth Massachusetts Regiment, April 19, 1861," *MHM,* 56 (1961), 39–71.

65. Charles H. Coleman and Paul H. Spence, "The Charleston Riot, March 28, 1864," *JISHS,* 33 (1940), 7–56; John F. Reed, "Riot in Illinois: An on the Scene Account of 1864 Draft Riots," *Manuscripts,* 4 (1951–1952), 23–27.

4. The Tragedy of Race

1. Ira Berlin, "The Revolution in Black Life," in Alfred F. Young, ed., *The American Revolution: Explorations in the History of American Radicalism* (Dekalb, Ill., 1976), 349–82; Berlin, *Slaves Without Masters: The Free Negro in the Antebellum South* (New York, 1974); Gary B. Nash, "Forging Freedom: The Emancipation Experience in the Northern Seaport Cities, 1775–1820," in Ira Berlin and Ronald Hoffman, eds., *Slavery and Freedom in the Age of the American Revolution* (Charlottesville, Va., 1983), 3–48; Nash, *Forging Freedom: The Formation of Philadelphia's Black Community, 1720-1840* (Cambridge, Mass., 1988); Benjamin Quarles, *The Negro in the American Revolution* (Chapel Hill, 1961); Quarles, "The Revolutionary War as a Black Declaration of Independence," in Berlin and Hoffman, eds., *Slavery and Freedom,* 283–301; Shane White, "'We Dwell in Safety and Pursue Our Honest Callings': Free Blacks in New York City, 1783–1810," *JAH,* 75 (1988), 445–70; White, *Somewhat More Independent: The End of Slavery in New York City, 1770–1810* (Athens, Ga., 1991).

2. Other than those cited above and below, these riots include incidents in New York (August 10, 1801; June 19, 1819; September 19, 1826; November 13–15, 1832; and April 12 and 20, 1837); Philadelphia (September 11 ca., 1824; April 16, 1830; May 4 ca., 1834; and June 16, 1835); Camden, N.J. (Dec. 11, 1832); Detroit (June 1833); Buffalo, N.Y. (June 19, 1834; July 1835); Marion, Ohio (September 1839); Carlisle, Penn. (June 3, 1843); southeastern Pennsylvania (several incidents in 1851); Boston (February 15 and April 1851). The most comprehensive survey of antebellum racial violence is John M. Werner, "Race Riots in the United States during the Age of Jackson, 1824–1849" (Ph.D. diss., Indiana University, 1973). This analysis relies heavily upon Werner even when it is not cited below. For incidents listed above see ibid., 41, 201, 237–38, 273. See also [New York] *Commercial Advertiser,* April 20, 1830, July 25, 30, 1833; *New York Evening Post,* April 19, 1830, Dec. 11, 1832, June 25, 30, 1833; *Morning Courier and New York Enquirer,* May 5, 1834; Paul A. Gilje, *The Road to Mobocracy: Popular Disorder in New York City, 1763–1834* (Chapel Hill, 1987), 147–53; Leonard L. Richards, *"Gentlemen of Property and Standing": Anti-Abolition Mobs in*

Jacksonian America (New York, 1970), 33; John C. Schneider, "Urbanization and the Maintenance of Order: Detroit, 1824–1847," *MiH,* 60 (1976), 263–65; Adrian Cook, *The Armies of the Streets: The New York City Draft Riots of 1863* (Lexington, Kentucky, 1974), 21.

3. *New York Evening Post,* Jan. 3, 18, 1820, June 25, 1825; [New York] *National Advocate,* January 3, 1820.

4. The most recent account is Thomas P. Slaughter, *Bloody Dawn: The Christiana Riot and Racial Violence in the Antebellum North* (New York, 1991). See also W. U. Hensel, *The Christiana Riot and the Treason Trials of 1851: An Historical Sketch,* 2nd rev. ed. (Lancaster, Pa., 1911); Jonathan Katz, *Resistance at Christiana: The Fugitive Slave Rebellion, Christiana, Pennsylvania, September 11, 1851—A Documentary Account* (New York, 1974); Roderick W. Nash, "The Christiana Riot: An Evaluation of Its National Significance," *Journal of the Lancaster County Historical Society,* 65 (1961), 65–91; Nash, "William Parker and the Christiana Riot," *JNH,* 46 (1961), 24–31. For an example of a racially mixed rescue in Syracuse, New York, on Oct. 1, 1851, see Galpin W. Freeman, "The Jerry Rescue," *NYH,* 26 (1945), 19–34; for a largely white crowd rescuing a black in Wellington, Ohio, in September 1858, see John Bach McMaster, *A History of the People of the United States: From the Revolution to the Civil War,* 8 vols. (New York, 1901–1914), VIII, 356. For cases in Boston see Leonard W. Levy, "The 'Abolition Riot': Boston's First Slave Rescue," *NEQ,* 25 (1952), 85–92; David R. Maginnes, "The Case of the Court House Rioters in the Rendition of the Fugitive Slave Anthony Burns, 1854," *JNH,* 56 (1971), 31–42.

5. Gilje, *Road to Mobocracy,* 153–59; Nash, *Forging Freedom,* 213.

6. Howard P. Chudacoff and Theodore C. Hirt, "Social Turmoil and Governmental Reform in Providence, 1820–1832," *Rhode Island History,* 31 (1972), 21–33; Robert J. Cottrol, *The Afro-Yankees: Providence's Black Community in the Antebellum Era* (Westport, Conn.), 50–57; Richard C. Wade, "The Negro in Cincinnati, 1800–1830," *JNH,* 39 (1954), 43–57; Carter G. Woodson, "The Negroes of Cincinnati Prior to the Civil War," ibid., 1 (1916), 1–22.

7. Gilje, *Road to Mobocracy,* 162–70; John H. Hewitt, "The Sacking of St. Philip's Church, New York," *Historical Magazine of the Protestant Episcopal Church,* 49 (1980), 7–20; Linda K. Kerber, "Abolitionists and Amalgamators: The New York City Race Riots of 1834," *NYH,* 48 (1967), 28–39; J. Thomas Scharf and Thompson Wescott, *History of Philadelphia, 1609–1884* (Philadelphia, 1884), I, 637–38; Sam Bass Warner, Jr., *The Private City: Philadelphia in Three Periods of Its Growth* (Philadelphia, 1968), 126–29; John Runcie, "'Hunting the Nigs' in Philadelphia: The Race Riot of August 1834," *PH,* 39 (1972), 187–218.

8. Leonard P. Curry, *The Free Black in Urban America: The Shadow of the Dream* (Chicago, 1981), 100–101; Iver Bernstein, *The New York City Draft Riots: Their Significance for American Society and Politics in the Age of the Civil War* (New York, 1990), 119–20; David R. Johnson, *Policing the Urban Underworld: The Impact of Crime on the Development of the American Police, 1800–1887* (Philadelphia, 1979), 31–32.

9. Chudacoff and Hirt, "Social Turmoil," *Rhode Island History,* 31 (1972), 21–33; Cottrol, *The Afro-Yankees,* 56–57; Richards, *"Gentlemen of Property and Standing",* 122–29; Woodson, "Negroes of Cincinnati," *JNH,* 1 (1916), 1–22.

10. Janet S. Hermon, "The McIntosh Affair," Missouri Historical Society, *Bulletin,* 26 (1970), 123–43; Clement Eaton, "Mob Violence in the Old South," *MVHR,* 29 (1942), 351–70.

11. Gilje, *Road to Mobocracy*, 147–50; Edward Channing, *A History of the United States*, V (New York, 1927), 134; [New York] *National Advocate*, July 23, 1819; Michael Feldberg, *The Philadelphia Riots of 1844: A Study of Ethnic Conflict* (Westport, Conn., 1975), 4.

12. Leonard Harding, "The Cincinnati Riots of 1862," *Bulletin of the Cincinnati Historical Society*, 25 (1967), 229–39; Williston Lofton, "Northern Labor and the Negro during the Civil War," *JNH*, 34 (1949), 257–62, 272; John C. Schneider, "Detroit and the Problem of Disorder: The Riot of 1863," *MiH*, 58 (1974), 4–24; Wood Gray, *The Hidden Civil War: The Story of the Copperheads* (New York, 1964; orig. pub. 1942), 99–100; Bernstein, *New York City Draft Riots*, 119–20; Frank L. Klement, *The Copperheads in the Middle West* (Chicago, 1960), 16.

13. Schneider, "Detroit and the Problem of Disorder," *MiH*, 58 (1974), 4–24.

14. The following discussion relies heavily upon Bernstein, *New York City Draft Riots*; and Cook, *Armies of the Streets*. See also *The Bloody Week! Riot, Murder & Arson, Containing A Full Account of this Wholesale Outrage on Life and Property . . .* (New York, [1863]); Charles Brace Loring, *The Dangerous Classes of New York and Twenty Years' Work Among Them* (New York, 1872); Joel Tyler Headley, *The Great Riots of New York, 1712–1873* (Indianapolis, 1970; orig. pub. New York, 1873); James McCague, *The Second Rebellion: The Story of the New York City Draft Riots of 1863* (New York, 1968); Ernest A. McKay, *The Civil War and New York City* (Syracuse, 1990), 195–215; James M. McPherson, ed., *Anti-Negro Riots in the North, 1863* (New York, 1969; orig. pub. 1863); Albon P. Man, Jr., "The Church and the New York Draft Riots of 1863," *Records of the American Catholic Historical Society of Philadelphia*, 62 (1951), 33–50; Man, "Labor Competition and the New York Draft Riots of 1863," *JNH*, 36 (1951), 375–405; William Frederic Reekstin, "The Draft Riots of July 1863 on Staten Island," *Staten Island Historian*, 19 (1958), 27–30; James F. Richardson, *The New York Police: Colonial Times to 1901* (New York, 1970), 124–48; [William Osborn Stoddard], *The Volcano Under the City, by a Volunteer Special* (New York, 1887).

15. Brace, *Dangerous Classes*, 29–31; Bernstein, *New York City Draft Riots*, 4, 60.

16. Bernstein, *New York City Draft Riots*, 17–42.

17. Cook, *Armies of the Streets*, 193–268.

18. This analysis of Reconstruction collective violence relies heavily upon George C. Rable, *But There Was No Peace: The Role of Violence in the Politics of Reconstruction* (Athens, Ga., 1984); Joel Williamson, *After Slavery: The Negro in South Carolina during Reconstruction, 1861–1877* (Chapel Hill, 1965); Eric Foner, *Reconstruction: America's Unfinished Revolution, 1863–1877* (New York, 1988); Allen W. Trelease, *White Terror: The Ku Klux Klan Conspiracy and Southern Reconstruction* (New York, 1971); Ted Tunnell, *Crucible for Reconstruction: War, Radicalism and Race in Louisiana, 1862–1877* (Baton Rouge, La., 1984); and Melinda Meek Hennessey, "To Live and Die in Dixie: Reconstruction Race Riots in the South" (Ph.D. diss., Kent State University, 1978). In the following discussion, unless one of these works was the most significant source for a riot, I do not cite it for each specific incident. Any analysis of Reconstruction riots, however, should begin with these works.

19. Quoted in Trelease, *White Terror*, 143–44.

20. Stanley F. Horn, *Invisible Empire: The Story of the Ku Klux Klan, 1866–1871*, 2nd ed. (Montclair, N.J., 1969; orig. pub. 1939).

21. Herbert Shapiro, "Afro-American Responses to Race Violence during Reconstruction," *Science and Society*, 36 (1972), 158–70.

22. Trelease, *White Terror*, 31, 130; Tunnell, *Crucible for Reconstruction*, 155–56; Hennessey, "To Live and Die in Dixie" (Ph.D. diss., Kent State University, 1978), 94–99.

23. Gene L. Howard, *Death at Cross Plains: An Alabama Reconstruction Tragedy* (University, Ala., 1984).

24. Jack D. L. Holmes, "The Effects of the Memphis Race Riot of 1866," *West Tennessee Historical Society Papers*, 12 (1958), 58–79; Holmes, "The Underlying Causes of the Memphis Race Riot of 1866," *THQ*, 17 (1958), 195–221; Bobby L. Lovett, "Memphis Riots: White Reaction to Blacks in Memphis, May 1865-July 1866," ibid., 38 (1979), 9–33; James Gilbert Ryan, "The Memphis Riots of 1866: Terror in a Black Community during Reconstruction," *JNH*, 62 (1977), 243–57; United States Congress, Special Committee, *Memphis Riots and Massacres, 1866* (Miami, Florida, 1969); Altina L. Waller, "Community, Class and Race in the Memphis Riot of 1866," *JSH*, 18 (1984), 233–46.

25. John Carver Edwards, "Radical Reconstruction and the New Orleans Riot of 1866," *International Review of History and Political Science*, 10 (1973), 48–64; Donald E. Reynolds, "The New Orleans Riot of 1866, Reconsidered," *LaH*, 5 (1964), 5–28; Gilles Vandal, "The Origin of the New Orleans Riot of 1866, Revisited," ibid., 22 (1981), 135–65; Vandal, *The New Orleans Riot of 1866: Anatomy of a Tragedy* (Lafayette, La., 1983).

26. Rable, *But There Was No Peace*, 77–78, 137–40, 183; Melinda Meek Hennessey, "Race and Violence in Reconstruction New Orleans: The 1868 Riot," *LaH*, 20 (1979), 77–91; Dale A. Somers, "Black and White in New Orleans: A Study in Urban Race Relations, 1865–1900," *JSoH*, 40 (1974), 19–42; Stuart Omer Landry, *The Battle of Liberty Place: The Overthrow of Carpet-Bag Rule in New Orleans, September 14, 1874* (New Orleans, 1955).

27. Melinda Meek Hennessey, "Racial Violence during Reconstruction: The 1876 Riots in Charleston and Cainhoy," *South Carolina Historical Magazine*, 86 (1985), 110–12; William C. Hine, "Black Organized Labor in Reconstruction Charleston," *LH*, 25 (1984), 515. Augusta, Louisville, Chattanooga, Norfolk, Alexandria, Knoxville, Nashville, Richmond, Mobile, and Savannah all experienced rioting during Reconstruction, which in some cases led to fatalities. G. David Garson and Gail O'Brien, "Collective Violence in the Reconstruction South," in Hugh Davis Graham and Ted Robert Gurr, eds., *Violence in America: Historical and Comparative Perspectives*, rev. ed. (Beverly Hills, Cal., 1979), 243–60; Holmes, "Underlying Causes," *THQ*, 17 (1958), 197; Sarah Woolfolk Wiggins, "The 'Pig Iron' Kelley Riot in Mobile, May 14, 1867," *Alabama Review*, 23 (1970), 45–55.

28. Theodore B. Fitz Simons, Jr., "The Camilla Riot," *Georgia Historical Quarterly*, 35 (1951), 116–25; Lee W. Formwalt, "The Camilla Massacre of 1868: Racial Violence as Political Propaganda," ibid., 71 (1987), 399–426; Lewis Nicholas Wynne and Milly St. Julien, "The Camilla Race Riot and the Failure of Reconstruction in Georgia," *Journal of Southwest Georgia History*, 5 (1987), 15–37.

29. James M. Wells, *The Chisolm Massacre: A Picture of Home Rule in Mississippi*, 2nd ed. (Washington, D.C., 1878).

30. Carolyn E. DeLatte, "The St. Landry Riot: A Forgotten Incident of Reconstruction Violence," *LaH*, 17 (1976), 41–49.

31. Manie White Johnson, "The Colfax Riot of April 1873," *LHQ*, 13 (1930), 391–427.

32. One study based mostly upon the reading of the *New York Times* listed 82 race-related riots between 1863 and 1883. Hennessey counted only 72 race riots during Reconstruction. My own count, based largely on secondary sources, revealed at least 375 race-related riots between 1865 and 1876. I suspect that careful examination of the sources available would bring the total even higher, yet still not bear full testimony as to the extent of this violence. Garson and O'Brien, "Collective Violence," in Graham and Gurr, eds., *Violence in America*, 2nd ed., 243–60; Hennessey, "To Live and Die in Dixie" (Ph.D. diss., Kent State University, 1978), 5, 454. See also John A. Carpenter, "Atrocities in the Reconstruction Period," *JNH*, 47 (1962), 234–47.

33. Barry A. Crouch, "A Spirit of Lawlessness: White Violence; Texas Blacks, 1865–1868," *JSH*, 18 (1984), 217–32.

34. Trelease, *White Terror*, 365.

35. Trelease, *White Terror*, 306, 323–24, 357–58; Rable, *But There Was No Peace*, 97, 117.

36. See also Ray Granade, "Violence: An Instrument of Policy in Reconstruction Alabama," *Alabama Historical Quarterly*, 30 (1968), 181–202; Melinda M. Hennessey, "Reconstruction Politics and the Military: The Eufaula Riot of 1874," ibid., 38 (1976), 112–25; Ralph L. Peek, "Lawlessness in Florida, 1868–1871," *Florida Historical Quarterly*, 40 (1961), 164–85; Harry P. Owens, "The Eufaula Riot of 1874," *Alabama Review*, 16 (1963), 224–37; Herbert Shapiro, "The Ku Klux Klan during Reconstruction: The South Carolina Episode," *JNH*, 49 (1964), 34–55; J. C. A. Stagg, "The Problem of Klan Violence: The South Carolina Up-Country, 1868–1871," *Journal of American Studies*, 8 (1974), 303–18.

37. In addition to the works already cited on the Klan see Barry D. Crouch, "Postbellum Violence, 1871," in Arthur M. Schlesinger, Jr. and Roger Burns, eds., *Congress Investigates: A Documentary History, 1792–1974* (New York, 1975), III, 1689–1846; and Francis B. Simkins, "The Ku Klux Klan in South Carolina, 1868–1871," *JNH*, 12 (1927), 606–47; Charles L. Flynn, Jr., "The Ancient Pedigree of Violent Repression: Georgia's Klan as A Folk Movement," in Walter J. Fraser, Jr., and Winfred B. Moore, Jr., *The Southern Enigma: Essays on Race, Class, and Folk Culture* (Westport, Conn., 1983), 189–98.

38. Quoted in Vernon Burton, "Race and Reconstruction: Edgefield County, South Carolina," *JSH*, 12 (1978), 34–35.

39. The figures listed here were derived form several sources. James Elbert Cutler used the *Chicago Tribune* and other sources to compile a comprehensive list to 1903. The National Association for the Advancement of Colored People added to that list as reported in several sources. Frank Shay has a list that goes to 1937. Thereafter, lynching, which was already on the wane, declined precipitously. See Cutler, *Lynch-Law: An Investigation into the History of Lynching in the United States* (Montclair, N.J., 1969; orig. pub. 1905), 155–92; Donald L. Grant, *The Anti-Lynching Movement: 1883–1932* (San Francisco, 1975); Shay, *Judge Lynch: His First Hundred Years* (Montclair, N.J., 1969; orig. pub. New York, 1938). See also Walter White, *Rope and Faggot: A Biography of Judge Lynch* (New York, 1929), 227–69; National Association for the Advancement of

Colored People, *Thirty Years of Lynching in the United States, 1889–1918* (New York, 1969; orig. pub. 1919); Southern Commission on the Study of Lynching, *Lynchings and What They Mean: General Findings of the Southern Commission on the Study of Lynching* (Atlanta, [1931]); Daniel T. Williams, "The Lynching Records of Tuskegee Institute," in Williams, comp., *Eight Negro Bibliographies* (New York, 1970). The best account on lynching is W. Fitzhugh Brundage, *Lynching in the New South: Georgia and Virginia, 1880–1930* (Urbana, Ill., 1993). My analysis of southern race relations relies upon Herbert Shapiro, *White Violence and Black Response: From Reconstruction to Montgomery* (Amherst, Mass., 1988); Joel Williamson, *The Crucible of Race: Black-White Relations in the American South Since Emancipation* (New York, 1984); and Neil R. McMillen, *Dark Journey: Black Mississippians in the Age of Jim Crow* (Urbana, Ill., 1989). Unless one of these works was a significant source for a riot, I do not cite it for each specific incident.

40. Mary Church Terrell, "Lynching from a Negro's Point of View," *North American Review*, 178 (1904), 859–60; Shapiro, *White Violence*, 89, 111–13; Williamson, *Crucible of Race*, 204–205; McMillen, *Dark Journey*, 234; "The Waco Horror," *Crisis*, 12 (July 1916), Supplement, 1–8; quotation is from British writer Stephen Graham and is cited in Shapiro, *White Violence*, 146.

41. Winfield H. Collins, *The Truth About Lynching and the Negro in the South: In Which the Author Pleads that the South Be Made Safe for the White Race* (New York, 1918), 65.

42. Quoted in Frenise A. Logan, *The Negro in North Carolina, 1876–1894* (Chapel Hill, 1964), 186. See also Eric Anderson, *Race and Politics in North Carolina, 1872–1901: The Black Second* (Baton Rouge, La., 1981), 321–23.

43. John Carlisle Kilgo, "An Inquiry Concerning Lynchings," *South Atlantic Quarterly*, 1 (1902), 7.

44. Henderson M. Somerville, "Some Co-Operating Causes of Negro Lynching," *North American Review*, 177 (1903), 506–12.

45. Edward L. Ayers, *Vengeance and Justice: Crime and Punishment in the 19th-Century American South* (New York, 1984), 252–53; William F. Holmes, "Moonshining and Collective Violence: Georgia, 1889–1895," *JAH*, 67 (1980), 600; Ida B. Wells, "Southern Horrors: Lynch Law in all its Phases," in Ida B. Wells-Barnett, *On Lynching: Southern Horrors, A Red Record, Mob Rule in New Orleans* (Salem, N.H., 1991; orig. pub. as *Southern Horrors*, 1892), 6–12.

46. Cutler, *Lynch-Law*, 155–92; NAACP, *Thirty Years of Lynching*; White, *Rope and Faggot*, 252–53.

47. Robert Seitz Frey and Nancy Thompson-Frey, *The Silent and the Damned: The Murder of Mary Phagan and the Lynching of Leo Frank* (Lanham, Md., 1988), 93; Louis R. Harlan and Pete Daniel, "A Dark and Stormy Night in the Life of Booker T. Washington," *Negro History Bulletin*, 33 (1970), 159–61.

48. Ida B. Wells, *Crusade for Justice: The Autobiography of Ida B. Wells*, Alfreda M. Duster, ed. (Chicago, 1970), 61–66.

49. William Warren Rogers and Robert David Ward, *August Reckoning: Jack Turner and Racism in Post–Civil War Alabama* (Baton Rouge, La., 1973).

50. *NYT*, Feb. 23, 1898; Wells, *Autobiography*, 252; George Brown Tindall, *South Carolina Negroes, 1877–1900* (Columbia, S.C., 1952), 255–56.

51. McMillen, *Dark Journey*, 140; Grant, *Anti-Lynching*, 4; Walter White, *A Man Called White: The Autobiography of Walter White* (New York, 1948), 40–43.

52. William F. Holmes, "Whitecapping: Agrarian Violence in Mississippi, 1902–1906," *JSoH*, 35 (1969), 165–85; Holmes, "Whitecapping in Mississippi: Agrarian Violence in the Populist Era," *Mid-America*, 55 (1973), 134–48; Holmes, "Moonshining and Collective Violence," *JAH*, 67 (1980), 589–611; Holmes, "Moonshining and Law Enforcement in Turn of the Century Alabama," in Merle Black and John Shelton Reed, eds., *Perspectives on the American South: An Annual Review of Society, Politics, and Culture*, I (New York, 1981), 71–80; Michael J. Cassity, *Chains of Fear: American Race Relations Since Reconstruction* (Westport, Conn., 1984), 35–48; Grant, *Anti-Lynching*, 4–5; Madeline Noble, "The White Caps of Harrison and Crawford County, Indiana: A Study in Violent Enforcement of Morality" (Ph.D. diss., University of Michigan, 1973), 156–57.

53. Ayers, *Vengeance and Justice*, 253–55.

54. Quoted in McMillen, *Dark Journey*, 227–28.

55. McMillen, *Dark Journey*, 225–28; John Rogers, *The Murders of Mer Rouge: The True Story of an Atrocity Unparalleled in the Annals of Crime* (St. Louis, 1923), 33–35.

56. W. Fitzhugh Brundage, "The Darien 'Insurrection' of 1899: Black Protest during the Nadir of Race Relations," *Georgia Historical Quarterly*, 74 (1990), 234–53; Brundage, *Lynching*, 133–36.

57. Shapiro, *White Violence*, 28; George C. Wright, *Racial Violence in Kentucky, 1865–1940: Lynching, Mob Rule, and Legal Lynchings* (Baton Rouge, La., 1990), 169–70.

58. McMillen, *Dark Journey*, 226; Grant, *Anti-Lynching*, 120.

59. See, for example, Vernon Lane Wharton, *The Negro in Mississippi, 1865–1890* (Chapel Hill, 1947), 106–16; Logan, *Negro in North Carolina*, 117–18, 125–27; and McMillen, *Dark Journey*, 226–27, 263–67.

60. For a discussion of varieties of lynchings see Brundage, *Lynching*, 17–48. For a discussion of lynchers see Shay, *Judge Lynch*, 84–98; Raper, *Tragedy of Lynching*; and McMillen, *Dark Journey*, 238–45. For women and children in lynch mobs see *Crisis*, 11 (Jan., 1916), 145–46.

61. Quoted in Williamson, *Crucible of Race*, 128. See his discussion of Felton, ibid., 124–30.

62. On southern violence see Richard Maxwell Brown, *Strain of Violence: Historical Studies of American Violence and Vigilantism* (New York, 1975); H. C. Brearley, "The Pattern of Violence," in W. Y. Couch, ed., *Culture in the South* (Chapel Hill, 1934), 678–92; Dickson D. Bruce, Jr., *Violence and Culture in the Antebellum South* (Austin, Tex., 1979); John Shelton Reed, "To Live—and Die—in Dixie: A Contribution to the Study of Southern Violence," *Political Science Quarterly*, 86 (1971), 429–43; Reed, "Below the Smith and Wesson Line: Reflections on Southern Violence," Black and Reed, eds., *Pers. on the Amer. South*, I, 9–22; Charles S. Sydnor, "The Southerner and the Laws," *JSoH*, 6 (1940), 3–23. On honor see Ayers, *Vengeance and Justice*; and Bertram Wyatt-Brown, *Southern Honor: Ethics and Behavior in the Old South* (New York, 1982).

63. For a sampling of this literature see Richard P. Bagozzi, "Populism and Lynching in Louisiana," *ASR*, 42 (1977), 355–59; H. M. Blalock, Jr., "Percent Black and Lynchings Revisited," *Social Forces*, 67 (1989), 631–33; Allison Davis, "Caste, Economy, and Violence," *AJS*, 51 (1945), 7–15; Carl Iver Hovland and Robert R.

Sears, "Minor Studies of Aggression: VI. Correlation of Lynchings with Economic Indices," *Journal of Psychology,* 9 (1940), 301–10; James M. Inverarity, "Populism and Lynching in Louisiana, 1889–1896: A Test of Erikson's Theory of the Relationship between Boundary Crises and Repressive Justice," *ASR,* 41 (1976), 262–80; Alexander Mintz, "A Re-Examination of Correlations between Lynchings and Economic Indices," *Journal of Abnormal and Social Psychology,* 41 (1946), 154–60; Whitney Pope and Charles Ragin, "Mechanical Solidarity, Repressive Justice, and Lynchings in Louisiana," *ASR,* 42 (1977), 363–69; Stewart E. Tolnay, E. M. Beck, and James L. Massey, "Black Lynchings: The Power Threat Hypothesis Revisited," *Social Forces,* 67 (1989), 605–23; Ira M. Wasserman, "Southern Violence and the Political Process," *ASR,* 42 (1977), 359–62.

64. On the issue of sex and lynching see the African-American critics of lynching in White, *Rope and Faggot,* 54–81; Wells, "Southern Horrors," in Wells-Barnett, *On Lynching,* 7–12. See also Jacquelyn Dowd Hall, "'The Mind that Burns in Each Body': Women, Rape, and Racial Violence," in Ann Snitow, Christine Stansell, and Sharon Thompson, eds., *Powers of Desire: The Politics of Sexuality* (New York, 1983), 328–49.

65. Williamson, *Crucible of Race,* 109–223.

66. In addition to the works already cited on developments in race relations in this period, see Chicago Commission on Race Relations, *The Negro in Chicago: A Study of Race Relations and a Race Riot in 1919* (New York, 1968; orig. pub. Chicago, 1922); Gilbert Osofsky, *Harlem: The Making of a Ghetto, Negro New York, 1890–1930,* 2nd ed. (New York, 1971); Allan H. Spear, *Black Chicago: The Making of a Negro Ghetto, 1890–1920* (Chicago, 1967); C. Vann Woodward, *Origins of the New South, 1877–1913* (Baton Rouge, La., 1951); Woodward, *The Strange Career of Jim Crow,* 2nd rev. ed. (New York, 1966). The best studies on this race rioting are Elliott Rudwick, *Race Riot at East St. Louis, July 2, 1917* (New York, 1972; orig. pub. Carbondale, Ill., 1964); Roberta Senechal, *The Sociogenesis of a Race Riot: Springfield, Illinois, in 1908* (Urbana, Ill., 1990); and William M. Tuttle, Jr., *Race Riot: Chicago in the Red Summer of 1919* (New York, 1970).

67. Allen D. Grimshaw, "Actions of Police and the Military in American Race Riots," *Phylon,* 24 (1963), 271–89; Grimshaw, "Lawlessness and Violence in America and Their Special Manifestations in Changing Negro-White Relationships," *JNH,* 44 (1959), 52–72; Grimshaw, "Urban Racial Violence in the United States: Changing Ecological Considerations," *AJS,* 66 (1960), 109–19; Bernard F. Robinson, "The Sociology of Race Riots," *Phylon,* 2 (1941), 162–71. For surveys of race rioting see Arthur I. Waskow, *From Race Riot to Sit-In, 1919 and the 1960s: A Study in the Connections between Conflict and Violence* (Garden City, N.Y., 1966); Lee Erskine Williams II, "Racism and Race Riots, 1919" (Ph.D. diss., Mississippi State University, 1975); Lee E. Williams and Lee E. Williams II, *Anatomy of Four Race Riots: Racial Conflict in Knoxville, Elaine (Arkansas), Tulsa, and Chicago, 1919–1921* (Jackson, Miss., 1972). In the following discussion, unless one of the surveys was a significant source for a riot, I do not cite it for each specific incident.

68. Helen G. Edmonds, *The Negro and Fusion Politics in North Carolina, 1894–1901* (Chapel Hill, 1951), 147–77; Harry Hayden, *The Story of the Wilmington Rebellion* (n.p., 1936); Logan, *Negro in North Carolina*; Jerome A. McDuffie, "Politics in Wilmington and New Hanover County, North Carolina, 1865–1900: The Genesis of a

Race Riot" (Ph.D. diss., Kent State University, 1979); H. Leon Prather, Sr., *We Have Taken a City: Wilmington Racial Massacre and Coup of 1898* (Rutherford, N.J., 1984); Henry Litchfield West, "The Race War in North Carolina," *Forum*, 26 (1899), 578–91.

69. Charles Crowe, "Racial Violence and Social Reform: Origins of the Atlanta Riot of 1906," *JNH*, 53 (1968), 234–56; Crowe, "Racial Massacre in Atlanta, September 22, 1906," ibid., 54 (1969), 150–73; White, *A Man Called White*, 3–12.

70. John Hope Franklin, *From Slavery to Freedom: A History of Negro Americans*, 3rd ed. (New York, 1969; orig. pub. 1947), 433–522; W. E. Burghardt DuBois, *The Souls of Black Folk: Essays and Sketches* (New York, 1953); August Meier and Elliott Rudwick, "Black Violence in the 20th Century: A Study of Rhetoric and Retaliation," Hugh Davis Graham and Ted Robert Gurr, eds., *Violence in America: Historical and Comparative Perspectives* (Washington, D.C., 1969), 307–16; Rudwick and Meier, "Negro Retaliatory Violence in the Twentieth Century," *New Politics*, 5 (1966), 41–51.

71. *NYT*, July 26–28, 1900; Ida B. Wells-Barnett, "Mob Rule in New Orleans: Robert Charles and His Fight to the Death . . ." in Wells-Barnett, *On Lynching*; William Ivy Hair, *Carnival of Fury: Robert Charles and the New Orleans Race Riot of 1900* (Baton Rouge, La., 1976); Williamson, *Crucible of Race*, 201–209.

72. Martha Gruening, "Houston," *Crisis*, 15 (Nov. 1917), 14–19; Robert V. Haynes, *A Night of Violence: The Houston Riot of 1917* (Baton Rouge, La., 1976); Rudwick and Meier, "Negro Retaliatory Violence in the Twentieth Century," *New Politics*, 5 (1966), 41–51; Edgar A. Schuler, "The Houston Race Riot, 1917," *JNH*, 29 (1944), 300–38. Compare this incident to the shooting that occurred in Brownsville in which the guilt of the black troops is in doubt. Ann J. Lane, *The Brownsville Affair: National Crisis and Black Reaction* (Port Washington, N.Y., 1971); John D. Weaver, *The Brownsville Raid* (New York, 1970).

73. For examples of racial unrest in the North before the 1890s see *NYT*, March 5, 1886; Roger Lane, *Roots of Violence in Black Philadelphia, 1860–1900* (Cambridge, Mass., 1986), 45–46, 62.

74. *Outlook*, 74 (1903), 867; Shapiro, *White Violence*, 122, 487, n. 5; Grant, *Anti-Lynching*, 120; Wells, *Autobiography*, 309–20.

75. Dennis B. Downey and Raymond M. Hyser, *No Crooked Death: Coatesville, Pennsylvania, and the Lynching of Zachariah Walker* (Urbana, Ill., 1991); Eric F. Goldman, "Summer Day," *American Heritage*, 15 (June 1964), 50–53, 83–89; Theodore Roosevelt, "Lynching and the Miscarriage of Justice," *Outlook*, 99 (1911), 706–707; Sterling D. Spero and Abram L. Harris, *The Black Worker: The Negro and the Labor Movement* (New York, 1931), 212, 250; Paul M. Angle, *Bloody Williamson: A Chapter in American Lawlessness* (New York, 1952), 89–116, 281–83; Victor Hicken, "The Virden and Pana Mine Wars of 1898," *JISHS*, 52 (1959), 263–78; John H. Kaiser, "Black Strikebreakers and Racism in Illinois, 1865–1900," ibid., 65 (1972), 313–26; *NYT*, Nov. 11, 1898; ibid., April 11, 1899; William M. Tuttle, Jr., "Labor Conflict and Racial Violence: The Black Worker in Chicago, 1894–1919," *LH*, 10 (1969), 408–32; Tuttle, *Race Riot*, 108–56. On similar labor-based race rioting in the South see David Montgomery, "Violence and the Struggle for Unions in the South, 1880–1930," in Black and Reed, eds., *Pers. on the Amer. South*, I, 35–47.

76. Gilbert Osofsky, "Race Riot, 1900: A Study of Ethnic Violence," *Journal of Negro Education*, 32 (1963), 16–24; Osofsky, *Harlem*, 46–50; Citizens' Protective League, *Story of the Riot* (New York, 1969; orig. pub. New York, 1900); *NYT*, August 16, 1900.

77. James L. Crouthamal, "The Springfield Race Riot of 1908," *JNH*, 45 (1960), 164–81; Senechal, *Sociogenesis of a Race Riot*, esp. 123–57.

78. William M. Tuttle, Jr., "Views of a Negro during 'The Red Summer' of 1919," *JNH*, 51 (July 1966), 209–18.

79. Rudwick, *Race Riot*, 49–50; [W. E. B. DuBois and Martha Gruening], "The Massacre of East St. Louis," *Crisis*, 14 (Sept. 1917), 219–38.

80. Robert Asher, ed., "Documents of the Race Riot at East St. Louis," *JISHS*, 65 (1972), 327–36; Rudwick, *Race Riot*, 41–94; *Crisis*, 14 (Aug. 1917), 175–78; [DuBois and Gruening], "Massacre," ibid. (Sept. 1917), 219–38.

81. Racial disturbances also took place in New York City (1917), Waco, Texas (1917), Lexington, Kentucky (1917), Chicago (1917), Chester, Pennsylvania (1917), Youngstown, Ohio (1917), Philadelphia (1918), Camp Merritt, New Jersey (1918), Dewey, Oklahoma (1918), New London, Connecticut (1919), Bisbee, Arizona (1919), Washington, D.C. (1919), Knoxville, Tennessee (1919), Omaha, Nebraska (1919), Millen, Georgia (1919), Charleston, South Carolina (1919), Philadelphia (1919), Longview, Texas (1919), Port Arthur, Texas (1919), Norfolk, Virginia (1919), Argo, Illinois (1919), Syracuse, New York (1919), Ocmulgee, Georgia (1919), Wilmington, Delaware (1919), Waukegan, Illinois (1920), and Chicago (1920). *Crisis*, 14 (July 1917), 145, 264, 302–303, 313; ibid., 15 (Nov. 1917), 36; ibid., 16 (Oct. 1918), 297; Chicago Commission on Race Relations, *Negro in Chicago*, 53–67; Haynes, *Night of Violence*, 319; Spear, *Black Chicago*, 213; Spero and Harris, *Black Worker*, 280–81; Tuttle, "Labor Conflict," *LH*, 10 (1969), 424; Waskow, *From Race Riot to Sit-In*, 12–37, 105–18, 304–307; Williams, "Racism" (Ph.D. diss., Mississippi State University, 1975), 158–98; Rudwick, *Race Riot*, 58–73; Vincent P. Franklin, "Philadelphia Race Riot of 1918," *PMHB*, 99 (1975), 336–50; Williams, "Racism" (Ph.D. diss., Mississippi State University, 1975), 13–157; Michael L. Lawson, "Omaha, A City in Ferment: Summer of 1919," *NH*, 58 (1977), 395–417.

82. Chicago Commission on Race Relations, *Negro in Chicago*; Carl Sandburg, *The Chicago Race Riots: July 1919* (New York, 1919); Tuttle, *Race Riot*.

83. Richard C. Cortner, *A Mob Intent on Death: The NAACP and the Arkansas Riot Cases* (Middletown, Conn., 1988); O. A. Rogers, Jr., "The Elaine Race Riots of 1919," *Arkansas Historical Quarterly*, 19 (1960), 142–50; Walter F. White, "'Massacring Whites' in Arkansas," *Nation*, 109 (1919), 715–16; and Todd E. Lewis, "Mob Justice in the 'American Congo': 'Judge Lynch' in Arkansas during the Decade after World War I," *Arkansas Historical Quarterly*, 52 (1993), 156–84.

84. Scott Ellsworth, *Death in a Promised Land: The Tulsa Race Riot of 1921* (Baton Rouge, La., 1982); R. Halliburton, Jr., "The Tulsa Race War of 1921," *Journal of Black Studies*, 2 (1972), 333–57; Halliburton, *The Tulsa Race War of 1921* (San Francisco, 1975); Walter F. White, "The Eruption of Tulsa," *Nation*, 112 (1921), 909–10.

5. Brink of Anarchy

1. The best surveys of labor violence remain Philip S. Foner, *History of the Labor Movement in the United States*, 6 volumes (New York, 1947–1982); David Montgomery, "Strikes in Nineteenth-Century America," *Social Science History*, 4 (1980), 81–104; Philip Taft, "Violence in American Labor Disputes," *Annals of the American Academy of Political and Social Science*, 364 (1966), 127–40; and Taft and Philip Ross, "American

Labor Violence: Its Causes, Character, and Outcome," in Hugh Davis Graham and Ted Robert Gurr, eds., *The History of Violence in America: Historical and Comparative Perspectives* (New York, 1969), 281–395. This analysis of labor rioting relies upon these and the other works cited in this note. In the following discussion, unless one of these works was a significant source for the specific incident, I do not cite it. See also Louis Adamic, *Dynamite: The Story of Class Violence* (New York, 1931); Jeremy Brecher, *Strike!* (Boston, 1972); John R. Commons et al., *History of Labour in the United States*, 4 vols. (New York, 1918–1935); Melvyn Dubofsky, *Industrialism and the American Worker, 1865–1920* (Arlington Heights, Ill., 1975); P. K. Edwards, *Strikes in the United States, 1881–1974* (New York, 1981); E. T. Hiller, *The Strike: A Study in Collective Action* (Chicago, 1928); Rhodri Jeffreys-Jones, *Violence and Reform in American History* (New York, 1978); Sidney Lens, *The Labor Wars: From the Molly Maguires to the Sitdowns* (Garden City, N.Y., 1973); David Montgomery, "Violence and the Struggle for Unions in the South, 1880–1930," in Merle Black and John Shelton Reed, eds., *Perspectives on the American South: An Annual Review of Society, Politics, and Culture,* I (New York, 1981), 35–47; David Montgomery, *Workers Control in America: Studies in the History of Work, Technology and Labor Struggles* (Cambridge, 1979); Patricia Cayo Sexton, *The War on Labor and the Left: Understanding America's Unique Conservatism* (Boulder, Col., 1991); and Samuel Yellen, *American Labor Struggles* (New York, 1936). See also H. M. Gitelman, "Perspectives on American Industrial Violence," *Business History Review,* 47 (1973), 1–23.

2. Quoted from *The Nation* in Lens, *Labor Wars,* 58.

3. The best narrative of the railroad strike is Robert V. Bruce, *1877: The Year of Violence* (Chicago, 1989; orig. pub. 1959). See also Gerald G. Eggert, *Railroad Labor Disputes: The Beginnings of Federal Strike Policy* (Ann Arbor, 1967), 24–53; Walter Licht, *Working for the Railroad: The Organization of Work in the Nineteenth Century* (Princeton, 1983), 244–72; Nick Salvatore, "Railroad Workers and the Great Strike of 1877: The View from a Small Midwest City," *LH,* 21 (1980), 522–45; Shelton Stromquist, *A Generation of Boomers: The Pattern of Railroad Labor Conflict in Nineteenth-Century America* (Urbana, Ill., 1987). For the nineteenth-century perspective see Joel Tyler Headley, *Pen and Pencil Sketches of the Great Riots* (New York, 1882), 337–560; James Dabney McCabe, *The History of the Great Riots . . .* (Philadelphia, [1877]).

4. The best modern account is Paul Krause, *The Battle for Homestead, 1880–1892: Politics, Culture, and Steel* (Pittsburgh, 1992). See also Linda Schneider, "The Citizen Striker: Workers' Ideology in the Homestead Strike of 1892," *LH,* 23 (1982), 47–66; Leon Wolff, *Lockout, the Story of the Homestead Strike of 1892: A Study of Violence, Unionism, and the Carnegie Steel Empire* (New York, 1965); David P. Demarest, Jr., and Fannia Weingartner, *"The River Ran Red": Homestead 1892* (Pittsburgh, 1992). For the contemporary perspective see Arthur G. Burgoyne, *The Homestead Strike of 1892* (Pittsburgh, 1979; orig. pub. 1893); Myron R. Stowell, *"Fort Frick" or the Siege of Homestead: A History of the Famous Struggle . . .* (Pittsburgh, 1893).

5. For a good narrative see Almont Lindsey, *The Pullman Strike: The Story of a Unique Experiment and of a Great Labor Upheaval* (Chicago, 1942). See also Stanley Buder, *Pullman: An Experiment in Industrial Order and Community Planning, 1880–1930* (New York, 1967), 147–201; Eggert, *Railroad Labor Disputes,* 152–225.

6. For a comprehensive account see George S. McGovern and Leonard F. Guttridge, *The Great Coalfield War* (Boston, 1972), 122–29, 172–79, 210–40. See also Graham Adams, Jr., *Age of Industrial Violence, 1910–1915: The Activities and Findings of the United States Commission on Industrial Relations* (New York, 1966), 146–60, 170–75; George P. West, *Report on the Colorado Strike: United States Commission on Industrial Relations* (Washington, D.C., 1915), 104–106, 126–38; H. M. Gitelman, *Legacy of the Ludlow Massacre: A Chapter in American Industrial Relations* (Philadelphia, 1988), 1–30; Zeese Papanikolas, *Buried Unsung: Louis Tikas and the Ludlow Massacre* (Salt Lake City, 1982).

7. For a survey of West Virginia mining problems see David Alan Corbin, *Life, Work, and Rebellion in the Coal Fields: The Southern West Virginia Miners, 1880–1922* (Urbana, Ill., 1981), 218–24. See also Winthrop D. Lane, *Civil War in West Virginia: A Story of the Industrial Conflict in the Coal Mines* (New York, 1921); Richard D. Lunt, *Law and Order vs. The Miners: West Virginia, 1907–1933* (Hamden, Conn., 1979), 120–44; and Lon Savage, *Thunder in the Mountains: The West Virginia Mine War, 1920–1921* (Pittsburgh, 1990; orig. pub. 1985). See also Gordon B. McKinney, "Industrialization and Violence in Appalachia in the 1890s," in J. W. Williamson, ed., *An Appalachian Symposium: Essays Written in Honor of Gatis D. Williams* (Boone, N.C., 1977), 131–44.

8. This discussion draws on several sources, including Ruth A. Allen, *The Great Southwest Strike* (Austin, Tex., 1942); Eggert, *Railroad Labor Disputes*, 60–80; Harry Frumerman, "The Railroad Strikes of 1885–86," *Marxist Quarterly*, 1 (1937), 394–405; Rowland Berthoff, "The Social Order of the Anthracite Region, 1825–1902," *PMHB*, 89 (1965), 261–91; Harold K. Kanarek, "The Pennsylvania Anthracite Strike of 1922," ibid., 99 (1975), 207–25; Grace Palladino, *Another Civil War: Labor, Capital, and the State in the Anthracite Regions of Pennsylvania, 1840–68* (Urbana, Ill., 1990); A. C. Hutson, Jr., "The Coal Miners' Insurrections of 1891 in Anderson County, Tennessee," *East Tennessee Historical Society's Publications*, 7 (1935), 103–21; Hutson, "The Overthrow of the Convict Lease System in Tennessee," ibid., 8 (1936), 82–103; Willard Heaps, *Riots, U.S.A.* (New York, 1966), 100; Robert David Ward and William Warren Rogers, *Labor Revolt in Alabama: The Great Strike of 1894* (University, Alabama, 1965), 76–78, 110–12; Victor Hicken, "The Virden and Pana Mine Wars of 1898," *JISHS*, 52 (1959), 263–78; John H. Keiser, "Black Strikebreakers and Racism in Illinois, 1865–1900," ibid., 65 (1972), 313–26; Paul M. Angle, *Bloody Williamson: A Chapter in American Lawlessness* (New York, 1952), 3–71, 277–79.

9. Historical analysis of these strikes can be found in Sarah M. Henry, "The Strikers and Their Sympathizers: Brooklyn in the Trolley Strike of 1895," *LH*, 32 (1991), 329–53; Ken Fones-Wolf, "Mass Strikes, Corporate Strategies: The Baldwin Locomotive Works and the Philadelphia General Strike of 1910," *PMHB*, 110 (1986), 447–57; Robert E. Zeigler, "The Limits of Power: The Amalgamated Association of Street Railway Employees in Houston, Texas, 1897–1905," *LH*, 18 (1977), 71–90. For contemporary reports see New York State, *Report of the Special Committee of the Assembly Appointed to Investigate the Causes of the Strike of the Surface Railroads in the City of Brooklyn* (Albany, 1895); *NYT*, Jan. 15–Feb. 21, 1895; Harold J. Howland, "The War in Philadelphia," *Outlook*, 94 (March 5, 1910), 522–25; Edmund Levinson, *I Break Strikes: The Technique of Pearl I. Bergoff* (New York, 1935),

49–50, 89–104. For examples of other violent trolley strikes see *Outlook*, 74 (1903), 544; *NYT*, March 5–7, 1886, Oct. 22, 1888, July 17, 24, 1899, Aug. 6, 1920; Harold E. Cox, "The Wilkes-Barre Street Railway Strike of 1915," *PMHB*, 94 (1970), 75–94.

10. Levinson, *I Break Strikes*, 70–88. For other examples see Paul Avrich, *The Haymarket Tragedy* (Princeton, 1984), 189–91; Daniel Eli Burnstein, "Progressivism and Urban Crisis: The New York City Garbage Workers' Strike of 1907," *Journal of Urban History*, 16 (1990), 386–423; Robert J. Embardo, "'Summer Lightening,' 1907: The Wobblies in Bridgeport," *LH*, 30 (1989), 518–35; Henry B. Leonard, "Ethnic Cleavage and Industrial Conflict in Late 19th Century America: The Cleveland Rolling Mill Company Strikes of 1882 and 1885," ibid., 20 (1979), 524–48; Daniel J. Walkowitz, *Worker City, Company Town: Iron and Cotton-Worker Protest in Troy and Cohoes, New York, 1855–84* (Urbana, Ill., 1978).

11. For a good recent account see Christopher Waldrep, *Night Riders: Defending Community in the Black Patch, 1890–1915* (Durham, N.C., 1993). See also James O. Nall, *The Tobacco Night Riders of Kentucky and Tennessee, 1905–1909* (Louisville, Ky., 1939). For other examples of rural collective violence see Tomás Almaguer, "Racial Domination and Class Conflict in Capitalist Agriculture: The Oxnard Sugar Beet Workers' Strike of 1903," *LH*, 25 (1984), 325–50; George L. Bell, "The Wheatland Hop-Fields' Riot," *Outlook*, 107 (1914), 118–22; Woodrow C. Whitten, "The Wheatland Episode," *PHR*, 17 (1948), 37–42.

12. A good comprehensive account is Michael A. Gordon, *The Orange Riots: Irish Political Violence in New York City, 1870 and 1871* (Ithaca, 1993). See also Joel Tyler Headley, *The Great Riots of New York, 1712–1873* (New York, 1970; orig. pub. New York, 1873), 289–306; Gustavus Myers, *History of Bigotry in the United States* (New York, 1943), 212–13.

13. Headley, *Great Riots*, 289–306.

14. For a good recent account see Harold W. Aurand, *From the Molly Maguires to the United Mine Workers: The Social Ecology of an Industrial Union, 1869–1897* (Philadelphia, 1971). See also James Ford Rhodes, "The Molly Maguires in the Anthracite Region of Pennsylvania," *AHR*, 15 (1910), 547–61; Anthony Bimba, *The Molly Maguires* (New York, 1932); F. P. Dewees, *The Molly Maguires: The Origin, Growth and Character of the Organization* (Philadelphia, 1877).

15. John P. Beck, "They Fought for Their Work: Upper Peninsula Iron Ore Trimmer Wars," *MiH*, 73 (1989), 24–31; Sterling D. Spero and Abram L. Harris, *The Black Worker: The Negro and the Labor Movement* (New York, 1931), 198–99.

16. *NYT*, Nov. 11, 26, 1920.

17. By comparison 9,438,480 immigrants came to the United States between 1840 and 1880. Some 7,661,264 came from Germany, Ireland, Great Britain, and Sweden-Norway. Immigration figures from U.S. Department of Justice, Immigration and Naturalization Service, *1984 Statistical Yearbook of the Immigration and Naturalization Service* ([Washington, D.C., 1984]), 2–4.

18. Quoted in Demarest and Weingartner, eds., *"The River Ran Red"*, 10.

19. Victor R. Greene, *The Slavic Community on Strike: Immigrant Labor in Pennsylvania Anthracite* (Notre Dame, Ind., 1968), see esp. 129–31, 138–43, 171–73, 190; Berthoff, "The Social Order of the Anthracite Region, 1825–1902," *PMHB*, 89

(1965), 261–91; Michael Novak, *The Guns of Lattimer: The True Story of a Massacre and a Trial, August 1897–March 1898* (New York, 1978); *NYT,* Oct. 11, 1900.

20. *NYT,* April 7, 11, 1900; Burnstein, "Progressivism and Urban Crisis," *Journal of Urban History,* 16 (1990), 386–423; Levinson, *I Break Strikes,* 41–44; Adams, *Age of Industrial Violence,* 114–15, 197; Taft, "Violence," *Ann. of the Amer. Acad. of Pol. and Soc. Sci.,* 364 (1966), 135–36; United States Bureau of Labor, *Report on Strike of Textile Workers in Lawrence, Mass. in 1912: Senate Documents, 62d Congress, 2d Session, Vol. 31* (Washington, D.C., 1912), 44–45.

21. Greene, *Slavic Community,* 142–43; McGovern and Guttridge, *The Great Coalfield War,* 172–76.

22. Herbert G. Gutman, "Work, Culture, and Society in Industrializing America, 1815–1919," *AHR,* 78 (1973), 531–88; Leonard, "Ethnic Cleavage," *LH,* 20 (1979), 524–48.

23. Almaguer, "Racial Domination," *LH,* 25 (1984), 337–40; Aurand, *From the Molly Maguires,* 122–23; Robert P. Ingalls, *Urban Vigilantes in the New South: Tampa, 1882–1936* (Knoxville, Tenn., 1988), 43–50, 63–69.

24. Leonard Pitt, "The Beginnings of Nativism in California," *PHR,* 30 (1961), 35; John Bach McMaster, *A History of the People of the United States: From the Revolution to the Civil War,* 8 vols. (New York, 1901–1914), VIII, 63.

25. Robert W. Blew, "Vigilantism in Los Angeles, 1835–1874," *Southern California Quarterly,* 54 (1972), 25–26.

26. Roy T. Wortman, "Denver's Anti-Chinese Riot, 1880," *Colorado Magazine,* 42 (1965), 275–91.

27. The best accounts of the anti-Chinese movement are Alexander Saxton, *The Indispensable Enemy: Labor and the Anti-Chinese Movement in California* (Berkeley, 1971), 200–208; and Robert Edward Wynne, *Reaction to the Chinese in the Pacific Northwest and British Columbia, 1850 to 1910* (New York, 1978), 103. See also Lynwood Carranco, "Chinese Expulsion from Humboldt County," *PHR,* 30 (1961), 329–40.

28. Saxton, *Indispensable Enemy,* 6, 72–73, 114–16; Wynne, *Reaction to the Chinese,* 13–19, 32–34; Hubert Howe Bancroft, *The Works of Hubert Howe Bancroft: Popular Tribunals, vol. 2,* XXXVII (San Francisco, 1887), 706–707; Bruce, *1877,* 268–70.

29. For a modern account of the Rock Springs massacre see Craig Storti, *Incident at Bitter Creek: The Story of the Rock Springs Chinese Massacre* (Ames, Iowa, 1991). See also [Isaac H. Bromley], *The Chinese Massacre at Rock Springs, Wyoming Territory, September 2, 1885* (Boston, 1886); Clayton D. Laurie, "Civil Disorder and the Military in Rock Springs, Wyoming: The Army's Role in the 1885 Chinese Massacre," *Montana,* 40 (summer 1990), 44–69.

30. Jules Alexander Karlin, "The Anti-Chinese Outbreaks in Seattle, 1885–1886," *Pacific Northwest Quarterly,* 39 (1948), 103–30; Karlin, "The Anti-Chinese Outbreak in Tacoma, 1885," *PHR,* 23 (1954), 271–83; Clayton D. Laurie, "'The Chinese Must Go': The United States Army and the Anti-Chinese Riots in Washington Territory, 1885–1886," *Pacific Northwest Quarterly,* 81 (1990), 22–29; Wynne, *Reaction to the Chinese,* 99–103, 173–206, 243–83, 318–19. See also Carlos A. Schwantes, "Protest in a Promised Land: Unemployment, Disinheritance, and the Origins of Labor Militancy in the Pacific Northwest, 1885–1886," *Western Historical Quarterly,* 13

(1982), 373–90; W. Thomas White, "Race, Ethnicity, and Gender in the Railroad Work Force: The Case of the Far Northwest, 1883–1918," ibid., 16 (1985), 265–83.

31. Wynne, *Reaction to the Chinese*, 337–38; John G. Bitzes, "The Anti-Greek Riot of 1909—South Omaha," *NH*, 51 (1970), 199–224.

32. Quotations from John E. Coxe, "The New Orleans Mafia Incident," *LHQ*, 20 (1937), 1089. See also ibid., 1067–1110; Richard Gambino, *Vendetta: A True Story of the Worst Lynching in America*... (New York, 1977); J. Alexander Karlin, "New Orleans Lynchings of 1891 and the American Press," *LHQ*, 24 (1941), 187–204; John S. Kendall, "'Who Killa De Chief?'" ibid., 22 (1939), 492–530; John V. Baiamonte, Jr., "'Who Killa de Chief' Revisited: The Hennessey Assassination and Its Aftermath, 1890–1891," *LaH*, 33 (1992), 117–46.

33. *NYT*, Aug. 6–7, 1920.

34. *NYT*, Aug. 5, Sept. 27, 1898.

35. Juanita Brooks, *The Mountain Meadows Massacre* (Norman, Ok., 1962; orig. pub. 1950); Edward L. Ayers, *Vengeance and Justice: Crime and Punishment in the 19th-Century American South* (New York, 1984), 256; Marshall Wingfield, "Tennessee's Mormon Massacre," *THQ*, 17 (1958), 19–36.

36. *NYT*, Sept. 27, Oct. 9, Nov, 7, 1900, April 7, 1905.

37. Herbert G. Gutman, "The Tompkins Square 'Riot' in New York City on January 13, 1874: A Re-examination of its Causes and its Aftermath," *LH*, 6 (1965), 44–70.

38. The most important account is Avrich, *The Haymarket Tragedy*. See also Henry David, *The History of the Haymarket Affair: A Study in the American Social-Revolutionary and Labor Movements* (New York, 1936); Bruce C. Nelson, *Beyond the Martyrs: A Social History of Chicago's Anarchists, 1870–1900* (New Brunswick, 1988).

39. For the best recent general survey of the IWW see Melvyn Dubofsky, *We Shall Be All: A History of the Industrial Workers of the World* (New York, 1969). See also Foner, *History of Labor*, IV; Patrick Renshaw, *The Wobblies: The Story of Syndicalism in the United States* (New York, 1967). In the following discussion, unless one of these works was the most significant source for a riot, I do not cite them for each specific incident.

40. Dubofsky, *We Shall Be All*, 199–209, 227–90, 294–98; see also U.S. Bureau of Labor, *Report on Strike*; Steve Golin, *The Fragile Brigade: Paterson Silk Strike, 1913* (Philadelphia, 1988); Anne Huber Tripp, *The IWW and the Paterson Silk Strikers of 1913* (Urbana, Ill., 1987); Bell, "The Wheatland Hop-Fields' Riot," *Outlook*, 107 (1914), 118–22; Whitten, "The Wheatland Episode," *PHR*, 17 (1948), 37–42; and Neil Bitten, "Riot, Revolution, Repression in the Iron Range Strike of 1916," *Minnesota History*, 41 (1968), 82–94.

41. The best discussion of opposition to World War I remains H. C. Peterson and Gilbert C. Fite, *Opponents of War, 1917–1918* (Madison, Wis., 1957). For the Green Corn rebellion see ibid., 39–41; and Garin Burbank, *When Farmers Voted Red: The Gospel of Socialism in the Oklahoma Countryside, 1910–1924* (Westport, Conn., 1976), 133–56.

42. *NYT*, Feb. 20, 22, 1917; Leslie Marcy, "Food Riots in America," *International Socialist Review*, 17 (1917), 582–87; William Frieburger, "War, Prosperity and Hunger: The New York Food Riots of 1917," *LH*, 25 (1984), 217–39; Dana Frank, "Housewives, Socialists, and the Politics of Food: The 1917 New York Cost-of-Living Protests," *Feminist Studies*, 11 (1985), 255–88.

43. Norman H. Clark, *Mill Town: A Social History of Everett, Washington* . . . (Seattle, Wa., 1970), 186–213.

44. John H. Lindquist and James Fraser, "A Sociological Interpretation of the Bisbee Deportation," *PHR*, 37 (1968), 401–22.

45. Quoted in Dubofsky, *We Shall Be All*, 392. See also Arnon Gutfeld, "The Murder of Frank Little: Radical Labor Agitation in Butte, Montana, 1917," *LH*, 10 (1969), 177–92.

46. Dubofsky, *We Shall Be All*, 445–68.

47. Peterson and Fite, *Opponents of War*, 115, 146, 199.

48. Peterson and Fite, *Opponents of War*, 152, 153, 201; *NYT*, March 26, 1918.

49. Peterson and Fite, *Opponents of War*, 32, 45–46, 168–69, 199; *NYT*, July 2, 1917.

50. Robert L. Morlan, *Political Prairie Fire: The Nonpartisan League, 1915–1922* (Minneapolis, 1955), 175–78.

51. Peterson and Fite, *Opponents of War*, 4, 32; Morlan, *Political Prairie Fire*, 174–75.

52. Peterson and Fite, *Opponents of War*, 202–205; *NYT*, April 5, 1918; *Crisis*, 16 (June 1918), 88.

53. Quoted in Peterson and Fite, *Opponents of War*, 205–207.

54. Quoted in ibid., 212. See also ibid., 208–21.

55. Robert K. Murray, *Red Scare: A Study in National Hysteria, 1919–1920* (Minneapolis, 1955); Stanley Coben, "A Study in Nativism: The American Red Scare of 1919–20," *Political Science Quarterly*, 79 (1964), 52–75; *NYT*, May 2, 1919.

56. Peterson and Fite, *Opponents of War*, 289. See also ibid., 285–96; Murray, *Red Scare*, 87–90; William Pencak, *For God and Country: The American Legion, 1919–1941* (Boston, 1989), 144–69.

57. Murray, *Red Scare*, 182–89.

58. The best general accounts of the second Klan are David M. Chalmers, *Hooded Americanism: The First Century of the Ku Klux Klan, 1865–1965* (Garden City, N.Y., 1965); and Kenneth T. Jackson, *The Ku Klux Klan in the City, 1915–1930* (New York, 1967). There have been several good local studies, including Charles C. Alexander, *The Ku Klux Klan in the Southwest* ([Lexington, Ky.], 1965); Alexander, *Crusade for Conformity: The Ku Klux Klan in Texas, 1920-1930* ([Houston], 1962); Robert Alan Goldberg, *Hooded Empire: The Ku Klux Klan in Colorado* (Urbana, Ill., 1981); William D. Jenkins, *Steel Valley Klan: The Ku Klux Klan in Ohio's Mahoning Valley* (Kent, Oh., 1990); Leonard J. Moore, *Citizen Klansmen: The Ku Klux Klan in Indiana, 1921–1928* (Chapel Hill, 1991). See also William Pierce Randel, *The Ku Klux Klan: A Century of Infamy* (New York, 1965); "The Rise and Fall of the KKK," *New Republic*, 53 (Nov. 30, 1927), 33–34.

59. Alexander, *Crusade*, 10; Chalmers, *Hooded Americans*, 60–62.

60. Jackson, *Ku Klux Klan in the City*, 53–54, 134–35, 167–68, 171, 177, 179, 181; Chalmers, *Hooded Americanism*, 178–79, 238–40, 251–52, 263, 272; "The Klan as the Victim of Mob Violence," *Literary Digest*, 78 (Sept. 8, 1923), 12–13; Jenkins, *Steel Valley Klan*, 117–39; Alexander, *Crusade*, 37; Alexander, *Ku Klux Klan in the Southwest*, 99; Angle, *Bloody Williamson*, 172–91, 200–206, 285–86.

61. For a discussion of the negative view of disorder and rioting in the nineteenth and early twentieth centuries see Gregory W. Bush, "Heroes and the 'Dead Line' Against Riots: The Romantic Nationalist Conception of Crowd Behavior,

1840–1914," *Hayes Historical Journal*, 8 (1989), 34–57; Paul Boyer, *Urban Masses and Moral Order in America, 1820-1920* (Cambridge, Mass., 1978); Eugene E. Leach, "Mastering the Crowd: Collective Behavior and Mass Society in American Social Thought, 1917–1939," *American Studies*, 27 (1986), 99–114; Eric H. Monkkonen, *The Dangerous Class: Crime and Poverty in Columbus, Ohio, 1860–1885* (Cambridge, Mass., 1975); Monkkonen, "A Disorderly People? Urban Order and Disorder in the Nineteenth and Twentieth Centuries," *JAH*, 68 (1981), 539–59.

62. Paul A. Gilje, *The Road to Mobocracy: Popular Disorder in New York City, 1763-1834* (Chapel Hill, 1987), 267–82.

63. The best accounts on the origins of the police are Roger Lane, *Policing the City: Boston, 1822-1885* (Cambridge, Mass., 1967); James F. Richardson, *The New York Police: Colonial Times to 1901* (New York, 1970). See also Celestine Estelle Anderson, "The Invention of the 'Professional' Municipal Police: The Case of Cincinnati, 1788 to 1900" (Ph.D. diss., University of Cincinnati, 1979); A. E. Costello, *Our Police Protectors: History of the New York Police from the Earliest Period to the Present Time* ([New York], 1885); Gilje, *Road to Mobocracy*, 267–82; David R. Johnson, *Policing the Urban Underworld: The Impact of Crime on the Development of the American Police, 1800–1887* (Philadelphia, 1979); George Austin Ketcham, "Municipal Police Reform: A Comparative Study of Law Enforcement in Cincinnati, Chicago, New Orleans, New York, and St. Louis, 1844–1877" (Ph.D. diss., University of Missouri, 1967); Wilbur R. Miller, *Cops and Bobbies: Police Authority in New York and London, 1830–1870* (Chicago, 1977); Edmund E. Radlowski, "Law and Order at Cripple Creek, 1890–1900," *Journal of the West*, 9 (1970), 346–55; John C. Schneider, *Detroit and the Problem of Order, 1830–1880: A Geography of Crime, Riot, and Policing* (Lincoln, Neb., 1980).

64. Richardson, *New York Police*, 82–108; Paul O. Weinbaum, "Temperance, Politics, and the New York City Riots of 1857," *New York Historical Society Quarterly*, 59 (1975), 246–70.

65. Richardson, *New York Police*, 214–83; Lane, *Policing the City*, 180–219.

66. Corbin, *Life, Work, and Rebellion*, 200–202; Lane, *Civil War in West Virginia*; Lunt, *Law and Order*, 97–100; Gutman, "The Tompkins Square 'Riot,'" *LH*, 6 (1965), 44–70; Avrich, *The Haymarket Tragedy*; Citizens Protective League, *Story of the Riot* (New York, 1969; orig. pub. 1900); Gilbert Osofsky, "Race Riot, 1900: A Study of Ethnic Violence," *Journal of Negro Education*, 32 (1963), 16–24. For the earlier impact of official opposition to lynching in some states see Ann Field Alexander, "'Like an Evil Wind': The Roanoke Riot of 1893 and the Lynching of Thomas Smith," *VMHB*, 100 (1992), 173–206; and David A. Gerber, "Lynching and Law and Order: Origin and Passage of the Ohio Anti-Lynching Law of 1896," *OH*, 83 (1974), 33–50.

67. *Outlook*, 74 (1903), 724. An article in the *Literary Digest* in 1925 cited that only sixteen lynchings had occurred in 1924 and stressed how, reflecting new attitudes, police and public officials had interceded forty-five times to stop lynching. "The Passing of Judge Lynch," *Literary Digest*, 84 (Jan. 31, 1925), 30–31. See also John D. Wright, Jr., "Lexington's Suppression of the 1920 Will Lockett Lynch Mob," *RKHS*, 84 (1986), 263–79.

68. Eric H. Monkkonen, *Police in Urban America, 1860–1920* (Cambridge, 1981); Adrian Cook, *The Armies of the Streets: The New York City Draft Riots of 1863* (Lexington, Ky., 1974), 19; *NYT*, Jan. 28, 1900, May 30, 1920.

69. Randolph Bartlett, "Anarchy in Boston," *American Mercury*, 36 (1935), 456–64; Richard L. Lyons, "The Boston Police Strike of 1919," *NEQ*, 20 (1947), 147–68.

70. Dewees, *Molly Maguires*; Rhodes, "The Molly Maguires," *AHR*, 15 (1910), 547–61; Robert P. Weiss, "Private Detective Agencies and Labour Discipline in the United States, 1855–1946," *Historical Journal*, 29 (1986), 87–107; Levinson, *I Break Strikes!*; William Beck, "Law and Order during the 1913 Copper Strike," *MiH*, 54 (1970), 275–92.

71. Howland, "War in Philadelphia," *Outlook*, 94 (1910), 523.

72. Bruce Smith, *The State Police: Organization and Administration* (Montclair, N.J., 1969; orig. pub. 1925), 29–41, 54–65. For reference to "cossacks" see Adamic, *Dynamite*, 163, 263, 286–87, 327.

73. Quoted in Charles A. Peckham, "The Ohio National Guard and Its Police Duties, 1894," *OH*, 83 (1974), 51.

74. Henry A. Bellows, *A Treatise on Riot Duty for the National Guard* (Washington, D.C., 1920), 28.

75. On the architecture of armories see Robert M. Fogelson, *America's Armories: Architecture, Society, and Public Order* (Cambridge, Mass., 1989). On the role of the national guard in supressing strikes see Robert W. Coakley, "Federal Use of Militia and the National Guard in Civil Disturbances: The Whiskey Rebellion to Little Rock," in Robin Higham, ed., *Bayonets in the Streets: The Use of Troops in Civil Disturbances* (Lawrence, Ka., 1969), 17–34; Clarence C. Clendenen, "Super Police: The National Guard as a Law-Enforcement Agency in the Twentieth Century," ibid., 85–111; Jim Dan Hill, "The National Guard in Civil Disorders: Historical Precedents," ibid., 61–84; Jerry M. Cooper, "The Wisconsin National Guard in the Milwaukee Riots of 1886," *Wisconsin Magazine of History*, 55 (1971), 31–48; Martha Derthick, *The National Guard in Politics* (Cambridge, Mass., 1965); Ronald M. Gephart, "Politicians, Soldiers and Strikes: The Reorganization of the Nebraska Militia and the Omaha Strike of 1882," *NH*, 46 (1965), 89–120; John K. Mahon, *History of the Militia and the National Guard* (New York, 1983); Peckham, "The Ohio National Guard," *OH*, 83 (1974), 51–67; Kent D. Richards, "Insurrection, Agitation, and Riots: The Police Power and Washington Statehood," *Montana*, 37 (autumn 1987), 10–21; Robert Reinders, "Militia and Public Order in Nineteenth-Century America," *Journal of American Studies*, 11 (1977), 81–101; United States War Department, War Plans Division, *Military Protection: United States Guards, The Use of Organized Bodies in the Protection and Defense of Property during Riots, Strikes, and Civil Disturbances* (Washington, D.C., 1919).

76. Jerry M. Cooper, *The Army and Civil Disorder: Federal Military Intervention in Labor Disputes, 1877–1900* (Westport, Conn., 1980); Cooper, "The Army as Strike-breaker—The Railroad Strikes of 1877 and 1894," *LH*, 18 (1977), 179–96; Barton C. Hacker, "The United States Army as a National Police Force: The Federal Policing of Labor Disputes, 1877–1898," *Military Affairs*, 33 (1969), 255–64; United States Senate, 57th Congress, 2nd Session, *Federal Aid in Domestic Disturbances, 1887–1903* (Washington, D.C., 1903).

77. See, for example, Luke Grant, *The National Erectors' Association and the International Association of Bridge and Structural Ironworkers: United States Commission on Industrial Relations* (Washington, D.C., 1915), 111–13.

78. Bellows, *Treatise on Riot Duty*, 94–143, esp. 123. See also Eugene E. Leach, "The Literature of Riot Duty: Managing Class Conflict in the Streets, 1877–1927," ms. dated July 1990.

79. J. S. Tunison, *The Cincinnati Riot: Its Causes and Results* (Cincinnati, 1886); Steven J. Ross, *Workers on the Edge: Work, Leisure, and Politics in Industrializing Cincinnati, 1788–1890* (New York, 1985), 264–69.

6. Democracy Entrenched

1. Irving Bernstein, *Turbulent Years: A History of the American Worker, 1933–1941* (Boston, 1971), 220–25, 236–38, 241–43, 267–83; Walter Galenson, *The CIO Challenge to the AFL: A History of the American Labor Movement, 1935–1941* (Cambridge, Mass., 1960), 428–29, 478–79; Philip A. Korth and Margaret R. Beegle, *I Remember Like Today: The Auto-Lite Strike of 1934* (East Lansing, Mich., 1988); Samuel Yellen, *American Labor Struggles* (New York, 1936), 324–58.

2. Bernstein, *Turbulent Years*, 243–49.

3. The workers in Homestead did not sleep in the plant, but did cordon it off and prevented strikebreakers from entering either the town or the plant. This action was not a sit-down in the 1930s sense, but it had the same effect. For an overview of the sit-down see Sidney Fine, *Sit-Down: The General Motors Strike of 1936–1937* (Ann Arbor, 1969), 121–23. The number of sit-downs is cited from Bernstein, *Turbulent Years*, 500. See also Sidney Lens, *The Labor Wars: From the Molly Maguires to the Sitdown* (Garden City, N.Y., 1973), 333–34, 351–55; George D. Blackwood, "The Sit-Down Strike in the Thirties," *South Atlantic Quarterly*, 55 (1956), 438–48; Melvyn Dubofsky, "Not So 'Turbulent Years': Another Look at the American 1930's," *Amerikastudien/American Studies*, 24 (1979), 5–20; Edward Levinson, *Labor on the March* (New York, 1938), 141–86.

4. Quotation from Bernstein, *Turbulent Years*, 534; and Fine, *Sit-Down*, 239. On Murphy's position see Bernstein, *Turbulent Years*, 530–35, 540–46; Fine, *Sit-Down*, 148–55, 239–57, 293–95.

5. Bernstein, *Turbulent Years*, 529–40; Fine, *Sit-Down*, 1–13, 197–98, 212–14, 266–72; Galenson, *CIO Challenge*, 134–38.

6. Quotation from Bernstein, *Turbulent Years*, 541.

7. Bernstein, *Turbulent Years*, 485–90; Donald G. Sofchalk, "The Chicago Memorial Day Incident: An Episode of Mass Action," *LH*, 6 (1965), 3–43.

8. Bernstein, *Turbulent Years*, 675–80; Fine, *Sit-Down*, 330–41. See also Harold S. Roberts, *The Rubber Workers: Labor Organization and Collective Bargaining in the Rubber Industry* (New York, 1944).

9. For a comprehensive discussion of Midwest farmer radicalism see John L. Shover, *Cornbelt Rebellion: The Farmers' Holiday Association* (Urbana, Ill., 1965). For incidents discussed in text see ibid., 32, 117–19, 130. See also James O. Babcock, "The Farm Revolt in Iowa," *Social Forces*, 12 (1934), 369–73; J. Craig Jenkins and Charles Perrow, "Insurgency of the Powerless: Farm Worker Movements (1946–1972)," *ASR*, 42 (1977), 249–68; Rodney D. Karr, "Farmer Rebels in Plymouth County, Iowa, 1932–1933," *Annals of Iowa*, 47 (1985), 637–45; A. William Hoglund, "Wisconsin Dairy Farmers on Strike," *Agricultural History*, 35 (1961), 24–34; Lowell K. Dyson,

Red Harvest: The Communist Party and American Farmers (Lincoln, Neb., 1982), 101–108.

10. Howard Kester, *Revolt among the Sharecroppers* (New York, 1969; orig. pub. 1936), 83–84; Herbert Shapiro, *White Violence and Black Response: From Reconstruction to Montgomery* (Amherst, Mass., 1988), 246–50; Louis Canter, *A Prologue to the Protest Movement: The Missouri Sharecropper Roadside Demonstrations of 1939* (Durham, N.C., 1969); Bernstein, *Turbulent Years,* 165–68.

11. Bernstein, *Turbulent Years,* 222–25, 236–44 485–90; and Sofchalk, "Chicago Memorial Day," *LH,* 6 (1965), 3–43.

12. American Civil Liberties Union, *Violence in Peekskill: A Report of the Violations of Civil Liberties at Two Paul Robeson Concerts Near Peekskill, N.Y., August 27th and September 4th, 1949* (New York, [1950]); Shapiro, *White Violence,* 378–88. For a similar incident see Robert C. Myers, "Anti-Communist Mob Action: A Case Study," *Public Opinion Quarterly,* 12 (1948), 57–67.

13. American Civil Liberties Union, *Violence at Peekskill,* 19.

14. Ronald H. Bayor, *Neighbors in Conflict: The Irish, Germans, Jews, and Italians of New York City, 1929–1941* (Baltimore, 1978), 155–65.

15. Maurico Mazón, *The Zoot-Suit Riots: The Psychology of Symbolic Annihilation* (Austin, Tex., 1984); Steve Chibnall, "Whistle and Zoot: The Changing Meaning of a Suit of Clothes," *History Workshop,* 20 (1985), 56–81; Stuart Cosgrove, "The Zoot-Suit and Style Warfare," ibid., 18 (1984), 77–91; Ralph H. Turner and Samuel J. Surace, "Zoot-Suiters and Mexicans: Symbols in Crowd Behavior," *AJS,* 62 (1956), 14–20.

16. Daisy Bates, *The Long Shadow of Little Rock: A Memoir* (New York, 1962); Shapiro, *White Violence,* 412–16; Michael R. Belknap, *Federal Law and Southern Order: Racial Violence and Constitutional Conflict in the Post-Brown South,* (Athens, Ga., 1987), 44–52.

17. Bates, *Long Shadow,* 62.

18. For a detailed overview of the civil rights movement see Taylor Branch, *Parting the Waters: America in the King Years, 1954–63* (New York, 1988).

19. John Hope Franklin, *From Slavery to Freedom: A History of Negro Americans,* 3rd ed. (New York, 1969), 433–652.

20. Gunnar Myrdal, *An American Dilemma: The Negro Problem and Modern Democracy* (New York, 1944).

21. For a general discussion of the decline of lynching see W. Fitzhugh Brundage, *Lynching in the New South: Georgia and Virginia, 1880-1930* (Urbana, Ill., 1993), 161–244; Donald L. Grant, *The Anti-Lynching Movement: 1883–1932* (San Francisco, 1975); Jacquelin Dowd Hall, *Revolt Against Chivalry: Jesse Daniel Ames and the Woman's Campaign Against Lynching* (New York, 1979); Robert L. Zangrando, "The NAACP and a Federal Antilynching Bill, 1934–1940," *JNH,* 50 (1965), 106–17; Zangrando, *The NAACP Crusade Against Lynching* (Philadelphia, 1980). See also Jesse Daniel Ames, *The Changing Character of Lynching: Review of Lynching, 1931–1941; With a Discussion of Recent Developments in this Field* (Atlanta, 1942); Henry E. Barber, "The Association of Southern Women for the Prevention of Lynching, 1930–1942," *Phylon,* 34 (1973), 378–89; James Harmon Chadburn, *Lynching and the Law* (Chapel Hill, 1933); Commission on Interracial Cooperation, *The Mob Still Rides: A Review of the Lynching Record, 1931–1935* (Atlanta, 1936); James Weldon Johnson, "Lynching—

America's National Disgrace," *Current History*, 19 (1924), 596–601; National Association for the Advancement of Colored People, *Thirty Years of Lynching in the United States, 1889–1918* (New York, 1969; orig. pub. 1919); Lewis T. Nordyke, "Ladies and Lynchings," *Survey Graphic*, 28 (1939), 683–86; Arthur F. Raper, *The Tragedy of Lynching* (Montclair, N.J., 1969; orig. pub. Chapel Hill, 1933); John Shelton Reed, "An Evaluation of an Anti-Lynching Organization," *Social Problems*, 16 (1968), 172–82; Southern Commission on the Study of Lynching, *Lynchings and What They Mean: General Findings of the Southern Commission on the Study of Lynching* (Atlanta, [1931]); Ida B. Wells, *Crusade for Justice: The Autobiography of Ida B. Wells*, Alfreda M. Duster, ed. (Chicago, 1970).

22. NAACP, *Thirty Years of Lynching*, 29; "The Passing of Judge Lynch," *Literary Digest*, 84 (Jan. 31, 1925), 30–31; Ralph Ginzburg, *100 Years of Lynching* (New York, 1962), 181–252.

23. Joe Jordan, "Lynchers Don't Like Lead," *Atlantic Monthly*, 177 (1946), 103–108; John D. Wright, Jr., "Lexington's Suppression of the 1920 Will Lockett Lynch Mob," *RKHS*, 84 (1986), 263–79.

24. Virginius Dabney, "Dixie Rejects Lynching," *The Nation*, 145 (1937), 579–80; [Mississippi Bar Association], *Mississippi and the Mob* (Jackson, Miss., [1925]).

25. Quotation from *Birmingham (Alabama) Post*, Oct. 27, 1934 and reprinted in Ginzburg, *100 Years of Lynching*, 221–24. See also James R. McGovern and Walter T. Howard, "Private Justice and National Concern: The Lynching of Claude Neal," *The Historian*, 43 (1981), 546–59; McGovern, *Anatomy of a Lynching: The Killing of Claude Neal* (Baton Rouge, La., 1982).

26. Stephen J. Whitfield, *A Death in the Delta: The Story of Emmet Till* (New York, 1988). See also Howard Smead, *Blood Justice: The Lynching of Mack Charles Parker* (New York, 1986).

27. Thomas F. Parker, ed., *Violence in the U.S.: Volume 1: 1956–1967* (New York, 1974), 61–68.

28. Belknap, *Federal Law and Southern Order*, 29, 70–105, 120; Richard Maxwell Brown, "Southern Violence vs the Civil Rights Movement, 1954–1968," in Merle Black and John Shelton Reed, eds., *Perspectives on the American South: An Annual Review of Society, Politics and Culture*, I (New York, 1981), 49–69; Branch, *Parting the Waters*, 164–68; Numan V. Bartley, *The Rise of Massive Resistance: Race and Politics in the South during the 1950's* (Baton Rouge, La., 1969), 64; August Meier and Elliott Rudwick, *CORE: A Study in the Civil Rights Movement, 1942–1968* (New York, 1973); Parker, ed., *Violence . . . Vol. 1*, 6, 13–48, 68–74.

29. For general surveys of this racial violence during World War II see James Albert Burran III, "Racial Violence in the South during World War II" (Ph.D. diss., University of Tennessee, 1977); Pete Daniel, "Going among Strangers: Southern Reactions to World War II," *JAH*, 77 (1990), 886–911; and Harvard Sitkoff, "Racial Militancy and Interracial Violence in the Second World War," *JAH*, 58 (1971), 661–81.

30. Burran, "Racial Violence" (Ph.D. diss., University of Tennessee, 1977), 47–51, 141–46, 212–14; Sitkoff, "Racial Militancy," *JAH*, 58 (1971), 668; Thomas Sancton, "The Race Riots," *New Republic*, 109 (July 5, 1943), 9–13.

31. Sitkoff, "Racial Militancy," *JAH*, 58 (1971), 671; Daniel, "Going among Strangers," ibid., 77 (1990), 906–907; Burran, "Racial Violence" (Ph.D. diss., University of Tennessee, 1977), 104–26, 164–85.

32. Dominic J. Capeci, Jr., and Martha Wilkerson, *Layered Violence: The Detroit Rioters of 1943* (Jackson, Miss., 1991); Alfred McClung Lee and Norman Daymond Humphrey, *Race Riot* (New York, 1943); L. Alex Swan, "The Harlem and Detroit Riots of 1943: A Comparative Analysis," *Berkeley Journal of Sociology*, 16 (1971–1972), 73–93; B. J. Widick, *Detroit: City of Race and Class Violence*, rev. ed. (Detroit, 1989), 99–112.

33. Dominic J. Capeci, Jr., *Race Relations in Wartime Detroit: The Sojourner Truth Housing Controversy of 1942* (Philadelphia, 1984); David Allan Levine, *Internal Combustion: The Races in Detroit, 1915–1926* (Westport, Conn., 1976), 153–98; Walter White, "The Sweet Trial," *Crisis*, 31 (Jan. 1926), 125–29; William Gremley, "Social Control in Cicero," *British Journal of Sociology*, 3 (1952), 322–38.

34. Capeci and Wilkerson, *Layered Violence*, 9–12; Swan, "Harlem and Detroit Riots of 1943," *Berk. J. of Soc.*, 16 (1971–1972), 73–93.

35. For a recent study see Cheryl Lynn Greenberg, *"Or Does It Explode?" Black Harlem in the Great Depression* (New York, 1991). See also *The Complete Report of Mayor LaGuardia's Commission on the Harlem Riot of March 19, 1935* (New York, 1969).

36. The best modern study of this riot is Dominic J. Capeci, Jr., *The Harlem Riot of 1943* (Philadelphia, 1977). See also Kenneth B. Clark, "Group Violence: A Preliminary Study of Attitudinal Pattern of Its Acceptance and Rejection: A Study of the 1943 Harlem Riot," *Journal of Social Psychology*, 19 (1944), 319–37; Clark and James Barker, "The Zoot Effect in Personality: A Race Riot Participant," *Journal of Abnormal and Social Psychology*, 40 (1945), 143–48; Swan, "The Harlem and Detroit Riots of 1943," *Berk. J. of Soc.*, 16 (1971–1972), 73–93; Walter White, "Behind the Harlem Riot," *New Republic*, 109 (Aug. 16, 1943), 220–21.

37. The literature on the major ghetto riots is huge. For a sampling of this literature see Nathan Cohen, ed., *The Los Angeles Riots: A Socio-Psychological Study* (New York, 1970); Jerry Cohen and William S. Murphy, *Burn, Baby, Burn! The Los Angeles Race Riot August, 1965* (New York, 1966); Robert Conot, *Rivers of Blood, Years of Darkness: The Unforgettable Classic Account of the Watts Riot* (New York, 1968); Frederic C. Coonradt, *The Negro News Media and the Los Angeles Riots* ([Los Angeles], 1965); *McCone Commission Report: Complete and Unabridged Report by the Governor's Commission on the Los Angeles Riot* (Los Angeles, 1965); Tom Hayden, *Rebellion in Newark: Official Violence and Ghetto Response* (New York, 1967); Nathan Wright, Jr., *Ready to Riot* (New York, 1968); Sidney Fine, *Violence in the Model City: The Cavanagh Administration, Race Relations, and the Detroit Riot of 1967* (Ann Arbor, 1989); John Hersey, *The Algiers Motel Incident* (New York, 1971; orig. pub. 1968); Herbert G. Locke, *The Detroit Riot of 1967* (Detroit, 1969); Peter H. Rossi, ed., *Ghetto Revolts* (New Brunswick, 1973); Van Gordon Sauter and Burleigh Hines, *Nightmare in Detroit: A Rebellion and Its Victims* (Chicago, 1968). For a description of the major riots see *The Kerner Report: The 1968 Report of the National Advisory Commission on Civil Disorders* (New York, 1988; orig. pub. 1968); Parker, ed., *Violence . . . Vol. 1*, 104–11, 181–99.

38. Leon Freidman, ed., *Violence in America: Final Report of the National Commission on the Causes and Prevention of Violence*, I (New York, 1983; orig. pub. 1969), xx.

39. Thomas F. Parker, ed., *Violence in the U.S.: Volume 2, 1968–1971* (New York, 1974), 15–34; Ben W. Gilbert et al., *Ten Blocks from the White House: Anatomy of the Washington Riots of 1968* (New York, 1968).

40. *Kerner Report,* 362–89; Leon Friedman, ed., *Violence in America: Mass Media and Violence,* VI (New York, 1983; orig. pub. 1969), 103–20.

41. For a sample of the discussion on the political causes of these riots see Joseph Boskin, *Urban Racial Violence in the Twentieth Century,* 2nd ed. (Beverly Hills, Cal., 1976); Joe R. Feagin and Harlan Hahn, *Ghetto Revolts: The Politics of Violence in American Cities* (New York, 1973); Robert M. Fogelson, *Violence as Protest: A Study of Riots and Ghettos* (Garden City, N.Y., 1971); Ted Robert Gurr, *Why Men Rebel* (Princeton, 1970); Morris Janowitz, "Patterns of Collective Racial Violence," in Hugh Davis Graham and Ted Robert Gurr, eds., *Violence in America: Historical and Comparative Perspectives* (Washington, D.C., 1969), 317–39; Louis H. Masotti and Don R. Bowen, eds., *Riots and Rebellion: Civil Violence in the Urban Community* (Beverly Hills, Cal., 1968); Richard E. Rubenstein, *Rebels in Eden: Mass Political Violence in the United States* (Boston, 1970); Jerome H. Skolnick, *The Politics of Protest* (New York, 1969).

42. *Kerner Report,* 203–482. See also Barbara Ritichie, *The Riot Report: A Shortened Version of the Report of the National Advisory Commission on Civil Disorders* (New York, 1969); Freidman, ed., *Violence in America; McCone Commission Report.* For an evaluation of these reports see Daniel Calhoun, "Studying American Violence," *Journal of Interdisciplinary History,* 1 (1970), 163–85; and Anthony M. Platt, *The Politics of Riot Commissions: A Collection of Official Reports and Critical Essays* (New York, 1971). See also Kenneth O'Reilly, "The FBI and the Politics of the Riots, 1964–1968," *JAH,* 75 (1988), 91–114.

43. Fogelson, *Violence as Protest,* 86–90; E. L. Quarantelli and Russell R. Dynes, "Property Norms and Looting: Their Patterns in Community Crises," *Phylon,* 31 (1970), 168–82; Quarantelli and Dynes, "Looting in Civil Disorders: An Index of Social Change," in Masotti and Bowen, eds., *Riots and Rebellion,* 131–41.

44. E. J. Hobsbawm and George Rudé, *Captain Swing* (New York, 1968), 79–80; Eugene D. Genovese, *Roll, Jordan, Roll: The World the Slaves Made* (New York, 1974), 613–15.

45. Fogelson, *Violence as Protest,* 90–94.

46. Parker, ed., *Violence . . . Vol. 1,* 104, 181, 188, 196–97; Parker, ed., *Violence . . . Vol. 2,* 15–30.

47. *Life,* 63 (July 28, 1967), 16–28.

48. *Kerner Report,* xix.

49. Friedman, ed., *Violence in America,* I, xx; Parker, ed., *Violence . . . Vol. 1,* 104, 181, 194; Parker, ed., *Violence . . . Vol. 2,* 15.

50. *Time,* July 25, 1977. See also Robert Curvin and Bruce Porter, *Blackout Looting! New York City, July 13, 1977* (New York, 1979).

51. For a survey of this violence joining rioting with other manifestations see Friedman, *Violence in America* (16 volumes). See also Truman Capote, *In Cold Blood: A True Account of a Multiple Murder and Its Consequences* (New York, 1965).

52. For surveys of this movement see Todd Gitlin, *The Sixties: Years of Hope, Days of Rage* (Toronto, 1987); Allen J. Matusow, *The Unraveling of America: A History of Liberalism in the 1960s* (New York, 1984); Edward P. Morgan, *The 60s Experience: Hard Lessons about Modern America* (Philadelphia, 1991); James Miller, *"Democracy Is in the Streets": From Port Huron to the Siege of Chicago* (New York, 1987); William L.

O'Neill, *Coming Apart: An Informal History of America in the 1960's* (Chicago, 1971); Tom Shachtman, *Decade of Shocks: Dallas to Watergate, 1963–1974* (New York, 1983).

53. W. J. Rorabaugh, *Berkeley at War: The 1960s* (New York, 1989), 20–22, 30–34.

54. Gitlin, *Sixties,* 177–88; Miller, *"Democracy Is in the Streets,"* 226–36.

55. Friedman, ed., *Violence in America,* IV, 72–74; Morgan, *The 60s,* 118–20.

56. Kenneth J. Heineman, *Campus Wars: The Peace Movement at American State Universities in the Vietnam Era* (New York, 1993), 34, 40, 130, 173–77, 186–87, 192, 202, 212–13.

57. Gitlin, *Sixties,* 249–54; Rorabaugh, *Berkeley,* 116–18; Parker, ed., *Violence . . . Vol. 1,* 251–54.

58. Norman Mailer, *The Armies of the Night: History as a Novel, the Novel as History* (New York, 1968), 240.

59. Parker, ed., *Violence . . . Vol. 1,* 253–54; O'Neill, *Coming Apart,* 339–44; Morgan, *The 60s,* 152–54.

60. Gitlin, *Sixties,* 306–309; Parker, ed., *Violence . . . Vol. 2,* 61–66.

61. Miller, *"Democracy Is in the Streets,"* 283–310; Walter Schneir, ed., *Telling It Like It Was: The Chicago Riot* (New York, 1969); John Schultz, *No One Was Killed Documentation and Meditation: Convention Week, Chicago, August 1968* (Chicago, 1969); David Lewis Stein, *Living the Revolution: The Yippies in Chicago* (Indianapolis, 1969); Daniel Walker, *Rights in Conflict* (New York, 1968).

62. Miller, *"Democracy Is in the Streets",* 302–306.

63. Gitlin, *Sixties,* 377–408; Parker, ed., *Violence . . . Vol. 2,* 149.

64. Heineman, *Campus Wars,* 214–17; Parker, ed., *Violence . . . Vol. 2,* 102–108.

65. Rorabaugh, *Berkeley,* 160–66; Gitlin, *Sixties,* 353–61; Parker, ed., *Violence . . . Vol. 2,* 113–14, 156–58.

66. Parker, ed., *Violence . . . Vol. 2,* 159–62; Heineman, *Campus Wars,* 245.

67. Sources on Kent State include Scott L. Bills, ed., *Kent State / May 4: Echoes through a Decade* (Kent, Oh., 1982); Peter Davies, *The Truth About Kent State: A Challenge to the American Conscience* (New York, 1973); Joseph Kelner and James Munves, *The Kent State Coverup* (New York, 1980); James A. Michener, *Kent State: What Happened and Why* (New York, 1971); Robert M. O'Neil et al., *No Heroes, No Villains: New Perspectives on Kent State and Jackson State* (San Francisco, 1972).

68. Heineman, *Campus Wars,* 249.

69. Parker, ed., *Violence . . . Vol. 2,* 168–71; O'Neil et al., *No Heroes, No Villains.*

70. See the photographs published in Davies, *Truth about Kent State,* 61–137, esp. photograph 53.

71. Parker, ed., *Violence . . . Vol. 2,* 167.

72. Barbara Epstein, *Political Protest and Cultural Revolution: Nonviolent Direct Action in the 1970s and 1980s* (Berkeley, 1991), 58–156.

73. Elizabeth Adell Cook, Ted G. Jelen, and Clyde Wilcox, *Between Two Absolutes: Public Opinion and the Politics of Abortion* (Boulder, Co., 1992), 1–2; Marian Faux, *Crusaders: Voices from the Abortion Front* (Seacaucus, N.J., 1990), 116–99; *Facts on File: Weekly World News Digest With Cumulative Index* (1988), 778. See also Randall A. Terry, "Operation Rescue: The Civil Rights Movement of the Nineties," *Policy Review,* 47 (1989), 82–83.

74. Donn Teal, *The Gay Militants* (New York, 1971), 17–23, 197–200; Leigh W. Rutledge, *The Gay Decades: From Stonewall to the Present: The People and Events that Shaped Gay Lives* (New York, 1992), 1–3, 51, 67, 160.

75. Susan E. Davis, ed., *Women Under Attack: Victories, Backlash and the Fight for Reproductive Freedom* (Boston, 1988), 57–60; Epstein, *Political Protest*, 163–65.

76. *Norman (Oklahoma) Transcript*, Sept. 4, 10, 1989; *NYT*, July 29, 1992; *Facts on File* (1991), 158–59.

77. Jon Hillson, *The Battle of Boston* (New York, 1977), esp. 15–22; Ronald P. Formisano, *Boston Against Bussing: Race, Class, and Ethnicity in the 1960s and 1970s* (Chapel Hill, 1991); Emmett H. Buell, Jr. and Richard A. Brisbin, Jr., *School Desegregation and Defended Neighborhoods: The Boston Controversy* (Lexington, Mass., 1982).

78. Michael Newton and Judy Ann Newton, eds., *Racial and Religious Violence: A Chronology* (New York, 1991), 605–11; *Facts on File* (1989), 34.

79. Elizabeth Wheaton, *Codename Greenkil: The 1979 Greensboro Killings* (Athens, Ga., 1987), 83–94, 123–64.

80. *Facts on File* (1987), 51. The settlement of the case was announced in May 1993. National Public Radio, May 13, 1993.

81. Bruce Porter and Marvin Dunn, *The Miami Riot of 1980: Crossing the Bounds* (Lexington, Mass., 1980). *Facts on File* (1982), 979; ibid. (1984), 211–12; *NYT*, Jan 23, 1989.

82. Newton and Newton, ed., *Racial and Religious Violence*, 601, 606; *Newsweek*, May 20, 1991; *NYT*, May 7–8, 1991, July 7–8, 1992.

83. *NYT*, Nov. 1, 1986, Aug. 30, Nov. 1, 1989; *Norman (Oklahoma) Transcript*, Sept. 5, 1989, June 15, 1992. A largely white crowd fought police at Jones Beach, New York on the July 4 holiday. *NYT*, July 3 and 4, 1989.

84. *Facts on File* (1989), 319.

85. Philip Gourevitch, "The Crown Heights Riot and Its Aftermath," *Commentary*, 95 (1993), 29–34; *NYT*, May 14, 1990, April 8, 1992; *Facts on File* (1986), 982; ibid. (1989), 658.

86. *NYT*, May 1–8, 1992. For an analysis of the riot see Robert Gooding-Williams, ed., *Reading Rodney King, Reading Urban Uprising* (New York, 1993); and Haki R. Madhubuti, ed., *Why L.A. Happened: Implications of the '92 Los Angeles Rebellion* (Chicago, 1993).

87. On the riots elsewhere see *NYT*, May 3, 1992.

88. See the casualty list in *Newsweek*, May 18, 1992, 47.

89. *NYT*, May 3, 1992.

Epilogue

1. While crowd violence was limited, bloodshed from other sources was still possible. There was a certain amount of state-sanctioned violence from police and other authorities in the South. White extremists also used isolated acts of terror such as bombings and even abduction and murder. But this study does not focus on all violence, only collective action by crowds.

Appendix

1. Leonard L. Richards, *"Gentlemen of Property and Standing": Anti-Abolition Mobs in Jacksonian America* (New York, 1970), 10–19; David Grimsted, "Ante-Bellum Labor: Violence, Strike, and Communal Arbitration," *JSH,* 19 (1985), 5–28.

2. Leonard Richards based his count of riots in the 1830s on perusal of *Niles' Weekly Register,* while his larger count of abolition riots was based on a reading of abolitionist papers like *The Liberator.* Richards, *"Gentlemen of Property and Standing,"* 15, n24.

3. Paul A. Gilje, *The Road to Mobocracy: Popular Disorder in New York City, 1763–1834* (Chapel Hill, 1987), 246–53; and Peter George Buckley, "To the Opera House: Culture and Society in New York City" (Ph.D. diss., State University of New York, Stony Brook, 1984). See also Richard Moody, *The Astor Place Riot* (Bloomington, Ind., 1958); David Grimsted, *Melodrama Unveiled: American Theater and Culture, 1800–1850* (Chicago, 1968); and Bruce A. McConachie, "The 'Theatre of the Mob': Apocalyptic Melodrama and Preindustrial Riots in Antebellum New York," in McConachie and Friedman, eds., *Theatre for the Working-Class Audiences in the United States, 1830-1980* (Westport, Conn., 1985), 17–46.

4. Richards, *"Gentlemen of Property and Standing,"* 10–19; Carl E. Prince, "The Great 'Riot Year': Jacksonian Democracy and Patterns of Violence in 1834," *Journal of the Early Republic,* 5 (1985), 1–20.

5. According to my count, which focuses more on New York City and is less comprehensive than Grimsted's, there were 64 riots in 1828 and 44 riots in 1829, as compared to 58 riots in 1834 and 56 riots in 1835.

Index

PAUL A. GILJE is Professor of History at
the University of Oklahoma and author of
*The Road to Mobocracy: Popular Disorder
in New York City, 1763-1834.*